# Paradigms of
# Clinical
# Social Work

# Paradigms of Clinical Social Work

### Edited by

### *Rachelle A. Dorfman, M.S.S.*

BRUNNER/MAZEL *Publishers* • New York

**Library of Congress Cataloging-in-Publication Data**

Paradigms of clinical social work.

  Bibliography: p.
  Includes index.
  1. Social case work. 2. Social case work—United
States. I. Dorfman, Rachelle A. II. Title: Clinical
social work.
HV43.P35  1988     361.3'2      88–2879
ISBN 0–87630–512–5

Copyright © 1988 by Rachelle A. Dorfman

*Published by*
BRUNNER/MAZEL, INC.
19 Union Square
New York, New York 10003

MANUFACTURED IN THE UNITED STATES OF AMERICA

10  9  8  7  6  5  4  3  2  1

To Frances and Frank Abramson,
parents beyond compare

# FOREWORD

In the mid-1920s, leaders of the social work profession gathered together for a series of meetings to attempt to define what was generic in social casework, what was its essential and identifying core, and what was specific or specialized in the young and growing profession.* Their concern was to unite a profession that had grown up in separate fields of practice, in different organizations, often with only tenuous connections. Among the group at Milford were educators and leaders from the world of practice. The educators were eager to identify what could be taught to all students to give them flexibility as they moved into the profession. The practitioners also wanted to be assured, upon hiring recent graduates, that the new recruits would have an identifiable body of knowledge and skills upon which they could build, but they also hoped graduates would have some specialized knowledge related to the agency's purpose and area of practice.

The Milford Conference ended with a conviction that social casework as a professional practice, as a method, is generic and that fields of practice are specific with additional special knowledge and skill requirements. Some current developments in our now infinitely more complex profession echo the vision of the Milford Conference. The 1981 Curriculum Policy Statement of the Council on Social Work Education, which guides and shapes curriculum development and structure in all accredited schools of social work, takes the position that the first year of graduate education should be directed to the mastery of a common core of knowledge, skills, and values that are shared by and identify all social

---

* American Association of Social Workers (1929). *Social Casework: Generic and Specific: An Outline. A Report of the Milford Conference*. Studies in the Practice of Social Work, Number 2, New York.

work practitioners. It requires the second year be devoted to more specialized training which may be defined in many ways: by field of practice, by method, by population served, by social problem. The National Association of Social Workers has organized its program around five commissions representing five broad but specialized fields of practice.

But underneath these tidy and perhaps necessary organizational arrangements are deep and widespread differences. The differences are not simply related to the requirements of different fields of practice or problem foci, but are differences in world view, in knowledge base, and in methodology.

Almost 60 years have passed since the publication of the Milford Conference Report. As one views the fascinating and varied array of approaches to clinical social work presented in this volume, one becomes acutely aware that we must continue to ask the same questions asked by the Milford Conference leaders. The answers, however, will not be so simple.

What is common among the presentations of practice in this volume? How is the clinical social worker to be identified? Are the variations "specializations" or are they different and even mutually exclusive or competitive conceptions? And, as an educator for clinical practice excited by these rich and persuasive presentations, I find myself asking, What should we teach? How should we choose?

Some critics have condemned the divergence and divisions within the field, bemoaning our seemingly permanent professional identity crisis and accusing the profession of faddism and even of a lack of intellectual integrity. Although the enormous variation in the field does pose problems, it could not have been otherwise unless we closed ourselves off from the changing world and the ever-expanding knowledge available to us.

Two essential and, I believe, defining characteristics of the profession have led us to this point. In fact, it may be the very nature of our identity that makes it nearly impossible to establish a clear identity. First, the boundaries of our concern are drawn wide. The profession is characterized by its attention to *person-in-situation*, to both the individual and the environment and the transactions that occur. This definition of the unit of attention thus may include concern with the deepest level of the individual's inner experience, the poisonous effect on our environment of the threat of nuclear war and mass destruction, and the transaction between the inner life and the threat of annihilation. Our practice with its potential for broad and multiple concerns must therefore be informed by knowledge from all of the social sciences, to some extent from the physical sciences, and hopefully, at least in part, from the arts and the humanities. Thus, it is that social workers have been borrowers of knowledge from many fields. Their intellectual and conceptual boundaries have not only been wide but they have also been open. In the past 20 years, with an explosion of knowledge in every field, social work has been inundated with new information, new concepts, new theory. The response of an open system to multiple inputs of energy and information from its environment, if it is able to integrate these inputs, is to become increasingly differentiated. This volume presents a picture of that differentiation and leads us to ask, as Mary Richmond did 65 years ago, What is Social Casework?

First, we may ask, do the conceptions presented here share any common ground? As we explore the varied pictures of practice we find that each author embraces social work's traditional unit of attention, person-in-situation, and each agrees that help and/or change takes place in the context of a relationship between the clinical social worker and the client system (individual, family, or group). Beyond those areas of agreement, differences emerge. The view and definition of person-in-situation varies from author to author, and each elects to emphasize, focus, or limit in a different way. The relationship, its nature and its degree of salience, is also differently defined. Further, different authors rely on different explanatory systems and make use of different data.

Some social workers have attempted to minimize the divergence in the profession, claiming that although differences in conceptualization may be striking, in actual practice people who seem to *think* differently probably *do* about the same thing. This volume challenges that myth by presenting each of the authors with a case. Clearly, not only do the different professionals think differently about the Shore family, they also would do very different things.

A second characteristic and fundamental principle of social work practice has been that we start where the client is. However, it also becomes clear in this volume that we start where the worker is, that it is the professional's construction of reality, the professional's world view, that directs the practice. It is clear that the members of this family would have had a very different experience depending on whose office they happened to find themselves in. It is far less clear, however, which experience would have been more useful or more helpful or what the outcomes of the various experiences might have been.

How can the practitioner, the educator, the student of practice make use of the rich and varied fare that the editor has gathered and laid before us? First, we can learn, we can be exposed to the creative thinking that is expanding the intellectual boundaries of the profession. We can learn about what colleagues are doing, the questions they are asking, and the answers they are discovering. Rachelle Dorfman establishes the context for our explorations by reviewing the history of clinical practice and we are then introduced to the Shore family. In the second part of this volume we are taken on a guided tour through some of the major practice models. We find comfort in the more familiar approaches such as the psychosocial, problem-solving, and task-centered practice models. We are reminded again of the power of the group for healing and learn of the newest developments in the application of modern psychodynamic thinking to practice. A model based on some of the major Adlerian concepts is presented. We experience the precision and certainty of radical behaviorism and come to know about the impact of cognition on the development and the resolution of problems. Finally, we focus on the intimate or social environment as the context for change through structural family therapy and psychosocial rehabilitation, that new-old model for helping the chronically mentally ill.

As we complete this portion of our journey, we may ask, How is it possible to translate these many models, or even some of them, into our daily practice? The cognitive dissonance generated as we are exposed to these different approaches is stimulating and growth-producing as long as distance is maintained and we do not have to commit ourselves to action. However, as we begin to consider how we might work with the Shore family, choices must be made. Pondering the questions of application and integration, we move on to the final section of the volume, to a different level of conceptualization. We are now asked not just to think about clients and about practice, but to think about how we think. To some extent, the final chapters offer ways of considering the models presented earlier. For example, the eco-systems perspective presents an overarching systemic framework of assessment that may include, according to Carol Meyer, multiple theories and models with the view that through this evaluative way of thinking, the profession may be unified. Other authors suggest other epistemologies, other ways of thinking. The chapter on existential practice suggests that we abandon theorizing, categorizing, diagnosing, and making our own meanings, that we attend to the immediacy of the client's experience in the world, the meaning the client makes of that experience, and the shared experience of worker and client.

The constructivist developmental paradigm calls our attention to the ways individuals develop systems of meaning and suggests, following the work of Piaget and the sociocognitive developmentalists, that no matter what model of practice we are using, we must learn to assess clients' developmental levels in terms of how they think and how they make meanings. In other words, we are asked to think about how we think clients think and their ways of knowing the world.

Thinking and knowing is also the focus of the chapter on cybernetic epistemology, a chapter which, drawing on the work of Gregory Bateson and what has been called "The New Epistemology," suggests the circular thinking processes and thinking tools that must be utilized to move to a truly ecological perspective, to translate into thinking and into practice "the roundness of life."

The final chapter suggests yet another epistemological stance, a position deeply rooted in the traditional American philosophical positions of pragmatism and utilitarianism. Extolling an eclectic position, Hugh Rosen suggests that practitioners may develop a personal philosophy of practice, drawing upon the many models available and tailoring the practice to fit the needs of the particular client in a particular situation at a particular time. The selection of techniques and strategies should be based, not deductively from the theoretical models or constructs but inductively through empirical research. The author suggests that theories are like maps—they are only good if they get you where you want to go.

This volume, in a series of thoughtful and well-presented chapters, brings to us the variety, the richness, and the options available in clinical social work practice today. It is an outstanding contribution to the profession. It does not answer the questions raised by the Milford Conference, and I doubt if those questions could be answered at this time. It does not define the common identity shared by all clinical social work practitioners beyond a focus on person-in-situation and the salience of the worker-client relationship. And, although it does not move us towards unification of the profession, it does present us with some ways to think about the profession and, perhaps even more important, ways to think about how we think. Thoughtful examination of the theory, knowledge, and epistemological positions that support clinical practice today can only lead us to a greater critical awareness of the constructions of reality and of the profession that we each bring to our practice.

**Ann Hartman, D.S.W.**
*Dean*
*Smith College*
*School for Social Work*

# CONTENTS

# ACKNOWLEDGMENTS

This book has come to be because of the unique contributions of many people. I thank Hugh Rosen, my friend and mentor, whose fertile mind has stimulated and intellectually challenged me beyond what I ever thought possible. I am grateful to Jay S. Efran, who helped clarify theoretical points and lovingly made sure that my head stayed the right size. Without the encouragement and editing skills of Elsa R. Efran, there would be no book. Daniel Efran, as well, contributed significantly to the clarity and logic of the text.

Thanks also to Judith Kasser, Elizabeth W. Horton, and Milton Speizman, who shared their experiences and provided their expertise. I am grateful to my editor, Ann Alhadeff, for her constant support, and to Tonya Meadows for cheerfully keeping track of the massive amount of correspondence it took to organize the project. The contributors deserve a special thank-you for doing it "my way" and for having to deal with my countless deadlines.

I am especially grateful for the patience and love of my children, Holly and Jeff (Holly for her uncanny ability to spell words she has never heard before, and Jeff for his good nature despite "no dinner, no clean socks, and a preoccupied Mom"). And to my parents, colleagues, friends, students, and clients, who endured the loss of my full attention during the year I was possessed with the work—my heartfelt appreciation.

R. A. D.

# ABOUT THE EDITOR

**Rachelle A. Dorfman, M.S.S.,** completed her undergraduate work at Hahnemann University and received her master's degree from the Bryn Mawr Graduate School of Social Work and Social Research. She is currently a doctoral candidate in Psychoeducational Processes at Temple University.

Dorfman is Assistant Professor and Assistant Director of the Mental Health Technology Baccalaureate Program in the School of Allied Health Professions, Hahnemann University. She maintains a part-time private practice in suburban Philadelphia, PA.

# ABOUT THE CONTRIBUTORS

**Terry Eisenberg Carrilio, Ph.D.,** is currently Director, Program Development and Research, Big Brothers/Big Sisters of America. She also maintains a small private practice in Philadelphia, PA. Carrilio has been a Lecturer at Bryn Mawr Graduate School of Social Work and Social Research and at the University of Pennsylvania. She has worked with groups for interfaith couples and is currently doing research on working and parenting. She has written articles on social work practice, research, and developmental theory.

**Sophie Freud, Ph.D.,** is Professor of Social Work and Chair of the Human Behavior Sequence, Simmons College School of Social Work, Boston, MA. Since 1976, she has also been on the faculty of Harvard Extension Evening University, where she teaches courses on the psychology of women. She has lectured and led workshops throughout the United States and has written widely on such topics as the psychology of women, sexuality, parenting, life-cycle crises, mental health education, and the passion experience. In addition, Freud has published approximately 50 book reviews. She is the author of *My Three Mothers and Other Passions* (in press).

**Donald F. Krill, M.S.W.,** is Professor, The Graduate School of Social Work, University of Denver, CO. He is also the Director of the Family Therapy Training Center, University of Denver, and maintains a private practice in clinical social work. He is a consultant and teacher in Wellness programs. Krill is the author of *Existential Social Work* and most recently *The Beat Worker: Humanizing Social Work Practice and Psychotherapy.* He entertains groups with an act entitled "Interludes of Magical and Psychological Trickery."

**Jay Lappin, M.S.W.,** is Senior Trainer, Family Therapy Training Center, Philadelphia Child Guidance Clinic, Philadelphia, PA. He has lectured throughout the United States and has written about various aspects of family therapy, including ethnicity, runaways, and stages of treatment. He is an approved supervisor and board member of the American Association for Marriage and Family Therapy in New Jersey and a contributing editor of the *Family Therapy Networker.* His private practice is in Collingswood, NJ.

**Robert F. Massey, Ph.D.,** is Visiting Professor of Counseling and Marriage and Family Counseling at Queens College, City University of New York, and Professor of Psychology at St. Peter's College, Jersey City, NJ. He is a licensed psychologist as well as a licensed marriage and family therapist. He has taken courses with Kurt and Alexandra Adler. Massey's publications include articles about family systems theory and therapy, personality theories, and social psychology. He is the author of *Personality Theories: Comparisons and Syntheses.*

**Carol H. Meyer, D.S.W.,** is Professor of Social Work, Columbia University, New York, NY. She is on the editorial boards of the *British Journal of Social Work* and the *Journal of Women in Social Work* and is former editor-in-chief of *Social Work.* She is the author of *Staff Development in Public Welfare Agencies, Social Work Practice: A Response to the Urban Crisis, Social Work Practice: The Changing Landscape,* and *Clinical Social Work in the Eco-systems Perspective.*

**Catherine P. Papell, D.S.W.,** is Professor Emerita of Social Work, formerly Director of the Division of Direct Practice, and Acting Associate Dean, School of Social Work, Adelphi University, Garden City, Long Island, NY. She is a member of the board of directors of the Association for the Advancement of Social Work with Groups, Inc., and is a family therapist with the Nassau County Medical Center Alcoholism Outpatient Clinic. She is co-editor (with Beulah Rothman) of the journal, *Social Work with Groups.* She has also co-authored (with Beulah Rothman) "Mainstream Model" and "Social Group Work Models: Possession and Heritage," which appeared in the *Journal of Education for Social Work.*

**William J. Reid, D.S.W.,** is Professor, School of Social Welfare, Rockefeller College of Public Affairs and Policy, The State University of New York at Albany. He is editor of the series in International Social Welfare, associate editor of the *Journal of Continuing Social Work Education,* and member of the editorial board of the *Journal of Social Service Research.* He is the author of *Family Problem Solving, Task-Centered Casework,* and *Research in Social Work.*

**Hugh Rosen, D.S.W.,** is Professor, Director of Mental Health Technology Programs, and Associate Dean of Student Affairs, School of Allied

Health Professions, Hahnemann University, Philadelphia, PA. He is also a member of the board of the Piaget Society. Rosen is the author of *Pathway to Piaget: A Guide for Clinicians, Educators and Developmentalists, Development of Sociomoral Knowledge: A Cognitive-Structural Approach,* and *Piagetian Dimensions of Clinical Relevance.* He maintains a limited private practice in Philadelphia.

**Beulah Rothman, D.S.W.,** is Distinguished Professor, Barry University School of Social Work, Miami, FL. She is Director of the Ph.D. program in social work. She is co-editor (with Catherine P. Papell) of the journal, *Social Work with Groups,* and is a member of the board of directors of the Association for the Advancement of Social Work with Groups, Inc. Rothman is co-author (with Catherine P. Papell) of "Mainstream Model" and "Social Group Work Models: Possession and Heritage," which appeared in the *Journal of Education for Social Work.* She is the Director of the Florida Center for Group Work Studies.

**Bruce A. Thyer, Ph.D.,** is Associate Professor, University of Georgia School of Social Work, Athens, GA. He is a licensed social worker in Florida, where he maintained a private practice. He is the author of *Treating Anxiety Disorders* and co-editor of *Psychiatric Clinics of North America: Anxiety Disorders* and *Progress in Behavioral Social Work.*

**Francis J. Turner, D.S.W.,** is Professor and Chairman of Social Work, York University, Toronto, Ontario. He was formerly the Executive Vice-president, Laurentian University, Sudbury, Ontario, and Moses Distinguished Visiting Professor (1984–85) at Hunter College, New York City. He is editor of *International Social Work.* Turner is also the author of *Differential Diagnoses and Treatment in Social Work, Social Work Treatment, Adult Psychopathology,* and *Psychosocial Therapy.*

**Fred D. Wright, Ed.D.,** is Lecturer, Department of Psychiatry, School of Medicine, University of Pennsylvania, Philadelphia, PA. He is also Director of Training and Education at the Center for Cognitive Therapy, Philadelphia, PA. His recent publications include "Treatment of Test Anxiety" and "Overcoming Procrastination" (co-authored with Patrick Grecco). Both chapters appear in *Clinical Application of Cognitive Therapy with College Students* (in press), edited by Arthur Freeman, Ed.D., ABPP, and Suzanne Boyle, Ph.D.

**Polly Young-Eisendrath, Ph.D.,** is Guest Lecturer in Human Development, Bryn Mawr College, and was formerly Assistant Professor, Bryn Mawr Graduate School of Social Work and Social Research. She is an A.C.S.W. social worker as well as a licensed psychologist. She is Chief Psychologist at Clinical Associates West, P.C., Bala Cynwyd, PA. Young-

Eisendrath is a Jungian analyst and is a graduate of the Inter-Regional Society of Jungian Analysts. She is the co-editor (with James Hall) of *The Book of the Self: Person, Pretext, Process,* co-author (with Florence Wiedemann) of *Female Authority: Empowering Women Through Psychotherapy,* and author of *Hags and Heroes: A Feminist Approach to Jungian Psychotherapy with Couples.*

# INTRODUCTION

At one time, most social workers conceptualized their clients and their clients' problems from a single therapeutic paradigm—psychoanalysis. In the early years of the profession, social workers gravitated to psychoanalysis because its theories about the unconscious and the impact of childhood experiences, as well as its view of the human experience, helped them to understand confusing aspects of their clients' behavior. Eventually other paradigms emerged, offering expanded or different views. Some—for example, psychosocial therapy and brief task-centered therapy—had their roots in social work, while others—for example, behavior therapy and cognitive therapy—had their roots in the behavioral sciences.

Social workers responded to these developments by seeking advanced training in the new paradigms and attending seminars and conferences in which the theories and techniques emanating from the new paradigms were discussed and demonstrated.* They also read voraciously.

A number of books present or compare therapeutic paradigms, but only a handful have been written by clinical social workers from a social work perspective. One of the major values embraced by that perspective is self-determination: that is, social workers want their clients to be able to make a wide range of well-informed choices predicated on a solid foundation of information (about themselves, the available resources, and the situation at hand). Because we wish no less for the practitioner, we present here the paradigms in the same spirit. In the same way that a social worker might encourage a client to consider information, this

---

* On December 11, 1985, for example, 1,567 social workers joined 5,500 other professionals in Phoenix for "The Evolution of Psychotherapy," a conference featuring the masters of the leading psychotherapy paradigms (J. Zeig, personal communication, June, 1987).

book is designed to encourage the reader in the scholarly endeavor of considering and comparing the various paradigms.

To facilitate comparison, I asked each contributor to follow the same framework, which is reproduced below:

Introduction

The Concept of the Person and the Human Experience (the underlying philosophical position of the paradigm regarding its view of the person and the human experience)

Historical Perspective (overview of origins and development of the paradigm)

Key Theoretical Constructs (the explanation of problems, symptoms, and disease, and the theory of change identified with this approach)

Assessment

Treatment of Choice (applicability of the paradigm for client, setting, and situation)

The Therapeutic Process (techniques and methods, course of treatment, and therapist-client relationship)

Limitations of the Model (major problems and issues, failures, under-developed areas)

Research

Summary

References

Almost from the beginning, I realized that although a common framework would be useful, it would also be problematic. The various levels of development among paradigms is often given as one of the reasons why others have abandoned the idea as not possible (see, for example, Turner, 1979). In addition, contributors tend to use frameworks in distinctive ways: Some emphasize assessment, others focus on therapeutic process or research. Nevertheless, I persisted with my initial plan, because the value of being able to compare aspects of therapeutic paradigms far outweighs any "unbalance" in presentation.

I felt that the commonality of social work training, education, and values among the contributors would make the book particularly useful to clinical social workers. Once again, I kept to my original plan, with two exceptions. Robert Massey, a psychologist, wrote the Adlerian chapter, because he is an expert in Adlerian theory and because he convinced me that he had started his career 18 years ago as a caseworker in New Jersey. Fred D. Wright, a psychologist, who wrote the cognitive therapy chapter, made no such claim. Nevertheless, as the Director of Training and Education at the Center for Cognitive Therapy in Philadelphia (home base for cognitive therapy), he was an expert whom I could not turn away.

I wanted to establish a context in which to place the paradigms and to have a mechanism that would organize them into a cohesive work. The historical perspective presented in Chapter 1 traces the evolution of clinical social work and thus serves as the context for the rest of the book. Chapter 2, "The Case," is the core of the book; here the Shores (a real family) are described in depth. In each of the following chapters (Chapters 3–15), I invited the contributors to use material from the Shore family case study to illustrate the theory and practice of their paradigms. Some discussed the family as a unit; others focused primarily on one or two members (e.g., Young-Eisendrath has emphasized the marital couple, largely excluding the two children). In every situation, I admonished the contributors to resist the temptation to try to "solve" the case.

I am indebted to the Shores for sharing their secrets, including some of the most painful moments in their lives, especially when they knew that their words would appear in print to be read by other family members, as well as total strangers. During the 20 hours of interviews, I found it difficult to refrain from being "therapeutic" and to concentrate solely on helping them to tell their stories. For me, it was a lesson in listening. For the Shores, the experience of telling their story (without therapeutic intervention) and later receiving the written account of it was enlightening and emotionally moving; much later it became evidence of change. After the manuscript was complete, I visited again with the Shores. The Epilogue is a brief account of the Shore family one year later.

The paradigms could have easily been organized alphabetically, chronologically, or by common roots (e.g., psychoanalytic, behavioral, humanistic). As I read the chapters, however, I noticed other distinctions and organized them along those lines. The paradigms in Part II are somewhat more discrete and are more likely to offer specific techniques, whereas the "metaparadigms" in Part III have a higher level of complexity and abstraction. The metaparadigms do not identify specific techniques; instead they provide frameworks from which techniques can be created.

In the final chapter (Chapter 16), Rosen speculates on the influences that determine why a practitioner will learn and continue to practice one therapeutic approach over another. He argues persuasively—as others have—for an eclectic approach to practice. However, Rosen goes further by supplying a set of guidelines to evaluate other paradigms, enabling the practitioner to construct his or her "personal philosophy of practice."

Finally, I decided on the title, *Paradigms of Clinical Social Work*. The term *paradigm* has been popularized in the behavioral sciences by Kuhn (1972). In his own work, Kuhn, a student of the history of science, has used the term in several ways. For the purpose of this book, however, it is defined as a "conceptual-interpretive framework—an interlocking network of presuppositions, assumptions, attitudes, beliefs, premises, expectations, and values. It is a construal of reality that orients a person to the world and guides him or her in the selection of problems and methodology for conducting research programs" (Rosen, see p. 392, this volume).

The majority of paradigms that I selected did not have social work roots. Nevertheless, I have associated them with clinical social work practice: first, because clinical social workers are interested in them, and second, because each of them supports (however differently) the person-in-situation focus that has always been at the heart of social work practice.

My intent has been to respond to a need in a creative way. I want to caution the reader, however, that this book is meant only to whet the appetite—to provide a starting point from which to explore unfamiliar paradigms more deeply and to begin to savor their richness.

R. A. D.

## REFERENCES

Kuhn, T. S. (1972). *The structure of scientific revolutions* (2nd ed.). Chicago: University of Chicago Press.

Turner, F. J. (1979). Interlocking perspectives for practice. In F. J. Turner (Ed.), *Social work treatment* (2nd ed., pp. 535–546). New York: The Free Press.

# Paradigms of
# Clinical
# Social Work

# PART I
# History and Case

# 1

# Clinical Social Work: The Development of a Discipline

*Rachelle A. Dorfman, M.S.S.*

Although the profession of social work is young—less than 100 years old—the practice of helping others is ancient. There have always been people willing to devote large portions of their lives to alleviating human suffering. This chapter will focus on some of the people who were instrumental in the development of the profession, as well as on some early efforts to help the poor, which eventually expanded to include help for all socioeconomic classes and for emotional as well as social problems. In addition, the chapter will trace the development of social consciousness and social welfare that laid the foundation for the contemporary practice of clinical social work, a field that has been called an entirely separate discipline (Alexander, 1977), a specialization of social work (Strean, 1978), and a movement (Briar, 1983).

We know from the anthropological record that prehistoric peoples engaged in cooperative and helping behaviors that contributed to their survival in a harsh environment. Nevertheless, this account begins arbitrarily at a more recent point, 4,000 years ago, with Hammurabi, the king of Babylon, who declared—in a sweeping gesture of social consciousness—that he would protect every widow and orphan in Babylon. Two thousand years after Hammurabi's reign, the Greeks were supporting their dependent citizens in the same manner and teaching their children that it was better to give than to receive.

Similar teachings can be found in ancient religious writings. For example, the Old Testament says, "Thou shalt not harden thine heart nor

3

shut thine hand from thy poor brother" (Deuteronomy, 15:7). Farmers are told that after they harvest their fields, they should not return to fetch a forgotten sheaf, but should leave it in the field "for the stranger, for the fatherless, and for the widow" (Deuteronomy, 24:19). The Talmud, a collection of Jewish law and tradition, excuses no one from giving: "Even a poor person who is kept alive by tzedakah funds [charity] must give tzedakah from what he receives" (Shulchan Aruch, Yoreh De'ah, 248:1). Other examples can be found in the Koran, the Islamic holy book, which exhorts Muslims to donate a portion of their assets to the poor. The Christian world regards charity as the supreme virtue, demonstrated in the passage: "And now abideth faith, hope, charity, these three; but the greatest of these is charity" (I Corinthians, 13).

## ENGLISH AND AMERICAN ANTECEDENTS

When the Christian church was small, most of the help for the needy came from relatives and friends. By the sixth century, however, Christianity dominated Europe and the monasteries became centers for relief of the poor. Not only was relief given at the monastery door, but, in the prototype of modern outreach services, monks went into the community to perform charitable acts.

The plague, the famines of the 15th century, and the dismantling of the feudal system (which meant the loss of the master's caretaking) contributed to a tremendous rise in unemployment, homelessness, and crime. By 1536, England turned Protestant and relief of the poor was secularized. Monasteries were dissolved and the monks, whose work was to aid the poor, instead joined the ranks of the poor.

In the following decades, suffering and social disorder became widespread. Probably moved more by fear of insurrection than benevolence, English lawmakers wrote The Poor Law of 1601. This landmark in public welfare legislation stood nearly unchanged in England for the next 250 years and was a major influence on American social welfare policy:

> In short, people were expected to look out for themselves and their families. If they got into trouble, they would first turn to their relatives and neighbors, just as we do today. If these resources were inadequate, the community was morally obliged to share with them through the poor law, but on the other hand, officials were justified in seeing that individuals or members of the family did not evade their responsibilities. (Leiby, 1978, p. 40)

In colonial America, poor children were apprenticed to tradesmen and many people who were unable to care for themselves were literally "farmed out" to the lowest bidders at town meetings. The able-bodied were put to work; the old and incapacitated were granted small amounts of money (outdoor relief) or were placed in institutions (indoor relief). For a time, indoor relief was the favored method of dealing with the poor, and hundreds of almshouses were built.

At first, indoor relief seemed more humane than farming-out or meager outdoor relief. Although the intent may have been humane, conditions inside these institutions deteriorated rapidly. Children, criminals, the mentally ill, and epileptics were housed amid filth, disease, hunger, and violence. Spurred by reports of these conditions, reformers demanded that children be removed from the poorhouses and that state and federal governments provide aid to improve the quality of care for those who remained.

## SCIENTIFIC CHARITY

The Civil War brought with it a temporary reversal in charitable practices: Outdoor relief replaced indoor relief as the favored method of dealing with the poor. Large amounts of public and private funds were appropriated to help sick and destitute soldiers and military families. After the war, private agencies multiplied, particularly in the larger cities. In 1878, in Philadelphia alone, there were 800 such groups (Trattner, 1979). Despite the great number of agencies, relief was chaotic and ineffective.

In that era, it was assumed that people are by nature lazy and self-indulgent and that if they are given relief, they will become demoralized parasites, unwilling to work. (That assumption persists in some circles even today.) Herbert Spencer, the English philosopher, applied Darwin's theory of evolution to social conditions. He believed that there was a natural evolutionary process toward higher forms of social life and that, if left alone, the lower forms (i.e., the needy) would die out. He and other "Social Darwinists" felt that it would be unnatural (or worse, would lead to a disastrous weakening of the species) if the poor were given relief, because then they would become *irreversibly* dependent (which translated to "unworthy"). Spencer and his followers believed that minimal volunteer charity was justified only because it encouraged the development of Christian virtue in the *givers*. They believed that moral failure was the cause of poverty and distress and that for everyone— *except* the "unworthy" (irreversibly dependent)—moral uplift was the remedy.

Charity workers had to first distinguish the worthy from the unworthy (an impossible task) and then employ "benevolent stinginess" (Lubove, 1965), which meant that, for their own good, the needy were given little financial assistance. Next, the charity workers had to devise and implement a method for moral correction to elevate those who were deemed morally deficient but "worthy" nevertheless.

By the last part of the 19th century, there had been an unprecedented rise in the number of charities, but there was no corresponding increase in their effectiveness. At the same time, however, the intellectual community was developing a new respect for science and the doctrine of single causation—the idea that every effect could be traced to a cause. If the cause could be uncovered, the cure could be revealed. This philosophy suggested that science might lead to a cure-all for all kinds of human problems. Charity workers began to think that this linear scientific model might also provide them with solutions to social ills (Germain, 1970).

With missionary zeal and high expectations, *scientific* charity was born in the United States with the emergence of the Charity Organization Societies (COS). The first COS was established by an Episcopalian minister, Stephen Humphreys Gurteen, and his businessman parishioner, T. Guilford Smith, as a response to the destitution and ineffective relief in Buffalo, New York, in 1876.* Gurteen spent the summer of 1877 in London, studying the Society for Organizing Relief and Repressing Mendacity. He returned to model the first American COS after the London society.

The stated objective of the COS was to eliminate sentimental almsgiving and replace it with scientific investigation and businesslike organization and efficiency. District agents in each COS registered each case (to eliminate duplication of services) and then determined the worthiness of the applicants. Thorough investigation and the assessment of individual needs were primary functions. Money was rarely given. Instead, referrals were made to agencies with specialized services. Leiby (1978) has pointed out that the best part of the work—probably because it was the most intellectually stimulating—was the case conferences held by volunteer district committees. Professionals, society women, and knowledgeable community members were invited to discuss cases and formulate recommendations. In keeping with the COS motto, "Not alms, but a friend," the committee frequently assigned a "friendly visitor" to the family.

Friendly visitors were respectable, successful, and "moral" volunteers who would befriend needy families and, by their example, attempt to guide the families out of poverty and suffering. The relationship between friendly visitor and needy person was by no means equal, but it was supposed to be reciprocal: "The poor were to learn diligence, abstinence, and thrift, as basic to self-support" (Lewis, 1977, p. 97) "and the rich

---

* Earlier, the New York Association for Improving the Conditions of the Poor (A.I.C.P.), established in 1843, had also advocated the organization of charities. It developed some of the principles seen in the COS, such as investigation, volunteer visitors, moral exhortation, and limited relief.

might benefit from examples of courage and good cheer displayed by the poor" (Lubove, 1965, p. 114). Mutual understanding between the classes was supposed to reduce friction and foster social harmony.

Robert Treat Paine, a COS spokesman from Boston, said that friendly visiting was "the only hope of civilization against the gathering curse of pauperism in the great cities" (Lubove, 1965, p. 5). Although it did not turn out to be the salvation of civilization, friendly visiting was an appealing, if idealistic, concept. It is at this point that one can begin to recognize systematic investigation, attention to individual needs, case conferences, and the therapeutic relationship as the embryonic form of casework as we think of it today.

By 1900, the role of the paid agent was upgraded and the role of the volunteer visitor was diminished, probably because it was difficult to recruit enough volunteers to fill the need and because COS leaders were interested in promoting the professionalization of the discipline of "Applied Philanthropy" (the infant social work). However, the main reason for the decline of the importance of the volunteers was that after extensive contact with the needy, people in the COS movement realized that poverty had more to do with social, economic, and psychological factors than with personal moral shortcomings. They began to have serious doubts about the effectiveness of friendly visiting. It was difficult to maintain the belief that poverty was unrelated to the massive cyclic economic depressions in the latter part of the 19th century: "If moral failure was not the cause of poverty, then friendly visiting was not the solution" (Popple, 1983, p. 75).

## THE SETTLEMENT MOVEMENT

Many people thought that the "solution" to poverty could be found in a new ideology, the short-lived settlement movement, which arose at the same time as the COS. From the outset, settlement workers concentrated on *environmental* determinants. Although they did not deny that personal shortcomings contributed to poverty, they relegated them to a minor role.

In the late 19th and early 20th century, the larger American cities were overcrowded and filthy. Immigrants in pursuit of a better life flooded the urban areas: 14 million came between 1860 and 1900, another 9 million between 1900 and 1910. Most immigrants worked as unskilled laborers in factories, subject to the brutal working conditions and periodic layoffs that kept them locked into poverty.

During this period, the nation's universities were also expanding, and a large group of young men and women began to graduate and seek roles in the new industrialized society. There was no clear place for them—big business was at the top and organized labor was at the bottom. Many of these idealistic men and women became alienated from society as it then existed, and sought to change it by becoming social reformers. The settlement movement provided them with a meaningful niche (Hofstadter, 1956).

The charity workers had taken a friendly but unquestionably superior position in their efforts to change the individual, whereas these young men and women claimed equality with the poor and chose to live in neighborhood settlement houses in the heart of the poor communities. Their client was the *community*, not the individual. As the movement progressed, involvement extended from the neighborhood to the city, the state, the nation, even the world. Instead of moral exhortation, the "treatment" was activism: creating day-care centers, libraries, dispensaries, employment bureaus, literacy classes, art classes, and social and recreational activities and clubs. The settlement workers obtained playgrounds, gymnasiums, garbage collection, and public bathhouses for their communities. They became "spearheads for reform" (Davis, 1967), becoming involved in the labor movement and in activism for civil rights.

The first American settlement, the Neighborhood Guild, was founded in New York City in 1886 by Stanton Coit, a young American who had spent three months in England living at Toynbee, the first English settlement house. (Again, this is evidence of the English influence on American social welfare policies and programs.) Coit was impressed by the university students he saw who were living and working among the poor, attempting to create small-town neighborliness in the midst of the London slums. The idea spread rapidly in America. By 1897 there were 74 settlements, in 1900 over 100, and by 1910 over 400.

One of the most well-known of the settlement houses was Hull House in Chicago, which was founded in 1889 by another Toynbee visitor, Jane Addams. Many Hull House programs became models for other settlements. Addams' work ranged from the mundane (she was the trash inspector in her Hull House neighborhood) to the lofty (she was president of the Women's International Peace Conference at The Hague).

Although much has been written about Jane Addams, she still remains an enigma (Davis, 1973). She has been depicted as suprahuman, saintlike, and as a symbol for the Progressive Era. Historians have speculated on what motivated her to devote her entire life to political action. Among the speculations are rebellion against family pressure to be the "maiden aunt" (Lasch, 1965), guilt because of her material comfort in the face of the social ills of the period, her early feelings of uselessness and depression, or (as she wrote in her autobiography) "a conversion experience" that occurred shortly after she witnessed the slaughter of animals at a bullfight in Madrid (Addams, 1910).

Perhaps all of the explanations are valid. At any rate, Addams was a college-educated woman who was uninterested in marriage and family in an era that offered her few other opportunities or occupations. Like many other Victorian women of her upper-middle-class background and privilege, for a while (eight years of her early adulthood) she languished with illnesses, neurotic breakdowns, and invalidism, mixed alternately with abortive attempts to further her education.

Addams' "creative solution" (Davis, 1973) to her long search for something to do that had value and meaning, her growing awareness of the gap between the classes, and perhaps some righteous indignation about what she observed in the industrialized cities contributed to her founding of Hull House. Jane Addams was a tireless activist for peace as well as social reform, and in 1931 she received the Nobel Peace Prize for her work.

The settlement movement declined after World War I. The poor were still present, but they were less visible in the postwar posterity, and fewer university students volunteered for settlement work. (Most preferred more exotic endeavors in foreign countries or were attracted to a broader array of lifestyles and an increasing number of professional opportunities.) The "other" social workers—COS workers—continued to push for professional status, a preoccupation that the settlement workers did not share and that probably hastened their demise. Instead of agents for community *change*, the surviving settlements evolved into community *service* agencies (e.g., "Y"'s, neighborhood centers, and community centers).

Although the settlement movement was a comparatively short-lived outgrowth of early social work, it played an important role in the development of clinical social work (or, as it was then called, casework). For example, charity workers facing the environmental factors of inadequate housing and sanitation, unemployment, and other consequences of explosive industrialization, immigration, and urbanization in the early 20th century, had difficulty maintaining the notion that moral failings were the cause of poverty and distress. At first, they held fast to their beliefs, engaging in bitter disputes with the settlement workers in the same manner that holders of a scientific paradigm resist new evidence of an alternative paradigm (Kuhn, 1962). However, the settlement movement provided the irritant and the debate for the holders of the moral-failings viewpoint, and thus contributed to the dramatic paradigmatic shift in social work—from an individual moral-failings approach to a person-in-situation approach.

## THE PROFESSIONALIZATION OF SOCIAL WORK

With the decline of the settlements, social reform drew less attention, and social workers instead focused their attention on a relentless quest for professionalization. Their major obstacle lay in social work's broad practice base. Although workers developed expertise in diverse settings and situations, they were unable to claim a unified integrated method of practice.

In 1915, Abraham Flexner, a well-known critic of the medical profession and an authority on professional education, was invited to address the National Conference of Charities and Correction. His topic was "Is Social Work a Profession?" Flexner's answer was a resounding "no." Flexner defined the concept "profession" for the first time, thereby outlining what the social workers would have to do to achieve their goal. Central to his definition was that a profession must "possess an educationally communicable technique" (1915, p. 581). Furthermore, he said, "The occupations of social workers are so numerous and diverse that no compact purposefully organized educational discipline is feasible" (1915, pp. 585–588).

If it was not a profession, what was it? Flexner concluded that social workers, although kind and resourceful, were merely mediators. They did not utilize technical skills of their own but simply directed others to appropriate services. Social workers responded to Flexner by attempting to delineate and develop a method that would be uniquely and clearly their own.

Mary Richmond, a prominent Baltimore COS leader, deserves the credit for eventually formulating the method called for by Flexner. Her book, *Social Diagnosis* (1917), was the culmination of painstaking efforts to make the theory and method of social casework "educationally communicable."

Inspired by medical colleagues, Richmond's social casework was scientific in its conception. She presented directions for investigation, diagnosis, and treatment. The emphasis was sociological, attending to the influence of the environment on individual personality development and adjustment.

*Social Diagnosis* was acclaimed both inside and outside the social work ranks, as social workers committed themselves to the idea that social ills can be changed by changing the individual through interventions in the environment. Its acceptance paved the way for social work's professional status and for Mary Richmond to become the leading figure in the field.

Richmond had been a frail, sickly child. She spent much of her youth preoccupied with books, at a time when girls were not encouraged in scholarly pursuits (Pumphrey, 1956). When she was 27, she happened to see an advertisement for an administrative position with the Baltimore COS. It was difficult for her to conceive of leaving her secure bookkeeper's salary of $50.00 per month, especially because she hadn't the slightest idea about what a COS was or what it did, or if she would like the work or have an aptitude for it. "Scientific" even then, Richmond researched the COS organization and concluded that it was a risk worth taking.

During her career, she rose from that obscure administrative assistant-ship to a position of leadership—and changed the face of social work by transforming charity work into a profession. In 1900, she left Baltimore to direct the Philadelphia COS. She remained there until 1909, when she accepted the post of director of the Charity Organization Department of the Russell Sage Foundation in New York City. At the foundation, she dedicated herself to raising social work standards. She remained with the foundation until her death in 1928.

During those initial 30 years of the 20th century, the discipline grew dramatically. It became a full-fledged profession with four clearly defined specialized fields of practice: medical, school, psychiatric, and family social work. It formed its own professional associations—the American Association of Hospital Social Workers in 1918, the American Association of Social Workers in 1920, the American Association of Visiting Teachers in 1922, and the American Association of Psychiatric Social Workers in 1924—and it developed its own professional standards.

Once the uniform practice base had been established, the next concern was the expertise that social workers were developing in the specialized fields of practice. Were there enough commonalities among the specialties to retain the concept that social work was one profession? The Milford Conference, a group of agency executives and board members who met periodically for five years, affirmed in its report in 1929 that indeed there was a "generic social case work" that was "more substantial in content and much more significant in its implications for all forms of social case work than were any of the specific emphases of the different case work fields" (NASW, 1974, p. 3). Thus, by 1930, social work had developed a base of generic skills and a social casework core. Although casework remained the dominant social work method, later other methods—group work, community organization, administration, and research—were added.

Social casework thrived during and after World War I as workers began to become involved with "clients" (Richmond's term) above the poverty level. However, the sociological approach to social casework was to be short-lived. Workers became puzzled once again by the clients who did not improve. Socioeconomic factors did not seem to explain all the distress they saw.

Meanwhile, Freud and psychoanalysis "had become almost a national mania" (Trattner, 1979, p. 213). Psychoanalysis seemed to offer everything the caseworkers needed. Its emphasis on *internal* forces that acted on the individual seemed to explain the failure of social casework for many "resistant" clients. Psychoanalysis was "scientific" and provided a the-oretical base complex enough to please even a critical Abraham Flexner. When social workers embraced psychoanalytic principles, they felt that they were elevated from identification with "do-gooder" charity work-ers to the status of the psychiatrists and the psychologists who were also enamored of Freud's understanding of personality and human behavior.

## THE DEPRESSION YEARS

Both the prosperity of the 1920s and the belief expressed by President Herbert Hoover that the country was near the "final triumph" over poverty came crashing down with the stock market in 1929. The Depression that followed lasted a decade. By 1932, 12,000,000 people were unemployed, 5,000 banks had closed, and 32,000 businesses had failed (Popple, 1983). The amount of destitution and suffering rose to new heights.

During the Depression, Hoover's attitude about public relief (the dole)—that it was demoralizing to recipients, morally wrong, and counter to natural forces—fell out of favor. When Franklin D. Roosevelt took office in 1933, he instituted his own philosophy, which, beginning with the 1933 Federal Emergency Relief Act, provided a wide range of public welfare programming.

Roosevelt's "New Deal" changed the role of social workers again, and once more they adjusted their understanding of human suffering.* Many social workers became interested in social reform and old-fashioned relief. They could not deny the impact of the socioeconomic environment on the emotional well-being of the individual. As Paul Kellogg, editor of *Survey,*** said, "You cannot deal effectively with an inferiority complex on an empty stomach" (Trattner, 1979, p. 238).

As part of the New Deal, social worker Harry Hopkins formulated Regulation Number I. This legislation ended the relief-giving function of private agencies by withdrawing public funds earmarked for relief and redistributing them to public agencies. The public agencies were required to hire one social worker for every 20 employees, which increased the number of social work jobs from 40,000 in 1930 to 80,000 in 1940 (Trattner, 1979). The workers not employed in government service (those remaining in private agencies) continued to practice casework. At this point, the profession had expanded in the public and private sector and approached individual problems from a sociological, economic, and psychological perspective. The former linear approach to client problems

---

* Popple (1983) makes the well-taken point that the reason why social work is a profession in constant flux is because, unlike medicine or law, it is embedded in an institutional context and interacts with that context as part of its mission. As political, social, and economic institutions change over time, so must the profession. For a summary of the societal forces that have affected the practice of social work during the last 20 to 30 years, see Ginsberg (1987).

** *Survey* (published from 1907 to 1952) was a social work journal that had a profound influence on American public and private social welfare policy.

had been replaced by a multidetermined, systematic, individualized person-in-situation approach.

A much less positive development occurred during that period which, to some extent, still plagues the profession. Two types of workers emerged—the graduate-level social worker and the untrained public welfare social worker. Most graduate-level workers were not willing to fill the large number of low-paying welfare positions. Even if that were not the case, there were too few social workers to fill all the openings. The workers who did seize the opportunity were usually without degrees or specialized training.

Although the professional organizations accepted welfare as a field of practice, they were unwilling to accept the untrained public welfare workers as members of their associations. This situation generated the development of undergraduate social work education, but eventually, 30 years later, it caused dissension within the profession when the professional associations reversed their decision and permitted social workers with BSWs to join their organizations.

## THE DIAGNOSTIC-FUNCTIONAL CONTROVERSY

Social work—never a profession to shy away from controversy or differing philosophies within its own house—became embroiled in yet another debate that began during the Depression era: the debate between the "diagnostic" and "functional" approaches. Like other internal disputes of the past decades, this one lasted many years. Although the debate was at times heated, always lively, and sometimes dangerously divisive, it ultimately served to further influence social work values, principles, and methods.

In the 1920s, casework had become identified with the psychoanalytically oriented approach, which emphasized diagnosis based on an investigation of the history of the client and treatment based on the client's uncovering and understanding of his or her early childhood experiences. It relied on Freudian concepts, including the unconscious, transference, resistance, and psychic determinism. These ideas eventually came to be called the "diagnostic school."

However, many social workers became discontented with the traditional Freudian approach to practice and the mechanistic, deterministic view that portrayed human beings as prey to the dark forces of the unconscious and the harsh restrictive influences of early internalized parental injunctions (Smalley, 1970). In the 1930s, a group of faculty members at the University of Pennsylvania School of Social Work, led by Virginia Robinson and Jessie Taft, and which included Kenneth Pray, Almena Dawley, Harry Aptekar, Grace Marcus, and Ruth Smalley, developed another approach to practice, which came to be called the "functional school." They were influenced by the theories of Mead, Dewey, Lewin, and especially Otto Rank (a former disciple of Freud's who had also taught at Penn). The first exposition of this approach was in Robinson's (1930) *A Changing Psychology of Social Work*.

The functional school adopted an optimistic view of human beings (first developed for psychotherapy by Rank) that people were not (as orthodox Freudians would support) the end products of their pasts, but were capable of continually creating and re-creating themselves. In the functional school, the focus was on the relationship between the worker and the client. That relationship, it was theorized, was the context in which the client's innate power for growth and choice would be fostered and released. This meant that the responsibility for "treatment" was the client's, not the social worker's. In fact, the word "treatment" was never used. In its place was the term "helping process." Within a time-limited helping process, the client and social worker would attend only to the client's immediate issues. There was no exploration of the past, no interpretation, and no setting of treatment goals. Most important, there was no diagnostic labeling. The worker in the functional school was not concerned with a specific outcome, because, in the context of the helping relationship, the client's growth could not be predicted. It was believed that gains from the experience could be used in the wider spectrum of the client's life.

The central tenet of functionalism had to do with the importance of the *function* of the agency in which the helping process took place. The client had to work within the boundaries of the agency's function, and therefore had to adjust to limits in the same way that a person must adjust to the social structures of society (Yelaja, 1986). Unlike the followers of the diagnostic school, the functionalists felt that the agency setting supplied "focus, direction, and content to the worker's practice" (Smalley, 1970, p. 80). This aspect of functionalism was developed by Jessie Taft and owes much of its conception to the context of the times. Because of the social and economic hardships of the Depression, agencies were forced to reassess their purposes and services and thus developed a sensitivity to outer realities (Taft, 1939).

On the other hand, the diagnostic school (which included Gordon Hamilton, Florence Hollis, Lucille Austin, Fern Lowery, and Annette Garrett) argued that despite the rise of the welfare state and governmentally mandated agency functions, social workers were professionals—not merely employees—and as such needed to be autonomous in their work. To them, agency function was merely an incidental factor of practice.

Even though the diagnostic school eventually accepted a more optimistic view of human beings (based on ego psychology), the rift remained deep and the bitter debate lasted about 25 years. Graduates of the "functional" schools had trouble obtaining jobs in the "diagnostic" agencies, and vice versa (Ehrenreich, 1985). Helen Perlman (whose problem-solving approach contributed to some resolution between the two schools) described an incident at a social work conference in Atlantic City: "A group of us went into a restaurant and a very bright waiter met us at the door and asked: 'What side of the room do you want to sit on, the diagnostic or the functional?' " (Gottesfeld & Pharis, 1977, p. 109).

When the dust finally settled in the 1950s, functionalism had faded, but it left social work practice enriched with many of its theories, attitudes, and techniques, including the concepts of process and the therapeutic relationship as an impetus for growth and change (Goldstein, 1973).

## POST-WORLD WAR II

In the 1940s and 1950s, national prosperity seemed to return in full. Once again, social workers, economists, and most Americans believed that poverty, even if not fully eradicated, was a minor problem. It appeared that the political system, especially the Social Security Act, would take care of the public welfare.

The pattern was predictable. With the glow of prosperity, interest in social issues declined and attention was turned once more to individual treatment. There was no shortage of clients or lack of support for the return to an individual focus. The wartime effort had uncovered a startling number of young recruits with psychological dysfunctions that were amenable to casework. In addition, middle-class clients began to seek help from family service agencies. The government passed the National Mental Health Act in 1946 and established the National Institute of Mental Health (NIMH) in 1949, which funded and supported research and training.

During the post-World War II period, graduate-level social workers made headway in resolving their professional association membership concerns and establishing their dominance over their less credentialed counterparts. The accrediting body for undergraduate programs (the American Association of Schools of Social Administration) and the accrediting body for graduate programs (The American Association of Schools of Social Work) merged to form the temporary National Council of Social Work Education. This new organization sponsored a major study of social work education, the Hollis-Taylor Report (1951), which recommended that social work training be confined to the graduate level. As a result, the National Council of Social Work Education was dissolved and replaced in 1952 with the Council on Social Work Education, which accredited only graduate programs.

In 1955, seven separate associations of social work specializations merged to form the National Association of Social Workers (NASW). Social workers who did not have advanced degrees were not welcome. This policy effectively disenfranchised the majority of social workers in the public sector, few of whom had master's degrees.

Before long, however, MSWs were to be involved again in the public sector, and the "invisible poor" (Harrington, 1962) were to become a social issue. The professional association membership controversy would also surface again, next time with dramatic consequences.

## THE 1960s AND 1970s

Poverty in America, which had really never completely disappeared, reappeared as a social and political issue in the 1960s. In 1962, President John F. Kennedy evoked an essentially old remedy by signing the Social Service Amendments into law. The legislation provided increases in individual social services to welfare recipients that were supposed to help the poor lift themselves out of poverty.

Congress measured the success of this program by the number of people who became self-supporting. Unfortunately, the welfare rolls grew larger rather than smaller, causing policymakers and others to look askance at social work (particularly casework) and to question its effectiveness, especially since the government was allocating funds to send welfare workers back to school for their MSWs (thus creating *more* social workers).

During the next administration, President Lyndon B. Johnson took his turn at solving the welfare problem by declaring a "War on Poverty." In July 1964, the Economic Opportunity Act established the Office of Economic Opportunity, VISTA, the Job Corps, Upward Bound, the Neighborhood Youth Corps, Operation Head Start, and the Community Action Program. At first, social workers were not involved in these programs. However, their expertise was sorely needed and they soon became deeply involved. Nevertheless, the programs were not successful in the way that Congress measured success. Trattner (1979) writes that they failed because they were designed not to change society, but to change its victims.

This was an unstable time for social work. All sorts of schisms and divisions developed within the profession. Until the post–World War II era, social work had been defined exclusively along the *method* lines of casework, group work, and community organization. As social work settings multiplied, social work was redefined along a number of lines of overlapping specialized *fields* of practice—for example, mental health, schools, and aging.

Moreover, there were also theoretical divisions. Caseworkers not only claimed allegiances to the diagnostic and functional models and to Perlman's problem-solving model (1957) but also embraced a number of models gleaned from psychological and behavioral theorists (Northen & Roberts, 1976; Roberts & Nee, 1970; Thorman, 1981; Turner, 1974, 1979, 1986). Although separate and distinct direct practice models proliferated, there was an escalation of an earlier search for an underlying common base to all aspects of social work practice.

The idea that there was a generic foundation to all social work practice was hardly new.* It had originated from the Milford Conference of the 1920s. In fact, it may have been the glue that for 50 years held together—however loosely—a "profession in disarray" (Kahn & Kammerman, 1979, p. 3). During the 1960s and 1970s, there were several attempts to first *define* a common base of social work practice (Bartlett, 1958, 1970; Gordon, 1962, 1969; Gordon & Schutz, 1977) and then to *delineate* a unified or integrated theory of social work knowledge, purposes, values, and skills (Goldstein, 1973; Meyer, 1983; Middleman & Goldberg, 1974; Pincus & Minahan, 1973; Siporin, 1975).

## FROM CASEWORK TO CLINICAL SOCIAL WORK

The workers who remained in "direct practice" (a term which encompassed individual, group, and family treatment) became increasingly alienated from their counterparts who were focused on large-scale social change. The differences between the proponents of direct practice (by the late 1960s called "clinical social work") and social reform became so great that eventually many workers left the NASW to form societies for clinical social work.

After the painful assaults endured by social work during the 1960s, the concept of casework had gone underground. It emerged, transformed, into two new concepts: *social work practice*, an umbrella term for multiple services, interventions, and tasks, but which does not clearly distinguish direct from indirect practice (Meyer, 1983); and the *practice of clinical social work*, which was formally recognized as a specialty by NASW in 1978 and later defined as follows:

> Clinical social work shares with all social work practice the goal of enhancement and maintenance of psychosocial functioning of individuals, families, and small groups. Clinical social work practice is the professional application of social work theory and methods to the treatment and prevention of psychosocial dysfunction, dis-

---

* For a discussion of the generic-specific concept in social work practice and education, see Bartlett (1959).

ability, or impairment, including emotional and mental disorders. It is based on knowledge of one or more theories of human development within a psychosocial context.

The perspective of person-in-situation is central to clinical social work practice. Clinical social work includes interventions directed to interpersonal interactions, intrapsychic dynamics, and life support and management issues. Clinical social work services consist of assessment; diagnosis; treatment, including psychotherapy and counseling; client-centered advocacy; consultation; and evaluation. The process of clinical social work is undertaken within the objectives of social work and the principles and values contained in the NASW Code of Ethics.*

The use of the word "clinical" (which has Greek roots and literally means "at the bedside") to describe a type of social work practitioner and practice has been controversial. Nearly everyone—advocates as well as detractors—has an opinion about it. The California Society of Clinical Social Work (the first society formed to reflect the new emphasis) was the first to use the term as a professional title (Alexander, 1977). Members retained the "social work" to maintain identity with the parent field; "clinical" was added to describe the individual, family, and group method of practice.

Some critics believe that the term "clinical" is inadequate because it represents only the treatment aspect of practice, ignoring the components of prevention and provision of concrete services. However, even though a particular case may not need prevention or provision, it is the traditional social work three-pronged approach to clients that differentiates "clinical" social workers from other psychotherapists (C. Papell, personal communication, August, 1986). In essence, clinical social work is indeed "psychotherapy plus" (Hollis, 1972).

Other critics are offended by the medical connotation of "clinical." They feel that social workers who use it "put on airs" in an attempt to obtain the same high status enjoyed by psychiatrists and psychologists. Many others feel that it is an elitist euphemism for graduate-level social work (Meyer, 1983).

Supporters, however, generally agree that despite its ambiguity and imprecision, the term accurately reflects the "hands on" quality of practice and "until we get a better one, it's all we have" (J. Kasser, personal communication, January, 1987).**

One needs to go beyond discussions of semantics and become familiar with the origins of the clinical societies to get a true sense of the identity

---

* This definition was approved by the NASW Board of Directors, in June, 1984.
** Judith Kasser was the first president of the Pennsylvania Society for Clinical Social Work and a member of one of the early boards of the Federation. She is currently the Executive Director of the Jewish Family and Children Service of Greater Boston.

of the clinical social worker. The founding members of the clinical societies felt strongly that the NASW, as a result of the social climate of the late 1960s and early 1970s, was biased toward social change. Although the majority of clinical social workers valued social reform, they believed that it should be a personal choice and not a professional mandate: Social reform, although important, neglected the essentials. (For example, although a depressed welfare mother's situation might improve through progressive welfare reform, her depression might persist unless she received clinical attention.) Consequently, clinical social workers felt that the NASW was "de-skilling" the profession and no longer represented their interests. Moreover, they felt that schools of social work were "focusing on the need for social change at the expense of preparation for clinical practice" (Horton, 1987, p. 2).

From inside and outside the profession, critics were asking, "What good is casework? What good does it do to spend time in clean little offices with one person or one family when people are starving out there?" The sentiment was that even if casework works, it is a "drop in the bucket." Clinical workers feared that if they did not do something drastic soon, there would be no casework. They were certain that their work was special and different from the work of psychiatrists and psychologists (J. Kasser, May, 1987, personal communication). They wanted more than the right to practice; they wanted to be respected, credible, and legitimized.

Licensure and regulation were a way to protect the consumer and, at the same time, to legitimize the profession. The rationale was that "If we as a profession are disenfranchised, disempowered, have no status, and accept inequality for ourselves, how can we help others? No one will listen to us because no one will care what we have to say" (J. Kasser, personal communication, May, 1987). Clinical social workers were especially distressed that, in 1970, the NASW accepted members with BSW degrees—the first professional association ever to *lower* entrance requirements. Moreover, the NASW supported multilevel licensing, which meant the possibility of licensing of BSWs and paraprofessionals to provide specialized clinical services for which they were not adequately prepared.

Although these general concerns were widely shared, some specific events precipitated the organization of many of the state societies. For example, in California, the stimulus was a 1966 ruling by the state attorney general that defined psychotherapy as a "medical" specialty. This ruling endangered the freedom of clinical social workers to practice in that state. In Massachusetts, clinical social workers felt a lack of support from the state NASW chapter in their efforts to lobby for federal appropriations for mental health services (Pharis, 1973).

Opponents of the clinical societies feared an irrevocable split in the profession and were angered by what they perceived to be elitist and self-serving behavior. However, both sides were deeply committed to what they believed. Proponents of each group wanted the freedom and the professional support to do their work and to educate and train social work students in relevant programs of study.

The clinical societies multiplied rapidly. In the spring of 1971, a group of clinical social workers from Chicago met with social workers from other states to organize yet another society and discuss the clinical social work movement. The result of that meeting was the formation of the National Federation of Societies for Clinical Social Work. The founding members (California, Illinois, Kentucky, Louisiana, New York, and Texas) met again in Houston a few months later to ratify their constitution.

## CURRENT ISSUES AND TRENDS

Regulation of the profession remains a primary concern. In 1971, only three jurisdictions (California, New York, and Puerto Rico) had licensing or certification for clinical social workers, whereas in 1987, 45 states have some type of regulation. However, there is no uniform national regulatory process, which means there is a "patchwork of state regulation" (Horton, 1987), ranging from simple one-time registration with no exams to quite stringent criteria that may include written exams, oral exams, investigation of practice, or renewal procedures.

There are currently clinical societies in 30 states and jurisdictions, with approximately 10,000 to 13,000 members. The Federation, as well as NASW (with 55 chapters and 108,000 members), continues to press for licensure, but perhaps because there has been some success in this area, many clinical workers have shifted their focus to securing third-party reimbursements and to upgrading professional education (Pharis & Williams, 1984).

The NASW and the Federation are entering a new phase in their relationship. In 1975, the Federation had provided start-up funding for the establishment of an independent clinical social work registry, the National Registry of Health Care Providers in Clinical Social Work. In 1986, the National Registry offered an advanced certification program for clinical social workers who have had five years of clinical experience and who pass an examination in clinical social work practice. The NASW, which sponsors a similar registry (the NASW Register of Clinical Social Workers), announced a "diplomate" program with similar requirements. In response to this apparent duplication, a committee (composed of members from both the National Registry of Health Care Providers in Clinical Social Work and the NASW) was established. As a result of negotiations, that committee created the American Board of Examiners in Clinical Social Work, which combined the two programs into a single, independent, advanced credential—"Board-certified Diplomate in Clinical Social Work."

Another joint venture of national scope has been a collaboration between the NASW and the Federation to develop a system for peer review—a task that will continue to present a major challenge to the field in an era of competition for low-cost, high-quality health care (Jackson, 1987). Although it seems clear that both organizations will continue to exist independently of each other, these initial steps may usher in other joint efforts in the next decade and may be a "major step toward achieving a more unified, and thus stronger, voice for the profession" (Harris, 1987).

In a period of changing health care delivery systems, a "stronger voice" will be not only an asset, but a necessity. With the trend toward prepaid health plans and scarce health care funds, clinical social workers are likely to have an even greater role in the provision of mental health services. They already constitute the largest group of professional outpatient psychotherapists (Goleman, 1985).

One reason why there are so many outpatient social worker psychotherapists is that their salaries (or, in the case of private practitioners, their fees) are lower than those of psychiatrists and psychologists. Nevertheless, health care organizations may be tempted to cut costs even further by hiring social workers who do not have adequate clinical training or experience. In the light of this possibility, the Federation has recommended that minimal professional standards for practice be established for all allied health care personnel, including clinical social workers (Horton, 1987).

The growth of private practice is another recent trend. The traditional concern about private practice has been that it is unsuitable for a profession whose origins are in serving the poor and disadvantaged. Another concern is that "private" settings may cause practitioners to become disconnected or isolated and thus lose sight of social work purposes and values. They might come to "look" more like high-status psychologists and psychiatrists than social workers. Young people who are attracted to the profession might be motivated more by materialism than idealism (Land, 1987).

The response to these concerns is that anyone can have social and emotional problems; therefore, clinical social work should serve people from all socioeconomic classes. That stance is supported by the move toward coverage of clinical social work by private and public health insurance plans. Such coverage would mean that more potential clients would have a choice about where to go for treatment (agency versus private practice) as well as a choice of provider (psychiatrist, psychologist, or clinical social worker).

Still another recent trend is the "emerging domains of practice" (Waring, 1983), that is, the development of specialties within clinical social work. Not only are there expanded opportunities in mental health settings, the health care system in general is increasingly requiring clinical social workers, especially in areas of preadmission and discharge service for hospitalized patients, health education, and genetic and family planning counseling (Waring, 1983). In addition, industries have begun to recognize the relationship of the quality of work life to emotional and social well-being (and vice versa). The way in which these two factors impact on employee productivity and effectiveness has resulted in the growth of "employee assistance programs" staffed primarily by social workers. Clinical social workers are also taking a fuller role in the field of substance abuse, the expanding field of corrections, and in services in the courts, police departments, and victim-oriented settings (Waring, 1983).

One of the most important recent trends in clinical social work has been the growth of a pluralistic approach to clinical practice. That trend was my impetus for compiling this book. Today, social workers are less inclined to identify with and practice from a single therapeutic model. In one national survey, for example, 84% of the clinical social worker respondents indicated more than one theoretical orientation (Jayaratne, 1982). The trend is toward technical eclecticism and theoretical integration (Siporin, 1985).

## CONCLUSION

The discipline of clinical social work is still developing. From its early days, its course has been marked by its shifting focus on individual and social change and constrained by its embeddedness in the social, economic, and political climate. Its strength, however, lies in its commitment to its person-in-situation approach as well as its consistent values. Despite the debate and controversy, the schisms and divisions, one objective has remained constant—the dedication to helping people live happier, healthier, and more meaningful, productive, courageous, and caring lives. As long as people need help, social work practice and clinical social work should continue to thrive and to serve.

## REFERENCES

Addams, J. (1910). *Twenty years at Hull House.* New York: Macmillan.
Alexander, J. (1977). Organizing for excellence. *Clinical Social Work, 5,* 363–366.
Bartlett, H. M. (1958). Toward clarification and improvement of social work practice. *Social Work, 3,* 3–9.
Bartlett, H. M. (1959). The generic-specific concept in social work education and practice. In A. J. Kahn (Ed.), *Issues in American social work* (pp. 159–190). New York: Columbia University Press.
Bartlett, H. M. (1970). *The common base of social work practice.* Washington, DC: National Association of Social Workers.

Briar, S. (1983). Practice trends. In S. Briar, A. Minahan, E. Pinderhughes, & T. Tripodi (Eds.), *Supplement to the encyclopedia of social work* (17th ed., pp. 106–111). Silver Spring, MD: National Association of Social Workers.

Davis, A. F. (1967). *Spearheads for reform: The social settlement and the progressive movement, 1890–1914.* New York: Oxford University Press.

Davis, A. F. (1973). *American heroine: The life and legend of Jane Addams.* New York: Oxford University Press.

Ehrenreich, J. H. (1985). *The altruistic imagination: A history of social work and social policy in the United States.* Ithaca, NY: Cornell University Press.

Flexner, A. (1915). Is social work a profession? *Proceedings of the National Conference of Charities and Corrections.* Chicago: The Conference.

Germain, C. (1970). Casework and science: A historical encounter. In R. W. Roberts & R. H. Nee (Eds.), *Theories of social casework* (pp. 3–32). Chicago: University of Chicago Press.

Ginsberg, L. H. (1987). Economic, political, and social context. In A. Minahan (Ed.), *Encyclopedia of social work* (18th ed., pp. xxxiii–xli). Silver Spring, MD: National Association of Social Workers.

Goldstein, H. (1973). *Social work practice: A unitary approach.* Columbia: University of South Carolina Press.

Goleman, D. (1985, April 30). Social workers vault into a leading role in psychotherapy. *New York Times*, p. 17.

Gordon, W. E. (1962). A critique of the working definition. *Social Work, 7*, 3–13.

Gordon, W. E. (1969). Basic constraints for an integrative and generative conception of social work. In G. Hearn (Ed.), *The general systems approach: Contributions toward a holistic conception of social work* (pp. 5–11). New York: Council on Social Work Education.

Gordon, W. E., & Schutz, M. L. (1977). A natural basis for social work specialization. *Social Work, 22*, 422–426.

Gottesfeld, M. L., & Pharis, M. E. (1977). *Profiles in social work.* New York: Human Services Press.

Harris, D. V. (1987). Joint committee gets approval. *NASW News, 32*(1), 1.

Harrington, M. (1962). *The other America: Poverty in the United States.* New York: Penguin Books.

Hofstadter, R. (1956). *The age of reform.* New York: Knopf.

Hollis, E. V., & Taylor, A. L. (1951). *Social work education in the United States.* New York: Columbia University Press.

Hollis, F. (1972). *Casework* (2nd ed.). New York: Random House.

Horton, E. W. (1987, February). *Clinical social work in health and mental health: Description of the profession and recommendations for study.* A report prepared for The Institute of Medicine, National Academy of Sciences, on behalf of the National Federation of Societies for Clinical Social Work. Minneapolis, MN: National Federation of Societies for Clinical Social Work.

Jackson, J. A. (1987). Clinical social work peer review: A professional leap ahead. *Social Work, 32*, 213–220.

Jayaratne, S. (1982). Characteristics and theoretical orientation of clinical social workers: A national survey. *Journal of Social Service Research, 4*(2), 17–30.

Kahn, A. V., & Kammerman, S. B. (1979, November). *The personal social services and the future of social work.* Paper presented at the NASW Professional Symposium, San Antonio.

Kuhn, T. (1962). *The structure of scientific revolutions.* Chicago: University of Chicago Press (Phoenix ed.).

Land, H. (1987). The effects of licensure on student motivation and career choice. *Social Work, 32*(1), 75–77.

Lasch, C. (1965). *The new radicalism in America, 1889–1963.* New York: Knopf.

Leiby, J. (1978). *A history of social welfare and social work in the United States.* New York: Columbia University Press.

Lewis, V. (1977). Charity organization society. In J. B. Turner (Ed.), *Encyclopedia of social work* (17th ed., pp. 96–100). New York: National Association of Social Workers.

Lubove, R. (1965). *The professional altruist: The emergence of social work as a career 1880–1930.* New York: Atheneum.

Meyer, C. H. (1983). Selecting appropriate practice models. In A. Rosenblatt & D. Waldfogel (Eds.), *Handbook of clinical social work* (pp. 731–749). San Francisco: Jossey-Bass.

Middleman, R., & Goldberg, G. (1974). *Social service delivery: A structural approach to social work practice.* New York: Columbia University Press.

National Association of Social Workers (NASW). (1974). Social case work: Generic and specific: A report on the Milford Conference. Washington, DC: Author. (Reprint of original work published in 1929)

Northen, H., & Roberts, R. W. (1976). The status of theory. In R. W. Roberts & H. Northen (Eds.), *Theories of social work with groups* (pp. 368–394). New York: Columbia University Press.

Perlman, H. (1957). *Social casework: A problem-solving process.* Chicago: University of Chicago Press.

Pharis, M. E. (1973). Societies for clinical social work. *Social Work, 18*(3), 99–103.

Pharis, M. E., & Williams, B. E. (1984). Further developments in societies for clinical social work: A ten-year follow-up study. *Clinical Social Work, 12*(2), 164–178.

Pincus, A., & Minahan, A. (1973). *Social work practice: Method and model.* Itasca, IL: Peacock.

Popple, P. R. (1983). Contexts of practice. In A. Rosenblatt & D. Waldfogel (Eds.), *Handbook of clinical social work* (pp. 70–94). San Francisco: Jossey-Bass.

Pumphrey, M. W. (1956). *Mary Richmond and the rise of professional social work in Baltimore: The foundations of a creative career.* Unpublished doctoral dissertation, Columbia University.

Richmond, M. (1917). *Social diagnosis.* New York: Russell Sage Foundation.

Roberts, R. W., & Nee, R. H. (Eds.). (1970). *Theories of social casework.* Chicago: University of Chicago Press.

Robinson, V. (1930). *A changing psychology in social casework.* Chapel Hill: University of North Carolina Press.

Siporin, M. (1975). *Introduction to social work practice.* New York: Macmillan.

Siporin, M. (1985). Current social work perspectives on clinical practice. *Clinical Social Work, 13*(3), 198–216.

Smalley, R. E. (1970). The functional approach to casework practice. In R. W. Roberts & R. H. Nee (Eds.), *Theories of social casework* (pp. 77–128). Chicago: University of Chicago Press.

Strean, H. S. (1978). *Clinical social work.* New York: The Free Press.

Taft, J. (1939, June). *Function as the basis of development in social work process.* Paper presented at the meeting of American Association of Psychiatric Social Workers, National Conference of Social Work.

Thorman, G. (1981). *Guide to clinical social work.* Springfield, IL: Charles C. Thomas.

Trattner, W. I. (1979). *From poor law to welfare state* (2nd ed.). New York: The Free Press.

Turner, F. (Ed.) (1974). *Social work treatment.* New York: The Free Press.

Turner, F. (Ed.) (1979). *Social work treatment* (2nd ed.). New York: The Free Press.

Turner, F. (Ed.) (1986). *Social work treatment* (3rd ed.). New York: The Free Press.

Waring, M. L. (1983). Emerging domains of practice. In A. Rosenblatt & D. Waldfogel (Eds.), *Handbook of clinical social work* (pp. 1024–1035). San Francisco: Jossey-Bass.

Yelaja, S. A. (1986). Functional theory for social work practice. In F. Turner (Ed.), *Social work treatment* (3rd ed., pp. 46–68). New York: The Free Press.

# 2

# The Case

*Rachelle A. Dorfman, M.S.S.*

## The Family

The problems of the Shore family are common ones. Among them are unemployment, illness, and the worrisome behavior of the children. What is uncommon is that despite the frequent help from various social services, the problems never get resolved and the family members never seem to function free from symptoms. Individually and collectively, their lives are marked by crisis and emotional distress.

Nancy is 43; her husband Charley is 51. The children are Rena, 18, who was adopted as a baby, and Michael, 12. Until recently, the entire family lived in the two-unit duplex they own. Nancy, Charley, and Michael still live in the second-floor apartment. Rena, who had occupied the first-floor apartment by herself since she was 13, has moved out; she lives nearby and is "on her own." Charley has been chronically unemployed for four years; the family survives largely on the disability checks Nancy has received every month for the last 10 years.

Nancy is a large woman. She calls herself "grossly obese" and makes frequent apologies about her appearance. Her hair is graying and her figure is decidedly matronly, but her flawless skin and the gap between her front teeth give her a youthful quality. The only reservation she has about being interviewed is, "After it's done, I will probably run from social worker to social worker trying to do everything suggested."

For most of her 23-year marriage to Charley, "trying to get everything fixed" has been her full-time job. She is at her best during family crises: "Then," she says, "I take control. I no longer dread the terrible things that might happen because they have already happened. It is the waiting for the crisis to occur that makes me worry." Her anxiety often turns

# The Shores (1936-1987)

| Year | # yrs. married | Nancy | Charley | Rena | Michael |
|------|------|------|------|------|------|
| 1936 | | | Born | | |
| 1944 | | Born | | | |
| 1954 | | | Joins Air Force | | |
| 1955 | | Father leaves | | | |
| 1958 | | | Discharged from Air Force (age 22) | | |
| 1959 | | Moves to present house (age 15) | | | |
| 1962 | | -------------- Nancy and Charley meet -------------- | | | |
| | | (age 18) | (age 26) | | |
| 1964 | | | Mother dies in accident shortly before wedding | | |
| | | ------------ Nancy and Charley marry ------------- | | | |
| | | (age 20) | (age 28) | | |
| 1968 | 4 | -------------- Decide to adopt a child -------------- | | | |
| 1969 | | | | Adopted (6 weeks old) | |
| 1974 | | | | Begins kindergarten ("gifted" program) | |
| 1975 | 11 | ------------------ Michael conceived ------------------ | | | Born |
| | | | | | Circumcision hemorrhages (8 days old) |
| 1976 | | | | | Develops asthma (6 months old) |
| 1977 | | Receives first disability check | | | |
| 1980 | | | | | Begins kindergarten |
| 1981 | 17 | Second back operation (age 37) | Expected to be breadwinner (age 45) | Moves downstairs (age 12) | Placed in learning disability class |
| | | "Gram" dies | | | |
| 1982 | | Grandfather dies | Begins to perform in comedy club | Lives downstairs alone (age 13) | |
| 1983 | | | Chronic unemployment begins | | |
| 1984 | | | | Acts in dinner theatre | |
| 1985 | | | Hits boss; is fired | Runs away twice | |
| | | | Psychotic break (Bipolar depression) | Becomes interested in finding birth mother | |
| | | | | Beaten by Charley (after fight with parents) | |
| | | | | Drops out of high school | |
| 1986 | | | Enters chef school | Drops out of college | |
| 1987 | 23 | | Attends vocational rehab program | Moves to apartment | |

*Note.* The idea for constructing a "time line" about the Shore family came from Jay Lappin, M.S.W.

into panic. She becomes nearly immobilized. Unable to leave the house, she chain-smokes and imagines the worst of all possible outcomes. Anxiety attacks occur daily.

There is no shortage of crises. Recurring flare-ups of a back injury that Nancy suffered as a young nurse incapacitate her without warning, confining her to bed for weeks or months. The flare-ups are not the only crises. Three times, doctors predicted that Michael, asthmatic since early infancy, would not survive until morning. Twice Rena ran away from home and was missing for several days.

The small apartment reverberates with the sounds of their crises. One typical scenario began with an argument. Rena, then 16, lunged forward to hit her mother. Charley, in frustration and fury, pulled Rena away from Nancy and beat her, bruising her face badly. It was on that evening, two years ago, that Nancy and Charley told Rena she would have to leave when she turned 18.

A new problem with a potential for crisis is emerging. The downstairs apartment, which is now vacant, has never been occupied by strangers. (Before Rena, Nancy's elderly grandparents lived there.) Because they need the money, Nancy and Charley have decided to rent it to a young couple. Nancy is anxious about being a landlord. She is trying to train Charley and Michael to keep their voices down and their steps light. She wishes that her family lived downstairs and the tenants lived upstairs, and says, "I'd rather they walk on me than we walk on them." Again, she fears the crises that are certain to erupt.

Rena has been in her own apartment a few blocks away for three months. Nancy worries about that, too. She feels that as an adopted child, Rena is especially sensitive to being "put out." Nonetheless, she still argues with Rena about her "laziness" and failure to finish anything, but there is less explosiveness now that she is on her own.

Despite some relief in the tension at home since Rena left, Nancy is still anxious and often depressed. She has gained 15 pounds, sleeps poorly, cannot concentrate, and is forgetful. Most of the time, she stays inside. Outside, she feels that people make disparaging remarks about her; only at home does she feel safe. Her days are filled with baseball games on TV, soap operas, needlepoint, and worrying about what will happen next.

Charley is blond, tall, and broad-shouldered. It is not difficult to imagine that he was once quite an appealing young man. When he was 27, his dreams and schemes interested and excited Nancy. Occasionally, he still talks of outlandish inventions and "get-rich-quick" schemes. The difference is that his wife no longer believes in him or his dreams. To her, they are annoying at best and embarrassing at worst.

Charley says, "All I ever wanted was to be somebody. I just want to be known for something, to have someone walk by my house and say,

'That's Mr. Shore's house.'" He boasts about the time he went to California "to become a movie star" and of all the rich and famous people he knew and still knows. He speaks wistfully of "just-missed" opportunities for stardom and of inventions that no one took seriously. He likes being interviewed, saying, "It's exciting." Nancy reminds him that the interview is for a clinical book, not a Broadway play.

Five years ago, Charley performed on amateur night at a downtown comedy club. Nearly every Thursday night since then, he has performed for free in front of a live audience, using the name Joe Penn. His pride is unbounded when he is recognized in public as Joe Penn. Occasionally, someone will even ask for his autograph.

His wife supports this activity because it makes him happy, but her perspective on his act is somewhat different from Charley's. The show embarrasses her. She says that while it is true that the audience laughs, they laugh at Charley, not at his jokes: "He is not funny," she maintains. Charley's defense is that probably Nancy's favorite comedian's wife doesn't think her husband is funny either.

Over the years, Charley has had scores of jobs. He was a salesman, a janitor, a self-employed carpet cleaner. Even though he lost jobs regularly, he had little difficulty finding a new one. Four years ago that situation changed. He began to experience long periods of unemployment. Several times in the last three months, Charley has mentioned suicide, always in response to a suggestion that he, like Nancy, should get on disability because of his "condition." Charley says that he would rather die first. Although he seems serious about this statement, he has no plan or means in mind.

The "condition" is the Bipolar depression that was diagnosed two years ago at the time of his first and only psychotic break and consequent four-week hospitalization: "I always got depressed," he recalls, "but that was different. That time I really went off." Remembering his grandiosity and manic behavior, he says, "I guess you do those things when you are sick." He is maintained on lithium.

A "firing" precipitated his break. He had completed an expensive cooking course and was determined to prove he could "make it" in his first cooking job. He says he hit the chef when he could no longer tolerate the man's calling him names. (His bosses had complained that Charley was too slow and talked too much.)

Since his illness, he has had fewer grand ideas; he just wants a job he can hold. When he does allow himself to dream, mostly he dreams the way he did when he was a child, quietly and by himself. He likes to daydream while he works, which affects his performance. He was fired from his last janitorial job for forgetting to lock all the doors and for not cleaning thoroughly.

Presently, Charley attends a vocational rehabilitation program where he receives minimum wages for training in janitorial services, a job he says he already knows how to do. The program's goals are to develop the work skills and interpersonal skills needed for employment and to place him successfully in a job. Nancy is pessimistic about the outcome. She is angry because no one will tell her the results of his psychological testing. She says that if she knew for certain that Charley wasn't capable of holding a job, perhaps she wouldn't be so angry with him.

About Nancy, Charley says, "She is the best wife in the world, the same as my mother. She even worries like my mother, but I don't always like that because I don't feel like a man." The duplex they own was given to them by Nancy's Aunt Flo. While Charley appreciates the generosity, he says, "*I* wanted to do that. *I* wanted to buy the house."

Nancy agrees that she is parental. She prefers to handle important matters herself, not trusting Charley's competence with dollars, documents, or decisions. She complains that when she sends Charley to the store for two items, he invariably comes home with one of them wrong. But most of all, she complains about not having enough money to pay the bills: "I worry and he doesn't give a damn." Charley says privately, "I worry, too, but I act like I don't because there is nothing I can do."

The couple frequently fights about Charley's compulsive lying. He tells Nancy what he believes she wants to hear, claiming he doesn't want to upset her with the truth. He says he would like to stop but he doesn't seem able to.

Charley usually stiffens as soon as he approaches the front door of his house: "Will there be a problem? Will Nancy complain about bills? Will Michael come home from school beaten up? They will want me to solve the problems. But I can't."

Being a father has been especially difficult. Charley and his son bicker and fight like small boys. Nancy finds herself storming in, breaking them up, and scolding them both. She says that each one fights for her attention, trying to outdo the other.

Because father and son tend to relate to each other like siblings, therapists who worked with the family in the past attempted to restructure the relationship by suggesting that Charley teach Michael how to fish and play miniature golf. Charley and Michael always return home from such outings angrily blaming each other for ruining the day. Nancy says, "The whole time they are out, I am in a knot worrying that they are going to come up the steps screaming. I am never disappointed." She wants Charley to act more like a father. Charley wants that, too. "But," he says, "sometimes you just don't think about what you're doing when you do it."

Twelve-year-old Michael is tall and gangly. When he speaks, one can hear the phlegm rattle in his chest. It seems as though his voice is echoing through the mucus. His habitually knitted brow and his glasses make Michael appear to be very intense. He talks about "feeling funny" and "feeling bad." He feels bad because "asthma has taken away part of my life." His theory is that God gives everyone something he or she is terrific at. He says, "I haven't found mine yet—the asthma keeps me from it. I can't be a great athlete because I can't run fast. I can't have a puppy because I would wheeze. I just want to be good at something." According to his theory, God also puts a scar on everyone. People have to overcome their scars before they can find their special thing. Michael says asthma is his scar and he is waiting to outgrow it so that he can "find himself."

In the meantime, he is unhappy and lonely. Attempts to make friends are unsuccessful. He feels that even when he tries to behave himself, it is useless because his reputation prevents the other kids from relating to him in a new way. They still tease and pick on him. If someone hits him, he neither hits back nor runs away. He just "stays."

When he is not being "silly," he is more successful in relating to adults. Always attuned to the news, he usually knows what is current in world events, politics, and business. He sympathizes with underdogs and victims and talks about becoming a psychologist so that he can help them. He is fiercely patriotic and always truthful. When asked why he tells the truth when a lie would avoid trouble, he says, "I am a Boy Scout; I cannot tell a lie."

Scouting is the highlight of his life, but there is trouble there, too. Camping trips require a level of coordination, self-control, and social skills that he doesn't have. He gets reprimanded when he puts his tent up wrong or ties his neckerchief incorrectly. When this happens, he says, the other scouts laugh and he feels like a fool.

In junior high, Michael is in a learning disability class. Although learning disabilities and special classes are part of his history, the current placement was not made because of them; tests show that he has overcome or outgrown any learning disability he had. The problem that still lingers and prevents him from being "mainstreamed" is his poor social judgment. The same behaviors he calls "silly," his teachers have called "bizarre." These include touching others, making strange noises and motions, and laughing too loud or at the wrong time.

Last summer, Michael went to overnight camp. This spring, his parents received a disturbing letter from the camp. Michael was not invited back. The reason given was more than the typical foul language and mischief of 12-year-old boys. Counselors complained that at mealtimes he played with the utensils and plates, poured things into the pitchers and bowls, and threw food. He did not get along with the other campers and was seen as the instigator of most of the problems that occurred that summer. The staff felt that when he wanted to behave, he could, and that he willfully chose to misbehave.

Michael reports the situation differently. One moment he says that he acts "silly" because he falls under the influence of others. A moment later he suggests that he acts that way so that others will like him. Still later he says, "I don't really want to act like that. It's really kind of stupid. I don't know why I do it."

Michael is ambivalent about his sister's leaving. He agrees that it is more peaceful at home, but now his parents are fussing about him more than ever. Nancy estimates that she spends "80% of her worrying time" agonizing about what will become of Michael.

Rena, four blocks away in a basement efficiency apartment, has agonies of another sort. She is attractive, intelligent, and talented. Everyone, including Rena, always expected that she would be successful. But in the last few years, no matter how promising her beginnings, eventually she either quits or fails at everything she starts.

With 31 cents in her purse and no job, she is overdrawn at the bank and can't pay her bills. She has taken loans to pay for college courses she never completed. Rena feels old and tired.

Her parents used to call it laziness when she refused to go to school and stayed in bed until mid-afternoon. They thought she was lazy when she dropped out of high school, got a G.E.D., and enrolled in pre-med— only to drop out of that. They believed that if they allowed her to remain at home, she would "vegetate" and do nothing at all.

Nancy pressures Rena to "go to therapy" because she has come to believe that there must be something more seriously wrong with Rena than "laziness." Rena has agreed to go for therapy, partly because one usually does what Nancy wants. "Mother," she explains, "has a way of making you feel so bad and guilty, you finally either do what she wants or are mad because she makes you feel so bad." She has also agreed to go because she is lonely and confused. Unfortunately, there is a waiting list for outpatient services at the community mental health clinic— and Rena's name is at the bottom of that list.

Nevertheless, it seems that the therapeutic process has already begun. Rena writes her thoughts in her journal every day, and spends hours wondering about why she is the way she is. She is happy to be interviewed because she says she needs to talk about "this stuff."

She remembers when she didn't want to talk about "this stuff" or even think about it. At 16, when the adoption agency, at her request, sent some information about her birth mother, she forced herself not to think about it. Now she intends to find out about herself, even if it means thinking about painful things.

Like Michael, Rena has some theories. The first one is that she is so accustomed to living with problems and crises that she must create them when they do not exist: "Just look at my life. It is the only way I know how to live. When things are going well, I can't stand it." As proof, she describes her brief college experience. Her attendance was excellent; the work was easy for her. Then she met a boy. Not long after that, she dropped out, blaming it on him. She claims she merely needed an excuse to "mess up" and he was a convenient one.

She calls her second theory "the adoption." Even if her adoption explanation is a "cop-out," she feels that it gives her a starting point from which to consider her life. She notes that she has patterned her life in much the same way as her birth mother did. Her birth mother didn't get along with her parents and was a high school dropout. Like Rena, she picked boyfriends who seemed worse off than herself.

Rejection is another thing Rena thinks about: "I push people so much with my demands that they eventually drop me like a hot potato. Then I can say, 'See what they did to me. They left me out in the cold.'" Sometimes generous to a fault, but more often selfish and demanding, she offers her relationship with her adoptive parents as proof of how she forces her own abandonment.

The most recent project Rena has started is the search for her birth mother: "I want to know her, see what she looks like, talk to her. I would like to sing for my mother." Rena wonders about her birth mother's approval: "She didn't like me before. Will she like me now?"

An attorney is helping Rena through the morass of conflicting state and agency policies that keep her from finding her birth mother. Meanwhile, she attends meetings of adoptees, birth mothers, and adoptive mothers, at which members share information and discuss feelings. Rena is usually found in the hallway asking questions of birth mothers. She asks, "Do you ever think of your kid? How could you do it? Didn't you care?"

## Family History

*Nancy*

Cute and precocious, Nancy was the cherished only child, only grand-child, and only niece of doting adults. She remembers those early years, the years before age 11, as golden. Although her mother, an exceptionally beautiful and somewhat self-centered woman, was often away socializing with a large circle of friends, there were always Aunt Flo and Gram to shower her with attention, affection, and gifts.

Little Nan was seldom childish, so the adults took her with them to the theater, the ballet, and fancy restaurants. Her manners were beyond reproach. To the delight of the grown-ups, she always cleaned her plate. She remembers, "They thought it was so cute because I ate everything and, at that age, never got fat."

Her earliest memory is of when she was five: "I remember going to a store and getting a fried egg sandwich. I had to go a different way because I wasn't allowed to cross streets. Nobody was with me. A dog chased me home and tried to take my sandwich. I remember the smell of the sandwich and the dog chasing me. I was worried more about the dog biting my sandwich than biting me! That must have been the first clue to what food was going to be in my life."

Another memory is from the same period: "My father was a waiter. It was a big deal waiting for him to come home at night. He would bring food from the restaurant and we would all be together to eat it."

Her father was a shadowy figure. Between his job and his gambling, he was rarely home. Still, she felt closer to him than to her mother. One night, when she was 11, her parents told her that her father was leaving. It was difficult to understand—her parents never argued. Years later, she learned that the leaving was precipitated by gambling debts to "the mob." Her mother was either unable or unwilling to go.

Although Aunt Flo and Gram still bought her beautiful clothes and knit her angora sweaters, the golden years were over. Mother had to work now, so she was away more than ever, which seemed "just fine" with Mother. Nancy is convinced that her mother never wanted her, a fact which her mother denies. They moved several times in the next few years; Nancy remembers each place in great detail.

The first two summers after the marriage broke up, Nancy's father drove a thousand miles to get her and take her back with him for a visit. Her most vivid memory is from the second visit, when she was 12. She wanted to buy something at the pool, so she went to the hotel room to ask her father for money: "My father was lying in bed undressed and his 'wife-to-be' was ironing, with nothing on from the waist up. That is when I realized he was sleeping with her. Before then, I didn't know anything about that."

After that summer, her father stopped coming for her and stopped calling. He remarried and had more children, but Nancy did not find that out until later. She remembers wondering why he didn't love her. She confided only to Aunt Flo's dog. The poodle would lie by her side as she alternately wept and fantasized about her father's return. Finally, when Nancy was 14, a relative had a chance meeting with her father and reported his whereabouts. She called him immediately.

Nancy feels that if she had not initiated that contact, she would never have heard from him again. Today, when he visits Nancy (about once a year), he talks about his three wonderful children, especially his eldest daughter, Sandy. Nancy cringes every time. Her father has *four* children— *she* is the eldest. She is bitter and resentful.

When Nancy was 15, her family moved into the duplex she still lives in. Gram lived downstairs with Grandfather, and Mother and Nancy lived in the upstairs apartment. The arrangement worked well. Nancy continued to spend a good deal of time with her beloved Gram. She made friends in the new school and began to date.

By high school, Nancy was overweight. Mother, however, was still "movie star" beautiful. Nancy says, "Boys would come over to see me, but they soon liked my mother better." She felt like an ugly duckling next to her seductive mother clad in tight sweaters.

After high school, Nancy went to nursing school on a full academic scholarship. For the first time, she lived away from home. "All I wanted," she recalls, "was to take care of people." She learned how to do that in the exciting atmosphere of the hospital, where she developed lifelong friendships with other nurses and doctors. Some of those doctors are involved now with Michael's treatment.

She calls the nursing years "the best years": "I felt so good about myself, totally in control. I was a damn good nurse. I was capable of handling anything that happened."

The only nursing she has done since injuring her back was part-time, "under-the-table" work in an old-age home. During that 18-month period, she retained none of her old confidence. She feared that at any moment a situation would arise that she could not handle. But, as usual, when emergencies did occur, she handled them quite well. Back pain and the threat of losing her disability payments because she was working "illegally" forced her to quit.

Following every flare-up of her injury, Nancy repeats the same pattern. Once the pain subsides, she feels a welling of desire to return to school for an advanced degree in nursing and to ultimately return to her profession. She calls nursing schools and fills out applications; twice she made appointments with admissions counselors.

Eventually, a pall of gloom comes over her because she again realizes the full extent of her physical limitations. The flare-ups are unpredictable and keep her off her feet for months. Even between acute phases, she is unable to sit for more than short periods without pain. The possibility of completing a graduate degree, much less maintaining a career, appears remote. When Nancy again realizes this, she relinquishes her dream and returns to "earth" and to the family's problems.

### Charley

Charley's childhood lacked the comforts of Nancy's. He had few possessions and his clothes were never "right." He felt loved by his mother, but he was hardly the center of anyone's attention. His father, a one-time amateur boxer, was a "tough little guy." He dealt with Charley the same way he dealt with problems on the street—with his fists.

Charley's mother and father fought constantly. Although Father never hit his wife, Mother was known to have taken more than a few swings at Father. Charley remembers one night when he was five years old. His father came home drunk, having gambled away his money. "Mom knocked him out cold." The scariest scene from his childhood was the night that his father got out his gun to "kill" his boss, whom he accused of cheating him. Charley doesn't remember the outcome; he only remembers the grey shiny gun.

By contrast, most memories of his mother are pleasant ones: "One day when I was about six, I was watching Mother scrub the floor. There was an awful smell of ammonia. She stopped working, turned on the radio, and put her feet up. She said her feet were hurting. I rubbed her feet."

Another memory from the same period was from the first grade: "Whenever my friend and I would see each other, we would fall on the floor and wrestle. I remember my first-grade teacher, Miss Brown. She used to stick her long nails in our backs when she grabbed us. We had this cloakroom; there were little hooks on the walls. This one time, my friend and I were wrestling in the cloakroom. Miss Brown grabbed us both and hung us up on those little hooks."

When Charley was six, his sister Pat was born. Two years later his sister Louise was born. Charley says he was a lousy brother to his cute kid sisters, always hitting them. He recalls a stunt he pulled on Pat, when he was 17 and she was 11. She was with a group of friends and he was with a group of boys. Unexpectedly, they met on the subway. Always playing the clown, Charley took his shoes and socks off, saying that they were on backwards. His companions roared; Pat was red-faced.

Like Michael, Charley was teased daily by the other kids. He got beaten up regularly, until he managed to trade a prized toy for protection from a gang of four brothers. At 18, miserable and fed up with the fighting at home and on the streets, he enlisted in the Air Force. He proudly reports that he held that job for four years, the longest of any job. He still talks about the Air Force shows he performed in and drops names of the famous people he met during his enlistment.

After his discharge, he went to California. Charley paints the service years and the California period with a flourish. However, when he speaks of his Hollywood adventures and the starlets he dated, the details seem vague and much less compelling than the other details of his life.

## Courtship and marriage

Nancy and Charley's first date was at a picnic in the park arranged by mutual friends. They did not expect to be alone, but before they realized it, their friends had left for another picnic. Nancy will never forget those first few hours together. "He was so funny and handsome. He was different from anyone I had ever experienced. He told me he had been in the movies in Hollywood. He had ideas, inventions, and plans to have his own business. I believed everything he told me." Although he was only a delivery man for a florist shop, Nancy recalls, "he explained that he was learning the business to open his own shop."

Nancy promised to marry Charley in spite of her mother's and Aunt Flo's prediction that he would never make a decent living. Nancy wanted to prove them wrong. Two years after the picnic, they were married.

Charley's mother was struck and killed by a car shortly before the wedding. His father eventually remarried; he died of a heart attack several years ago.

The early years of the marriage were relatively free from the problems that currently plague them. Although Charley went from job to job, it didn't worry them. Nancy was more than willing to support the family by working at what she loved most—nursing.

They originally had a rich social life. Over the years, however, they lost many of their friends. Nancy feels that their friends left because, as they matured, they had less and less in common with Charley, who remained a "kid."

The couple's first problem was that Nancy could not become pregnant. Because of Charley's low sperm count and Nancy's irregular ovulation, pregnancy was nearly impossible. After four years, doctors suggested adoption. They had been married five years when they adopted six-week-old Rena. Six years later, Michael was conceived.

## Rena

Gram called her "the angel from heaven." Once again there was an only child, an only grandchild, and now an only *great*-grandchild as well. It was easy for the adults to dote on her; she was an exceptionally pleasant baby. At five months, Rena was standing. At 11 months, she could name the artist of each painting and print on Gram's walls.

Rena's early memories all include family members. She recalls playing a game with her father when she was just a toddler. She would sit on a special chair while he would go away and come back again. She recalls beckoning him to reappear. She also recalls a family vacation when she collected "teeny tiny" shells of different colors by the water's edge. When the vacation was over, she put them in a jar and took them home with her. She can still hear her mother screaming from the bathroom where Rena kept her "shells" in a jar of water, "Charley, Charley, these shells are moving!" Her father flushed what turned out to be snails down the toilet. Rena says she was very upset for a very long time.

Charley and Nancy knew that she was bright, but at first they did not realize the extent of her giftedness. At age five, she bypassed the regular kindergarten program and entered a "mentally gifted" first grade. At a very young age, Rena began to "belt" out songs like a nightclub performer. Her parents remember other parents asking her for her autograph after an elementary school pageant. Everyone was impressed by her talent and was certain that she would have a future in show business.

She also displayed an unusual artistic talent, wrote poetry and short stories, and had an extraordinary mechanical ability. The latter annoyed Charley, because she was able to "fix anything" and he was not.

Birthdays, a happy time for most children, were unhappy for Rena. She moped about, looking sad and distracted. Eventually, she revealed that she always thought about her birth mother on that day, and wondered if her mother thought about her, too.

In grade school, there was some foreshadowing of her "not finishing anything." Then, however, when she dropped activities before completion, she always replaced them with others that were more challenging. Now she drops them in failure and despair.

The calm of her grade school years gave way to a turbulent preadolescence and adolescence. Rena says of herself at 12, "I was a different person. I was good in school and never got into trouble. All the elders loved me. I was very intelligent and could talk to anyone about anything. But, like Michael, the kids didn't like me." She spent most of her time downstairs with Gram and Great-grandfather or with Aunt Flo.

Things were not going too well at home, either. Nancy had undergone one back operation and was facing a second. After that second operation, it was clear that she would never be able to stand the rigors of nursing again. Charley had to be the breadwinner. Michael was sick very often at that point, but the most difficult problem of all was Gram's death.

Rena's relationship with her great-grandmother had been unusually close. She spent more time in Gram's apartment than in her own family's. When Rena got yelled at, Gram would scream upstairs, "Don't touch that angel from heaven!" Several times, Gram slipped child abuse literature under the door. Rena said Gram was the only one in the whole world who ever loved her.

Shortly after Gram's funeral, Rena—who had been sharing a room with Michael—moved downstairs with her great-grandfather. It seemed a logical and convenient solution to the lack of space and privacy for a developing young girl. A year later, Great-grandfather died, and Rena stayed downstairs alone, sleeping in Gram's bed. Her parents now regret the arrangement. They point to the deterioration in her behavior that followed.

At first things went exceedingly well. Rena, on a whim, auditioned for a role on a proposed TV series and was one of the six finalists chosen in a national search. All the finalists were invited to New York for a screen test with a major television network. Charley was beside himself with aspirations to manage Rena and make her a star. The entire family was given the "star treatment." Unfortunately, Rena was told that she was "too cute" for the part.

Shortly after that experience, Rena won the leading role in the school play. As Dorothy in "The Wizard of Oz," she sang and danced and won the admiration of the entire school.

When the excitement of those two events passed and life returned to normal, Rena began to cut school. Then the fighting began in earnest. She refused to go to school or to keep the downstairs apartment clean. Charley and Nancy threatened, pleaded, punished, and hit. Twice Rena ran away. When she returned, she always promised to do better.

When she was 15, she got a part in a local dinner theater. Charley and Nancy allowed her to do the weekend performances if she attended school. When she was caught cutting again, her parents had her withdrawn from the company. They feel that she has never forgiven them for that.

Eventually Rena quit school. Now a few years older, she speaks of her shame and once more verbalizes her resolve to "do better."

*Michael*

Michael has been hospitalized 14 times and has spent hundreds of hours in hospital emergency rooms for asthmatic status, a type of asthma which gets out of control. (Sufferers are often near death as doctors struggle to bring it under control.) When Michael has an asthma attack, Nancy works closely by phone with the pediatrician monitoring his condition; she injects him with adrenalin and helps him to breathe with a nebulizer. Michael's earliest memory is of not being able to breathe, crying, "Gimme air, gimme air." He says, "Once, an ugly lady came in and gave me a shot instead. I wanted to hit her and tell her I didn't need the shot. I am perfectly fine."

Nancy claims that Michael was born unlucky. When he was only eight days old, he hemorrhaged from a circumcision wound. Asthma first appeared when he was six months old, and he was sickly and prone to high fevers throughout infancy. Nancy worried that he might not grow up at all. Now she worries about what his life will be like. Despite frequent illnesses, he was a happy baby. He walked, talked, and reached all the developmental milestones on schedule.

His worrisome health continued through the toddler stage. At two and a half, he had his first grand mal seizure and has been on seizure medication ever since. Doctors hold the medication responsible for at least a portion of his behavior problems, specifically the hyperactivity, but no one is quite certain just how much of his problem can be attributed to adverse side effects.

His behavior was first identified as problematic in kindergarten. After two months of first grade, he was transferred from the regular classroom to an LD classroom. Teachers said he could not follow instructions and seemed "lost" and confused. The report from the school psychologist stated that he had fine and gross motor coordination problems.

At 12, Michael feels that he is different from the rest of the kids. However, he refuses to accept his very real physical limitations; despite constant failure and rejection, he continues to try out for the track and softball teams. On the other hand, he acknowledges his difference and alienation and says, "Sometimes I feel that I should be in another country or in another time zone. I wish I could start my life over again." He likes the idea of having his story in a book because people "pity the underdog."

# PART II
## *Paradigms*

# 3

# Mental Structures and Personal Relations: Psychodynamic Theory in Clinical Social Work

*Polly Young-Eisendrath, Ph.D.*

Nancy and Charley Shore have frequent fights about Charley's "compulsive lying." Oddly enough, Charley knows he is lying, claiming that he "doesn't want to upset" Nancy with the truth. According to the case description, he says he would like to stop, but he doesn't seem to be able to. From this statement, we could say that Charley is aware of a conflict within his own desires: He wants to tell the truth, but he doesn't tell the truth. As the case report shows, the Shores have been influenced by psychodynamic theory in their ordinary conversations about themselves. They evaluate each other's actions and motivations, make self-reflective judgments about their own intentions, and they are sometimes aware of inner conflict.

Conversations about personal life among North Americans frequently contain sophisticated allusions to psychodynamic concepts that have become part of the popular domain. These concepts include resistance, repetition compulsion, unintended (or unconscious) meanings, and ideals of autonomous individuality. Although speakers may not know the theoretical terms, their analyses of themselves are infused with meanings from psychodynamic theories. In such conversations, "madness" is held at arm's length and confusions are examined from a clinical distance, with almost analytical precision.

We have arrived here from diverse ethnic and cultural backgrounds. Perhaps these differences predispose us to embracing a theory of self-reflection that is grounded in principles of individual freedom through conscious awareness. In any case, as a society, we have adopted a manner of talking about ourselves that prominently features psychodynamic ideas.

This mode of analysis of personal life emerged in Europe only about a hundred years ago. It is indeed remarkable that we Americans have adopted its central tenets into our everyday conversations in such a brief period of time. We will not address here the process by which psychodynamic theory has affected our society, but Bellah and his colleagues have done part of that work for us (Bellah, Madsen, Sullivan, Swidler, & Tipton, 1985). According to them, our society, which is predicated on personal freedom, equality, retributive justice, and the pursuit of individual happiness, has enshrined ideals of autonomous individuality. These ideals are frequently explained and supported by concepts from psychodynamic theory.

I consider it an impossible task to describe the influence of psychodynamic theory on clinical social work, because much of our thinking and relating has been influenced by psychodynamics even before we entered social work. My solution to this problem is to give a personally biased account of how I use psychodynamic theory—how I teach it, apply it, and converse in it—even while the theory is in the midst of major changes and conflicts. My supervision of clinical social workers has helped me to single out books and articles that practitioners find most useful; I will refer to these throughout this chapter.

So that we can begin with a common language, I will define *person* and *self* as I currently use them. Assumptions and concepts within psychodynamic theory have been misleading regarding these two central concepts. I hope to unravel some of the knots that currently keep psychodynamic theory tied to a mechanistic or materialistic model of mind. My own use of psychodynamic concepts is framed by the person-in-situation reasoning of social work practice, and it is influenced by the work of some contemporary social philosophers. The central role of the social environment in the evolution of personal being has been usefully articulated by Strawson (1959), MacMurray (1961), and Harré (1984).

Strongly influenced by these authors, I define *person* to be a primary, first-order experiential construct. The term, as used in ordinary conversation, refers to an animated being who has learned a theory about it*self*. The physical characteristics of persons are ubiquitous and publicly visible; we recognize a person as a spirited, embodied being with a particular form. Certain powers are universally assigned to persons in all instances, no matter what the culture or society. First, a person is endowed by other persons to be a point of action—to be able to move about and to be a physical location—as well as to intend, will, and choose in a way that is consonant with personal power. Second, a person is assumed to have a point of view, to have a kind of individual subjectivity that is known to us in terms of cognition, mentality, and perception. Through our relationships with other persons, we all acquire the means to define ourselves and others as makers and doers. Through kinesthetic, gestural, and symbolic communication, we develop *person*-ality as a condition shared among us. There is no knowledge or experience of being a person that is first learned alone and then attributed to others. In order to experience ourselves as persons, we need the reflections, definitions, and perceptions of others *on an ongoing basis* throughout our life cycle.

A *self*, on the other hand, is secondary to personal being. Through commerce with a culture of persons, we acquire a *theory* about our own subjectivity, about our individual experiences. Beliefs about autonomy, self-reflection, motivations, intentions, and the like are acquired through communications with one's immediate family, one's "tribe," and society in general. Beliefs about self strongly determine how persons relate to one another, especially as adults. As Harré says, "A person is a being who has learned a theory, in terms of which his or her experience is ordered" (1984, p. 20). At this point in time, we must assume that neither other animals nor organisms hold theories about themselves from which much of their reality is constructed. Theories of self are exclusively a characteristic of the personal world, whereas language and other symbolic expressions probably belong also to the world of animals.

As North Americans, we tend to believe that our definition of a self as an autonomous and unique individual *is* reality. Ethnocentrism frequently enters into conversations about self as we dispute the concerns of personal freedom in terms of inherent, self-reflective individual consciousness. Consider our conflicts with the Soviets and Chinese, for example, concerning such ideals as uniqueness, freedom of choice, and self-awareness. Partly because we have absorbed psychodynamic concepts into our theory of self, we tend to believe that separate and autonomous selves are the truest, least contestable aspects of personal reality. In other words, *as a society* we predicate our personal existence on certain ideals of uniqueness, personal power, and freedom of choice, assuming that because we have separate physical bodies, we are endowed with separate and original minds. As Michael Shore, who is only 12 years old, puts it, "God gives everyone something he or she is terrific at."

Clinical social work relies on an ethic of self-determination and on principles of an autonomous self. An example of such an emphasis can be found in the California Society for Clinical Social Work Code of Ethics. As Lemmon (1983) states in a summary of the code, the clinical social worker "is identified with and upholds the concept of improving the mental health and social functioning of individuals" and "is re-sponsible for special self-awareness so as to prevent the intrusion of [the clinician's] personal needs into the professional relationship" (p. 858). These statements imply normative standards for mental health and self-awareness. In social work (in North America) we have relied heavily upon principles of an autonomous self that sometimes contrast with our psychosocial orientation regarding the influence of social conditions, class, and economic and related factors. As we shall see, frequently our use of psychodynamic concepts has shaped a project of individual mastery or identity (e.g., our use of ego psychology), over and above our desires for collective social change, contextual analyses, and rational communities.

If we are to accomplish our goals of social change, communion, and community among diverse peoples, we must examine our use of psy-chodynamic theory. We first need to remember that personal identity and individuality are very new ideas within the history of human societies. According to Swan (1985), the first use of the word "identity," defined as it is today, was recorded in 1570. Swan also notes that the notion of personal "individuality" (in terms of a unique and separate being) makes its first recorded appearance in 1638, in poetry. Thus, the idea of an individual self is not quite 350 years old—not even as old as Harvard University—and therefore deserves to be used cautiously and imaginatively, in recognition of its potentially weak survival.*

Clients themselves regularly present complaints in terms of limitations and fears concerning self-determination. Nancy Shore says that in times of crisis, "I take control. I no longer dread the terrible things that might happen because they have already happened. It is the waiting for the crisis to occur that makes me worry." She imagines herself and her family to be the target of her problematic "control." For Nancy, the idea of *control* is loaded with ambivalent meaning—as loaded as it is within psychodynamic theory, in which it is used to describe both *effective* adaptation (e.g., mastery and self-control of impulses) and *ineffective* adaptation (e.g., over-controlling and rigid defenses).

## THE CONCEPT OF THE PERSON AND THE HUMAN EXPERIENCE

As we have seen, a basic premise of self in North America is *autonomy*. Persons are expected, as adults, to be self-controlling, self-determining, and individually responsible for an internalized morality and ethics.

Some "selves," however, are expected to be inherently more capable of self-determination than other selves. Implicitly and explicitly, we have

---

* For a further discussion of these issues, see Jaynes (1976), Broughton (1986), and Young-Eisendrath & Hall (1987).

*androcentric* norms for mental health, health, leadership, relationship, and mastery. Androcentrism refers to reasoning based on a male point of view—generally from the point of view of the "healthy" (normative) white male—that derives from men's experiences of themselves and others. Studies of Americans' expectations of "ideal" women and men, conducted by Broverman, Broverman, Clarkson, Rosenkrantz, and Vogel in 1970, and by Broverman, Vogel, Broverman, Clarkson, and Rosenkrantz in 1972, present empirical evidence of the collective prejudices we share about gender differences. These studies show that we expect men to be stronger, more objective, more competent, and more independent than women. More significant for this discussion, we expect women (ideally) to be less competent and more passively dependent than "healthy adults," when gender is eliminated on the questionnaire form. In other words, ideally women are assumed to be less capable than men in willing and directing their own lives. Our theories of female and non-white selves are organized in such a way as to explain the inferior self-determination of these people. They are expected to have less-than-ideal selves.

Women and people of color frequently find themselves in difficult circumstances regarding their knowledge and perspectives on reality. What they say or offer is questioned simply because they are assumed to be inferior (in self attributes) *or* because they are assumed to be *compensating* for their inferiority. The double bind of the inferior self is forcefully present in most conversations about self-determination, mastery, and freedom of choice. If a "less-than" person presents knowledge, perceptions, or experience in a forceful, insistent manner, that person will frequently be interpreted as compensating (e.g., being overcontrolling, too rigid, or too emotional). If such a person behaves in a non-self-determining manner, she or he will be more readily accepted as authentic, but will be assumed to be less intelligent, less objective, less competent, and so on—whatever falls into the stereotype of that person's gender, race, or class.

Until recently, all forms of psychodynamic theory have been infused with androcentric reasoning about autonomous individuality. Ideals of separation and individuation, mastery, rationality, and individual freedom have been the cornerstones for most psychodynamic theories of self. Sullivan's interpersonal theory and Jung's analytical psychology have been exceptions to some degree, as we shall see. In both of these systems of thought, ideals for collective functioning and dialectical balance have replaced ideals of individual autonomy. Still, these theories are constrained by androcentrism regarding certain concepts of femininity, women's abilities, and the value of intuitive relatedness. As we survey the history of psychodynamic theory, we should keep in mind the limitations I have briefly identified. We will return to them in the final section.

## HISTORICAL PERSPECTIVE

The history of psychodynamic theories and methods could hypothetically be traced all the way back to the ancients, who used introspective debate, such as the Socratic method, to explore cultural and intellectual issues. The method of contained dialogue, or rhetorical influence through disciplined conversation, is in evidence both in the traditions of confessional practices and scholarly exercises.

However, the specific history of the psychodynamic theory of psychological processes usually begins with the work of Freud and Breuer in the last decade of the 19th century. Because psychodynamic concepts are so intrinsically tied to the methods that historically evolved for the treatment of personal difficulties, I have combined my summary of key concepts with a historical review of major elements in the development of psychodynamics over the last hundred years.

## KEY THEORETICAL CONSTRUCTS*

### Freud's Theories

Because I presume that practice is the foundation of theory, I will begin by recalling that the 19th century practices of mesmerism (later called hypnosis) and exorcism were the primary interpersonal arenas in which early psychodynamic theory was forged. The essential features of these practices are captured by a modern definition of psychotherapy: "a planned, emotionally charged, confiding interaction between a trained, socially sanctioned healer and a sufferer. The interaction is focused on the relief of the sufferer's distress, primarily through symbolic communications, but sometimes through touching" (Frank, 1971, p. 10).

Hypnotists used the term *rapport* to describe the dynamic energy that was thought to move between the healer and the sufferer. This "influence" was later called *transference* in psychoanalysis.

In 1893–95, Breuer, a physician friend and mentor of Freud, collaborated with Freud on the book, *Studies in Hysteria* (Breuer & Freud,

---

* I have drawn upon many sources for my account of psychodynamic theory. Some of these are particularly relevant to social work practice. I especially recommend the following: 1) for a foundational history of psychodynamic thought, Ellenberger (1970); 2) for a sound contextual understanding of object relations theory, Greenberg and Mitchell (1983); 3) for an understanding of the paradigms of psychoanalysis, Loevinger (1976); 4) for a comprehensive tracing of the interface between clinical social work practice and psychodynamic theories, the relevant selections from Rosenblatt and Waldfogel (1983) (for example, see pp. 266–279, 361–381, 401–419, and 623–649); 5) for a useful reworking of ego psychology into an active, personal language, Schafer (1978); 6) for a classic reading of the influence of ego psychology on social work practice, Wood (1971); 7) for a complete review of interpersonal theory, Sullivan (1953); and finally 8) for contemporary feminist revisions of psychodynamic theory, Chodorow (1978), Baker Miller (1976), Irigaray (1985a, 1985b), Young-Eisendrath and Wiedemann (1987), and Young-Eisendrath (1984).

1893–1895/1955), which contains a description of therapeutic methods along with some psychological theory. Breuer and Freud made special use of hypnotic trance: Rather than "suggesting away" symptoms, as other physicians had done, they used the trance state to induce a patient to remember previously forgotten ideas. Working with his famous patient Anna O. (who was actually a social worker, Bertha Pappanheim), Breuer discovered the "talking cure" as a treatment for hysteria. Hysteria, which literally means "wandering womb," was a particularly female malady that presented as a collection of symptoms that appeared to be physical but that had no physical cause. Common manifestations of hysteria included paralysis, muteness, deafness, respiratory disturbances, and blindness. Under the influence of the "cathartic method" of suggestion, the patient could talk freely about the memories of traumatizing events (usually from early childhood) that had apparently contributed to the manifestation of symptoms. Freely talking and reliving the emotional impact of the lost idea were vehicles of cure. The re-association of affect and idea was called "abreaction" by Breuer and Freud; they considered it to be the keystone of the cathartic method. Even then, however, Freud observed that the patient often resisted the cure; at a critical point in treatment, the patient would block associations, wander off the subject, or speak about attractions to the doctor. Freud decided that these "resistances" and "defenses" were evidence of a mental force that conflicted with the patient's desire to remember and be cured.

Through these early practices, Freud revealed what would become evidence for the central idea of later psychodynamic theory: conflicting or opposed mental forces or desires within an individual. The desire to remember was in conflict with the desire to forget early traumatic events. Freud's training and practice as a research neurologist prompted him to conceive of this conflict as taking place within a mental space, between energies or forces that he represented as brain events. At about the time that he and Breuer were writing their book, Freud was also working on an extensive map of the mind as a topography of forces and structures that could be explained in terms of biological functions.

Two renditions of Freud's observations and ideas were beginning to emerge. One was an account of people talking freely and rendering symbolic meaning within an emotionally charged relationship; the other was of mental spaces and energies. The latter represents the greater part of our inheritance from psychodynamic theory.

Along with Loevinger (1976), we shall call the first major phase of Freud's work his "trauma theory" period. Trauma theory describes the reliving of actual traumatic events (usually sexual abuse) that have interfered with a person's development. This period ended formally with the publication of *The Interpretation of Dreams* (Freud, 1900/1953). Heralding both an interpretive method for understanding dreams (which could be translated into understanding symptoms, everyday jokes, and slips of the tongue) and a complete model of mental spaces and forces, this book introduced many new elements that became central aspects of psychodynamic theory.

Between 1900 and 1920, Freud wrote about a theory of instinctual conflict that Loevinger (1976) and others have called the "dual drive theory." Unconscious motives and meanings were seen as products of opposing instinctual forces—for example, love and hate, narcissism and relatedness. Freud also described conflicts between opposing thought forms, which resulted in competing constructions of reality and competing perceptions. One form of thought, as revealed through dreams, was a "primary process" that Freud assumed was the chronologically earliest form of mental process, also called "hallucinatory wish-fulfillment." Primary process thinking is characterized by associations of sensations and images through contiguity, similarity, and proximity. These associations are clusters of images (visual, auditory, tactile, etc.) around significant emotional experiences. These images can result in distortions (hallucinations) that replace conscious perceptions of external reality. In Freud's view, infants had to distinguish gradually between hallucination and reality perception. This procedure resulted in a "reality principle," a method of constructing "secondary process" thinking according to the forms of time, space, and causality that are considered to be a part of rational life. Moreover, primary and secondary mental processes continued as competing thought forms during adult life.

Freud showed how to uncover rational meaning in dream thoughts by translating primary process into secondary process thinking. From his self-analysis of his own dreams and from his work with patients, Freud came to believe that his earlier theory of traumatic injury in early life was incorrect. With a new method of interpretation in hand, he now formulated a theory of infantile wishing and fearing. Infantile wishes and fears, especially regarding sex and aggression, were the cornerstone of Freud's second period of psychoanalytic theory. These unconscious or repressed desires and motivations were in conflict with the dictates of morality in civilized life, resulting in both symptomatic behaviors and dreams that contrasted with conscious rationality.

In 1905, Freud published his essays on sexuality (Freud, 1905/1953) and amended his earlier trauma theory of psychopathology. Although actual traumatic abuse of a child could produce later symptoms, adult psychopathology was more often related to conflicts between infantile desires and the constraints of reality. Freud developed a *genetic model* of three periods of infantile sexuality that were in evidence still in adult functioning:

1. The *oral* period is roughly the first year of life, when the infant experiences tension between nurturant pleasures and fearful needs

or overwhelming anxieties. Basic survival needs for food and security are primary motivating forces that connect the infant to the mother.

2. The *anal* period is from about two to three years of age, and involves conflicts between the child's desire to submit to and be protected by the parent, and the parent's dominance of the child's eliminatory processes and free movement. The child's desires (e.g., to be approved and to be physically active) frequently seem in opposition to the parents' desires (e.g., to restrict the child's movement and to discipline the child's body).

3. The *phallic* or *Oedipal* period occurs from about three to four or five years of age. This phase of development is the basis of what is now known as the classic "conflict theory" of psychoanalysis; it focuses on the child's fantasies of romantic love with the parents, which are opposed to the aggressive threats of parental discipline. At this stage, the child has loving feelings for the parent as a *whole person* (instead of loving just part of the parent, such as the breast). The child is also aware of basic structural body differences, and knows, for example, that males have penises and that females do not. Furthermore, children are aware of their relative smallness in the face of their parents' much greater strength and powers. Freud describes an Oedipal love affair between the male child and the mother, and between the female child and the father. A necessary outcome of this period—renouncing romantic love for the parent of the opposite sex—permits the child to be receptive to being educated as a member of society. Resolution of the Oedipal conflict is significantly different for boys and girls, as we shall see.

In *The Interpretation of Dreams*, Freud presented a schematic model of primary and secondary thought forms, which he called the *topographic model*. Throughout the second period of psychoanalysis, Freud revised and elaborated this map, and attempted to systematize it in a series of essays that are usually called his "papers on metapsychology" (Rickman, 1975). Responses to distress, such as mourning, sexual wishes, fears, and feelings of aggression, were cast as mental energies, powered by drives and organized around the idea of *opposition*.

The metapsychological theory of psychoanalysis relies on assumptions of mental energies and mind spaces. It is frequently used as the primary model for discussions of psychodynamics, and infuses our language with terms like defenses, structure, unconscious, and conscious, entities that have no immediate referents in our experience. These energies and entities are assumed to exist within an individual mind. The *fallacy of individualism*—the belief that because we have separate bodies, we have separate, unique, individual minds—is an assumption that continues to be problematic in psychodynamic theory. This fallacy leads us to study human behavior in terms of an individual mental space.

Metaphors of mental spaces and energies have tended to be fashioned according to the cultural dictates of particular eras. In Freud's time, his theoretical discussions were empowered by references to physical and biological materialism and to Newtonian physics. Now that we have transcended these models, Freud's discussions seem outdated.

However, two elements of Freud's formal theory continue to trouble us in clinical work: the disease model of interpersonal disturbance and the fallacy of individualism. We have translated his ideas of opposing mental forces and spaces into discussions about symptoms and causes of mental disease. We then talk about certain interpersonal processes in terms of the "damage" done to the mental spaces within the individual. This tendency to describe things according to psychodynamic theory makes our interpretations of people's interactions almost impossible to translate directly into ordinary language. We have developed a psychodynamic language, with specialized referents, which we can share only in part with our clients, if we can share it at all.

In the second period of the development of psychoanalysis, Freud shifted his clinical work more toward interpretation, using the models he had constructed. More than in the earlier period, he imposed his meanings on patients' free talk. By and large, this was a curative move, because he was able to persuade people that their distresses were meaningful and that they could make rational connections between the gaps in their experiences. One form of interpretation became primary: the account of the conflictual triangle of the Oedipal relationship (two parents and one child). This conflict was seen as the major transition to be mastered in order for an individual to pass from childhood into adulthood. Freud's interpretation was androcentric, based on observations about himself and the contributions of males to society and culture. So much has been written on this topic that I need not go into detail here, but I recommend a volume of essays edited by Garner, Kahane, and Sprengnether (1985) as fundamental to understanding the evolution and meaning of the Oedipal complex for clinical work, in both Freud's time and now.

According to psychodynamic theory, the major tasks of the mature personality involve love and work as contributions to society. Freud believed that motivations to succeed in these activities were in conflict with infantile wishes, especially the sexual and aggressive wishes of the Oedipal period. The resolution of the Oedipal conflict prominently involves the child's willingness to replace wishes and fears with realistic ideals for development.

For the little boy, this involves turning away from romantic love for his mother and identifying with his father, taking his father as an "ego ideal" or a template for future achievements. The penis is the special focus of fantasies about the father, and the enormous (from the child's perspective) force of the father's aggression is the focus of fear. The boy fears that his father might castrate or otherwise brutally punish him if the boy were to make actual moves to possess his mother; at the same time, the boy admires the greater strength and larger penis of his father. By renouncing his romantic wishes, the boy acknowledges his father's greater strength and power; by idealizing the father, the boy looks forward to his own eventual possession of a big penis and a woman like his mother. From this point on, the boy can take the initiative to become a man and a father.

The girl has a more difficult time resolving her wishes and fears from this earlier period, because neither she nor her mother possesses great strength or a penis. The girl's tasks are also to renounce her romantic love for her father and to idealize her mother. Two major obstacles often prevent a satisfactory outcome of the idealization of the mother. First, the mother is the object of primitive sexual fantasies for both male and female infants. The girl has to transfer her sexual feelings from her mother to her father in order to feel the conflict between her own wishes and aggressions. If she does not make this step, she will always remain undifferentiated from her mother and will remain in love with her own female self; her narcissism will be primary (that is, she will be doomed to love herself and unable to love another).

Even when a girl is able to feel a captivating love for her father, she will still have difficulty identifying with her mother; she will be disappointed—even enraged—that neither she nor her mother possesses a penis (a source of sexual gratification and a visible body part). In the best of outcomes, the girl can only partly idealize her mother and partly surrender her love for her father. This love will be replaced by the desire to become a mother herself and have a male baby. Because her mother represents no ideals for culture or achievement, however, the girl will have little identification with the ideals of her society, *unless* she identifies with her father.

Identification with her father will predispose her poorly for adult life as a mother. Because of unresolved castration rage, the girl develops a "castration complex" and "penis envy" as neurotic problems more frequently than the boy develops an "Oedipus complex" or "castration anxiety." Hence, more women seek psychoanalytic treatment (as well as other forms of psychological treatment) in adulthood.

Indeed, this idea about an early lack of an adequate female image for maturity has been carried over into many psychodynamic theories about female inferiority. The crucial element of many psychodynamic theories of female development is that all girls and women *compensate* for primary psychological inadequacies in ways that are distorted, troubling, and/or regressive. In the psychodynamic literature, women are frequently described in terms of compensating for some basic incompleteness. Their desires and manner may be characterized as needy, controlling, manipulative, or domineering, *or* as aloof, passive, enraged, depressed, and depleted. Within psychodynamic theories of female development, we are lacking an ideal female self, complete without compensation, primarily because the female self has been predicated on a fundamental lack or inadequacy.

Following the publication of Freud's *Beyond the Pleasure Principle* (1920/1955), another major theoretical development took place that has had much influence on clinical social work. Whereas all of Freud's earlier contributions stressed *unconscious* mental events, this later work turned toward *consciousness* and is part of what is called his "ego psychology." In 1920, Freud dismissed the efficacy of the initial model of a *pleasure principle* (as opposed to a reality principle) as the major explanatory principle for human motivation. He then introduced the idea of a psychobiological principle of aggressiveness and destructiveness that he called the "death instinct." He also began to formulate a concept of *mastery* as the development of conscious control (responsibility).

In our dreams, relational patterns, accidents, and acting out of impulses, we often repeat earlier injuries. According to Freud, this occurs because we are trying to master the anxiety that surrounds these events in order to experience personal control. Freud's first formal attempt to trace the dynamics of a new model of mind, which by then included the principle of mastery, came with the publication of *The Ego and the Id* (1923/1961). This new model, which is frequently cited as the basis of all psychodynamic theory, is known as the *structural model;* it introduced the concepts of the ego, id, and superego.* The structural model is a map of the "residues" of early relationships that are constantly being reconstructed within the individual mind. For example, parents demand that the child curb its impulses in order to be loved, and the child then demands this of itself, setting up guiding ideals for conduct. The intrapsychic structure of personality is the residue of early interpersonal relationships.

The famous dictum of Freud's ego psychology has become the principle of much clinical social work. In Freud's language, rather than in his translators' terms, it states, "Where 'it' happens to me, I will become the master." In other words, psychoanalysis will attempt to influence a person towards active mastery of a situation in which the person feels overwhelmed, dominated, or oppressed by circumstances.

The final piece of Freud's ego psychology was added in 1926 in his paper on anxieties, inhibitions, and symptoms (1926/1959). Here Freud developed a "signal theory" of anxiety that reversed his earlier theory

---

* Incidentally, most of us now know that Freud did not use these abstract terms which his English translators imposed on "das ich" (the I), "das es" (the it), and "das über ich" (the over-I).

from the dual-drive period. He had previously assumed that repression was a defense against remembering traumatic ideas, and that anxiety emerged as an indication that unconscious emotion was bound up with the repressed idea. In terms of his ego psychology, Freud *now* assumed that anxiety precipitated repression and was often the occasion of repression. Intense anxiety, experienced as fear, was a signal to a person's sense of "I"; it was a danger signal. Consequently, the person would unconsciously defend against anxiety by either blanking out a perceptual event, denying its effect, or otherwise forgetting it.

The complex evolution of psychoanalytic ego psychology is a major chapter in clinical social work history because of its profound influence on psychiatric social work in the United States. In 1936, Anna Freud published *The Ego and the Mechanisms of Defense* (1936/1946), which continues to be widely read among social workers. In 1939, the year of Freud's death, Hartmann published *Ego Psychology and the Problem of Adaptation* (1939/1958), which elaborated and extended principles of mastery through metapsychological concepts. Erikson's *Childhood and Society*, published in 1950, was an especially influential translation of ego psychology into psychosocial terminology, although it is principally remembered for its rendering of Freud's theory of infantile sexuality into a model of life development through the mastery of conflicts. Unfortunately, even with the assistance of Erikson's translation of Freud's ideas, social workers have continued to use ego psychology in a way that is plagued by the mechanistic language of metapsychology. Concepts such as defenses of the ego, the structural model, and the conflicts of drives are often reified or are used in an unexamined way, which is confusing to client and social worker alike.

Two contemporary theorists of ego psychology have expanded the work of Erikson and have provided a less problematic language for considering ego mastery as the active desire to control one's impulses, wishes, and fears. The first is Vaillant (1977), who has done substantial research on defense mechanisms and has ordered them into a structural hierarchy of relational patterns. The second is Schafer (1978), who has reworked the entire metapsychology into an action language that is effective in both its clinical applications and its theoretical clarifications.

These theorists permit us to grasp what is useful in ego psychology and help us to understand it in terms that can be clearly communicated to other professionals and clients. Schafer, especially, clarifies the domain and boundaries of personal responsibility, a key concern in social work. Claiming and enacting personal responsibility is perhaps the central curative outcome of psychoanalytic forms of treatment, both classical and modern. Describing how the transformation from passive experience to active mastery takes place within treatment, Schafer states:

In one way or another and more and more, the analysand sees himself or herself as being the person who essentially has been doing the things from which he or she was apparently suffering upon entering analysis, and from many other problems as well that will have been defined only during the analysis itself.

. . . Analysis also establishes progressively that it is the analysand who, unconsciously and painfully, has been arbitrarily but understandably assuming responsibility for both the fortunate and unfortunate happenings of life. By the term *happenings* I am referring to those events over which in actuality the analysand as child or adult had little or no control. (pp. 180–181)

We see how Rena Shore is attempting to cope with her personal responsibility for relationship when she says, "I will push people so much with my demands that they eventually drop me like a hot potato. Then I can say, 'See what they did to me. They left me out in the cold.' " She expresses a conflict about how she behaves with other people, a conflict that she recognizes as a pattern (i.e., making demands of others versus doing something else) but seems helpless to change. If Rena increased her understanding about what she is and is not responsible for in her expectations of friends and authority, her mastery of her circumstances would probably also increase.

We could also analyze Rena's statement in terms of her defense against trusting others and her unintentional desire to dominate them (in the same way that she might have been dominated by the desires and needs of her parents at a time in her life when she had little ability to satisfy their expectations). Looked at in this way, Rena has been, since childhood, in an "identification with the aggressor," a repetition compulsion to reenact what she passively endured.

## Object Relations Theory

Another major branch of psychoanalytic psychology developed in what has been called "the British School." This work initially evolved from the contributions of Melanie Klein in the 1940s and 1950s, but has continued into the present. Klein formulated her conceptions about human development primarily through her psychoanalysis of children, even very young children (e.g., 2 years old). Theorists such as Winnicott, Fairbairn, Guntrip, and Jacobson—and later Mahler, Kernberg, and Kohut—extended the psychoanalytic theory of *object relations*. The history of this branch of theory is complex and multifaceted. Its findings were originally opposed and rejected by classical psychoanalysts and were then gradually embraced, although they are still frequently criticized in terms of classical theory.

From about the 1940s on, some analysts began to work on the idea that the primary dyadic relationship of infant and parent is more influential in adult development than is the triadic relationship of the Oedipal conflict. Much of the evidence for this view comes from analyzing the dreams and fantasies of young children, and from observing the synchronized interactions of infants and mothers during the first three years of the children's lives. Some contributors to object relations theory also call their work "ego psychology" (e.g., Blanck & Blanck, 1974), but they assume that ego (as the expression and image of "I") develops almost from the beginning of life and that it is filled with the attributes and behaviors of adult caretakers.

By and large, object relations theory is an interpretive clinical method that uses the *tools* of psychoanalysis, but modifies the rules and symbolic meaning of *interpretations*. Images of exaggerated power, beauty, aggression, and achievement—especially as these are expressed and expected in relationships with other adults—are interpreted in terms of primary-process hallucinatory wish fulfillment. For example, recall that Charley Shore told Nancy during their courtship that he had been "in the movies in Hollywood" and then continued to imagine himself as a movie star (with no realistic possibility of becoming one). We might interpret his behavior as a residue of an early relationship in which he believed himself to be special or felt that he had to be the "star" in order to be loved. Object relations theorists stress the "primitive" or infantile aspects of overwhelming emotions. Winnicott, especially, considers the defenses of psychotic disturbances, such as splitting into all-good and all-bad, denial of external reality, and auditory hallucinations, to be organized against the *re*-experiencing of primitive "agonies" of infancy: falling apart, falling forever, being out of relation to one's body, and feeling entirely alienated.

Because many object relations theorists maintain a belief in a *drive* or *structural* model of mind, they continue to talk in terms of conflicts of drives, forces, and part-persons (such as ego and id). American psychiatrist Harry Stack Sullivan is an exception; the central feature of his work was the *interpersonal* origin of the self. Sullivan (1953) offers a definition of personality that distinctly contrasts with the psychoanalytic model of individual mind: "The developmental history of the personality . . . is actually the developmental history of interpersonal relations" (p. 30). His only concept of individual subjectivity is that of a "self system," a patterning of habitual actions and thoughts around certain assumptions, expectations, and logic that is born out of anxiety in interpersonal relating. These "security operations" are efforts to avoid anxiety, which Sullivan interprets as a threat to self-esteem.

Sullivan's model of therapeutic influence includes the idea that the healer, as well as the sufferer, should participate in the process of change.

Together they communicate in three competing modes of reality: *syntaxic, parataxic,* and *prototaxic.* The syntaxic mode is a form of communication that is perfected through the use of a shared symbolic system, such as language, that permits a *consensual validation* of one's experiences and thoughts, which are validated intersubjectively as good, true, and so forth. This mode is comparable to Freud's reality principle, although it does not rest on any particular cultural categories of space, time, or causality. The parataxic mode is based on images and ideas that take shape in early relationships and are not directly communicable through syntaxic means; they always remain somewhat idiosyncratic and hence may provoke *distortions* in consensual meaning. Comparable to Piaget's (e.g., 1936) preoperational thought and to Freud's concept of primary process, the parataxic mode is organized by emotionally charged images and ritualistic actions. (For example, Michael Shore's belief that his asthma is a punishment from God is parataxic.) The prototaxic mode is least accessible to words and is expressed through movement, gesture, facial expression, and bodily functions (such as yawning). Nancy's compulsion to eat could be considered a prototaxic expression that has emotional meanings which could not be adequately captured by words.

Sullivan can be considered an object relations theorist, even though his assumptions rest entirely on interactional principles. Unlike other object relations theorists, he has no model of mental energies, spaces, or structures that are entirely private and individual.

## Adler's and Jung's Theories

Two other psychodynamic theorists have made significant contributions to social work practice—Adler and Jung. Adler broke with Freud's psychoanalytic circle in 1911 and founded his own school of individual psychology. Grounded in theories of social being and convinced of the influence of class and cultural differences, Adler developed a personality theory that emphasized conscious functioning, long before Freud's ego psychology took shape. Freud felt that Adler's concept of life style and his insistence on the unity and coherence of personality were incompatible with psychoanalysis. Many of Adler's ideas and methods of carrying out the clinical interview have been adopted by social workers, without any recognition that they are Adler's. Because another chapter in this book is devoted entirely to Adlerian methods, I will focus mainly on Jung's analytical psychology in this section.

Jung also feuded with Freud, with whom he had collaborated from 1908 until 1913. Convinced of the radical significance of Freud's interpretations of unconscious meaning, Jung had become a member of Freud's circle of colleagues in 1907. He had also persuaded Bleuler, who was director of the Psychiatric Clinic at the City Hospital of Zurich, to adopt psychoanalytic methods and theory in clinical practice and research. Jung and Bleuler were influential psychiatrists prior to their association with Freud; they brought substantial outside validation and legitimacy to the Viennese group. However, neither Jung nor Bleuler ever entirely accepted Freud's major premises, and they both ultimately rejected the physicalistic reductionism and the dogmatism of Freud's theory of infantile sexuality (especially as it was applied in analyses of culture).

After his departure from Freud's psychoanalytic circle, Jung retired from professional life for about four years and then reemerged with a theory of personality development that is substantially different from Freud's and Adler's.

In the foreground of Jung's contributions to psychodynamic theory is the idea that the unity of personality is an achievement both in the moment and over time. Although everyone strives for a coherent and continuous sense of self, this state of being is not easily achieved. According to Jung, personality is organized around core images and states of emotional arousal. Core *emotional* states of human life, such as bonding and attachment, are expressed among humans everywhere in similar gestural and imaginary forms. Core *arousal* states include the predisposition to form unified *images* that are expressed as universal themes of emotional meaning in forms such as myths, art, rituals, and relationships. Jung used the word *archetype*, which means primary imprint, to describe a specifically human form for instinctual-emotional expression in human relationship. Archetypes constitute organizing principles for relating to self and world that are inherently given as predispositions to emote and respond in images. These images are filled out with actual experiences and strivings—what Jung called "psychological complexes"— that form the bases for personality. Such complexes include the structured images, ideas, and feelings that are associated with experiences of Self, Mother, Father, Child, and World. Prior to learning language or a shared symbolic system, an individual experiences these complexes as highly charged patterns of image, affect, and action (similar to Sullivan's parataxic mode and Piaget's preoperational thought). Complexes involve core arousal states of communication (such as attachment and aggression) and also core states of personal identity (such as self and other). Some complexes are more accessible to conscious awareness and language than others.

Jung's analytical psychology includes a basic premise of balance— between conscious and unconscious functions, between self and other, between culture and nature. Jung replaced the concept of *opposition* between these elements with the idea of a *dialectic*, a balanced interplay of opposites evolving towards a synthesis into a whole. His model of healthy personality is an interaction of complexes that influence each other, similar to the way in which people influence one another. Consequently, his method leads to an understanding of the meaning and expression of complexes, through which one can establish a "right attitude" or relationship to them. The development and welfare of one's personal being are dependent on a balanced interplay of the personal and the archetypal, of the individual and the collective. Interpersonal relationships offer the resistance and reflection necessary for a person to have access to complexes excluded from consciousness.

Jung's theory states that, especially in midlife, women and men confront the limitations of their own desires by means of relationships with valued partners, usually of the opposite gender. Jung described the outcome of love and conflict with a partner as the integration of a "contrasexual" complex. Women confront and integrate the meaning of their own masculinity as they recognize the real persons of the men onto whom they have projected the "animus" (repressed female masculinity). Men confront and integrate the meaning of "anima" as their male femininity as they recognize the real persons of women on whom they have depended and with whom they are bonded. In order to experience one's own repressed gender identity, one must necessarily withdraw the projection of the complex from the other and distinguish between what is latent in oneself and what is authentic and actual in the other.

Psychodynamic theory has an elaborate history and development that I have briefly characterized in terms of certain themes. I have been stressing how the fallacy of individualism creates a problematic error in much clinical theory and interpretation. Beginning with his models of mind, and ending with his principle of mastery, Freud tended to examine personal being as though it occurred in individual isolation. On the other hand, Freud's therapeutic methods were interactional and dialogical; he was as fascinated by narrative and symbolic meaning as he was concerned to present a scientific model of mental processes.

Because of Sullivan's and Jung's work, we are able to move beyond the tendency to construct individualistic models and to map mental spaces. In their theories, as well as in theories of modern ego psychology (e.g., Schafer, 1978), we can reclaim the interpersonal space as the primary condition of both psychotherapeutic intervention and psychodynamic theory. Similarly, object relations theorists and feminist revisionists of psychodynamics stress the contribution of dependence to development. Ideals of mature *dependence* are as essential for adulthood as ideals of mature *independence*.

Certain advantages of psychodynamic theory make it especially useful in contemporary clinical social work practice. Perhaps foremost is its long and interesting tradition, in comparison to other, more recent, theoretical approaches. Through sharing of information by practitioners, researchers, and clients, psychodynamic theory has evolved as a common language for expressing conflict and unresolvable dilemmas in human existence. Moreover, its framework for practice and theory has always been dialogical. Opportunities for talking freely about the symbolic significance of emotionally charged events are provided at every level—from the consulting room to the lecture room. Ruptures, disputes, and diversities among theorists have always been recast into renewed forms within the broad circle of basic principles of the theory.

What are these principles? The first is that personal being evolves through some kind of dialectic of stability and change, of predictable patterns of conflict with somewhat predictable emotional themes. The second is that these conflicts occur, and are even predestined to occur, right from the beginning of each person's existence. The third is that they are never resolved and are always motivating. We can think of psychodynamic theory as a project designed to capture the essential characteristics of a person. When or if the project is completed, we will have mapped the boundaries and domains of that individual's being in a way that distinguishes it from any other living being.

## ASSESSMENT

Psychodynamic assessment can take many forms, but it generally focuses on conflict: intrapersonal, interpersonal, or both. Adaptation to core conflicts, such as those articulated by Erikson, and the defense mechanisms that structure the adaptation, are areas for evaluation. I use a blending of psychodynamic categories and stage developmental theory (e.g., Loevinger's, 1976, ego development stages) to understand patterns of interpersonal functioning that are implicit in clients' actions and thoughts.

Two kinds of reflective activities are involved in assessment: *description* and *analysis.* Descriptions are the facts, data, evidence, impressions (visual and otherwise), and narrative histories presented by clients and other sources (e.g., schools). Analysis involves the process of organizing descriptions to fit a theoretical framework, which may then be used as a reference system to aid in making decisions. Analysis also attempts to sort descriptions into a shared language that practitioners can use to communicate with each other and their clients; such descriptions present more enduring "truths" than transitory data could present.

The line of reasoning that I follow in making an assessment is:

1. *Presenting problem*—stated in client's language;
2. *Personal data*—descriptions of identifying information, history, living situation, and the like, gathered from a variety of sources;

3. *Assessment of the person(s)*—analysis of the data and descriptions into a theoretical formulation from developmental and psychodynamic theories (or other theories of choice);
4. *Assessment of the problem for intervention*—reformulation of the presenting problem in theoretical terms, in light of the assessment of the person(s);
5. *Goals or objectives for intervention*—formulation of goals in client language, based on the reformulation of the problem and considering the practical limitations of the client's situation;
6. *Method of intervention*—deciding upon the means, time framework, and setting for reaching the short-term and/or long-term goals for intervention;
7. *Method of continuing reassessment*—finding a method for evaluating and reevaluating the effectiveness of the intervention in reaching its goals, which includes a final reevaluation of the person in terms of the original assessment.

Because of space limitations, I cannot give a *complete* assessment for the Shore family, but I will follow the procedure I have just outlined in a brief assessment of their case. Out of the varied collection of problems identified by members of the family, I have chosen two as representative presenting problems. The first is Nancy's worry that, after the initial interview, she will "probably run from social worker to social worker trying to do everything suggested." The second is Charley's observation that Nancy is like his mother, but, as he says, "I don't always like that because I don't feel like a man." These presenting problems indicate conflicts between a current attitude and a past orientation that now seems problematic. Nancy currently wants to cooperate with the interview, but believes that it may trigger her (past) desire to "fix" everything. Charley currently likes and admires Nancy's being the "best wife in the world," but believes he might feel like a son (as in the past) because Nancy seems to be more adequate than he is.

For a number of reasons, I would treat the parental couple as my clients. First and foremost, Rena and Michael exhibit a variety of age-appropriate, developmental competences that I believe could be adequately strengthened by clearing up some of the relational conflict between their parents. Rena is capable of leaving home successfully—and should do so with the support of her parents. Nothing in the case indicates to me that ethnic or interpersonal patterns would interfere with Rena's move into the world; she appears to have the physical and emotional health to cope with young adulthood. Michael seems more vulnerable, but his early development (reaching all milestones on schedule) and his intelligence indicate resources for further development. With realistic knowledge about Michael's physical limitations (presented as educational information during couples therapy), Nancy and Charley could guide him into a more satisfying adolescence. Keeping him out of therapy may strengthen this possibility.

From the data presented about the Shores as a couple, I would make the following psychodynamic and developmental analyses of Nancy and Charley, as in step 3 above.

## Nancy

Nancy's typical defense mechanisms include a mix of what Vaillant (1977) calls "neurotic" and "mature" defenses with one "immature" defense. Her *immature* defense against anxiety is *acting out*, exhibited primarily by her chain-smoking and overeating. According to Vaillant, this defense consists of impulsive behavior that rids one of anxiety prior to the felt experience or knowledge of conflict. Addictions are common expressions of this defense.

Nancy primarily uses neurotic defenses against anxiety. *Rationalization* for not returning to school for an advanced degree is evident in her accounts of illnesses and other barriers. Similarly, her concept of herself as an incessant worrier, supported by evidence from her past, functions as a rationalization for all kinds of fears and false starts. Additionally, *displacement* of her fears about her own inadequacies contributes to her obsessive concern about Michael and to her sitting at home and waiting "in a knot worrying" about what is happening to family members.

On the other hand, Nancy uses several *mature* defenses to cope with stress and anxiety. *Altruism* is primary: "All I wanted was to take care of people." Her worrying sometimes has the form of *anticipation* and results in useful planning and structuring; for example, she is "trying to train Charley and Michael to keep their voices down" in anticipation of new tenants in the downstairs apartment. She *sublimates* her anxieties by doing needlepoint and by keeping financial records. There are also evidences of *humor* (she makes jokes about her weight and her worrying) and *suppression* (she is able to set priorities regarding financial and health concerns).

Clearly, Nancy has competences that have emerged both in mothering and in nursing. Her academic scholarship, her ability to get jobs, and her lifelong friendships with other nurses and doctors are all important aspects of mastery of work and love as an adult. Finally, Nancy demonstrates some ability for insight about her own patterns and motivations. Both in describing conflicts and in remembering the past (e.g., the story about the sandwich and the dog), Nancy indicates that she is able to perceive patterns of past behaviors that contribute to current difficulties.

In terms of Loevinger's (1976) ego developmental stages, Nancy is using primarily *self-aware* functioning. This stage includes formal thought operations (inductive and deductive reasoning), multiplicity of norms and values, and concerns for one's identity (wanting to discover "who am I?"). Conflict between approval-seeking and autonomy, conflict between rules and self-chosen standards, and concerns about goals, successes, and the future are prominent aspects of this stage that fit with Nancy's presentation of herself.

## Charley

Charley's defenses against anxiety are primarily of the *immature* and *neurotic* type. His immature defenses include *denial* of external/interpersonal reality, *idealization, projective identification,* and *acting out.* Denial through fantasy is obvious in Charley's "get-rich-quick" schemes, his compulsive lying, his daydreaming, and his "just-missed" opportunities for stardom and inventive genius. Idealization and projective identification are prominent aspects of his relationship with Nancy. He calls her "the best wife in the world," but he can't stop lying to her. Charley appears to identify with being Nancy's son and to project the "mother" onto Nancy. He then seems unable to "solve the problems" and behaves toward Nancy as if he is another son, fighting for attention and trying to outdo Michael. To some extent, Charley elicits mothering behavior from Nancy and then feels helpless to take up parental roles himself. Finally, acting out his impulses, wishes, and fears is a major way in which Charley rids himself of feelings of conflict. Beating Rena, leaving and losing jobs, and getting fired for fighting are examples of acting out. (From the psychiatric classification of Bipolar Depression, we assume that Charley has also used *psychotic* defense mechanisms, including perhaps delusional projection, dissociation, or bizarre splitting, but we do not have direct evidence that this is a continuing situation.)

Neurotic defenses include *rationalization* and *reaction formation.* Rationalization is evident in his claims that he doesn't want to "upset" Nancy with the truth, and in his belief that Nancy's criticism of Joe Penn (his stage character) is typical of a comedian's wife. Reaction formation is likely to play an important part in Charley's portrayal of Joe Penn. His shame and resentment are expressed as a desire for approval for being funny; he is not sublimating his anxiety in humor.

Charley has fewer competences than Nancy, but he is motivated for some kind of employment and has some apparent charm and performance ability. It does not appear, however, that he has clearly mastered either love or work concerns of adult life. Furthermore, there is no evidence that he is capable of insight about his motivations or actions.

In Loevinger's terms, Charley is operating at the *self-protective* stage, most typical of ages four through six. Concrete and stereotyped thought, hedonistic motivations, avoidance of work (seeing all "work" as burdensome), fearing one's own feelings, and manipulating others through one's actions are prominent features of this stage that describe Charley's behaviors.

## TREATMENT OF CHOICE

In terms of psychodynamic features of development and interpersonal functioning, Nancy and Charley are in different worlds. We could offer explanations from object relations theory that would tie early patterns of interpersonal relating—and early traumas—to current functioning in both of these people. When it comes to our treatment decision, however, we know from the above assessment that most forms of psychodynamic therapy would *fail* with Charley, although Nancy might be helped by insight-oriented brief therapies such as rational-emotive therapy, gestalt therapy, transactional analysis, or other adaptations of psychodynamic approaches that focus on differentiation from family-of-origin problems. The "depth" psychotherapies—such as psychoanalysis or Jungian and object relational approaches—would not be indicated for Nancy, because they rely on an ability to sustain observational insight during emotionally charged therapy sessions. Nancy's health problems, family stresses, and low self-esteem make her an unlikely candidate for depth therapy. All forms of insight therapy are contraindicated for Charley while he is at the self-protective stage. As I have said elsewhere, therapists should "avoid the inadvertent consequences of assisting an extremely self-protective person in supposedly becoming more 'assertive' and in 'getting into feelings'—consequences which often lead to great confusion and manipulation of others by the client" (Young-Eisendrath, 1982, p. 332). Clients who are predominantly at preconformist stages, as Charley is, need to develop conformity and to experience the gratifications of rule-oriented behaviors. Without the sense of conformity, which comes through belonging, group-oriented values, and helpfulness, a person cannot develop either self-evaluated standards for behavior or the basis needed for insight.

My assessment of the problem to be treated here is *not* structural development or personality change, however. I would intervene on a time-limited basis to improve communicative practices, psychological know-how, and parenting skills, and to reinforce the use of higher level defense mechanisms within the interpersonal field of this couple. To deal with Nancy's problem of "trying to do everything suggested," I would make a contract that we work on specific chores and tasks over a six-month period. The tasks would be clearly outlined at the conclusion of each couple session. Because one of Charley's problems is that he does not "feel like a man," I would reinforce goals and reasons for job training as a means to support his ideals about masculinity. Later, those initial treatment goals would be further structured toward resolving conflicts about parenting and income management. The methods of evaluating these goals would be structured according to the specific treatment issues raised by the couple in the first therapeutic session.

## THE THERAPEUTIC PROCESS

In recent years, researchers of therapeutic outcome and process have increasingly moved towards delineating common strategies for therapeutic change that cut across theoretical orientations and methods. The work of Frank (1971), Goldfried (1982), and Strupp (1977) has especially influenced me in looking at some of these strategies. As a result, I have found that four basic "curative factors" of therapeutic influence appear to occur in all forms of therapy. I use these factors to guide my choice of interventions that will fit with particular client situations:

### 1. *Management of rapport or empathy in the interpersonal field*

The therapist establishes a basic *trust* or empathy with clients through the use of specific (e.g., joining skills, interviewing skills) and nonspecific (e.g., hope, suggestion, and authority) factors. After such trust has been established and is communicated, the therapist uses it to support, persuade, advocate, confront, and oppose various events within the therapeutic interactive field. With a couple, the therapist may act primarily to *manage* (that is, direct) the trust or rapport that is already present between the pair. Using and managing separation anxiety (by confronting loss and dependence) is a major component of rapport management in couple therapy.

### 2. *Structuring learning or educational activities within the interpersonal field*

The therapist instructs clients in new ways of thinking and acting that are appropriate to the tasks at hand. Different from "education" or "schooled" learning, therapeutic learning is matched to clients' functioning and intuitively "makes sense" to the clients. This kind of learning is accommodated to the clients' defenses, motivations, and conflicts, in a personally suited manner.

## 3. *Increasing clients' personal responsibility*

By clarifying, interpreting, and educating, the therapist functions to increase clients' understanding of responsibility and their ability to act responsibly. This central curative factor contributes to increased mastery, which can result in personality change, even when personality change is not the specific goal of therapy (as with the Shores). To increase clients' personal sense of agency in their lives, the therapist must understand the domain and boundaries of personal responsibility from the clients' point of view. Designing tasks and provoking reflection on mastery can have enduring effects on clients' abilities to feel and be in charge of their lives.

## 4. *Increasing the clients' frame of reference for meaning-construction*

Different from therapeutic learning, this factor concerns the clients' reasoning, logic, or cognitive structures. The therapist provides opportunities, through tasks, interpretations, and the like, for the clients to examine and reexamine assumptions, and to connect these to consequences of actions. By repeatedly covering certain themes—for example, the antecedents and consequences of acting out—clients develop a new interpretive framework for understanding their behaviors and the world in general.

Although, as I have noted, these factors are common to all forms of therapy, they are not always fully utilized in every approach. In the case of the Shore couple, I would review my plan for the use of psychodynamic techniques to be sure that my methods would encompass as many of these curative factors as possible.

From my assessment of Nancy and Charley, I had decided upon a time-limited, non-insight-oriented form of psychodynamic treatment. My major intervention tool, as outlined in the first factor, would be the available trust between Nancy and Charley; I would increase empathy by improving their ability to speak and listen to one another. New learning about parenting, increased responsibility-taking (for Charley, regarding job requirements; for Nancy, regarding achievement/career goals), and restructuring of defensive patterns between members (i.e., reinforcing higher level defenses such as anticipation, sublimation, and altruism) would be connected with the second, third, and fourth curative factors.

I have described techniques and methods for this form of couple therapy elsewhere (Young-Eisendrath, 1984) in detail, but I will briefly summarize here how I would proceed with the Shores.

Using Jung's theory of development in middle life, I would map the psychological complexes that characterize the interpersonal field of this couple. From the case description, I would guess that the "negative Mother complex" plays a major role in increasing fear and disrupting trust. This nonrational complex is organized around the negative pole of nurturance: suffocation, stagnation, and death. Separation anxiety and fears of engulfment are feelings associated with this complex; they are not feelings that are under personal control, but are enacted as part of an interpersonal field in which one member of the couple is projecting the complex and the other is identifying with it. As I have written elsewhere:

> [When a woman identifies with this complex, she] describes herself as a disaster: she is fat, ugly, stupid and unattractive in the extreme. Yet she also feels too powerful and may be apologetic about this. . . . She feels at fault for most of the misery in her family, but she does not know why. Often she openly calls herself a "bitch" or "nag" and finds that her partner readily agrees with her, confirming her self-hatred. (Young-Eisendrath, 1984, p. 66)

The other complex that seems to play an important role—and which complements the negative mother—is the "bully" or "negative son." This complex involves openly aggressive and threatening behavior of a "macho" type, which flares up in response to "overwhelming" experiences of the negative mother complex.

Assessing the interactive field of the couple would take place in an initial two-hour session, during which the members of the couple would engage in a variety of dialogical activities. At the end of this session, as I described above, a therapeutic plan would be drawn up and assessment of the members would be summarized.

A treatment plan is drawn up for six two-hour sessions, approximately a month apart. The sessions focus on the interpersonal field of the couple, using co-therapists trained in psychodynamic methods (especially Jungian methods). Interventions take place specifically through techniques that support, interpret, expand, and explore the dialogue of the couple. Homework is given after each session, and clients report on homework at the beginning of the next meeting. In general, emotions in the interpersonal field are "heated up" by interventions that increase separation anxiety (threats of separations, interpretations concerning grief and loss, etc.) and are "cooled down" by interventions that increase feelings of bondedness.

For the Shores, I would use primarily noninterpretive techniques, including the following:

1. *Doubling:* This is a psychodramatic intervention in which co-therapists sit behind clients and "speak out" as "alter egos." The wording and pacing are matched to clients, but the content is typically

shaped by the nonrational complexes that are dominating the couple's interactive field.

2. *Therapist assessment:* Using ordinary language, co-therapists dialogue about what they perceive to be happening between the members of the couple, emphasizing both nonrational complexes and curative factors for change.

3. *Empathy interview:* Co-therapists (usually gender-matched to the couple) interview each member of the couple while the other partner listens. Such interviews, which last about 10 minutes, focus on some aspect of confusion (usually projective identification) that is interfering with each person's listening to the other. The objective is to increase empathy for the partner being interviewed.

4. *Homework and wrap-up:* At the end of each session, there is a structured review of that session's content and key themes, as well as an explanation of the next homework assignment. Homework often includes reading or listening to tapes, as well as activities such as scheduling intimate time, cooperating in new methods of parenting, or trying out new ways of talking.

After six sessions, the couple (in this instance, the Shores) is evaluated in terms of the goals specified at the outset and additional concerns that have been raised during the six-month period. If all has gone well (as I would anticipate, based on the above plan and goals), they will be directed to return in six months for a follow-up session, which would be conducted in a manner similar to the initial assessment. If problems still existed (by then a year after the first intervention), another course of couple therapy would be instituted, or some other therapeutic approach would be recommended.

This active form of psychodynamic couple therapy utilizes concepts from object relations theory, ego psychology, Sullivan's interpersonal theory, and Jung's analytical psychology. It is relatively easy to learn and may be used with or without insight techniques.

Given the briefness and co-therapist arrangement of this form of treatment, the relationship between clients and therapists is generally "consultative." That is, the therapists are primarily consultants on the interpersonal field of the couple relationship. Although transference (and countertransference) issues can emerge, they are rare (much rarer than in individual intensive dynamic psychotherapy).

## LIMITATIONS OF THE MODEL

I have presented this particular model of psychodynamic treatment to respond to several of the limitations that are typically a part of the classical application of psychodynamic theory to social work practice. First, as I have tried to show, psychodynamic assessment permits a practitioner to be flexible and wide-ranging when matching treatment to the needs of clients. Because psychodynamic theory has a long and well-documented history of different (and competing) conceptual frameworks, it is closer to a paradigm (a broad sweep of conceptualizations) than many other theoretical formulations are. Second, when psychodynamic theory is freed from the language of mental structures and situated within the interpersonal (interactive) field, its explanatory power increases. Third, psychodynamic theory can be used for assessment without necessarily being applied to a treatment regime.

The central limitation of psychodynamic theory, from my point of view, is its androcentric bias. As I stated earlier in this chapter, theories that center on men's experience of themselves and their relationships tend to build dominance-submission and superior-inferior reasoning into self-concepts. A major disruptive effect of psychodynamic theories of family-of-origin patterning is the blaming of mothers, or the projection of the negative mother complex onto women who nurture. Elaborately rationalized blaming of women for being "toxic agents" (e.g., schizo-phrenigenic mothers) and for loving in the wrong ways (e.g., being fused with their children) has obscured the parts played by men and children in human development.

Unless we oppose the androcentric concepts and reasoning of psychodynamic theories, social workers can fall into reinforcing negative self-concepts in women and people of color. Irigaray (1985a), a psychoanalytic philosopher and feminist, connects the skeptical doubting of early philosophers with the general skepticism about women and mothers in psychodynamic theory. She claims that male theorists have gradually deprived the female and feminine of their intrinsic worth and truth, by identifying these progressively as incomplete and lacking. Ultimately, this symbolic *emptying* of the female person of her own worth leads to a fearful preoccupation about women's power, because, as she says, the woman who is "deprived of everything" must want "to take possession of everything" (Irigaray, 1985a, p. 167).

The model that I have presented for treating the Shores is grounded in feminist therapy. Recognizing the double bind of female gender identity, I can use a psychodynamic approach to interpersonal influence in a way that relieves some of the burden of internalized inferiority for those people who have "less-than" ideal selves. In the case of the Shores, I would be careful to validate Nancy's experiences and observations while I helped Charley to listen to her as a partner, not as a mother. At the same time, I would encourage Nancy to withdraw her idealizing projections onto Charley so as to free him from the pressures to be more than he is capable of being. These therapeutic moves would happen because of the methods I outlined and not because of techniques of interpretation.

Failures of psychodynamic theory to support social work practice have resulted primarily from androcentric errors and assumptions of mental separatism. In the account I have given, I have attempted to correct some of the biases that interfere with useful applications of psychodynamics to person-in-situation analyses.

## RESEARCH

Much useful clinical research has been carried out in the field of psychodynamic theory and therapy. It is hardly possible even to think about summarizing the extent and complexity of the findings. However, I can recommend three relatively recent books that offer empirical strategies for carrying out and applying psychodynamic theory to clinical research. The first is *Forms of Brief Therapy*, edited by Budman (1981), which describes a number of ongoing research projects on brief psychodynamic treatment. The second is the elaborate record of the research carried out over many years at the Menninger Foundation, *Forty-two Lives in Treatment* by Wallerstein (1986). Finally, *Patterns of Change* (Rice & Greenberg, 1984) offers a helpful and clear strategy for empirical research on psychodynamic process in treatment.

From my experience in reading, applying, and conducting research on psychodynamic theories of treatment, I am impressed by the amount of knowledge we already have about how and why treatment works. If one reviews even part of the material from the above three books, one is immediately aware of the empirical advantages of a hundred years of practice and observation using this approach. In my own practice, I keep careful records and conduct follow-up meetings with clients. These simple procedures lend much empirical information about my effectiveness and help me clarify my thinking.

## SUMMARY

I have attempted to show how I use and converse about psychodynamic principles in a revised manner suitable to values and orientations of clinical social work. By unraveling the knots of mental separatism—that is, exploring the *interpersonal* dynamics of conflict and change—and undoing the double binds of androcentrism, we can continue to tap into a rich tradition of intelligent interpersonal practice within a psychodynamic framework.

Psychodynamic assessment is the keystone of my decision-making about intervention. Because of the broad scope of psychodynamic theory,

I can fit my work into a larger systematic framework that is shared by many other practitioners and has been tried and tested.

In conclusion, I want to point out that it is within the *tradition* of psychodynamics that we find the most concern for making theory and therapy a dialogical process. Therapists themselves are encouraged to enter the clinical process as clients. Participating as a client, the therapist-in-training or therapist already in practice is exposed to the influences of psychodynamics from the other side.

From the point of view of psychodynamic theory, human development over the lifespan depends on successive integrations of conflicts into conscious awareness, increasing an individual's ability to live satisfactorily within the finite limitations of personal being. The ability to "listen" to the emotional and nonrational, as well as the rational, voices in oneself and others is the critical element of developing a symbolic life in adulthood. Psychodynamic therapies are designed especially to provoke and contain such conflict within a framework that moves the participants from action to symbol, from habit to awareness, and from impulse to choice.

## REFERENCES

Baker Miller, J. (1976). *Toward a new psychology of women*. Boston: Beacon.

Bellah, R. N., Madsen, R., Sullivan, W. M., Swidler, A., & Tipton, S. M. (1985). *Habits of the heart: Individualism and commitment in American life*. New York: Harper & Row.

Blanck, G., & Blanck, R. (1974). *Ego psychology: Theory and practice*. New York: Columbia University Press.

Breuer, J., & Freud, S. (1955). *Studies in hysteria* (Standard Ed., Vol. 2). London: Hogarth Press. (Original work published 1893–1895)

Broughton, J. (1986). The psychology, history and ideology of the self. In K. Larsen (ed.), *Psychology and ideology* (pp. 128–164). Norwood, NJ: Ablex.

Broverman, I. K., Broverman, D. M., Clarkson, R. E., Rosenkrantz, P. S., & Vogel, S. R. (1970). Sex-role stereotypes and clinical judgments of mental health. *Journal of Consulting and Clinical Psychology, 34*, 1–7.

Broverman, I. K., Vogel, S. R., Broverman, D. M., Clarkson, R. E., & Rosenkrantz, P. S. (1972). Sex-role stereotypes: A current appraisal. *Journal of Social Issues, 28*, 59–78.

Budman, S. (1981). *Forms of brief therapy*. New York: Guilford Press.

Chodorow, N. (1978). *The reproduction of mothering: Psychoanalysis and the sociology of gender*. Berkeley: University of California Press.

Ellenberger, H. F. (1970). *The discovery of the unconscious*. New York: Basic Books.

Erikson, E. H. (1950). *Childhood and society*. New York: Norton.

Frank, J. (1971). Therapeutic components shared by all psychotherapies. *Master lectures: Psychotherapy research and behavior change, 1*, 9–37. Washington, DC: American Psychological Association.

Freud, A. (1946). *The ego and the mechanisms of defense*. New York: International Universities Press. (Original work published in 1936)

Freud, S. (1953). *The interpretation of dreams* (Standard Ed., Vols. 4 & 5). London: Hogarth Press. (Original work published in 1900)

Freud, S. (1953). *Three essays on the theory of sexuality* (Standard Ed., Vol. 7). London: Hogarth Press. (Original work published in 1905)

Freud, S. (1955). *Beyond the pleasure principle* (Standard Ed., Vol. 18). London: Hogarth Press. (Original work published in 1920)

Freud, S. (1959). *Inhibitions, symptoms and anxiety* (Standard Ed., Vol. 21). London: Hogarth Press. (Original work published in 1926)

Freud, S. (1961). *The ego and the id* (Standard Ed., Vol. 19). London: Hogarth Press. (Original work published in 1923)

Garner, S. N., Kahane, C., & Sprengnether, M. (1985). *The (m)other tongue: Essays in feminist psychoanalytic interpretation*. Ithaca, NY: Cornell University Press.

Goldfried, M. (1982). *Converging themes in psychotherapy*. New York: Springer.

Greenberg, J. R., & Mitchell, S. A. (1983). *Object relations in psychoanalytic theory*. Cambridge, MA: Harvard University Press.

Harré, R. (1984). *Personal being*. Cambridge, MA: Harvard University Press.

Hartmann, H. (1958). *Ego psychology and the problem of adaptation*. New York: International Universities Press. (Original work published in 1939)

Irigaray, L. (1985a). *Speculum of the other woman* (G. C. Gill, Trans.). Ithaca, NY: Cornell University Press.

Irigaray, L. (1985b). *This sex which is not one* (C. Porter, Trans.). Ithaca, NY: Cornell University Press.

Jaynes, J. (1976). *The origin of consciousness in the breakdown of the bicameral mind*. Boston: Houghton Mifflin.

Lemmon, J. A. (1983). Legal issues and ethical codes. In A. Rosenblatt & D. Waldfogel (Eds.), *Handbook of clinical social work* (pp. 853–865). San Francisco: Jossey-Bass.

Loevinger, J. (1976). *Ego development*. San Francisco: Jossey-Bass.

MacMurray, J. (1961). *The form of the personal* (Vol. 1 & 2). Atlantic Highlands, NJ: Humanities Press.

Piaget, J. (1936). *The origins of intelligence in children*. New York: International Universities Press.

Rice, L., & Greenberg, L. S. (1984). *Patterns of change: An intensive analysis of psychotherapy process*. New York: Guilford Press.

Rickman, J. (Ed.). (1975). *A general selection from the works of Sigmund Freud*. Garden City, NJ: Doubleday.

Rosenblatt, A., & Waldfogel, D. (1983). *Handbook of clinical social work*. San Francisco: Jossey-Bass.

Schafer, R. (1978). *Language and insight*. New Haven, CT: Yale University Press.

Strawson, P. F. (1959). *Individuals*. London: Methuen.

Strupp, H. (1977). A reformulation of the dynamics of the therapist's contribution. In A. Gurman & A. M. Razin (Eds.), *Effective psychotherapy: A handbook of research* (pp. 1–22). New York: Pergamon.

Sullivan, H. S. (1953). *The interpersonal theory of psychiatry*. New York: Norton.

Swan, J. (1985). Difference and silence: John Milton and the question of gender. In S. N. Garner, C. Kahane, & M. Sprengnether (Eds.), *The (m)other tongue: Essays in feminist psychoanalytic interpretation* (pp. 142–168). Ithaca, NY: Cornell University Press.

Vaillant, G. (1977). *Adaptation to life*. Boston: Little Brown.

Wallerstein, R. (1986). *Forty-two lives in treatment*. New York: Guilford Press.

Wood, K. (1971). The contribution of psychoanalysis and ego psychology to social casework. In H. Strean (Ed.), *Social casework: Theories in action* (pp. 45–122). Metuchen, NJ: Scarecrow Press.

Young-Eisendrath, P. (1982). Ego development: Inferring the client's frame of reference. *Social Casework, 63,* 323–332.

Young-Eisendrath, P. (1984). *Hags and heroes: A feminist approach to Jungian psychotherapy with couples*. Toronto, Ont.: Inner City.

Young-Eisendrath, P., & Hall, J. (1987). *The book of the self: Person, pretext, process*. New York: New York University Press.

Young-Eisendrath, P., & Wiedemann, F. (1987). *Female authority: Empowering women through psychotherapy*. New York: Guilford Press.

# 4

# Adlerian Theory and Therapy

## *Robert Massey, Ph.D.*

A colleague recently remarked, "Most of us are more neo-Adlerian than we realize." A number of concepts first formulated by Alfred Adler (1870–1937) have seeped into contemporary understanding of social relations and therapy without being explicitly acknowledged. This is partly because in many ways Adler was ahead of his time. For example, as early as 1925 he commented on the social barriers to sex role equality and the psychological consequences that these had for cooperation between the sexes—an issue that we have only recently begun to fully address.

Adler's perspective was a *social* one (Massey, 1981). Whereas Freud emphasized psychophysiological variables and Jung stressed spiritual considerations, Adler accented psychosocial processes. Adler offers a "contextual psychology" rather than a reductionistic approach (Ansbacher & Ansbacher, 1956). In treatment and theory, Adler expressed respect for the processes that are unique to each individual. He pointed to the ways in which individuals and their contexts mutually influence each other. His search for patterns guided him towards holistic rather than atomistic explanations. He was interested in the dynamic unity of individuals and in how they function within their larger contexts.

Adler advocated holistic integration and a growth orientation to such an extent that Maslow (1962) credited him with being a forerunner of the "Third Force" in psychology. Adler also had some impact on the development of psychoanalysis. In 1909, Freud acknowledged borrowing the term "confluence of drives" from a 1908 paper by Adler, although Adler made the emphasis on the unity of personality a basic part of his theory and Freud remained a dualist (Ansbacher & Ansbacher, 1956).

At the same time, however, Freud rejected Adler's postulation of an "aggression drive," whereas later (in 1920 and 1923) Freud affirmed an "aggression instinct." In "Instincts and Their Vicissitudes" (1915/1957), Freud repeats Adler's earlier (1908) ideas about the "reversal of an instinct into its opposite" ("reaction formation") and "turning round of an instinct upon the subject" (e.g., repressed voyeurism converted into exhibitionism) (Adler, 1956, pp. 32–33).

Some common misconceptions—that Adler was a follower of Freud and that he was a "psychoanalytic deviant"—have hindered recognition of his contributions. After extensive research, Ellenberger (1970) commented:

> Contrary to common assumption, neither Adler nor Jung is a "psychoanalytic deviant," and their systems are not merely distortions of psychoanalysis. Both had their own ideas before meeting Freud, collaborated with him while keeping their independence, and, after leaving him, developed systems that were basically different from psychoanalysis, and also basically different from each other.
>
> The fundamental difference between Adler's individual psychology and Freud's psychoanalysis can be summarized as follows: Freud's aim is to incorporate into scientific psychology those hidden realms of the human psyche that had been grasped intuitively by the Greek tragedians, Shakespeare, Goethe, and other great writers. Adler is concerned with the field of *Menschekenntnis*, that is, the concrete, practical knowledge of man. . . . The reader must temporarily put aside all that he learned about psychoanalysis and adjust to a quite different way of thinking. (p. 571)

Because of tendencies to ostracize and anathematize unorthodox deviants, little interchange and cross-fertilization occurred between Freudians and Adlerians after Adler and Freud ceased to associate in 1909. Several therapists who trained in the Freudian tradition have modified psychoanalytic theory in a social/cultural direction. These revisionists are frequently called "neo-Freudian," yet can also justifiably be dubbed "neo-Adlerian" (Wittels, 1939). Bosshard (1931) referred to Harry Stack Sullivan as a neo-Freudian/neo-Adlerian, Sward (1945) regarded Karen Horney in this vein, and James (1947) viewed Horney and Erich Fromm in the same light. Ansbacher (1953), Munroe (1955), Sundberg and Tyler (1962), Rotter (1960), Thompson (1950), and Wolman (1960) concur in characterizing Sullivan, Horney, and Fromm as neo-Adlerians. Erik Erikson (Massey, 1986b) and Eric Berne (Massey, 1984, 1986d) have also contributed to the neo-Freudian and neo-Adlerian traditions.

## THE CONCEPT OF THE PERSON AND THE HUMAN EXPERIENCE

Appreciating Adler depends on understanding his world view. First, Adler dealt with humans as creative, indivisibly integrated, and unique individuals. He believed that people are "active" in responding to and constructing their own social environments. For Adler, people and social contexts are equally important and interactive. Environments influence people, and individuals are responsive to contextual influences.

Second, Adler advanced a *Menschekenntnis* approach to human functioning; his use of this term (literally, knowledge of human nature) falls within the tradition of Kant, Marx, and Nietzsche. On the conceptual level, *Menschekenntnis* connotes a concrete or pragmatic psychology; on the relational level, it means exercising an intuitive, practical understanding of persons. Adler's *Menschekenntnis* advances principles and methods that facilitate acquiring a practical knowledge of oneself and others. Adler could quickly draw accurate clinical conclusions about people within a short time of meeting them.

Ellenberger (1970) has delineated six axioms that form the basis of Adler's philosophy:

1. The "principle of unity" postulates that a human being is one and indivisible in mind-body functioning and in the operation of psychological processes.
2. The "principle of dynamism" emphasizes that life implies movement. Psychological movement entails intentionality (striving towards a goal) and freedom of choice.
3. The "principle of cosmic influence" stresses that a person is situationally influenced in many ways. Although each individual perceives the world in a unique way, we are all essentially interdependent. Thus Adler considered reflection on family and social structures, cultural processes, and ethical issues essential to his theorizing.
4. The "principle of the spontaneous structuration of the parts in a whole" is evidenced on the individual level when "all the components of the mind spontaneously organize and equilibrate themselves according to the individual self-set goal" (p. 610) and on the social level in the division of labor.
5. The "principle of action and reaction between the individual and [one's] environment" focuses on the continual adjustment and readjustment between persons and contexts. Adler viewed the power to modify a situation as a distinguishing capability of humans. He dealt primarily with social environments and offered a theory of the dynamics of interpersonal relationships.
6. Adler spoke of "the law of absolute truth." This embodies "a fictitious norm set for the conduct of the individual that consists of an optimal balance between the requirements of the community and those of the individual, in other words, between community feeling and legitimate self-assertion" (p. 610).

Third, Adler developed what Jaspers (1946/1963) called a "subjective psychology"—a study of the psyche as experienced or perceived from within. Subjective psychology contrasts with "objective psychology"— observation of the psyche as viewed by an outsider. Ansbacher and Ansbacher (1956), who collected, edited, and annotated Adler's writings, further defined subjective psychology. Subjective psychology, they pointed out, emphasizes the self, is holistic rather than atomistic, values personally experienced phenomenological descriptions over analysis into elements, presents a field theory rather than classification into definite categories, is more organismic than mechanistic, stresses motivation by pulls rather than by pushes, and understands through empathy rather than through reductionistic explanations. Subjective psychology favors "soft determinism," which views a person as formed more by the inner, choice-making processes, over "hard determinism," which construes an individual as shaped by external pressures alone. In another comparison, Allport (1961) has characterized subjective psychology as leaning toward an "idiographic" science (one that seeks principles applying to individual cases) rather than towards a "nomothetic" science that searches for generalized laws.

## HISTORICAL PERSPECTIVE

Adler was born in 1870 on the outskirts of Vienna. He had an older brother and four other siblings who grew to maturity. The family belonged to Vienna's Jewish community, but lived in a predominantly Gentile, semirural environment.

Adler's earliest memory was of himself at age two, all bandaged up because of rickets, sitting on a bench with his older brother, who could frolic with little effort. He recalled that everyone took good care of him (Bottome, 1957).

By the time he was five, Adler had decided to become a doctor. At 18, he entered the College of Medicine in Vienna and pursued the regular courses, including surgery. He gained his clinical experience at the Viennese Poliklinik, which served the poor, and then set up his practice in Vienna's Praterstrasse, a predominantly Jewish and lower-middle-class section (Wasserman, 1958). From the Prater (Vienna's amusement park), restaurant owners, artists, and acrobats came to Adler for treatment. He discovered that some of their displays of physical prowess were compensations for actual bodily weaknesses and defects. This insight developed into a main theme of his 1907 book, *The Study of Organ Inferiority* (Ansbacher & Ansbacher, 1956).

In 1897, Adler married Raissa Epstein, the daughter of a Russian merchant, whom he had met at a socialist political meeting. Adler was used to the lower-middle-class tradition of male dominance, but the independent, strong-willed, outspoken Raissa belonged to the intelligentsia, where women were accustomed to freedom and respect as peers. Her influence prompted him to both practice and promote equality between the sexes.

Adler first heard a lecture by Freud in 1899. The traditional story is that Adler defended Freud in the *Neue Freie Presse* after an attack on his *Interpretation of Dreams* and that Freud then invited Adler to meet with him. We know for certain that in 1902 Freud asked Adler and three others to join him on Wednesday evenings to discuss the problems of neurosis. Adler did not consider himself a disciple of Freud, was never psychoanalyzed, and differed both in theoretical emphases and in orientation to professional life. For example, Freud had upper-class clients and held Wednesday meetings in his home, whereas Adler treated common people and mingled with them in cafes, in which much of Vienna's intellectual and social life took place. Nevertheless, Adler was elected president of the Vienna Psychoanalytic Society in 1910, and he assumed joint editorship with Wilhelm Stekel of the *Zentralblatt für Psychoanalyse*, the official psychoanalytic journal. Challenged to present his views in 1911, Adler read two papers, "Problems of Psychoanalysis" and "Masculine Protest," subsequently published in 1914 under the titles "The Role of Sexuality in Neurosis" and " 'Repression' and 'Masculine Protest': Their Role and Significance for Neurotic Dynamics" (Adler, 1956). In the discussion on the papers, only Stekel, who generally opposed Adler, voiced the opinion that Adler's ideas did not conflict with Freud's. The vote on compatibility went against Adler 14 to 9 (Bottome, 1957), and attempts at a reconciliation failed. Adler resigned as president of the Psychoanalytic Society, and, later, to save Freud the embarrassment of having to withdraw, as editor of the *Zentralblatt*.

In 1912 Adler and his associates founded the Society for Free Psychoanalytic Research; in 1913 they changed the name to the Society of Individual Psychology. The new group eventually attracted members from other countries, and in 1923 the *Journal of Individual Psychology* added *International* to its title.

World War I had a decisive impact on Adler. Until that time he had spoken of the need for human cooperation; now he emphasized the absolute necessity of "social interest." He acted on his conviction that humans need to replace egocentricity with a goal of a universal community by involving himself in education. Otto Glockel, president of the Vienna Board of Education, wanted to reform the educational system and was introduced to Adler by Carl Furtmuller, his friend and biographer (Furtmuller, 1973). Between 1921 and 1934, Adlerians set up and ran more than 30 child guidance clinics in connection with the school system. Until 1927, Adler lectured every fortnight to parents and teachers from over 50 schools. He incorporated one or two demonstrations into each presentation.

From 1926 on, Adler spent an increasing amount of time lecturing in such cities as Berlin, Munich, Paris, London, Amsterdam, New York, Boston, Chicago, Detroit, Philadelphia, and San Francisco. In 1929, he was appointed clinical director of the Mariahilfe Ambulatorium, an outpatient facility for neurotics in Vienna. He lectured at Columbia University from 1929 to 1931. In 1932, he was selected for the first chair for medical psychology at Long Island University. While on a lecture tour in Scotland, in 1937, he collapsed and died from a heart attack.

The development of Individual Psychology was thrown into disarray when the Nazis closed down the child guidance clinics in Vienna and overran Europe. However, Adler had sown the seeds of his theory in the United States. Today, regional associations of the American Society of Adlerian Psychology exist in New York, Chicago, and Los Angeles. Adlerian groups are also active in Austria, England, France, Holland, Israel, and Switzerland.

As noted earlier, Ansbacher and Ansbacher (1956, 1973) edited and systematized Adler's writings in two volumes. The thoughts of other Adlerians are compiled in the volumes edited by Dreikurs, Corsini, Lowe, and Sonstegard (1959) and Adler and Deutsch (1959). Mosak and Mosak (1975) assembled a comprehensive *Bibliography for Adlerian Psychology.*

## KEY THEORETICAL CONSTRUCTS

### Adler's Conceptual Foundations

Adler's theory is built on four conceptual foundations:

1. People are *active* and *creative* in interpreting reality and in forming and pursuing styles of life that are unique to each of them.
2. The *social dimension* of human development is spotlighted. Adler conceived of people as significantly influenced by early family experiences, as embedded in community, and as having essential social needs for interpersonal connections. He considered each person's level of social cooperation as a barometer of mental health.
3. Behavior and its patterning are *goal-oriented.* The quality of a person's lifestyle goal distinguishes healthy development from mistaken development (in which an individual engages in negative interpersonal strategies).
4. A *person* is a *unity.* Adler named his approach "Individual Psychology" to emphasize the indivisibility and unity of a person, not isolation and separateness.

### The Person as "Active"

People engage in movement both physically and psychologically. Each member of the Shore family displays characteristic movements. Nancy moves with difficulty, affected by her obesity and back problems. As a comedian, Charley moves both athletically and lightly. Rena can move exuberantly and attractively, yet she draws away from significant people. Michael's movements are slowed by asthma and allergies.

Physical movement suggests psychological movement. Psychological movement involves temperament, a future orientation, and a style of relating to social realities. Through psychological movement, individuals direct their activities and interactions towards some esteem-enhancing goal. A person is not simply determined by genetic endowment and events, but selectively incorporates them into a consistent approach to living. Adler thus emphasized a "psychology of *use*, not possession." What matters most is not what one has, but what one does with it. This leaves an opening for an individual interpretation of reality. For instance, Nancy is beset with chronic problems, yet she prides herself on helping others. Charley has compiled a sporadic work record, yet he dreams of being a star actor. Rena rues the abandonment by her biological mother, yet she was adopted by a caring family. Michael is plagued with physical problems, yet he refuses to be defeated, passes them off as "his scar," and continues to try out for the track and softball teams.

### Style of life

Through psychological movement, people create styles of life that organize their energies in self-chosen directions. A style of life integrates the many aspects that are characteristic of an individual's life—constitutional makeup, physical reactions, self-image, attitude towards the world, interpersonal relations, and problem-solving strategies—into a self-consistent and accustomed pattern of behaving.

Nancy's style of life follows a "before and after" plot. Before age 11, she experienced the "golden years"; afterwards, there was struggle. In each area of Nancy's life, *before* a "nodal" event she displays enthusiastic initiative, and *after* this turning point she becomes discouraged. The pattern of beginning with energetic initiative and subsequently believing she has been thwarted becomes thematic in Nancy's psychological movement: She felt close to her father and later felt abandoned by him; she excelled as a student and nurse and felt defeated by a back injury; she chose Charley against the opposition of her family and then became annoyed and embarrassed by him; she wanted to be a mother so much that she adopted Rena and then was disappointed by her daughter's laziness and lack of accomplishments; she enjoyed a rich social life and then lost friends because of her perception that others thought of Charley as immature.

Each family member has created a style of life. Charley moves at his own pace, fantasizes about grand success, and remains generally undaunted (except during depressive periods) by a lack of appreciated accomplishments. He has preferred a certain isolation since at least the age of six, when his sister was born. His time theme is "when it happens" ("Some day I'll be great"). Rena is the gifted "angel from heaven" who never quite lets herself fit into earthly reality. Michael refuses to surrender to physical limitations but battles the odds in ways that alienate others. Together, the Shores have created a *family* style of life (Deutsch, 1967) around the motifs of disappointment and nonaccomplishment.

*Inferiority feelings and coping with them*

Beginning efforts in a particular area of endeavor may be impractical and faltering because of people's ineptitude or because the environment may be nonsupportive or overpowering. Hence, people experience feelings of inadequacy, insecurity, or inferiority.

There are several options to choose from in dealing with inferiority feelings. A person may give up, as Rena did after her rejection from the proposed television series and after her brief success in a school play. An individual may struggle against the inferiority feelings, as Michael does when he continually tries out for the track and softball teams despite physical limitations. A person may try to compensate for an inadequacy, as Charley does by performing on amateur night at a local comedy club, even though he did not make it to Hollywood. Inferiority feelings can crush active striving for fulfillment; we can see this when Charley flirts with committing suicide. An individual may capitalize on inferiority feelings and develop an inferiority complex, as Nancy does by defining herself as disabled and by allowing herself to panic as she waits for a crisis. In pursuit of competency, a person can overcome inferiority feelings by practicing a needed skill, making constructive changes, or discovering and exhibiting a positive aspect of some deviation from the usual. Unfortunately for the Shore family, "problems never get resolved," and the members do not overcome inferiority feelings.

## The Person as "Social"

Although unique, individuals are inevitably embedded in social reality. As infants, we are both helpless and dependent on the care of others. The expressed concern of others is necessary for our survival and growth. As we create styles of life, we are influenced by our *contexts*. In early life, we are shaped by the family context, and throughout life we fluctuate in our levels of esteem depending on how well we fulfill the social tasks of life. Adler viewed constructive contributions to community living as the criterion of mental health.

## Family constellation and birth order

Adler called the family context the "family constellation." He noted that, because the psychological situation often varies according to the child's position in a family constellation, each birth-order position frequently evokes certain personality traits. Only children and first children share some characteristics: They generally grow up more with adults than with other children and tend to display a heightened achievement orientation (Rothbart, 1971; also see Mosak & Mosak, 1975).

First children experience a "dethronement" when the second sibling arrives. For example, Charley has expressed his feelings of rivalry and resentment towards his younger sister. Even though he is now a parent, he still experiences rivalry towards Michael, as if he were a sibling. He also jealously resents Rena's mechanical competence.

When the oldest child experiences affection, he or she may strive to protect and help others, as Nancy has done; when encouragement is missing, the tendency to help may be lacking. Firstborns and lastborns especially run the risk of being favored and pampered. We can see this in Nancy and Rena, who were both doted upon and have some expectations of getting their own ways. Rena is in the unusual situation of being a double firstborn, both of her biological mother and of her adoptive parents. From her biological mother, she experienced rejection; from Nancy, acceptance. Rena's ambivalence (sometimes she basks in being favored, at other times she sees herself as the victim of rejection) is evidence of both kinds of treatment that she has received. In a sense, Michael is also a firstborn (his parents' first biological child), yet he also occupies the second (and last) position. Second children often take a different path from the first. Whereas Rena is bright, pleasant, artistic, and mechanical, Michael is intellectually inept, sickly, ungainly, and sports-minded. Middle children, born into a cluster of siblings, are often much more peer-oriented and easygoing than Michael is.

## Social interest

As a child creates a style of life in a family constellation, survival and nurturance depend on the expression of social interest by caregivers. If significant adults express sufficient social interest, a child lives in a context that fosters the buildup and enhancement of self-esteem. When caregivers lack social interest, the child's context is nonsupportive emotionally. This inhibits the development of personal talents and social skills, and a child becomes discouraged.

The proper development of social interest in a child results in respect for others' feelings and rights, understanding others' points of view, cooperation in friendships and tasks, and the emergence of positive ways to contribute to the general welfare and happiness of others. Adler considered social interest "the barometer of the child's normality" (1956, p. 154). Teamwork between parents serves as a guiding model for a growing child. A socially interested adult maintains an interdependent and mutually satisfying marital relationship; provides a context complete with necessities, guidance, and encouragement for children; works productively; and is involved constructively in the community.

Although Adler considered social interest to be an innate potential, he believed that it required encouragement from significant others for it to evolve appropriately. For example, when she was young, Nancy received some social interest, especially from Gram and Aunt Flo. However, her mother was competitive, her father distant and forgetful. Her self-esteem was wounded. Although she is generous in crises and performed well as a professional nurse, she has difficulty being an understanding and compatible wife, feels unloved in general and left out as a daughter, does not esteem her competencies, and lacks the courage to make positive changes in her present predicament.

## Tasks of life

*Friendship, work,* and *sexual love* are crucial to building self-esteem and to the evolution of social interest. Through these "three general social ties," an individual is linked to community (Adler, 1956, p. 131). Success in each enhances the self, furthers the striving for excellence, and benefits others. Failure in any of the areas reinforces inferiority feelings or prompts a vindictive striving for superiority, and undermines community living.

"We have always to reckon with others, to adapt ourselves to others and to interest ourselves in them. This problem is best solved by *friendship* [italics added], social feeling, and cooperation" (Adler, 1956, p. 132). The capacity for interpersonal relationships unfolds early in life—as early as age four or five. Children develop friendship bonds during training and education when they are related to as fellow subjects rather than as objects. Predisposed to feel inferior through smallness, clumsiness, or inexperience, a child must be taken seriously, not ridiculed or told lies that could aggravate these feelings. A child needs tenderness, security, and warmth. To thrive, a child must feel welcome. Adler prescribes guidance for the child, rather than punishment or humiliation: If parents default on providing tenderness, the child's life style may be oriented towards escaping interpersonal closeness. On the other hand, a pampered child, waited on by others and prevented from developing his or her own skills, will also not be prepared to contribute to cooperative living in an active and responsible manner. Young children manifest the early signs of social interest that are necessary for genuine friendship by their search for tenderness and in their use of language. This emerging social interest can evolve and extend to an increasing circle of people.

In the Shore family, each family member displays difficulty in gaining esteem and in practicing social interest through friendship. For instance, when Nancy was a young nurse (when her life was more successful), she developed friendships. Now she blames a lack of friends on Charley's immaturity. Her present relationships are more dependent (for example, she relies on her acquaintances in the medical field for help with Michael) and less self-affirming, self-assertive, and reciprocal. Charley, too, has few friends. As a child, he was teased and beaten up, and he bribed his way into being protected. The famous people he claims to know are more fantasies than realities. Rena also has trouble making friendships on her level; she has mostly associated with her elders. The boyfriends whom she has chosen have been unable to encourage her constructive development. Michael, too, has problems with friendships; he tends to antagonize rather than befriend.

Adler believed that we gain esteem and contribute to the community through the social task of *work*. Previously, work as a student and as a nurse served as the highlight of Nancy's life. She experienced self-confidence and proficiency while helping others. Now she has let physical symptoms deflect her from a socially useful pursuit of her talents. She has structured her finances around disability benefits, rather than around her productivity. Charley has dreamed and schemed and lost scores of jobs. Except for his four years in the Air Force, he has not prided himself on his work. Although interesting and entertaining for outsiders, his unpaid work as an amateur performer neither meets his ambitions nor helps support his family. His performances actually evoke his wife's derision when she perceives that the audience is laughing *at* him, not *with* him.

The third task of life is *sexual love*. Adler depicted love and marriage as "the most intimate devotion towards a partner of the other sex, expressed in physical attraction, comradeship, and the decision to have children . . . not a cooperation for the welfare of two persons only, but a cooperation also for the welfare of mankind" (1956, p. 432).

Nancy has experienced setbacks in this area. Instead of respecting her daughter's emerging sexuality, Nancy's mother competed seductively with her potential admirers. Nancy camouflaged her attractiveness by becoming overweight. She associated sexual awareness with rejection by her father, because she rarely saw him after she witnessed an erotic situation between him and his new lover.

Charley was also deprived of a positive example; he observed violence, rather than tenderness, between his parents. Generally, however, he has not been violent, except for the occasion on which he got "carried away" when protecting his wife from Rena. Indeed, he has curtailed his assertiveness to such an extent that he is depressed about his incompetence in handling any problems—marital, parental, or occupational.

It is difficult to imagine Nancy and Charley reveling in sexual encounters. More likely, their physical and psychological complaints lower their sense of attraction and attractiveness, provide excuses for avoiding each other, and inhibit their frequency and gratification in sexual relations. Nancy's looking down on Charley paired with his feelings of inferiority do not foster their mutual pleasuring.

At this point, Rena is also headed towards unsatisfactory relationships. Her choosing less talented boyfriends is a worrisome sign. Her search for her biological mother may reinforce her inferiority feelings by reminding her that she was unwanted or by leading her to a confrontation that would confirm her feeling of being unloved. On the other hand, a more optimistic possibility would be that the search for her biological mother and the return to her beginnings would help her to gain a more stable foundation for self-esteem.

When we look at how the Shore family has dealt with the three tasks of life, we see four people who have at times attained some levels of self-esteem, but who, for the most part, have stumbled over these challenges. In being defeated by these tasks until now, they have experienced lowered self-esteem, have underdeveloped their expressions of social interest, and have found their general social ties problematic.

## The Person as "Goal-directed"

Adler viewed behavior as goal-oriented. He postulated that each person strives for a goal of perfection. Each person defines what constitutes perfection. Adler considered the style of life to be organized around a self-chosen goal. Because an individual forms a style of life by age four or five, the goal is chosen early. A person's level of self-esteem is determined by the relative success in attaining the chosen goal through perfecting the social tasks of life.

Adler construed this goal as a "fictional final goal." Drawing on the ideas in Vaihinger's (1925) philosophy of "As If," Adler stated that the goals people devise for themselves may be unobtainable and remain unconscious, but insofar as the style of life seems oriented towards accomplishing them, they motivate a person. This goal or personality ideal does not always remain unconscious. A more self-aware person or a person who has made progress in therapy can become at least partially cognizant of it. The goal is likely to be kept unconscious if awareness of it might lead to a confrontation with reality that would prove it unjustifiable or if recognizing it might threaten the unity of the personality. The goal motivates a person to attain the position in life that he or she considers appropriate. A goal of perfection is often formulated when a person is experiencing some deficiency, lack, or inferiority, whether it be the helplessness of childhood, an organic ailment, or some obstacle to success in coping with the environment. Adler thought of such a predicament as generating the desire "to move from a minus to a plus situation." He considered this desire the fundamental human tendency.

During early childhood, a person sets goals that embody ideals of security, completion, and excellence. This goal of perfection gives direction to the whole personality, to expressive movements, to perceiving, thinking, feeling, and to a view of the world. Pursuit of one's goal provides the "psychological main axis" (Adler, 1956, p. 31) or "guiding line" (p. 99) that makes a style of life understandable. In light of those goals, a person constructs a schema for understanding and living life. This schema provides both an orientation to life's tasks and a way of understanding how best to strive for active mastery of the environment.

### Healthy and "mistaken" development

Healthy and neurotic development can be distinguished by the quality of the goal chosen. A fulfilled person pursues a goal of personal excellence and practices social interest. Healthy development is "socially useful." A neurotic person either capitalizes on inferiority feelings or disguises insecurity and vulnerability by striving for superiority. Neurotic development is "mistaken," because it furthers a "socially useless" goal that does not contribute to cooperation in community living.

Nancy's sense of inferiority stems originally from her feeling that her mother never wanted her and from the social psychological distance that her parents kept from her. When she was young, she compensated for this in seemingly positive ways by beginning to make friends, dating, and excelling academically. She was happiest when she was caring for others as a nurse, although actually she had been taking care of others for a long time. She cared for her mother by having to be more independent than a girl with a truly encouraging mother would need to be, and also by bringing home interesting guys, which allowed her mother to compete with her, rather than support her. She cared for her father by waiting patiently for him, when a father who was responsive to *her* needs would have provided for her more. She cared for Gram and Aunt Flo, who preferred that she give up her childhood so that she could be a companion to them.

Nancy gains control over other people by taking care of them. Controlling by rescuing gives her a sense of superiority and inflates her slender self-esteem. Even though Nancy attempts to compensate for her own inferiorities and tries to control people by offering to care for them, she herself, through her own overall condition, cries out for care.

Nancy has not reduced her weight, which might lessen her back discomfort. Adler (1956) conjectured that physical complaints and symptoms constitute "organ dialect" (p. 223). In some individuals, a bodily organ has some defect and receives some special attention during the development of a style of life. In other cases, inferiority feelings are manifested later on in life through bodily symptoms. Such symptoms express psychological problems and conflicts that an individual may not understand or may deny verbally. Nancy's back injury provides a metaphor for her problems in social adjustment: She tends to "break her back" rescuing others rather than discovering ways in which her own competence will shine independently while she interacts with others in mutual cooperation. We can view Nancy's back problems as a bodily statement about the "back-breaking" psychological burdens she had been carrying. Nancy's delay in becoming pregnant and her adoption of a child can be seen as a somatic distancing from, or ambivalence about, being involved in taking care of others.

Rena demonstrates that success does not automatically flow from talents but that an individual can choose to set a goal of becoming better at *not* using what he or she possesses. Apparent inferiority masks a superiority or disdain for normally expected productivity. Well-endowed with intelligence, several talents, and physical attractiveness, Rena has nonetheless experienced numerous failures. She has mistakenly "tried to become better at" being inferior. She internalizes and acts out the personally impoverishing aspects of the models in her context: Like her birth mother, she has not succeeded in school and has selected non-supportive boyfriends; like Nancy, she is overinvolved with crises and even generates them; like Charley, she has problems with peers and with productive work.

## "Safeguarding strategies"

When an individual is not making progress towards a goal of personal excellence, the most constructive approach is to figure out what the problem is or what one is capable of in a particular situation and to pursue realistic options effectively. A person may maneuver to conceal these deficiencies from himself or herself and others with "safeguarding strategies."

Through safeguarding strategies, people deflect responsibility for problem-solving away from themselves. These strategies serve as excuses for not accomplishing a task. By such safeguarding strategies, they either assert their superiority over others or emphasize that their inferiorities render them incapable of normally expected pursuits. Either way, the individuals are protected from an awareness of personal inadequacy, and other people are drawn in as foils or scapegoats to disguise low levels of self-esteem and of productivity.

Adler proposed six categories of safeguarding strategies: depreciation, accusation, self-accusation and guilt, distancing, anxiety, and exclusion.

1. *Depreciation* means to discount another's abilities, efforts, or accomplishments. Through depreciation, an individual with low self-esteem focuses on inadequacy in others and hopes to not have his or her own vulnerability discovered.
2. In *accusation,* an individual places blame on another in an attempt to distract attention from his or her own inadequacies.
3. The person who engages in *self-accusation* can elicit—from others—efforts that will take over the individual's responsibilities. Expressions of *guilt* can become justifications for one's inability to function as might be expected. (For example, Charley's self-criticism and guilt about not fulfilling his marital and parental obligations belittle and incapacitate him and invite Nancy's rescuing operations.)
4. Adler identified four modes of *distancing:* moving backward, standing still, hesitation, and construction of obstacles. Through *moving backward* an individual both avoids normal social obligations and exerts control over others. Such distancing includes suicide, agoraphobia, fainting, asthma nervosum, and migraine headaches. *Standing still* deters an individual "from moving closer toward the reality of life, from facing the truth, from taking a stand, from permitting a test or a decision regarding [his or her] value" (Adler, 1956, p. 274). An individual might stand still by suffering from insomnia that results in subsequent incapacity for work, by not succeeding in occupational and marital tasks, or by experiencing sexual dysfunctions.

   *Hesitation,* or a back-and-forth movement, results in the excuse of "being too late" and supports the fiction of "If I didn't have [this affliction], I would be the first" (1956, p. 275). The *if* clause usually contains an unfulfillable condition. Compulsions, pathological pedantry, fear of touching (which expresses distance spatially), extreme tardiness, and persistent noncompletion of tasks signify hesitation. In *constructing obstacles* (such as getting overtired or constipated, having headaches, or being moody), individuals set up tests that enable them to confirm their insufficiencies.
5. An individual may use *anxiety* as an excuse for not accomplishing esteem-threatening challenges or for not doing them well. Anxiety

intensifies the justification for distancing. Any exaggerated fear—whether of the past, of disease or death, or of gaining satisfaction only in the hereafter—hinders greater involvement in social reality.

6. The *exclusion tendency* eliminates from an individual's interest and sphere of activity any area of endeavor that appears too personally threatening. Nonperformance in school, having no occupation by age 30, indefinitely postponing marriage, and obsessive-compulsive rituals are examples of exclusion. Exclusions unduly limit activities and block the expression of social interest.

Rather than increasing self-esteem through the constructive use of talents and through contributing positively to a cooperative community, discouraged individuals use safeguarding strategies to evade real problems and slough off responsibilities.

The Shore family displays such maneuvers. Nancy believes, "Yes, I truly enjoy nursing and helping others, but my back problems prevent my gainful employment." Rena consoles herself with, "If only I had not been abandoned, I could have been consistently successful." Michael laments, "If only I didn't have asthma, I could be a great athlete and have a puppy like a normal boy." Charley views his comedy club performances as Joe Penn "as if" he is on his way to fame.

The use of "yes, but," "if only," and "as if" maneuvers implies that individuals involved in these strategies are interested in being aware of only certain types of information. Certain perceptions will advance the pursuit of a fictional final goal, and others will threaten its attainment. People tend to admit to awareness those things that bolster self-esteem and are congruent with their self-images. "Schemas of apperception" screen out that which is contrary to their senses of self and styles of life. What does not fit with their fictional final goals and self-chosen ways of maintaining self-esteem is also blocked from awareness through schemas of apperception. Subjective viewpoints may contain some early and persistent misinterpretations that hinder productive social living. Such blind spots about aspects of themselves and their interactions, which are readily noticed by others, comprise the "not understood."

When using a schema of apperception to pursue a neurotic goal of superiority, a person may seem to be on an idiosyncratic pathway that is disinterested in, oblivious of, or hostile towards others. These strategies represent the workings of a "private intelligence." In contrast, a socially interested person communicates with "common sense" or "shared understanding." For Charley, Rena, and Michael, constructive ways of making and keeping friends are part of the material that is "not understood" by each of them. Their ways of not connecting with others and of alienating some people represent the workings of "private intelligence" that has not learned to develop the kinds of friendly relationships that are built on and solidified by "shared understanding."

Through safeguarding strategies, an individual arranges interpersonal relationships to conceal personal inadequacies and deflated self-esteem. Other people are made to look bad or are manipulated to serve neurotic needs. By these arrangements, a person distracts others from noticing that he or she is not pursuing constructive solutions to problems. This diminishes positive social involvement.

"Neurotic arrangements" occur through safeguarding strategies and in connection with physical and psychological symptoms. Nancy's obesity and back problems, Charley's Bipolar depression, and Michael's asthma may all be legitimate somatic disturbances, yet they also provide complaints that can be manipulated for neurotic gains. Facing whatever inevitable or unalterable elements there are in these conditions and yet pursuing excellence and social interest require courage and optimism.

## The Person as "Unified"

Although he elaborated on several dimensions of human life, Adler insisted that each person acts as a dynamic *unity*. A person functions as a whole in several ways. First, in the early years, each person creates a unique style of life, which organizes and integrates personality tendencies into an overall, consistent life plan (see Figure 1).

Second, the style of life is oriented towards achieving a fictional final goal of excellence or superiority. Striving towards this goal unifies all of a person's psychological, interpersonal, and physical movements.

Third, a person's self-awareness generally embodies a coherent sense of historical continuity or unity of perspective that is guided by the individual's interpretation of constitutional capacities and of situational realities. These considerations lead an Adlerian therapist to deal with a client in a holistic rather than piecemeal way. A holistic approach seeks to discover the fictional final goal and the process of creating it so as to comprehend the overall life plan of the client. Understanding the style of life sheds light on why and how a person has chosen, in some ways, to follow a socially useful path and, in other ways, a mistaken one.

### ASSESSMENT

An Adlerian therapist assesses a case by examining several dimensions of an individual's personality structure and social relationships. Assessment includes analyzing (a) the organization and formation of a style of life, (b) the early origins of problems, (c) the level of self-esteem, (d) the social usefulness of the fictional final goal, (e) the quality of fulfilling

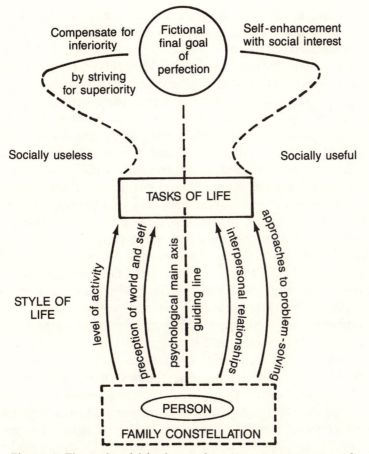

**Figure 1.** The style of life that each unique person creates, although influenced by a family context, is oriented towards a fictional final goal of perfection. The goal, and the approaches to the tasks of life, are healthy or mistaken, depending on whether they combine self-fulfillment with social interest or serve as compensations for inferiority feelings or superiority strivings. (From *Personality Theories: Comparisons and Syntheses*, p. 63, by R. F. Massey, 1981. New York: D. Van Nostrand. Copyright 1984 by R. F. Massey. Adapted by permission.)

the social tasks of life, (f) the degree of social interest, (g) the use of safeguarding strategies, and (h) the individual's level of courage and the overall optimistic or pessimistic outlook on living. Here, we will concentrate on the first two points, since we have discussed the others earlier.

## Life Style Analysis

Mosak and Shulman (1971) developed a systematic format to gather information for a life style analysis. A therapist first asks the client to name his or her brothers and sisters in order and to state how many years older or younger they are than the client. The client then specifies the main characteristics of each person at the time when the client was 12. The client makes comparisons (e.g., Who played together? Who was most like and who was most different from the respondent?) and ranks the siblings on 38 characteristics (including intelligence, athletic, easy-going, stubborn, shy). The therapist elicits information about parents: their ages, occupations, favorite child(ren), ambitions for the child(ren), which child is most like the parent, and the relationship between the parents. The therapist inquires into the individual's physical, school, social, and sexual development. The client is questioned about other important family information and about any additional parental figures. Finally, the client is invited to describe in as much detail as possible his or her earliest memories and their attendant feelings.

An abbreviated life style analysis of the Shores would show the following: Nancy would have no sibling descriptions to offer, nor vicarious sibling experiences with close cousins. The other three family members could give sibling descriptions. We have already referred to Nancy's early memories as showing a curtailed initiative, as submitting to limits (symbolized by not crossing streets and having someone else set her schedule), and as ascribing more importance to external than personal influences.

In Charley's memories, we see the themes of being beaten up (his father by his mother and him by other children—even his "friend"), of relying on magical solutions (a gun was purported to make problems go away), and of people getting hurt (his father in fights, his mother at work, himself at school—by at least one teacher). Charley could not rely on his elders for guidance and support. He expressed some sensitivity in helping his mother; however, this was a reversal of roles, the kind that wears children down rather than building them up so they will have the modeling and reserve of energy to be competent and nurturing. In his early years, Charley got "hung up" (symbolized by Miss Brown's punishment) rather than "helped up" (by encouraging elders), and he turned to clowning. Today Charley continues his life style themes: He entices Nancy to assault him verbally; he flirts with the magic of becoming famous as an actor; he is hurt psychologically and financially; and he has not learned how to establish cooperative relationships.

Rena's two early recollections show that she wants to control (she beckoned and her father reappeared) and that her initial interest and curiosity were washed away by Nancy's scare and Charley's complicity. Rena was so special that her father played with her, but he betrayed her. Her initiative was crushed as her inquisitive, knowledge-seeking self was discouraged. We see here the theme of promising beginnings marred by a lack of cooperation and unfulfilled talents. Is Rena attempting to make her adoptive parents feel guilty (as her birth mother may have felt guilty in conceiving her) by saying in her behavior, "See what you did to me!"? In any event, Rena is not taking control of her life nor becoming responsibly self-determining.

In Michael's sole reported memory we have evidence that "the first memory will show [the] fundamental view of life" (Adler, 1956, p. 351). Michael's "Gimme air!" asserts that life is difficult and the resources to survive are hardly available. A theme of interpersonal contrariness emerges in his remembering being given a shot by an unattractive nurse and his wanting to hit her when he thought he did not need it. Michael's concluding comment, "I am perfectly fine," either proclaims an unrealistic grandiosity or that he will eventually achieve success.

## Problem Children

Because Adler (1956) concluded that "By the time a child is five years old his attitude to his environment is usually so fixed and mechanized that it proceeds in more or less the same direction for the rest of his life" (p. 189), he focused on the strengths and weaknesses of early childhood. Adler (1956, 1933/1964b) looked especially for three classes of problems in childhood: *organ inferiority, pampering,* and *neglect.*

From very early on, Michael displayed organ inferiority. When he was only eight days old, he was in danger from hemorrhaging after his circumcision. Whether this simply introduced a theme of illness into his life or bodes ill for later sexual adjustment is unclear. His sexual maturity will certainly be complicated by his difficulty in getting along with peers. Blunted sexuality may further aggravate his problems. His asthma has certainly influenced his style of life. Asthma binds him dependently to his mother, curtails his normal athletic development, and interferes with his being like the other children, all of which undermine his self-confidence and self-esteem. Yet here we see how important subjective interpretation is, for Michael is not defeated for now. He still tries to achieve athletically, makes some attempts at befriending others, wants to be a good Boy Scout, and is developing interests (keeping current on world news, business, and politics) that may serve him well as an adult.

Adler found that "pampering" hinders a child's personal and social development. A pampered individual leans on others for success and expects them to help out. The pampered individual has a low level of both activity and social interest. A child needs warm encouragement and assistance with as-yet-undeveloped capabilities. A pampered child either is overindulged and rescued from age-appropriate responsibilities or is neglected and decides to act like royalty.

For example, Nancy was doted upon when she was a young child. Although somewhat distanced from her parents, she was the center of attention of other relatives. She benefited from this caring and learned adult ways. However, she did not have the opportunity to interact with siblings as peers, and other relatives buffered her from a harsher living situation. The effects of this shielding were aggravated when her father somewhat incomprehensibly departed and turned up later only sporadically. After her pampering stopped, she became less successful—first by becoming overweight, then by selecting a questionable partner and by having difficulty in mothering, and finally in not finding fulfillment in work. Nancy's style of life revolves around the theme of pampering—"being done for" or "doing for."

Like Nancy, Rena was doted upon. She was more overtly pampered by Gram, who dubbed her the "angel from heaven" and provided her parents with literature on child abuse when she was yelled at. Nancy and Charley believe they gave Rena too much free rein by letting her have her own apartment when she was 13. Rena has not learned to put as much of her own effort into projects as is necessary to accomplish them in line with her talents. Since Nancy has hovered over Michael for so much of his life and spends "80% of her worrying time" obsessing over him, Michael is in danger of deciding to overly rely on others.

Adler noticed that when children are deprived, are abused, or think they are neglected, problems may occur. Charley suffered from neglect. His father beat him, rather than encouraging him. Although, he felt, his mother loved him, she had to spend her time working rather than attending to him. With the birth of his sisters, he felt dethroned. Likewise, he felt deprived in terms of possessions, clothes, friends, and support from teachers. He has chosen to become a victim of neglect. He is jealous of Rena's mechanical ability, declines to derive satisfaction from constructive fathering, alienates Nancy as a source of appreciation, and disallows himself the gratification of succeeding as a worker.

The notion that the child's subjective interpretation is fundamental to how he or she handles each situation is apparent in Rena. Although not cared for by her biological mother, Rena was adopted into a home that desired and provided for her. Yet she mopes around on her birthdays, rather than celebrating with those who have loved her. She seems to continually turn potentially successful situations into failures and to set up rejection.

Adler placed a good deal of emphasis on courage. How much a person has been encouraged and how well the individual has used this needs to be noted. The person who has been encouraged to live a constructive style of life and who exercises courage in facing and fulfilling life's challenges and social tasks with others displays optimism. The discouraged individual, on the other hand, evidences a pessimism which depletes self-esteem and retards social interest. An Adlerian therapist gauges the degrees of courage, optimism, and pessimism in the client and observes to what extent "as if," "if only," and "yes, but" strategies are employed to compensate for inferiority feelings, low self-esteem, and a lack of social interest. The therapist then considers interventions for therapy based on the assessment.

## TREATMENT OF CHOICE

While focusing extensively on neurotics and problem children, Adler (1956, 1973) also commented on the therapy of delinquents, criminals, alcoholics, drug addicts, and insomniacs, as well as individuals with suicidal inclinations and sexual difficulties. Schizophrenics may also be treated with an Adlerian approach. Adler believed that their lofty and godlike goals are compensations for low self-esteem. While noting their greater distance from others and their break with "common sense," Adler recommended letting the patient demonstrate personal strengths and having a therapist maintain friendliness rather than the expected hostility.* Ansbacher (1974) concludes, "To date it is in educational counseling, child guidance, and family education where Adlerian psychology shows particular strength" (p. 100). He credits Dreikurs (1968; Dreikurs & Soltz, 1964) with contributing significantly to this impact.

Adler's work with children in connection with their parents and teachers remains a model for a family and systems orientation in therapy and for considering the wider context in dealing with individuals.

Adlerian therapy can occur one-on-one and in groups (where individual involvement in community is made more explicit and directly encouraged). Adlerian principles can also be used with members of a support group (such as for mothers of problem children), who can obtain emotional support and consider alternative solutions (Deutsch, 1959). Social clubs, in which inhibited and isolated individuals are encouraged to develop social skills and connections, can serve as an adjunct to therapy (Mohr & Garlock, 1959).

## THE THERAPEUTIC PROCESS

Adlerian therapy proceeds in four phases: (a) building a therapeutic relationship, (b) gathering data, (c) interpretation, and (d) active reconstruction (Ansbacher, 1974).

### Building a Therapeutic Relationship

Adler advised a therapist to develop empathy for a client and his or her total context. He viewed psychotherapy as "an exercise in cooperation

---

* Kurt Adler (1958), Alexandra Adler (1966), Papenek (1954), and Shulman (1968) have written further on treating schizophrenics.

and a test of cooperation" (1956, p. 340). He counseled tact and cautioned the therapist to avoid being contentious or pushy with clients. This tact, Adler believed, disarms a client and gives the responsibility for progress in therapy to the client, because "the actual change in the nature of the patient can only be his own doing" (1956, p. 336). Once a therapist has understood a client's goal and style of life, the therapist can then prod the client into a more socially useful direction. This is done by pointing out tendencies that are inimical to actualizing the client's own potential and to cooperating with others. Throughout the process, the therapist provides encouragement to stimulate the pursuit of excellence and to awaken social interest. The Adlerian emphasis on encouragement and social cooperation is embodied in the structuring of the sessions. Client and therapist sit and face each other; this puts them on the same physical level and invites a client to enter into a reasonable, cooperative relationship.

### Gathering Data

Before interpreting and intervening in a case, Adler examined a client's early recollections, birth order position, the impact of childhood disorders, and levels of self-esteem and social interest. He also inquired into *dreams*. He thought of night dreams and daydreams as further manifestations of an individual's self-consistent psychological processes. Dreams look forward (to attaining one's goals). The emotions and feelings in a dream may be more significant than the thoughts and pictures. Dreams convey metaphors and often embody inadequate, "as if" solutions to a problem, which emerge from a neurotic "private intelligence." When therapy is effecting positive change, dreams will probably reflect an increased courage in meeting the problems of living.

Adler (1956) explored whether a client becomes defeated by the traumas and frustrations of "exogenous factors" (p. 328) and uses them as excuses, or whether a client continues to build self-esteem and social interest despite them. He examined whether a person responds to organic ailments in a neurotic or a growthful way. Adler looked for consistency. He did not accept one element as predominant. He checked all impressions (about level of activity, verbalizations, expressive movement, social interactions, symptoms, subjective interpretations) against each other to understand the overall goal and style of life.

### Interpretation

Adler believed that "cure or reorientation is brought about by a correction of the faulty picture of the world and the unequivocal acceptance of a mature picture of the world" (1956, p. 333). A faulty picture results from a neurotic schema of apperception and the use of "private intelligence." Adler noted that "the uncovering of the neurotic . . . style of life . . . is the most important component in therapy . . . [because] the life-plan in its entirety can be kept intact only if the patient succeeds in withdrawing it from his own criticism and understanding" (1956, p. 334). Therefore, he concluded, the therapist's task is to explain to the client what the therapist thinks the client is really doing. Of course, doing that in a blunt, confrontive manner will not necessarily invoke insight. Adler advised, "A patient has to be brought into such a state of feeling that he likes to listen, and wants to understand. Only then can he be influenced to live what he has understood" (1956, p. 335).

Before making an interpretation, the therapist listens dialectically, in order to hypothesize the opposite of what the client is complaining about, for although the client "looks at his obstacles; we must look at his attempt to protect his fictive superiority and to rescue his ambition . . . [The client's excuse] always ends in, 'What couldn't I have accomplished were I not impeded by the symptoms?' " (1973, p. 199). A person with a neurotic orientation continually offers excuses for not engaging constructively in the challenges of living in the form of "if" statements ("I would ——, if ——"). For example, "I would have friends, *if* it weren't for Charley."

Adler wanted to arouse insight by this kind of interpretation: "The cure can only be effected by intellectual means, by the patient's growing insight into his mistake, by the development of his social feeling" (1933/1964b, p. 181). An Adlerian therapist might empathize with Charley on how vulnerable he must have felt as a child when his father bullied him and his teachers picked on him. The therapist would then attempt to have Charley understand that his fantasies of becoming famous have cushioned him against his feelings of hurt. By not accomplishing what he realistically could, he remains discouraged. This prevents him from offering Michael, Nancy, and Rena the encouragement they need. In turn, their appreciation would make him proud of himself and his efforts.

## Active Reconstruction

In Adlerian therapy, a cure—or even mere alleviation of symptoms—remains squarely in the client's hands. Cure involves valuing oneself and others, correcting mistaken perceptions, and putting insight into practice by actively reconstructing one's pattern of living in a direction that is positive for oneself and others. The neurotic tendency to maintain a dichotomized picture of the world and of others (everything is seen as above-below, victor-vanquished, masculine-feminine, nothing-everything) needs to change into a flexible mode of perception that views the variety and diversity of reality. A client must learn how to face the challenges of living and to increase self-esteem and social cooperation.

Recognizing and acting upon one's own responsibility also leads to cure. An Adlerian therapist encourages self-determination by asking, "What do *you* do?" in response to a client's complaint about another person or adverse circumstances (Dreikurs, 1967). Looking at one's own response rather than blaming other people or a given situation offers the possibility that one could make a different response.

Both insight and changes in behavior (which invite different responses from others) demonstrate that a client "is not merely a victim . . . but an active participant" (Dreikurs, 1967, p. 269). Cure entails surrendering the symptoms that have served as "arrangements" that excuse people from not meeting life's challenges and that protect their wounded self-esteem. Cure occurs when the neurotic eliminates the "but" from the "yes, but" formula and embraces the tasks of living with an esteem-building, interpersonally understood, and socially interested "yes!"

Adler conceived of therapy as reeducating people (especially those who have neurotic tendencies) in the art of living (Adler, 1964b). To complete an active reconstruction of a style of life, a client requires encouragement and may need confrontation (Garner, 1972; Shulman, 1971). Adler opposed the psychoanalytic notion of "transference," which is the projection of a client's infantile and sexual needs onto a therapist. He thought that this concept made a caricature of real emotion, shut off real possibilities of love, and reinforced submission and feelings of inferiority. However, he did advocate "transferring" the healthy features of the relationship between therapist and client back into everyday living (Adler, 1964a). He would minimize the significance of a symptom by not allowing a client to derive such triumph from it or by not over-emphasizing his (Adler's) power to cure it. At times, Adler found, a lighthearted approach—through humor, telling little jokes, or appearing pleasant rather than worried—was a valuable way to undercut resistance.

## Techniques

Adler pioneered in using several techniques that have since been explicitly labeled and are in current use:

1. *Paradox*—prescribing the intensification of an entrenched problem until the symptom-bearer gives it up (Frankl, 1969; Haley, 1976; Massey, 1986a). For example, to a bright girl who upset her family each morning with complaints about school, Adler advised fussing

even more and putting a sign above her bed, "Every morning I must torment my family as much as possible" (1956, p. 398).

2. *Going with the resistance*—not pressing for change with someone who resists therapeutic recommendations (Papp, 1980, 1983). To a depressed person, Adler would say, "Don't tax yourself, do only what you find interesting and agreeable these days," and if the patient countered that nothing was interesting, Adler would add, "Then at least . . . do not exert yourself to do what is disagreeable" (1929/1964a, p. 25).

3. *Dereflection*—focusing attention on someone else when self-absorbed thoughts seem to aggravate a problem (Frankl, 1969). Adler recommended to depressives brooding over their own troubles that they "consider from time to time how you can give another person pleasure" (1929/1964a, p. 25).

4. *Restraining change*—having the therapist be pessimistic about the possibility of change, so that a resistant client will counter by moving faster (Papp, 1980, 1983). To a depressive who had been instructed to become interested in someone else and who argued, "How can you expect me to give someone else pleasure when I have none myself?", Adler advised that a cure would take much longer than initially anticipated and stated, "Do not actually *do* anything to please anyone else, but just think out how you could do it" (1929/1964a, pp. 25–26).

## LIMITATIONS OF THE MODEL

The limitations of Adler's approach to understanding a person's style of life and context center around a lack of specificity, particularly in four areas—psychological processes, developmental progression, social interaction, and the later stages of therapy.

Adler spoke of broad psychological principles (perception, interpretation, creativity, valuing, and attribution processes). He did not define precisely how these processes operate, nor did he take into account how they may function differently, depending on the developmental stage of the individual. The work of Piaget (Elkind, 1974) on cognitive development, of Piaget (1933) and Kohlberg (1969) on moral judgment, and of Selman (1976) on social role-taking all suggest that important social psychological processes mentioned by Adler have developmental dimensions. How Adler's constructs emerge and function may well vary according to the developmental stage of the individual in question. The theory of Erik Erikson (1968), whose concepts parallel many of Adler's, adds a significant dimension to the Adlerian model by spelling out some ways in which developmental stages influence and modify social psychological processes (Massey, 1986b). The Gouldings (1978, 1979), working within the neo-Adlerian tradition of Berne's Transactional Analysis (Massey, 1986d), have developed techniques that utilize an understanding of the comparative inadequacy of rational processes in younger children, recollections of significant early scenes, and a client's current capacity to make more rational and fulfilling redecisions about goals and the direction of one's life.

Although Adler was a pioneer in addressing sociocultural issues in personality theory and therapy, he sketched the broad outlines rather than presenting the details. He described the overall dynamics of growthful and neurotic interpersonal patterns but provided no way of precisely depicting moment-to-moment interchanges. Berne (1961, 1964) spelled out some ways to depict the interplay of stimuli and responses in interpersonal interactions through his "analysis of transactions." Berne also provided a means of describing the goal and process of significant series of transactions through "analysis of time structuring." Although he stressed the importance of responding to the social challenges of living and alluded to the family context in which those challenges are faced, Adler focused mostly on an individual's perceptions and interpretations of social influences in creating a style of life. Ellenberger (1970) notes, "Neither Adler nor his disciples seem to have greatly investigated the varieties of interplay of two different styles of life. At least one attempt has been made by Dr. Eric Berne . . . [who] shows how rewarding it would be to make a systematic and scientific exploration of that little-known field" (p. 643). Through "script analysis," Berne (1972) offered a way to think about and diagram the dynamic interplay between primary socializers (generally parents and more indirectly grandparents) and an individual who is in the process of making basic life decisions.

Although Adler spotlighted the context of human development and sometimes utilized paradoxical interventions, he did not recognize what we now understand to be the mutual and reciprocal interconnections of persons joined together in systems. Understanding styles of life and assisting persons in correcting mistaken ways in living can be facilitated by uncovering their broader contexts and their systemic dynamics, such as "triangles" (Minuchin, 1974), "complementarities" (Minuchin & Fishman, 1981), and cross-generational "family loyalties" (Boszormenyi-Nagy & Spark, 1984; Bowen, 1976), which either support symptomatic patterns of behavior or provide crucial resources for change. Holistic systems thinking explains how *individuals* function interdependently in *contexts* (Massey, 1986c). Adler pointed to the importance of considering individuals in context, but did not touch on the dynamic interdependence of persons in context, which the more recent systems theorists have stressed.

In contemporary terms, we can categorize Individual Psychology as a "cognitive-behavioral" approach. Adler was interested in the cognitive functions (perception, interpretation, beliefs, ideas), and he looked for real behavioral change (he subscribed to the popular dictum, "Watch the hand, not the lips!"). As a largely cognitive-behavioral perspective, Individual Psychology could be found wanting by a psychoanalytic or a more existential approach. According to Fromm (1971), Adler stressed "modes of socialization" or relatedness but underplayed "modes of assimilation" (p. 142). Adler emphasized how persons interpret and use their constitutional as well as social realities, whereas in psychoanalysis the emphasis is more on how individuals are influenced and determined by these processes. An existentialist such as Frankl (1969) views Adler as embedded in social relations and as not helping persons to also integrate their philosophical and spiritual concerns in resolving their problems.

Finally, although Adler (1956, 1933/1964b, 1973) specified the initial stages of therapy in some detail (collecting early memories, etc.), he mainly provided general principles for how to proceed in the middle stages and was somewhat vague about the precise techniques to use. However, this is consistent with his stress on the uniqueness of each person, which the therapist would have to take into account in actual practice by tailoring each intervention to fit each client.

## RESEARCH

Adler and those interested in Individual Psychology have devoted themselves mostly to therapy and education and have focused less on formal research. The one variable that has received some experimental confirmation as a significant influence on personality is birth order. Schachter (1959) showed that birth-order position can impact on affiliative tendencies, especially in the face of fear. Zajonc (1983) indicated that birth order and the spacing of births exerts a substantial effect on the development of measurable intelligence and helps explain intergroup differences in scores. Vockell, Felker, and Miley (1973) and Ernst and Angst (1983) offer reviews of the literature on the area. Toman (1976) researched the consequences that would be likely to occur if men and women from varying family constellations and birth-order positions marry each other.

Several researchers have composed inventories to measure responses that pertain to some of Adler's variables. Reimanis (1965, 1966) designed a questionnaire to gauge memories about mother, father, siblings, and community. There are two measures of social interest: one by Greever, Tseng, and Friedland (1973), which assesses level of self-significance and involvement with work, friendship, and love; and a second by Crandall (1975), which compares sensitivity to characteristics and values more and less related to social interest. Massey (1986e) devised an inventory for expressing preferences for the various safeguarding strategies. Schutz (1967) assesses the quality of the parent-child relationship through one of his FIRO Awareness Scales, the LIPHE (Life InterPersonal History Enquiry) inventory.

## SUMMARY

Alfred Adler was a pioneer in the development of a social emphasis in diagnosis and therapy. He stressed that humans are born into social contexts and that responses to social situations are essential to personality development and functioning throughout the life cycle. He presented a balanced position by showing that one's constitutional endowments and social influences, as well as one's interpretation of these elements, all contribute to one's level of functioning. By creating a style of life that is directed towards a self-chosen goal, a person remains ultimately responsible for what happens. How one uses one's opportunities and talents makes the difference, not what aptitudes or circumstances one has at one's disposal.

Adler made clear distinctions between neurotic development and constructive development. A neurotic pattern centers around exaggerating inferiority feelings or compensating for them by striving for superiority. Safeguarding strategies camouflage injured self-esteem. Constructive development fulfills the twin criteria of enhancing personal self-esteem and expressing social interest. Self-esteem and community feeling are increased through friendship, productive work, and the mutuality of sexual love. Encouragement from others fosters constructive development and engenders the courage to face life's challenges.

Adler's legacy includes the valuable therapeutic technique of life style analysis. In addition, his work stresses the importance of understanding that early recollections illuminate current goal-directed motivations. Adler's social emphasis has gained increasing recognition and has enhanced other theories over the years. Adler deserves credit for inaugurating this trend.

## REFERENCES

Adler, Alexandra. (1966). Office treatment of the chronic schizophrenic patient. In H. Hoch & J. Zubin (Eds.), *Psychopathology of schizophrenia* (pp. 366–371). New York: Grune & Stratton.

Adler, A. (1908). Der aggressiontrieb im leben und in der neurose. *Fortschritte der Medizin, 26,* 577–584. As reprinted in *Heilen und bilden* (A. Adler & C. Furtmüller, Eds., 1914). Munich: Reinhardt.

Adler, A. (1956). *The individual psychology of Alfred Adler* (H. L. Ansbacher & R. R. Ansbacher, Eds.). New York: Basic Books.

Adler, A. (1964a). *Problems of neurosis: A book of case histories* (P. Mairet, Ed.). New York: Harper & Row. (Original work published 1929)

Adler, A. (1964b). *Social interest: A challenge to mankind* (J. Linton & R. Vaughan, Trans.). New York: Capricorn. (Original work published 1933)

Adler, A. (1973). *Superiority and social interest* (3rd ed.). (H. L. Ansbacher & R. R. Ansbacher, Eds.). New York: Viking.

Adler, K. (1958). Life style in schizophrenia. *Journal of Individual Psychology, 14,* 68–72.

Adler, K., & Deutsch, D. (1959). *Essays in Individual Psychology.* New York: Grove.

Allport, G. (1961). *Patterns and growth in personality.* New York: Holt, Rinehart, & Winston.

Ansbacher, H. (1953). "Neo-Freudian" or "Neo-Adlerian"? Report on a survey conducted among members of the American Psychoanalytic Association. *American Psychologist, 8,* 165–166.

Ansbacher, H. (1974). Goal-oriented Individual Psychology. In A. Burton (Ed.), *Operational theories of personality* (pp. 99–142). New York: Brunner/Mazel.

Ansbacher, H., & Ansbacher, R. (1956). See Adler (1956).

Ansbacher, H., & Ansbacher, R. (1973). See Adler (1973).

Berne, E. (1961). *Transactional Analysis in psychotherapy.* New York: Grove.

Berne, E. (1964). *Games people play.* New York: Ballantine.

Berne, E. (1972). *What do you say after you say hello?* New York: Grove.

Bosshard, H. (1931). [Review of *Socio-psychiatric research: Its implications for the schizophrenic problem and for mental health,* by H. S. Sullivan]. *American Journal of Psychiatry, 10,* 977–991.

Boszormenyi-Nagy, I., & Spark, G. (1973). *Invisible loyalties.* Hagerstown, MD: Harper & Row. (Reprinted by Brunner/Mazel, New York, 1984.)

Bottome, P. (1957). *Alfred Adler: A portrait from life* (3rd ed.). New York: Vanguard.

Bowen, M. (1976). Theory in the practice of psychotherapy. In P. Guerin (Ed.), *Family therapy* (pp. 42–90). New York: Gardner.

Crandall, J. (1975). A scale for social interest. *Journal of Individual Psychology, 31,* 187–195.

Deutsch, D. (1959). Didactic group discussions with mothers in a child guidance setting. In K. Adler & D. Deutsch (Eds.), *Essays in Individual Psychology* (pp. 247–255). New York: Grove.

Deutsch, D. (1967). Family therapy and family life style. *Journal of Individual Psychology, 23,* 217–223.

Dreikurs, R. (1967). *Psychodynamics, psychotherapy, and counseling: Collected papers.* Chicago: Alfred Adler Institute.

Dreikurs, R. (1968). *Psychology in the classroom* (2nd ed.). New York: Harper & Row.

Dreikurs, R., Corsini, R., Lowe, R., & Sonstegard, M. (Eds.). (1959). *Adlerian family counseling: A manual for counseling centers.* Eugene: University of Oregon Press.

Dreikurs, R., & Soltz, V. (1964). *Children: The challenge.* New York: Duell, Sloan, & Pearce.

Elkind, D. (1974). *Children and adolescents: Interpretative essays on Jean Piaget.* New York: Oxford University Press.

Ellenberger, H. (1970). *The discovery of the unconscious.* New York: Basic Books.

Erikson, E. (1968). *Identity, youth, and crisis.* New York: W. W. Norton.

Ernst, C., & Angst, J. (1983). *Birth order: Its influence on personality.* Berlin: Springer-Verlag.

Frankl, V. (1969). *The will to meaning.* New York: New American Library.

Freud, S. (1957). Instincts and their vicissitudes. In J. Strachey (Ed. and Trans.), *The standard edition of the complete psychological works of Sigmund Freud* (Volume XIV, pp. 117–140). London: Hogarth Press. (Original work published 1915)

Fromm, E. (1971). *The heart of man.* New York: Harper & Row.

Furtmuller, C. (1973). Alfred Adler: A biographical essay. In H. & R. Ansbacher (Eds.), *Superiority and social interest* (3rd ed., pp. 330–394). New York: Viking.

Garner, H. (1972). The confrontation problem-solving technique: Applicability to Adlerian psychotherapy. *Journal of Individual Psychology, 28,* 248–259.

Goulding, R., & Goulding, M. (1978). *The power is in the patient.* San Francisco: TA Press.

Goulding, M., & Goulding, R. (1979). *Changing lives through redecision therapy.* New York: Brunner/Mazel.

Greever, K., Tseng, M., & Friedland, B. (1973). Development of the Social Interest Scale. *Journal of Consulting and Clinical Psychology, 41,* 454–458.

Haley, J. (1976). *Problem-solving therapy.* New York: Harper & Row.

James, W. (1947). Karen Horney and Erich Fromm in relation to Alfred Adler. *Individual Psychology Bulletin, 5,* 105–116.

Jaspers, K. (1946). *Allegemeine psychopathologie* (4th ed.). (1st ed. published 1913). [English trans.: (1963). *General psychopathology* (7th edition). Chicago: University of Chicago Press.]

Kohlberg, L. (1969). Stage and sequence: The cognitive-developmental approach to socialization. In D. Goslin (Ed.), *Handbook of socialization theory and research* (pp. 347–480). Chicago: Rand McNally.

Maslow, A. (1962). *Toward a psychology of being.* New York: D. Van Nostrand.

Massey, R. (1981). *Personality theories: Comparisons and syntheses.* New York: D. Van Nostrand.

Massey, R. (1984, March). *Transactional Analysis: Integrating nexus of the neo-Freudian/ neo-Adlerian perspectives.* Paper presented at International Transactional Analysis Association Conference, Villars, Switzerland.

Massey, R. (1986a). Paradox, double-binding, and counterparadox: A Transactional Analysis perspective. *Transactional Analysis Journal, 16,* 24–46.

Massey, R. (1986b). Erik Erikson: Neo-Adlerian. *Individual Psychology, 42,* 65–91.

Massey, R. (1986c). What/who is the family system? *The American Journal of Family Therapy, 14,* 23–39.

Massey, R. (1986d, January). *Transactional Analysis vis-à-vis Individual Psychology: Theoretical and clinical comparisons.* Paper presented at the Winter Conference of the Transactional Analysis Association, Orlando, FL.

Massey, R. (1986e). *Safeguarding strategies inventory.* Unpublished manuscript.

Minuchin, S. (1974). *Families and family therapy.* Cambridge, MA: Harvard University Press.

Minuchin, S., & Fishman, H. C. (1981). *Family therapy techniques.* Cambridge, MA: Harvard University Press.

Mohr, E., & Garlock, R. (1959). In K. Adler & D. Deutsch (Eds.), *Essays in Individual Psychology.* New York: Grove.

Mosak, H., & Mosak, B. (1975). *A bibliography for Adlerian psychology.* New York: Wiley & Sons.

Mosak, H., & Shulman, B. (1971). *The life style inventory.* Chicago: Alfred Adler Institute.

Munroe, R. (1955). *Schools of psychoanalytic thought.* New York: Holt, Rinehart, & Winston.

Papenek, H. (1954). Dynamics and treatment of borderline schizophrenia from the Adlerian point of view. *American Journal of Individual Psychology, 11,* 60–70.

Papp, P. (1980). The Greek chorus and other techniques of paradoxical therapy. *Family Process, 19*(1), 45–57.

Papp, P. (1983). *The process of change.* New York: Guilford.

Piaget, J. (1933). *The moral judgment of the child.* New York: Free Press.

Reimanis, G. (1965). Relationship of childhood experience memories to anomie later in life. *Journal of Genetic Psychology, 106,* 245–252.

Reimanis, G. (1966). Childhood experience, memories, and anomie in adults and college students. *Journal of Individual Psychology, 22,* 56–64.

Rothbart, M. (1971). Birth order and mother-child interaction in an achievement situation. *Journal of Personality and Social Psychology, 17,* 113–120.

Rotter, J. B. (1960). Psychotherapy. *Annual Review of Psychology, 11,* 381–414.

Schachter, S. (1959). *The psychology of affiliation.* Stanford, CA: Stanford University Press.

Schutz, W. C. (1967). *The FIRO scales.* Palo Alto, CA: Consulting Psychologists Press.

Selman, R. (1976). Social-cognitive understanding: A guide to educational and clinical practice. In T. Lickona (Ed.), *Moral development and behavior: Theory, research, and social issues*. New York: Holt, Rinehart, & Winston.

Shulman, B. (1968). *Essays in schizophrenia*. Baltimore, MD: Williams & Wilkins.

Shulman, B. (1971). Confrontation techniques in Adlerian psychology. *Journal of Individual Psychology, 27*, 167–175.

Sundberg, N., & Tyler, L. (1962). *Clinical psychology: An introduction to research and practice*. New York: Appleton-Century-Crofts.

Sward, K. (1945). [Review of *Our inner conflicts* by K. Horney]. *Journal of Abnormal and Social Psychology, 41*, 496–499.

Thompson, C. (1950). *Psychoanalysis: Evolution and development*. New York: Hermitage House.

Toman, W. (1976). *Family constellation* (3rd ed.). New York: Springer.

Vaihinger, H. (1925). *The philosophy of "As If"; A system of the theoretical, practical, and religious fictions of mankind*. New York: Harcourt, Brace, & Co.

Vockell, E., Felker, D., & Miley, C. (1973). Birth order literature, 1967–1972. *Journal of Individual Psychology, 29*, 39–53.

Wasserman, I. (1958). Letter to the editor. *American Journal of Psychotherapy, 12*, 623–627.

Wittels, F. (1939). The neo-Adlerians. *American Journal of Sociology, 45*, 433–445.

Wolman, B. (1960). *Contemporary theories and systems in psychology*. New York: Harper.

Zajonc, R. (1983). Validating the confluence model. *Psychological Bulletin, 93*, 457–480.

# 5

# Psychosocial Therapy

*Francis J. Turner, D.S.W.*

Psychosocial therapy is an approach to the clinical practice of social work that in many ways can be called the *traditional* approach. Even though its roots go back to the early days of the profession, it has always striven to be as current as possible and has always drawn upon a broad base of knowledge sources. However, because of its long history and its connection with the early development of the profession, it is sometimes mistakenly viewed as no longer relevant, when in fact it is a system that has changed greatly and that continues to be at the cutting edge of contemporary practice.

## THE CONCEPT OF THE PERSON AND THE HUMAN EXPERIENCE

In its current perspective, psychosocial therapy takes a positive position about human nature: Individuals are inherently good and seek to better themselves within an awareness of and respect for the rights of others. But this perspective is not a naively romantic one. A broad range of significant factors mold and alter a person's potential, values, and aspirations. Thus, to understand people from a professional context, it is imperative that we take an approach that considers the spectrum of influences.

This multi-influence perspective is not a determining one. Each of us reacts to our life experiences in our own unique way. Even though we recognize some *common* influences on human development, and we are able to make generalizations about these patterns which assist us in understanding and helping clients, we still have an awareness of, and respect for, the *uniqueness* of each person. The many influences that shape our development are active throughout our lives, making us always capable of change.

Early in the development of the psychosocial approach, social workers believed that endowment and early history played a much more important role in the formation of problems. Over the years, this has been somewhat tempered by the accumulation of clinical experience, which has shown that many people are able to overcome the legacy of their pasts and bring about dramatic changes in their lives. Hence, inherent in the positive approach to human nature is an optimistic view that change is possible. Again, this optimism is not naive; proponents of psychosocial theory are aware of the tremendous amount of suffering and unrealized potential that occurs when people are deprived of experiences, goods, and services. A dramatic example of this is seen in the Shore family, of whom we will speak more in subsequent pages.

In psychosocial theory, values are an important concept. "Values" refers to those quasi-intuitive aspects of the personality that lead us to prefer some alternatives that we meet in day-to-day living over others, and which thus assist us greatly in making those many choices that are an ongoing part of living. The values that are of particular importance for this theory are those related to our perception of time, human activity, interpersonal relationships, and basic human nature (Kluckhohn and Strodtbeck, 1961).

From the perspective of relational values, psychosocial theory stresses the importance of each individual. Although they recognize the importance of familial and collateral values as primary factors in people's lives, psychosocial practitioners consider individual well-being to be their primary responsibility.

From the perspective of practice, the theory stresses *activity* as another prime value. That is, it emphasizes the responsibility of the practitioner to take whatever action is possible and available (and, of course, ethical) to help clients to achieve their goals.

## HISTORICAL PERSPECTIVE

The psychosocial model had its origins in the late 19th century, at the very beginning of the development of a scientific base for social work. Throughout its history, there have been two major consistent themes: One was an emphasis on the need to understand persons and groups from the twofold perspective of person and situation; the other was the view that the knowledge needed in order to conduct responsible practice should be drawn from a range of relevant disciplines. This latter point has resulted in an approach to practice that is open and inquiring, a system that continues to change, develop, and expand. I do not mean to suggest that the system is *completely* open to knowledge, regardless of source, or that it does not have its favorite theories. However, the psychosocial model has been ready to incorporate any new ideas and new methodologies that have proved to be useful and that are ethical.

Certainly this is a system that was, and continues to be, heavily influenced by psychoanalytic theory (see Chapter 1, p. 13). This was reflected in its earlier designation as "the Diagnostic School" in the famous Diagnostic-Functional controversy. However, although the Freudian influence on the development of the system was important, it has never been as all-pervasive as some of its critics allege. Throughout its history, the psychosocial model has integrated other theories. At times, the psychological or interior aspects of the person have received more attention than the social aspects. However, over the past 25 years, the focus has changed dramatically. During that time, we have become more comfortable with, and knowledgeable about, the social sciences and their strong potential for helping us to better understand and respond effectively to the needs of clients.

Within the profession of social work, important contributors to the development of psychosocial thinking included Richmond (1917, 1922), Hamilton (1951), Garrett (1958), Reynolds (1951), and Austin (1948). Influential works from other professions include those of Horney (1936), Sullivan (1953), Erikson (1963), and Hartmann (1958), as well as Parsons (Parsons & Shils, 1951), Merton (1957), and Kluckhohn (Kluckhohn & Strodtbeck, 1961).

However, Florence Hollis deserves the most credit for making the psychosocial approach a distinct theoretical system within social work. Although the term *psychosocial* had been used as a way of identifying a particular thrust of social work clinical practice, it was not generally associated with a specific approach to practice until after the publication of the first edition of *Casework: A Psychosocial Therapy* (Hollis, 1964). The development of the theory (and its commitment to still further development) can be observed in the two subsequent editions (Hollis, 1972; Hollis & Woods, 1981).

These later editions increased the knowledge base by incorporating ideas and concepts from other theories, including systems and role theory. Psychosocial therapy also became more sophisticated in its understanding of the impact of such factors as ethnicity, values, and power.

As I have noted, the term *psychosocial* was first used in a generic way to help connect the two essential components of practice; only later did it become identified with a particular system of practice within clinical social work. Now, however, the term is once again being used in a much broader context, as a means of avoiding a too narrow or too specialized approach to the human condition. This has occurred not only within social work but also in allied helping professions; there has been a growing recognition of the disadvantages of a too rigid compartmentalization of human knowledge.

## KEY THEORETICAL CONSTRUCTS

### Development of Personality

The unifying theme in the personality theory that underlies the psychosocial approach is that each person's history is "multi-influenced." Therefore, it is essential that we take a pluralistic perceptual approach in order to understand a person in his or her current context. Related to this concept of *plurality* is a corresponding concept of *individuality*, which holds that each person is influenced differently by the various events in his or her life. Hence, even though it is important to attempt to generalize about common experiences and situations, it is essential that we always take the individuality of each person into account in our assessments of significant factors in their psychosocial reality.

Psychosocial theory stresses the importance of dealing with the client in the *here and now*. Certainly, it is important for us to understand the client's earlier significant history, but only as a way of helping us understand its effect on the present. Therefore, in seeking to understand the Shore family, we need to take into account the references that Charley makes to his relationship with his own mother, as well as the adult role that Nancy displayed as a young girl, and we need to consider the impact of these factors on the current situation. A person's history not only provides information about events that have had an impact on that individual's life; it also tells us about the way in which his or her personality developed. And, although it is important for us to help our clients to deal with their current realities and reduce their stress and suffering in the present, we are equally interested in their futures. To this end, we should help them in a way that will enhance their ability to function more effectively and more satisfyingly—a way that also fosters the development of their potential.

As we know from the study of developmental psychology, many factors are involved in the development of personality. For example, even the parents' feelings towards their unborn child and the experiences of the pregnancy itself shape expectations about the child. If a pregnancy was unexpected, or if the mother experiences serious health problems, or if it upsets the marriage or the family's interaction, the child can begin to be seen in a negative light even before birth and will thus arrive with an already predetermined personality and perceived impact on the family. (Of course, these attitudes can also be in a positive direction.) The child's perceived personality influences the way in which the child is viewed in his or her early months, which in turn affects the way he or she is treated.

Needless to say, the culture into which the child is born has a great impact on determining the kinds of behaviors that are reinforced and the ways in which needs are recognized and met; it also prescribes who the caretakers will be and how care is to be provided. From the beginning of the child's life, the economic condition of the caretakers and the ethnic and cultural reality of the environment influence the behaviors, expectations, responses, and the sense of self which, taken together, begin to form the child's personality.

A person's development is also affected by his or her family structure, health, physical appearance, genetic endowment, birth order, sex, race, religion, ethnic identity, socioeconomic class, geographical location, life style, language, food habits, and the nature and location of housing.

Obviously, relationships with other family members, peers, friends, and co-workers play an important role in shaping the ways in which people develop and act. For example, parents and friends may or may not provide permanency, security, and consistency. We also cannot ignore relationships with the larger society, including school, work, religious structures, health and welfare systems, and government.

Sometimes overlooked is the influence that major historical events have on the development of personality. Often people who have lived through the same events display commonalities in some aspects of their personalities. For instance, we can often observe that some people who grew up during the Depression tend to be frugal and penny-conscious; people who survived the Holocaust tend to be tradition-oriented and history-oriented; and escaped refugees tend to be suspicious of government and officialdom.

Such a multifactored perception of personality development presents a tremendous challenge to us as practitioners. First, we must assess the differential impact, both positive and negative, of the many influences in the development of personality. Second, we must individualize each situation. This requires us to constantly try to make use of our understanding of the regularities in human development, while noting that within these generalities there are also individual differences. Third—and perhaps most essential to the psychosocial understanding of personality and problems—we must recognize that, just as a person's development may be influenced by many factors, a person's search for solutions may include many possibilities. This means that the practitioner can choose from among a rich and diverse range of interventions.

## Structure of Personality

According to psychosocial theory, all of the many influences that I have discussed have their impact upon a basic *structure* of personality. The essence of that personality is the sense of existence and identity that says, "I exist as a distinct human person." Within this awareness of existence is a realization that I have an intellectual apparatus that permits learning, experiencing, problem-solving, planning, dreaming, doing—in other words, an *ego*.

I am also aware that I have a will (an ability to choose to do some things and not to do others); that is, I have some control over my actions in most situations. I know that throughout my life I will do many things that I prefer not to do, or do not want to do, but I am aware that they are being done against my will. I am also aware that, as a part of my personality, I have a conscience, or *superego*—a part of me that helps me to decide what things are appropriate for me to do and what things I should not do even though I may still do them. At times, this decision to do or not to do is carefully thought out. At many other times, acceptable or unacceptable behavior is obvious to me without conscious thought.

I am also aware that a powerful part of my personality structure is my emotional nature. Emotions are the very complex system of powerful physical feelings experienced in different situations. These feelings can range from mild experiences of joy and sorrow to highly intense feelings of ecstasy, rage, despair, or depression. I know that at times I am not able to control these feelings. I am also aware that this "feeling" part of me can intrude on me in an often unexpected way, so that apparently small and insignificant events can trigger very strong and often surprising emotional responses within me.

I am aware that part of this emotional component consists of very strong likes and dislikes about a wide range of things, persons, activities, foods, places, and aspirations, the source of which I do not always fully understand. At times, this "unconscious" part of myself leads to feelings, activities, and decisions that may create problems and make me feel out of control. As powerful as some of these likes, dislikes, urges, and feelings are, I know that, if I wish, the thinking part of me will take control. I know that throughout my life the things I have learned, the patterns I have developed, the influence of others, and my own self-perception can reduce more and more the extent to which a part of me seems to be uncontrollable.

## Implications for the Case

As I have tried to show, the current psychosocial concept of personality combines psychoanalytic, cognitive, and learning theory concepts with an underlying optimistic existential view of people and potential. Much of this approach can be illustrated by examples from the Shore family case.

For example, Nancy's early history, including the relationship with her own mother, her only-child status, her father's abandonment and his subsequent denial of her existence as his first child, and her remaining in her childhood home are important factors in the development of the person she is now and the role she has chosen to play in the marriage. Her wish to care for others and her choice of a career in nursing are understandable in view of her past. She chose a husband who needed care and whose fantasies of "Hollywood and fame" fulfilled her own childhood fantasies. However, following her back injury, she was simultaneously a caretaker for her husband and children and a person who needed care herself.

Similar illustrations can be drawn from our knowledge of Charley's history and the subsequent history of the children and the family as a whole. We see a repetition, into the fourth generation, of some of the patterns that have produced problems over the years.

## ASSESSMENT

Assessment and diagnosis are an essential component of the psychosocial approach to practice. There is an ongoing commitment to understanding, evaluating, and identifying the critical variables in a particular case, and to determining the way in which those variables interact with and are involved in the client's problem. If we conduct our practices without relying on these judgments, either we do things without having an adequate basis for our actions, or we do the same things in all situations. Both these approaches are irresponsible.

Diagnosis is not a one-time act. Most situations that we deal with are complex and ever-changing, and therefore the process of diagnosis and assessment *must* be continuous. Diagnosis begins with our first glimpse of the client and the first sound of his or her voice. It continues even after the case is closed and we are writing up our reports.

Even though the assessment component of our intervention needs to be an ongoing process, it is also important that at several points throughout the life of the case we record our current assessment. This ensures both that we have a clear grasp of the situation and our role in it, and that others who may subsequently become involved in the case can have the benefit of our judgments about the situation, its essential components, and their interrelationship.

Diagnosis or assessment is not merely the recording of problems or weaknesses and the assigning of some label to the client. Appropriate professional intervention requires that we have an accurate assessment of not only the strengths of the person-in-situation but also the deficiencies of the person-in-situation. In many social work records, it is common to see accurate assessments of the problem areas in an individual, family, or community situation, with no indication of the areas of strength. This can result in a serious misunderstanding of situations or, even worse, a mismanagement of cases.

During the ongoing diagnostic process, there are three kinds of decisions or assessments that should be made about a person or persons. The first is, "How is this person like every other human being that I know?" In this regard, we make use of our general knowledge of human behavior and development. The second decision is, "How is this person like some other groups of people?" Here we begin to make use of our specific knowledge of influencing factors such as personality, culture, history, physical condition, values, sex, and economics, plus any others that may be relevant. This knowledge helps us to begin to see some of the differences that are to be found in this person. Third, "How is this person different from other people I have met?" This, too, is essential, because it makes use of our general knowledge of people and of specific subgroups in a way that permits us to individualize the client and thus better understand and work effectively and efficiently with him or her.

In the practice of psychosocial social work, both assessment and diagnosis are often difficult. The difficulty stems from the multifactor approach. The challenge of assessment grows as we become increasingly aware of the complexity of our clients' lives, the multiplicity of interacting influencing factors, and the difficulty of assessing accurately the differential impact of these factors. It is important to emphasize that the extent and content of this process need to be related both to the nature of the case and to the point where we are in the treatment process. Without understanding this and the ongoing nature of the process, we can find ourselves in the situation that used to be quite common in some settings: No intervention was begun with a client until a full diagnosis and history had been carried out. This frequently resulted in the denial of service to the client at a point at which it was most needed; it also led to the gathering and assessing of much information that was not needed if one considered what the client wanted to change. Nevertheless, this does not excuse us from attempting to understand and use appropriately all the facts that are available to us. Frequently, we will know very little about the client and will have to make decisions with the information obtained in a very brief contact. This certainly happens in crisis work and in other types of short-term treatment.

One of the early and ongoing questions we need to ask ourselves is, "What do we *not* know about the client and the situation?" Often we have so much information that we forget to ask about anything that might have been omitted. By asking this question, we are pushed to decide if it is necessary to investigate some unknown areas. An important aspect of this identification of significant gaps in knowledge is that it not only reveals further areas of stress or difficulty, but it also uncovers strengths and resources in clients' lives that may be called upon in a useful way.

In the case of the Shore family, there are several areas in which additional information might be useful both in assessment and in developing a treatment strategy. For example, we do not know about the family's ethnic identity, religion, and the neighborhood in which they live, nor a great deal about their economic situation, apart from some general information about the ongoing financial pressures due to lack of income. We have inadequate information about the nature of Nancy's back problem and the extent to which remedial steps could be taken if resources existed. Further, we know very little about the marital relationship, especially the sexual component.

The problems in this family are well described in the case summary. Members of the family appear to live in an ongoing series of crisis situations related to intrafamily relationships, role reversals, inadequate income, and many acute and chronic health-related conditions. Many of these problems originated in the history of the parents and continue to repeat themselves in the present. In addition to the family problems, there is a complex and not fully described marital situation that is marked by atypical role issues and unreal expectations of the partners to fulfill each other's fantasies and deprivations from the past. They also have few friends and a deteriorating employment picture.

From an individual perspective, each member of the family has personal problems and environmental problems; further stress results from the interaction between these two psychosocial components. Three of the four members of the family have some type of symptomatology that needs consideration: Nancy's back problem, Michael's asthma, and Charley's Bipolar depression (which at times has led to at least a mention of suicide, a fact in a case that always has to be viewed as serious).

Nevertheless, it is important to remember that there *are* some positives in this situation. The Shores are obviously intelligent people who have a concern about themselves. It is interesting to note that they somehow managed to have themselves selected for this project; they do attract help when it is needed. Nancy has a network of resources in the health field; Rena has been successful at getting admitted into programs in which she was interested. Overall, family members seem to have considerable social talents in verbalization, in entertaining, and in seeking resources. Even though they manifest moderately severe personality problems, they are apparently free of psychotic breaks with reality. Despite limited income and severe financial difficulties, they own their home.

Although there are health problems, they are not fully debilitating; most of the time each person can function in his or her respective role (the mother least so). The family appears able to survive in crisis situations; in fact, crisis seems to bring out some coping strengths, especially the mother's. There are some family bonds: For the most part, the family has stayed together. Even the daughter's living away from home appears to be more symbolic than real. Although they have not been too successful, family members still have aspirations for change and have kept to their value orientation of upward mobility. As problem-laden as they are, these family members do have some important things going for them as we consider them for treatment.

## TREATMENT OF CHOICE

According to psychosocial thinking, one of the significant environments in a client's life is the helping system and the ways in which it can be differentially viewed by the client. Thus, in considering the kind of help that a person needs, we need to take into account not only the nature of the service required but also the setting in which it is to be provided. By definition, psychosocial intervention is not limited to any particular kind of client, setting, or situation. It is a system of intervention that insists that each of these three variables is critical and needs to be carefully assessed and appropriately responded to. The theory does not hold that setting is not important, but rather that it can have a considerable impact, both positive and negative. It does not say that all clients can be helped equally. Indeed, there are people for whom we do not as yet have the requisite knowledge and skill to be of assistance; this is especially true of people whose cultures and belief systems differ from those of the predominant groups in our society. Nor does this system hold that we have ways of dealing with all the personal and situational problems that people face. For this reason, one of the important responsibilities of the psychosocial practitioner is to discover what it is that a client needs and where it can be found, even if it means seeking help at another setting or from a different discipline. The value system of psychosocial treatment teaches us to know our limitations as well as our potential. In the work with the Shores, for example, it would be important to develop liaisons with the physicians who were treating Nancy's back problems and Michael's asthma, the psychologist who had tested Rena, and the psychiatrist who was monitoring Charley's lithium.

## THE THERAPEUTIC PROCESS

One of the key components of psychosocial theory is that all aspects of the therapeutic process are viewed from a neutral perspective. That is, no form of intervention is to be considered more *inherently* worthy than any other; the test of its value is its relevance for, and influence on, the client and his or her situation. There was a time when this was not so, when the psychotherapeutic activities of the practitioner were seen as more valuable than was "mere" work with the environment; if this included work with the client's unconscious, it was seen as even more valuable.

Psychosocial treatment draws two important concepts from systems theory: *equifinality* and *multifinality*. Equifinality means that a particular outcome in a situation can be reached by means of different inputs; multifinality means that similar inputs can result in different outcomes. When applied to psychosocial treatment, this means that there is more than one way to treat a particular situation. In fact, similar treatment goals can be achieved by different routes; conversely, the use of similar approaches in cases will not always have the same outcome. We need to find a balance between an approach that seeks prescriptions for particular kinds of presenting situations and an approach that says that each case is so different that it is futile to seek formulas for intervention that are related to diagnosis.

These two concepts also help us understand that it is essential that we set clear treatment objectives. This means that although only a portion of the client's presenting situation is dealt with in the therapeutic process, there is some evidence that success in one area will carry over into other life areas as well.

As its name reflects, psychosocial treatment has a dual thrust: it seeks to bring about outer change in clients' significant environments and inner changes in clients' personality and behavior. In practice, this twofold approach is not seen in an either–or manner, nor does it assign more importance to either the *psycho* or *social* (inner or outer). Both forms of intervention are used in all but the rarest of instances. Because of the tendency within the literature to overvalue direct work with persons and undervalue work in the environment, less attention has been given to the differential roles and techniques used in this aspect of practice. Therefore, we have very little in our literature about specific and differential meanings of such things as money, food, gifts, and planned environmental techniques, but much more on interviewing, relationship, and the differential use of theories and methodologies. This is unfortunate, because money, food, gifts, and planned environmental techniques are powerful components of successful psychosocial intervention.

Hollis and Woods (1981) have made a major contribution to the psychosocial model by presenting this environmental component of practice from a threefold perspective: the range of resources that can be utilized, the types of communication used, and the variety of professional roles employed in behalf of our clients. Hollis and Woods identified six professional roles: *provider, locator, creator, interpreter, mediator,* and *aggressive intervener.* Since then, a further role of *broker* has been identified (Turner, 1986). The skilled practitioner makes creative use of these various roles to help the client identify and make optimum use of the helping network.

Hollis has also made a major contribution in direct services by helping specify the range of interactions between client and social worker during the therapeutic process (Hollis, 1968). The first of these is the sustaining procedures in which we convey to the clients our interest, our respect, and our understanding. The second type of interaction is direct influence—when we use the authority of the relationship to move clients in a particular direction or to address some particular aspects of their situation. The third type of treatment procedures are those that are designed to encourage clients to express their feelings—to talk about themselves and their significant realities.

However, we do more than just encourage clients to express their feelings and talk about them. We also help clients reflect about themselves and their realities. The fourth type of activity in treatment relates to the activities that lead clients to reflect on their current situations and the people in them.

In addition, we also attempt to have clients reflect on their behavior patterns and on those behaviors that might contribute to their present situations. Finally, we join with the clients in reflective thinking about their earlier life histories and the influence these have on their current functioning.

All methods of treatment are equally valued in the psychosocial approach. What makes any one method preferable to another depends on the presenting situation and the joint client-therapist assessment of what will be most effective. In the past, methods of intervention such as casework and group work were seen almost as separate specialties. There is no doubt that, in the early years of the psychosocial tradition, one-to-one intervention was the preferred method. This viewpoint has changed dramatically. It is now evident that some clients and some situations can benefit from one method of intervention more than another. Hence, a practitioner in the psychosocial tradition needs to be competent in working with individuals, dyads, families, groups, and community structures. This does not mean, however, that we all need to be equally competent in all methods, or that one should not specialize and develop skills in a particular model (for example, family therapy).

## Course of Treatment

When we discuss treatment, we customarily talk about its various phases, such as engagement, history-taking, assessment, diagnosis, treatment, termination, and follow-up. However, in practice, these phases are highly intertwined. Although intervention is seen as a process that does not lend itself to the regimentation of a structure that moves from history to assessment to diagnosis, and so on, this does not mean that there is not a structure and order to what we do with clients. Activities in the early phase of treatment ensure that we engage the client, that we give some immediate help, and that we assist the client in becoming involved in whatever process seems indicated. Throughout the life of the case, it is also important that we be aware of the necessity of encouraging the client to stay with the process, to understand the frustrations and impatience and questioning that can take place, and to begin to anticipate the termination. As the case draws to a close, we need to help the client deal with remaining material, understand the process, reinforce the gains that have been made, and anticipate the impending separation. In other words, just as there are *conceptual* parts to a case that need to be addressed throughout the duration of the case, there are also *temporal* phases that need to be understood differently and used for the client's benefit.

At one time, it was presumed that treatment had to be long-term. This has changed greatly; recently we have learned much about the powerful benefits of short-term intervention. We are now aware that a brief telephone conversation with a skilled therapist can have significant impact on a client. Thus, we can look at time as yet another treatment variable that must be used appropriately depending on the nature of the client, the request, the assessment, and the setting.

## Therapist-Client Relationship

One important resource in the armamentarium of the psychosocial therapist is the therapeutic relationship. Over the history of the helping professions, this relationship has been so important that it has taken on almost mystical proportions and has been viewed as the essence of treatment. The tremendous power and influence of "mind on mind," as Mary Richmond phrased it, have long been known (Richmond, 1922, p. 108). Often, people who have not had many happy relationships in their lives respond strongly to a concerned therapist. We also know that, when under stress, people respond to demonstrations of concern and competence. Thus, in situations in which they need professional assistance, clients quickly develop a bond with the therapist. When properly understood and utilized, that bond can be a powerful medium of influence and change.

Because of its potential for both helping and damaging clients, the therapeutic relationship has been given much attention in the literature. Throughout the history of psychosocial thought, it has been noted that clients transfer feelings and experiences from earlier relationships to their therapists. However, this is not one-sided; therapists may also transfer earlier feelings to their clients. For these reasons, psychosocial practice requires that trainees receive supervision to learn how to work effectively despite the often heavy emotional climate of the therapeutic relationship. Of course, this is not the only purpose of supervision. A related strong tradition in psychosocial practice is the use of professional consultation by all therapists, regardless of experience, which provides an opportunity to review cases, discuss practice issues, and hear other points of view.

The psychosocial approach to clinical practice fits well with the Shore family. Each family member could benefit from a sustained and consistent relationship with a therapist. An understanding of some of their earlier family history could help the parents and children reassess themselves and their demands on each other. An understanding of their present situation could help them put their pasts behind them, freeing them for more satisfying current lives.

The Shores appear to need some help in being individuals within a family and in functioning as a family unit. In this kind of situation, each family member could benefit, at least in the beginning, from an individual therapeutic relationship. Each person should have his or her own therapist, and there should also be one therapist who will work with all of the Shores as a family unit. The parents and children, especially Rena, need some help in sorting out who they want to be and where they want to go.

Nancy has found considerable satisfaction in the nursing profession. Are there ways in which she can still make use of this, in spite of her back problems? Charley also needs help in sorting out who he is, what he can do, what he wants to do, and what is available. The same applies to both children. This is a family with strong potentials, one that could benefit from an ongoing, multifaceted relationship with a setting such as a family agency. Because there is so much "growing up" to do, requiring long-term intervention, it would make more sense if the therapeutic relationship were primarily with the agency, and not with a single therapist. However, there should also be one person who could act as the coordinator of the intervention and the broker for other services (e.g., vocational help with the various family members).

## LIMITATIONS OF THE MODEL

Although psychosocial theory aims at being responsive to the whole range of situations that are met in social work practice, regardless of setting, it does not claim to be complete or universally effective. Some of the major problems that the system faces are those faced by the entire profession. One of the most humbling difficulties of this theory is the awareness of the complexity of variables with which we must deal. It is indeed a formidable challenge to attempt to assess the intricacies of personality with which we are faced in any presenting situation, to similarly differentially assess the significant environments and their interaction in the clients' lives, and to further assess the interrelationship of person and situation. Thus, one of our larger challenges is the development of strategies, conceptual frameworks, organizing concepts, and measurement instruments that will assist us in the critical assessment that is so essential to this system.

Similarly, we need to find ways of evaluating the differential impact of our psychosocial treatment techniques so that we may use them more precisely. We also need to find out which kinds of people and problems we are most able to help, and, of equal importance, about the kinds of situations we are least helpful in. Unlike our colleagues in medicine, we appear to be uncomfortable about declaring our lack of knowledge, whereas they quite openly declare to the public, "We do not know how to deal with such and such a situation. Please help us." We need to be more open about the gaps in our knowledge. If we proclaim our successes in our journals, we also need to report what it is that we do not do well.

## RESEARCH

The psychosocial system has long acknowledged the responsibility to develop our theory and practice from a research base. An increasing number of clinical articles written from a research perspective have appeared in the professional literature in the past 10 years; many of these have a specific psychosocial orientation (Ellison, 1983; Gibbs, 1982; Harel & Noelker, 1978). It is futile to expect research to answer the broad question, "Does psychosocial intervention work?" Such research is impossible. What *is* possible and necessary are hundreds of small, carefully designed projects that measure minute aspects of intervention. Out of these will develop a better formulated and better tested theory of intervention.

Although as psychosocial practitioners we have been interested in research and have been cognizant of our responsibility to commit significant resources to it, we have perhaps been naive in expecting too much of research. In the past, we have used inadequate resources and inappropriate designs to answer impossible research questions. I believe that we are now long past the point of asking such questions as "Does casework work?" and are aware that most clients who become involved in responsible, competent social work intervention are going to be helped to some extent. However, we are not yet able to be as precise about assessment, diagnosis, and intervention as we would like.

As I have mentioned, one of the problems in conducting research on psychosocial interventions has been the number of interacting variables with which we deal. In recent years, we have begun to appreciate the implications that the world of technology has, both for the provision of service and for research. In this regard, computers, which are available in ever-increasing numbers in our agencies, have tremendous potential to help us gather, analyze, and differentially assess the many aspects of treatment that we wish to study further.

Recent research has indicated that social workers need to be more attuned to the physical and biological realities of their clients (Johnson, 1984). In fact, it is possible that in time this system will more properly be called biopsychosocial theory.

We know also that many of the difficulties faced by our clients are the result of inadequate access to the goods and services of society, and that no amount of direct intervention on our part is going to be able to compensate for these lacks. Thus, as part of our analysis, we must determine the situations that, because of existing societal inequities, are beyond our ability to change.

## SUMMARY

Psychosocial thinking has helped shape the current practice of clinical social work. It is a system that is varied in its origins and complex in its knowledge base. It continues to evolve rapidly. Psychosocial practitioners can be proud of its accomplishments, while remaining aware of its deficiencies. We need to continue the restless search for better tested and better explicated knowledge and methods for intervening in the psychosocial realities of persons, groups, families, and communities.

Let me summarize what the psychosocial approach can offer clients such as the Shores. The case study introduced them this way: "The problems of the Shore family are common ones . . . unemployment, illness, and the worrisome behavior of the children. What is uncommon is that . . . the problems never get resolved." This is the kind of family that psychosocially oriented social workers have been working with for years; the Shores are replete with problems whose origins lie in history, heredity, health, personality, and the social reality in which they live. The accumulated practice wisdom and tested knowledge of the psychosocial tradition could be brought to bear to help them achieve a more satisfying and less stressful life style. However, this family could also expose the inadequacies of our knowledge and skills. Fortunately, it is also a family that brings many strengths and potentials to the therapeutic milieu.

Overall, my prognosis for this family would be optimistic. Indeed, they are to be commended for coming forward and standing as an example for all of us to think about. I wish them well in their futures.

## REFERENCES

Austin, L. (1948). Trends in differential treatment in social casework. *Journal of Social Casework, 29,* 203–211.

Ellison, E. S. (1983). Issues concerning parental harmony and children's psychosocial adjustment. *American Journal of Orthopsychiatry, 53*(1), 73–80.

Erikson, E. H. (1963). *Childhood and society* (2nd ed., rev.). New York: Norton.

Garrett, A. (1958). The worker-client relationship. In H. J. Parad (Ed.), *Ego psychology and dynamic casework* (pp. 53–72). New York: Family Service Association of America.

Gibbs, J. T. (1982). Psychosocial factors related to substance abuse among delinquent females: Implications for prevention and treatment. *American Journal of Orthopsychiatry, 52*(2), 261–271.

Hamilton, G. (1951). *Theory and practice of social casework* (2nd. ed., rev.). New York: Columbia University Press.

Harel, Z., & Noelker, L. (1978). Sector-related variation on psychosocial dimensions in long-term care for the aged. *Social Work in Health Care, 4*(2), 199–208.

Hartmann, H. (1958). *Ego psychology and the problem of adaptation.* New York: International Universities Press.

Hollis, F. (1964). *Casework: A psychosocial therapy* (1st ed.). New York: Random House.

Hollis, F. (1968). *A typology of casework treatment.* New York: Family Service Association of America.

Hollis, F. (1972). *Casework: A psychosocial therapy* (2nd ed.). New York: Random House.

Hollis, F., & Woods, M. E. (1981). *Casework: A psychosocial therapy* (3rd ed.). New York: Random House.

Horney, K. (1936). *The neurotic personality of our time.* New York: Norton.

Johnson, H. C. (1984). The biological bases of psychopathology. In F. J. Turner (Ed.), *Adult Psychopathology* (pp. 6–72). New York: The Free Press.

Kluckhohn, F. R., & Strodtbeck, F. L. (1961). *Variations in value orientations.* Evanston, IL: Row Peterson and Co.

Merton, R. K. (1957). *Social theory and social structure* (2nd ed.). New York: The Free Press.

Parsons, T., & Shils, E. A. (1951). *Toward a general theory of action.* Cambridge, MA: Harvard University Press.

Reynolds, B. (1951). *Social work and social living: Explorations in philosophy and practice.* New York: Citadel Press.

Richmond, M. (1917). *Social diagnosis.* New York: Russell Sage.

Richmond, M. (1922). *What is social case work?* New York: Russell Sage Foundation.

Sullivan, H. S. (1953). *The interpersonal theory of psychiatry.* New York: Norton.

Turner, F. J. (1986). *Social work treatment* (3rd ed.). New York: Free Press.

# 6

# Radical Behaviorism and Clinical Social Work

## *Bruce A. Thyer, Ph.D.*

Perhaps more than any other theory or model of clinical social work, the behavioral approach comes closest to following the tradition in our profession of striving for a person-in-environment perspective. It focuses upon enhancing the transactions that occur between individuals and their environments, upon improving the life skills of clients (which is designed to elicit a more favorable environment), and upon direct interventions that are designed to alter environments.

This central objective is poorly recognized by clinical social workers and others, because of a confusion between the stimulus-response psychology of Pavlov and Watson, which was prevalent during the 1920s and 1930s, and the far more sophisticated behavioral approach of Skinner. Pavlovian behavioral theory focuses on the role of environmental stimuli that elicit involuntary reflexive behaviors, whereas Skinnerian theory emphasizes how the *consequences* that have followed a person's actions in the past influence the form of his or her present activities. The following summarizes this view:

> Men act upon the world, and change it, and are changed in turn by the consequences of their action. Certain processes which the human organism shares with other species, alter behavior so that it achieves a safer and more useful interchange with a particular environment. When appropriate behavior has been established, its consequences work through similar processes to keep it in force. If by chance the environment changes, old forms of behavior disappear, while new consequences build new forms. (Skinner, 1957, p. 1)

## THE CONCEPT OF THE PERSON AND THE HUMAN EXPERIENCE

The philosophy of science that underlies behavioral social work is known as *behaviorism.* In the form advocated by Skinner—*radical behaviorism*—an attempt is made to account for human behavior without recourse to mental events that occur within the person. It is easy to see why this is called radical! Of course, not all behavioral social workers accept this view. Some advocate a variation called cognitive behaviorism (Wodarski, 1975), which seems more palatable to many clinicians, whereas others espouse a version called methodological behaviorism.*

Radical behaviorists view the contemporary person as the sum total of his or her individual learning history. Past actions that have been followed by rewarding consequences (reinforced) become more likely to occur again under similar circumstances; those actions that have been followed in the past by aversive consequences (punished) become less likely to occur under similar circumstances. Virtually all voluntary human behavior is seen to thus *operate* on one's environment, producing favorable or unfavorable consequences. Such actions are collectively known as *operant behavior* and develop through environmental shaping into that marvelously complex and idiosyncratic repertoire we call the human personality. In a behavioral model, almost all client problems are deemed to involve crucial operant elements. Behaviors that were adaptive in the past may be overtaken by a too rapidly changing physical or social environment and become maladaptive. Alternatively, trauma or deficits in a person's learning history may have left the person completely unable to cope with current environmental demands. In behavioral practice, intervention may focus either upon helping clients to change their psychosocial environment from a less punitive to a more reinforcing one, or upon helping clients change their own behavior, or both.

Certain problems of individual clients are seen as the products of Pavlovian-type learning processes, usually involving emotional or appetitive responses. Examples of such difficulties are phobic (Thyer & Curtis, 1985) or excessively fearful reactions (Shorkey & Taylor, 1973); sexual arousal difficulties such as psychogenic impotence or vaginismus; preferences for sexual stimulation through children, violence, or fetish objects; and the anticipatory nausea that occurs when cancer patients enter the chemotherapy clinic (Nesse, Carli, Curtis, & Kleinman, 1980). Because such reactions are relatively involuntary *responses* to environmental stimuli, they are collectively known as *respondent behaviors.*

A third relevant influence in accounting for human behavior may be labeled *biological factors.* Fatigue, diet, illness, injury, medications, allergies, hunger, thirst, pain, and so forth may all give rise to

---

* See Skinner (1974) for a review of these positions.

forms of problematic behavior that require appropriate assessment and intervention.

Behaviorists see these three factors as accounting for virtually all human behavior in its complex and manifold variations. Hypothetical constructs such as intrapsychic processes, cognition, will, and motivation are deemed to be either fallacious or more parsimoniously attributed to operant learning. This simplified model is presented in Figure 1, which illustrates how operant, respondent, and biological factors may overlap one another in giving rise to a given form of client behavior.

A behavioral approach theorizes that there are no essential or qualitative differences between what is labeled normal behavior and what is labeled abnormal (e.g., psychopathological). The same fundamental learning processes are believed to give rise to both. Practically speaking, this view is largely a matter of faith when dealing with real-life clients, but is a conviction supported by experimental research which clearly demonstrates how, in both laboratory and natural environments, complex human behavior is largely a function of past and present consequences.

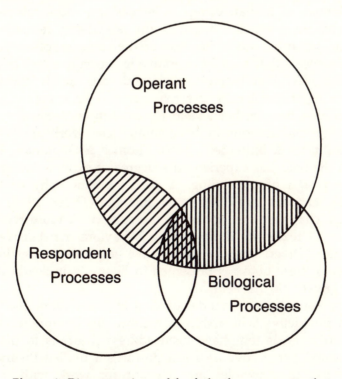

**Figure 1.** Diagrammatic model of the key processes that account for all human activity, according to the behavioral social work perspective.

## HISTORICAL PERSPECTIVE

Because the development of the formal principles of Pavlovian-type learning during the first decade of this century preceded the development of other behavioral theories, it is not surprising that behavioral interventions initially drew primarily upon respondent conditioning theory. Examples of these interventions include desensitization techniques for phobias, sexual dysfunctions, and other neurotic problems presumably mediated by anxiety; aversion therapy for alcoholism; and training in relaxation and assertiveness skills. All these methods are predicated upon the notion of using ostensibly Pavlovian procedures to establish counterconditioned emotional reactions to promote client psychosocial functioning. To varying degrees, these procedures have been found useful. Desensitization procedures and relaxation and assertiveness training are now an accepted part of the clinical skills of many social workers. On the other hand, aversion therapy for alcoholism is rarely used today.

The range of problems addressed by these behavioral approaches remained somewhat limited, compared to the broad array of client problems that social workers are called upon to alleviate, until Skinner and his colleagues began extending the laboratory findings of operant learning into the domain of human beings in increasingly more complex natural environments. In work that began in the late 1940s, researchers found that human behavior was a function of the same processes of learning (via consequences) that seemed operative in virtually every other animal species. The view that behavioral methods are merely theoretical extrapolations of animal-based research that had been conducted in laboratory contexts has not been valid for over three decades.

The earliest publications in behavioral social work appeared in the mid-1960s (Staats & Butterfield, 1965; Thomas & Goodman, 1965), and since then the field has experienced a degree of exponential growth that shows every sign of continuing. A partial bibliography of behavioral social work that was published some time ago (Thyer, 1981) cited over 350 articles, chapters, and books on the subject. A more recent review found over 50 textbooks devoted to a behavioral perspective in social work practice (Thyer, 1985). A cumulative graph depicting the years of publication of these books is presented in Figure 2; it clearly documents the rapid growth of the field.

No other contemporary model of clinical social work has generated this much productive scholarship. Moreover, the comprehensiveness of the substantive areas that have been addressed attests to the potential of a behavioral perspective as a step towards a unified theory of social work practice. Its principles are relevant for work with individuals, couples, families, small groups, organizations, and communities (see Rothman & Thyer, 1984; Thyer, 1987a; and Thyer, Himle, & Santa, 1986, for elaborations on this point).

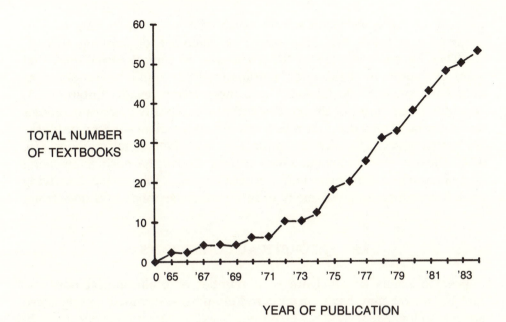

**Figure 2.** Cumulative graph of the years of publication of behavioral social work textbooks. A list of the titles is available from the author.

Two major figures who were instrumental in the shaping of behavioral social work as a practice perspective were Edwin Thomas and Richard Stuart. In early 1965, Thomas conducted a series of institutes aimed at educating field faculty and others in the elementary principles of behavior that had application in furthering the goals of social work practice. These lectures were subsequently published (Thomas & Goodman, 1965) and were soon followed by a second book edited by Thomas (1967) and sponsored by the Council on Social Work Education. Thomas and Stuart educated an influential cadre of doctoral students who became leading figures in the behavioral approach, including Rose, Gambrill, Levy, Sundel, Jayaratne, Butterfield, and Shorkey. Stuart's contributions have been in the areas of marital therapy (Stuart, 1980) and weight reduction (Stuart, 1978). Stuart is one of the country's foremost clinical researchers in these fields, and largely developed the eminently successful weight-loss-management program of Weight Watchers International, probably one of the greatest success stories in the history of disseminating behavioral methods to the public.

Behavioral approaches have had a major influence on clinical social work education and practice (Thyer & Bronson, 1981), as noted in recent reviews of outcomes in social work practice (Reid & Hanrahan, 1982; Rubin, 1985). Reid and Hanrahan (1982) conclude that "social workers are generating an empirical basis that supports claims to effectiveness for a broad range of methods" (p. 338). They also state that "the influence of the behavior modification movement is apparent and pervasive. The majority of the experiments involve evaluation of skills training or contingency contracting with the frame of reference of learning theory" (p. 329). By my count, 18 of the 29 studies of clinical social work that were evaluated by Reid and Hanrahan (1982) could be classified as behavioral social work. Likewise, in a more recent review, Rubin (1985) concluded that "most of the studies with unequivocally positive outcomes tested forms of practice that relied heavily on problem-solving and task-centered methods, usually in conjunction with behavioral methods" (p. 474). Clearly, the behavioral social worker enjoys the position of being part of a practice movement with a robust empirical foundation, a thriving clinical literature, and a diversity of intervention methods to choose from.

## KEY THEORETICAL CONSTRUCTS

Behaviorism is an amalgam of a number of philosophical positions that the reader may have encountered elsewhere. Included among these are the following:

### Determinism

Behaviorism contends most emphatically that all human behavior has potentially identifiable causes located within the past and present environment of the individual. In a sense, even one's genetic make-up is a product of the past environments experienced by our species and evolved through natural selection (Skinner, 1981). A person's current behavioral repertoire may also be said to be a product of an environmentally based natural selection that occurs within one's lifetime. Other approaches to clinical social work share this view of determinism to some degree. For example, psychoanalytic theory postulates a determinism of intrapsychic processes. Client-centered therapy hypothesizes a determinism that states that each of us is born with a *tendency* to grow in the direction of self-actualization. Determinism should not be confused with fatalism, the doctrine that contends that our fate cannot be avoided, no matter what we do (Grunbaum, 1953). As the behaviorist views it, determinism is an optimistic doctrine, always holding the potential for purposeful and positive change by human beings.

### Empiricism

This view suggests that clinical social workers should rely primarily upon objective data in decision making, preferably data obtained through experimental research. In practice, this means that the clinician turns first to empirically oriented treatment literature in order to find ways to accurately assess clients and effectively intervene with them. Another aspect of empiricism is the evaluation of one's own practice, often using single-system research designs (Thyer, 1986a).

## Operationism

This perspective suggests that the social worker should attempt not only to describe client problems in terms of observable behaviors, but also to develop treatment plans that can be conducted in a proceduralized manner. In practice, this means that social workers describe their assessment and treatment operations in such detail that the essential aspects of their practice activities could be replicated by their colleagues. In many respects, this principle is congruent with one suggested by Mary Richmond (1917/1935), the founder of social casework, who stated: "To say that we think our client is mentally deranged is futile; to state the observations that have created this impression is a possible help" (p. 335). Without operationism, social work will never be able to develop a scientific foundation for practice.

## Parsimony

The position of parsimony suggests that the clinical social worker should consider the simpler of the available and adequate explanations of a client's problem before seriously investigating etiological hypotheses of a more complex nature. For example, a clinical social worker who is asked to treat a mentally retarded person who repeatedly bangs her head should first rule out the possibility that the client is suffering from an infestation of ear mites, otitis media, or some other physical cause. Once this has been done, the clinician should examine other operant factors, such as the possibility that the head-banging is a means of obtaining attention or removing staff pressures to perform, or whether it is a by-product of boredom and fatigue. Only when these simpler explanations have been considered and discarded should the clinician seriously entertain more complex etiologies (e.g., intrapsychic conflict). In practice, a careful inventory of the potential biological, operant, and respondent etiologies almost always reveals the responsible maintaining factors. Epstein (1984) provides an excellent review of this principle of parsimony in psychological and clinical theorizing.

## Avoidance of Reification

Reification involves referring to, or employing, hypothetical entities as if they represent "real" things, in the absence of good evidence that the construct exists. It is all too easy to use terms such as id, motivation, the "family," oedipal conflict, and the like, and lose sight of the fact that these are only hypothetical constructs. One can avoid falling into the trap of reification by developing operational descriptions of client problems or characteristics, as described above. The problem with reification is that it often leads one to use the term in a causal or explanatory manner.

## Avoidance of Circular Reasoning

A circular explanation of client behavior is one wherein cause and effect are indistinguishable from one another. This most often occurs when the only evidence for the existence of a construct that has been used to explain a behavior is the very behavior one uses to infer the existence of the construct. For example:

*Statement*—"Mrs. Shore hates herself."
*Question*—"How do you know that?"
*Answer*—"Because she overeats to the point of gross obesity."
*Question*—"Why do you think she overeats?"
*Answer*—"Because she hates herself."

This type of reasoning and explanation is all too prevalent in clinical social work (and psychology, psychiatry, etc.) and is a form of pseudoexplanation. A noncircular explanation for Mrs. Shore's overeating *could* be that, as a child, she was strongly reinforced by grown-ups for eating "everything," a behavior that is now maladaptive.

These characteristic features of behaviorism—determinism, empiricism, operationism, parsimony, and the avoidance of reification and circular reasoning—coalesce into an optimistic framework for the behavioral social worker. The manifold social and personal problems that our profession attempts to alleviate are seen as potentially understandable phenomena, amenable to scientific scrutiny, analysis, and intervention. The focus is upon the detection of pragmatically manipulable causes, not specious relationships of little value to the practitioner.

The philosophy of behaviorism leads in a logical manner to its research counterpart, the experimental analysis of behavior. The application of behavior methods in real-life contexts has been found to yield effective and ethically sound solutions to a wide array of problems that have long been within the purview of the social work profession. Published examples of such well-controlled outcome studies include those that recount enabling the chronically unemployed to obtain and retain jobs (Azrin, Flores, & Kaplan, 1975; Jones & Azrin, 1973; Pierce & Risley, 1974); empowerment of the disenfranchised (Briscoe, Hoffman, & Bailey, 1975); and the reduction of crime (McNees, Egli, Marshall, Schnelle, & Risley, 1976), racism (Hauserman, Walen, & Behling, 1973), accidental trauma (Sowers-Hoag, Thyer, & Bailey, 1987), and contagious disease (Fawcett, 1977).

Despite the diversity of the problem areas that are currently being effectively addressed by behavioral methods, the general approach is predicated upon only four basic propositions:*

*1. Individuals, families, groups, communities, and entire societies engage in behavior*

In a strict sense, it is only the behavior of our clients that permits us to infer that clinical social work intervention is necessary. It is on the basis of what clients do, fail to do, or say, that problems arise. A given verbal or social interaction is seen as the sum of the behaviors of the individuals involved (Skinner, 1957), with the whole viewed as the sum of its parts—and no more. This seemingly heretical view applies equally to dyadic, family, group, or larger system phenomena. This perspective helps the practitioner avoid such errors as reification and circular reasoning (see p. 130) and keeps him or her focused on the practical concerns of helping people change.

By focusing upon a given client's behavior or upon the interactions of verbal and social behavior occurring among two or more individuals, the social worker becomes attuned to isolating the present contingencies of reinforcement and punishment that are assumed to be responsible for perpetuating problem behavior. We have excellent ideas about how to help people change their behavior, but we have no idea about how to directly alter internal, mental, cognitive, dispositional, or characterological constructs—characteristics that all are erroneously assumed to cause client problems. For instance, we cannot even agree about the *existence* of the superego, much less attempt to strengthen it or reduce its power. We can, however, help clients change the behaviors by which we infer the existence of the superego, defense mechanisms, family pathological processes, and the like.

As Hudson and Harrison (1986) note, "there are no techniques of intervention which will *directly* change any family attribute . . . all effective intervention techniques used by family therapists are aimed

---

* I have described these propositions in greater detail elsewhere (Thyer, 1987a).

fundamentally at changing the behavior of an individual who is a member of the group" (p. 89). By considering the purpose of social work treatment to be *behavior change*, one avoids the pitfalls of attributing reality status to fictitious "inner causes" or ascribing causal properties to such explanatory fictions.

## 2. All behavior is followed by consequences

Again, the emphasis is on the person's *past* history of reinforcement and punishment when facing similar situations. Note that the causative elements are *not* concepts such as purpose, intentions, cognitions, or willpower. Behaviorists recognize that these private events certainly *do* exist, but contend that such constructs do not add to our understanding of behavior (and therefore to our ability to predict and control it), since in themselves they arise from one's learning history. Likewise, it is incorrect to state that an individual behaves in a certain way now *in order* to obtain some reinforcer (or avoid some aversive stimulus) in the future. This latter pseudoexplanation attributes causative status to a *future* event, something that has never existed. Radical behaviorists consider such a view (i.e., about purposes and intentions, etc.) teleological and do not accept it as a viable cause of human behavior.

## 3. The consequences of a given behavior, to a very large extent, influence the future occurrence of that behavior

This viewpoint has been enumerated above.

## 4. The empirical analysis of the contingencies of which behavior is a function provides an effective intervention tool across all practice strata

Assessment and intervention are intimately interwoven in an applied behavioral analysis of a client problem. Information elicited by interviews is used to develop etiological hypotheses about the original and maintaining operant contingencies that may have given rise to the client's situation. The validity of these hypotheses is subsequently tested by the systematic alteration of the environmental contingencies experienced by the client, and the effects on behavior (and feelings) are carefully observed. I believe that the accuracy of the clinical social worker's etiological hypotheses is determined by whether or not the clinician successfully aids in the alleviation of client problems.

The focus, as mentioned earlier, may be upon environmental modification, upon client skill training designed to promote more effective environmental transactions, or upon both. For some problems of an affective or appetitive nature (anxiety, dysfunctional sexual arousal capacities, etc.), social work intervention based upon respondent methods may be appropriate (see Fischer & Gochros, 1977; Jackson & Smith, 1978; Thyer, 1983a).

The degree of sophistication of this behavioral approach to social work cannot be conveyed in this chapter, nor can important topics such as extinction, shaping, rule-governed behavior, schedules of reinforcement, or verbal behavior be addressed.*

## ASSESSMENT

A behavioral approach to clinical social work is by no means a mechanistic approach to assessment and practice. It requires as much clinical acumen and insight as other schools of practice, but it is distinguished by its characteristic reliance upon objective data—not solely upon logic or theory—to develop and test etiological hypotheses. I would like to illustrate this by examining what a behavioral social worker might offer the members of the Shore family.

The Shores certainly experience more than their share of life's problems, but then, such complex cases are commonly seen by clinical social workers. As with all efforts at effective therapeutic change, the focus of attention will be upon the strengths and weaknesses presented by *individuals*. Remember that behaviorists consider that the "family" per se is a metaphor; only the combined behaviors of Nancy, Charley, Michael, and Rena truly have an existence (Hudson & Harrison, 1986).

### Mrs. Shore

The case material on Mrs. Shore brings to our attention a number of serious problems of concern to the client. These include (in no particular order of priority) obesity, daily anxiety attacks, fears of leaving the home, chain-smoking, periodic back-pain flare-ups, worries over new tenants and family, depression, insomnia, lack of concentration, and bitter resentment over her father's treatment of her. Of course, prioritization of these problems would be a matter for the clinician to work out with Mrs. Shore. Since I have no way of knowing which of these difficulties the client wants help in overcoming, I will assume that she is concerned with all of them.

It is likely that Mrs. Shore meets the DSM-III-R criteria for Panic Disorder with Agoraphobia (American Psychiatric Association, 1987, pp. 238–239). We read that "her anxiety often turns into panic. She

---

* The reader is urged to consult primary references in the field for an amplification of these concepts (e.g., Skinner, 1953, 1957, 1969, 1971; Fischer & Gochros, 1975).

becomes nearly immobilized" and is "unable to leave the house . . . she imagines the worst of all possible outcomes. Anxiety attacks occur daily. . . . Most of the time, she stays inside . . . only at home does she feel safe."

This is a classic description of agoraphobia, a disorder (behaviorists might call it a metaphor) that is almost inevitably preceded by the onset of repeated episodes of apparently spontaneous panic attacks (Thyer & Himle, 1985). The usual sequence of events is that a person initially comes to fear and avoid the situations and circumstances associated with past panic attacks. Later, because of the seemingly random nature of the attacks, the person develops fears about entering situations from which escape might be difficult, or in which help might be unavailable, if such an attack should occur. Severe, chronic anticipatory anxiety is often the psychological sequela to spontaneous panic attacks; the individual comes to dread the onset of the next unpredictable episode (Thyer, 1986b, 1987b).

Assessment efforts with Mrs. Shore would probably begin with careful interviews designed to uncover the natural history of her panics and fears, including age of onset, apparent precipitants, waxing and waning of symptomatology, and possible substance abuse. One would also want to know if any members of her biological family have similar problems. Most cases of agoraphobia or panic disorder begin when clients are in their mid-twenties (Thyer, Parrish, Curtis, Cameron, & Nesse, 1985). A sizable percentage of these clients also abuse drugs or alcohol (Thyer, Himle, Curtis, Cameron, & Nesse, 1985; Thyer, Parrish, Himle, et al., 1986), and the condition seems to run in families (Ballenger, 1984).

Although the case material implies that Mrs. Shore's panic attacks are the result of periodic life and familial crises, such an interpretation is not supported by what is known about the etiology of anxiety attacks and agoraphobia (Curtis, Thyer, & Rainey, 1985; Thyer, 1986b, 1987b). Furthermore, although such an interpretation may be intuitively appealing, it is logically a specious line of reasoning. Most people in crisis feel anxious and agitated, but anxiety attacks themselves are a far more terrifying phenomenon. Such an interpretation fails to explain why such crises *specifically* result in panic, instead of in generalized anxiety, depression, hives, or an ulcer. The other members of the Shore family also have their share of living in a troubled psychosocial environment, but none of them appears to suffer from such panic attacks.

There are a number of specific assessment strategies available to help the clinical social worker develop an operational description of Mrs. Shore's difficulties. My book, *Treating Anxiety Disorders: A Guide for Human Service Professionals* (Thyer, 1987b), provides a checklist designed to help the social worker assess "anxiety attacks" and to clearly determine if a given client's experiences match those described by the DSM-III-R as a panic attack. The book also describes the use of client logs and diaries, which Mrs. Shore could use to record the frequency, duration, severity, and circumstances of her anxiety attacks. It would be important to have her distinguish between "spontaneous" panic attacks (those that catch her by surprise), provoked anxiety episodes (induced by actual or anticipated disturbing experiences), and generalized anxiety (a chronic state of agitated apprehension).

A number of rapid assessment instruments (Hudson & Thyer, 1986) are available for use with the anxious client. One that provides a measure of phobic avoidance *behavior* is the Mobility Inventory for Agoraphobia, developed by Chambless, Caputo, Jasin, Gracely, and Williams (1985). Measures that provide a quantified measure of anxious *affect* include the State-Trait Anxiety Inventory (Spielberger, Gorsuch, & Lushene, 1970), the Clinical Anxiety Scale (Thyer, 1987b), or the Zung Anxiety Scale (Zung, 1971). Mrs. Shore could be encouraged to systematically keep track of the amount of time she is out of the home, along with estimates of how fearful she was during each excursion.

These clinical assessment activities would aid in gathering the baseline information that is crucial for treatment and for outcome evaluation. In this case, the assessment period would be flexible, although it would probably take at least two weeks.

This focus on daily activities is also useful for assessing obesity problems like Mrs. Shore's. Stuart's (1967) program, for example, recommends that clients weigh themselves four times a day—after each meal and at bedtime. Mrs. Shore could be asked to begin weighing herself on a daily basis and to bring her weight record with her to each session.

To aid in the assessment of obesity problems, clients are often asked to complete food data sheets, on which they record the nature, quantity, and mode of preparation of the food they consume. They are also asked to record the circumstances under which eating is most likely to occur, and those under which it is less probable. Examples of the former situations might be "while watching TV" or "after a fight." Situations in which Mrs. Shore eats less might include "while reading nursing journals" or "when the refrigerator only has vegetables in it."

Mrs. Shore's other difficulties should also be assessed. Methods might include an evaluation of her assertiveness and communication skills (Arnow, Taylor, Agras, & Telch, 1985; Haimo & Blitman, 1985), which could bear on both her apparent agoraphobia and her fears of dealing with the new tenants. Treatment efforts aimed at alleviating her back problems, smoking, poor sleeping, or depression should wait until we have time to determine if the work that was targeted towards agoraphobia, panic attacks, and weight loss generalized to those areas. An effective weight reduction program might reduce her self-consciousness and perhaps improve her back problem (which her obesity probably exacerbates).

If her anxiousness were resolved, Mrs. Shore might also cut down on her smoking; it is known that clinically anxious individuals are more likely to smoke than are nonanxious ones (Hughes, Hatsukami, Mitchell, & Dalgren, 1986). Likewise, many of her other affective and psychological complaints (e.g., poor sleeping, difficulty concentrating, depression) may be improved following effective treatment for anxiety, since these conditions are often associated with the anxiety disorders, especially Agoraphobia and Panic Disorder (Cameron, Thyer, Nesse, & Curtis, 1986).

## Mr. Shore

The case material presents a somewhat more limited set of problems experienced by Mr. Shore. Among these are his apparent inability to keep a job, angry outbursts, compulsive lying, bickering with his son, and consideration of suicide when others suggest that he seek disability payments.

Although diagnosis on the basis of pharmacological response is always a risky proposition, the fact that Mr. Shore is "maintained" on lithium carbonate (along with what we know about him from his case material) makes it almost certain that he meets the DSM-III-R criteria for Bipolar Disorder.

Regrettably, very little empirical research has focused upon the objective assessment of manic phenomena. Assuming that Mr. Shore's manic-like behaviors were of concern to him (or at least that he could be persuaded by his family to seek treatment for them), a clinician might have to rely upon developing some form of idiosyncratic (to Mr. Shore) global rating scale, on which *Mrs.* Shore could periodically rate his degree of manic-like behaviors, speech, and the like. Bloom and Fischer (1982) and Hudson and Thyer (1986) discuss the construction of such global rating scales for assessment and practice-evaluation purposes.

Other measures of affect, such as rapid assessment instruments for depression, may be of use; examples are described by Bloom and Fischer (1982) and Levitt and Reid (1981). Such scales can assist clinicians in monitoring their clients' moods. For example, if Mr. Shore were to complete the Beck Depression Inventory twice a week throughout assessment and treatment, the resulting record of his mood swings and suicidal risk would be a valuable adjunct to clinical judgment.

Whenever clients are being maintained on medications, it is important to know if they are properly following the prescribed regimens. If they are not, any intervention efforts (behavioral or nonbehavioral) are likely to fail. Thus, determining medication compliance is a logical first step in assessment efforts. For example, with Mr. Shore, the clinician could implement a systemic monitoring program; this would only be done with his permission, and could involve him, or his wife, or both of them. Periodic assessment of lithium blood levels would be the ultimate criterion in determining whether or not his medication was being properly prescribed and taken. If Mr. Shore were not taking his lithium in an optimal manner, the clinician could suggest devising a treatment program that would ensure his compliance.

Again, a variety of diaries or logs could be used to keep a record of Mr. Shore's fights with his son, his angry urges or outbursts, and his compulsive lying. Indeed, the latter problem might be more accessible if Mr. Shore were to keep a *confidential* count of his lying episodes, which would be shared and discussed only with his therapist and not—at least initially—with other family members. Such diaries could review antecedents and consequences surrounding problematic behaviors and provide clues for the development of management strategies.

Mr. Shore's current job-finding skills could be assessed by determining how he would dress for and behave during an interview, prepare a resume, develop references, and so on. (In keeping with good behavioral practice, and also as a guard against Mr. Shore's exaggerating his abilities, the clinician should rely upon actual role-playing or on observations of Mr. Shore, not solely upon his verbal reports of his skills.) Deficiencies in any of these areas would lead quite naturally into the development of preliminary interventions.

## Michael

A number of the problems that Michael (age 12) displays are undoubtedly overlaid upon "normal" adolescent developmental phenomena (e.g., feeling unhappy or lonely, acting silly, and having poor self-control and social skills). Assessment efforts should be aimed at determining to what extent, if any, he significantly differs from his peers in these regards, before assuming that the above problems automatically require professional intervention in order to be resolved.

A number of his behaviors, such as emitting strange noises, making odd motions, touching others, and laughing inappropriately, are consistent with the DSM-III-R criteria for Tourette's Disorder. If this diagnosis were confirmed, there are some medications (e.g., haloperidol) that are useful in the treatment of Tourette-like behaviors. Various behavioral strategies (such as self-monitoring and systematic desensitization) developed by clinical social workers (Thomas, Abrams, & Johnson, 1971) may also be of value in this regard. In addition, the parents (and perhaps Michael) could be referred to various self-help and support groups devoted to Tourette's Disorder. Michael's case illustrates the importance of clinical social workers' possessing excellent diagnostic skills and a thorough familiarity with the DSM-III-R.

It is not clear when Michael last experienced a grand mal seizure, or if he is currently experiencing seizures. If they are continuing, the clinician should undertake an assessment to accurately determine Michael's medication compliance. As with Mr. Shore, the goal would be to improve less-than-optimal regimen compliance. If seizures are in abeyance and have not occurred for quite some time, the therapist could work with Michael's neurologist to see if a gradual fading program of anticonvulsant medication may be undertaken. The clinical social worker can be very helpful by providing the physician with details of the client's behavior and physical complaints. Concurrent with this, the clinician could implement a careful monitoring program aimed at detecting the emergence of epileptiform phenomena, and at diminishing the possible side effects of medication (e.g., the so-called hyperactivity mentioned in the case description). Any number of self-monitoring strategies (diaries, logs, critical incident recording forms) may be explained and used with Michael for this latter purpose. Structured observations obtained from his teachers and family would also be helpful. Again, Bloom and Fischer (1982) describe how this may be accomplished.

Because asthma has certain psychological aspects, a systematic monitoring program centered around Michael's asthma attacks is indicated. Michael and his family would be asked to retrospectively record the frequency, duration, intensity, and objective circumstances surrounding each asthma attack, in an attempt to reliably ascertain if the number of these attacks is increasing, decreasing, or remaining stable. Such information about the environmental antecedents and consequences of each attack may lead to the discovery of possible psychological precipitants. For example, it might be found that Michael's asthma attacks tend to occur when his parents are arguing. If so, the asthma-attack behavior may be reinforced by the immediate reduction in familial conflict, as everyone rushes around to assist Michael, fetch the nebulizer, get the car, and so forth. If this were the case, various behavioral strategies would be indicated, such as communication-skills training for Mr. and Mrs. Shore, with the goal of reducing Michael's asthma attacks as his parents come to bicker less frequently.

Assessment may also determine if Michael is adequately complying with any prescribed medical regimens designed to reduce the frequency of asthma attacks—for example, breathing exercises or avoidance of certain foods. Again, if his compliance is inadequate, behavioral strategies might improve his cooperation. Butterfield and Werkings (1981) and Shelton and Levy (1981) describe the conduct of such assessment and behavioral intervention methods from an empirically oriented clinical social work perspective.

## Rena

Many of Rena's problems are described in dispositional or trait language. We are told that she is "lazy," is lonely and confused, and fails at everything. She is also bankrupt, is preoccupied with her adoptive status, and is reportedly frequently rejected by others. The behavioral social worker shudders upon hearing client problems described in such dispositional terms. As a determinist, a behaviorist would hypothesize that Rena's so-called lazy behavior has had a history of being reinforced (perhaps by being "bailed out" by her parents?) or that productive behavior has had a history of being punished or subjected to extinction.

The case material does not provide enough information to support either contention. If blame were to be ascribed, one would certainly not want to add to Rena's burdens by labeling her lazy. Her past and present psychosocial environment is a far more culpable candidate. Furthermore, "laziness" may degenerate into a reification—"That Rena, she is just plain lazy"—as if laziness meant anything other than Rena's behaviors (or lack of behaviors). Once reified, laziness may be given causal status— "Rena didn't finish college because she is lazy"—a clear example of that explanatory fraud, circular reasoning.

It is not clear from the case material how Rena is supporting herself. She is living independently but does not have a job. She appears to lack many of the functional skills necessary for independent living, such as budgeting funds, obtaining and retaining employment, or maintaining a productive social life. It is easy to see how, in the absence of the skills that are necessary for the development of a reinforcing environment for oneself, a person could be lonely and confused, and perhaps preoccupied with the fantasy of being rescued from one's plight by, say, one's lost biological mother.

Initial assessment efforts should be aimed at exploring with Rena her interest in obtaining employment. An individual's vocational activities are important, not only for providing income, but also for consolidating one's identity and self-esteem and for giving structure to one's life. A clinician should have few qualms about suggesting to Rena the value of finding and maintaining a regular, productive, full-time job.

Schinke and Gilchrist (1984) are two social work practitioners who have developed and extensively tested a comprehensive behavioral program aimed at enhancing the life skills of adolescents. Their book includes chapters on enhancing interpersonal relationships, managing stress, anticipating employment, and building social responsibility—all of which seem relevant to working with Rena. A clinician might review the assessment strategies these authors provide, as well as those described and experimentally tested by Azrin et al. (1975), which are designed to promote employability. One suggestion might be that Rena explore enlistment in the military, which certainly provides an opportunity for the vocational training, structured life style, and independent living that she has thus far not experienced.

Rena's constant rejection by others suggests some social skills deficits. Perhaps, for example, she expresses her wishes in the form of aggressive demands instead of by assertive requests. The assessment of Rena's social skills may be conducted via direct observations of family interactions and by any number of validated pencil-and-paper rapid assessment instruments developed by social workers, such as assertion inventories (Gambrill & Richey, 1975; Gripton & Valentich, 1977) or Hudson's (1982) Index of Peer Relations. As we have seen before, such measures could be repeatedly administered before, during, and after treatment, to provide a means of evaluating client change. If social skills were determined to be a problem, the behavioral social work literature describes a number of interventions designed to help clients elicit a more reinforcing psychosocial environment (Rose & Schinke, 1978; Schinke, 1981).

The preceding discussion on clinical assessment strategies with the Shore family inevitably reflects my preferences. I have focused on the individuals in the family, not upon the communication patterns of any two or more members together. One reason for this is that I think that the atmosphere of chronic crisis in this family is largely due to the aggregated problems that each of the members experiences. If some of these difficulties could be effectively addressed, the verbal and nonverbal behaviors within the family would become more reinforcing and less aversive.

A second reason for my focus on the individual is that assessment methodology in clinical social work (both behavioral and nonbehavioral) is much less developed for the measurement of couples, groups, or families (Rose, 1981). Thus there is simply less empirical literature to draw on. Accordingly, in some cases the available assessment procedures dictate my areas of emphasis. For example, the measurement of depressive affect and behavior is well developed, while that for mania is virtually nonexistent, hence my descriptions of possible evaluation methods for Mr. Shore. This situation is, of course, a drawback in any empirically oriented approach to social work intervention, but it should improve as further additions are made to the practice research literature.

Traditionally trained clinical social workers may look somewhat askance at my emphasis on the concept of "countability" (i.e., developing operational descriptions of client problems). I would never contend that a client's skills on a role-playing test or scores on an assertiveness inventory convey all that we need to know about that client's social skills. But I do believe that, say, improvements on a client's scores on the validated Gambrill and Richey (1975) assertiveness inventory, coupled with clinical judgment, is a sounder basis for inferring important client change than is judgment alone. Actually, this notion of countability is quite consistent with the views of the founder of social casework, Mary Richmond, who suggested that "special efforts should be made to ascertain whether abnormal manifestations are *increasing* or *decreasing* in number and intensity, as this often has a practical bearing on the management of the case" (Richmond, 1917/1935, p. 435).

## TREATMENT OF CHOICE

As is evident from the preceding sections of this chapter, I believe that a well-trained behavioral social worker would have something to offer each of the Shores, individually. Because of space limitations, I have not addressed approaches that might be of value to the Shores *as a family;* these include marital treatment (Stuart, 1980; Thomas, 1977), family therapy (Jayaratne, 1978), group work (Rose, 1977), and parent training (Dangel & Polster, 1984). Each of these forms of intervention has been successfully employed by clinical social workers who have a behavioral focus, and a large number of well-controlled outcome studies document their effectiveness for certain problems. However, few comparative studies have looked at the relative effectiveness of, say, group versus individual treatment conducted by behavioral social workers; thus, no empirical guidelines are available at present to help in the selection of a specific treatment modality.

The behavioral social worker contends that virtually all human problems are amenable to behavioral analysis and intervention. This is because such social workers believe that their etiological formulations and treatment techniques are derived from fundamental principles that account for all human behavior. This viewpoint is demonstrated by the broad variety of human problems and clientele that behavioral practitioners have addressed, including the developmentally disabled, the psychotic, and the severely depressed, as well as those afflicted with the so-called neurotic conditions.

## THE THERAPEUTIC PROCESS

It is difficult to describe the conduct of behavioral social work in a general way, since by definition the treatment program is tailored in a meaningful manner to the unique characteristics of the clients and their problems. Certainly the behavioral social worker makes effective use of good clinical skills and relationship-building techniques, because these facilitate the conduct of treatment, client participation, and adherence to agreed-upon treatment plans. This is done, however, with a clear recognition that a good therapeutic relationship is a *necessary* but *insufficient* condition for effective behavioral change.

As in other types of social work, the first few sessions are likely to be devoted to information-gathering and evaluation—really finding out "where the client is at." This is done by developing, with client input, operational definitions of client problems, and by systematically and repeatedly measuring various aspects of these problems. Ideally, but not necessarily, such monitoring of client problems will be undertaken prior to the implementation of a formal program of treatment. Here, the empirical preferences of behavioral social workers come into play, as the practitioner draws upon the scientific practice literature, where available, in the selection of evaluation methods and preliminary intervention options. These are presented to the client for feedback and further ideas, until a mutually agreed-upon program of assessment and treatment is arrived at.

Once treatment has begun, the client and social worker periodically and jointly review the program's apparent effects on the target behaviors. Treatment that has positive effects is continued or augmented; after a fair trial, apparently ineffective interventions are altered or discontinued. Such decisions are based upon the "objective" *data,* coupled with clinical judgment and feedback from the clients and their significant others. After a problem has been alleviated, a program designed to maintain therapeutic gains may be necessary. For this purpose, assistance from others in the clients' psychosocial environment may be useful; this, of course, is also true during treatment.

## LIMITATIONS OF THE MODEL

As I have stated elsewhere (Thyer, 1983b), I believe that behavioral social work is the most optimistic, theory-rich, and empirically supported of all contemporary schools of social work intervention, and that it has the potential to lead the profession to the development of a comprehensive practice paradigm. Behavioral social work is, in my opinion, the *one* practice theory with applicability across all levels of intervention, ranging from clinical social work with individuals to the development of social welfare policy (Thyer, 1987a). This richness is evident in the professional literature (Thyer, 1981, 1985) and in the accumulating evidence that documents the effectiveness of behavioral interventions in the alleviation of problems of social and personal importance. I will not address here the corresponding paucity of positive outcomes in controlled research that evaluates the practices of other schools of clinical social work.

The major problem with a behavioral approach to social work practice, I feel, is that most educators and practitioners have an inadequate understanding of the model. Leading clinical social workers mistakenly identify Skinner as an SR (stimulus-response, i.e., Pavlovian) behaviorist (Strean, 1981), and equate behavioral methods to aversive control or the surreptitious manipulation of clients. As I hope I have illustrated, such contentions are entirely unfounded. The behavioral social worker is in complete agreement with the practice objectives, ethical standards, and value base of the profession at large.

Like all approaches to clinical social work (though perhaps less so than most), the behavioral perspective lacks an adequate foundation in the practice literature about many crucial areas important to social work practice. Little behavioral (or nonbehavioral) outcome research is being conducted in such fields as crisis intervention, grief counseling, community or organizational practice, or social welfare policy. Of course, the argument that "It hasn't been done" is not the same as "It can't be done," and continued research by behavioral social workers should see additional expansions of the field.

It is common both in the clinical social work literature and less formally in conversations with practitioners and academics for the view to be expressed that behavioral social work is somehow incongruent with traditional social work values, is manipulative of clients, and is neglectful of the role of interpersonal processes in fostering client change (Bruck, 1968; Strean, 1973, 1981; Watson, 1974). These factors are often presented as severely limiting the value of behavioral methods within social work practice. Fortunately, there appears to be little validity to such contentions, although it is certainly appropriate that various approaches to social work practice be subjected to ethical scrutiny. Any *effective* method of practice may be abused, not simply the behavioral methods.

As with other clinical social work methods, a behavioral approach is largely value-neutral, in that the theory and technology do not mandate what should be done or what the goals of treatment should be. Rather, it is an approach that is of great utility in helping social work clients achieve their goals, once they have been established. The process of goal selection—determining what behaviors should be valued or disavowed—is left to the discretion of the social worker, who is guided by professional ethical standards, legal mandates, and common sense. Behavioral social workers recognize the value of interpersonal process in developing and maintaining an effective clinical relationship. In fact, experimental studies have shown that clients perceive behavior therapists to be just as warm, empathic, and genuine as nonbehavioral therapists—in many cases, even more so (Fischer, Paveza, Kickertz, Hubbard, & Grayston, 1975; Sloan, Staples, Cristol, Yorkston, & Whipple, 1975).

A number of other authors have presented articulate rebuttals to these purported limitations of behavioral methods (Shaw, 1972; Carter & Stuart, 1970; Davison & Stuart, 1975; Wodarski, 1981), and the interested reader is referred to these primary sources for a more detailed discussion of the issues.

## RESEARCH

A thorough grounding in the findings of empirical social-science and behavioral-science research is a major characteristic of clinical social work conducted from a behavioral perspective. The social worker consults the practice-research literature for guidance in developing measurement procedures to assess client/environmental problems and also for suggestions about interventions that have been found to be effective with other clients who have experienced similar problems. Fortunately, the behavioral literature does provide such guidance for a large number of the problems and conditions that are addressed by clinical social workers. For those situations that have not yet been addressed by research, the behavioral social worker looks to the learning theory foundations for guidance for developing treatment plans.

Behavioral social workers also employ research in the systematic evaluation of their work, which in many instances involves the use of single-system research designs (Bloom & Fischer, 1982; Hudson & Thyer, 1986; Thyer, 1986a). Often, the clinical social worker can provide clear and convincing evidence to the larger social worker community that his or her clients are indeed benefiting from social work intervention.

I believe that the practices described above help us to bridge the lamentable gap that has existed for so long between social worker practitioners and their use of social work research. Throughout this chapter, I have extensively cited such practice-related research, which, when overlaid upon a foundation of professional social work training and clinical wisdom, greatly enhances the ability of our profession to effectively serve our clients.

## SUMMARY

The behavioral model of clinical social work has existed for the past two decades and has generated a large volume of practice and research literature that has demonstrated its effectiveness across a wide array of social and interpersonal problems. Behavioral social work is derived from contemporary learning theory and incorporates elements of respondent (Pavlovian) conditioning and observational learning, but it primarily draws upon the principles of operant conditioning. Operant behavior is seen as those human actions which are shaped and maintained by their environmental consequences; the behavioral approach focuses on helping clients to develop psychosocial environments that promote adaptive behaviors and reduce dysfunctional ones. Direct training in prosocial skills and abilities such as assertiveness, job interviewing, social interactions, and parenting practices is also heavily relied upon.

Assessment and treatment in behavioral social work focus upon both the client's abilities and the role of the client's environment in maintaining problems. Intervention is often targeted to both of these areas, providing the model with a true person-in-situation perspective.

Through this approach, behavioral social work has become an accepted method of clinical practice which is richly rewarding to its practitioners. Few professional experiences can match seeing one's clients undergo meaningful and positive change in their lives. After all, isn't that what social work is all about?

## REFERENCES

American Psychiatric Association. (1987). *Diagnostic and statistical manual of mental disorders* (3rd ed., revised). Washington, DC: Author.

Arnow, B. A., Taylor, C. B., Agras, W. S., & Telch, M. J. (1985). Enhancing agoraphobia treatment outcome by changing couple communication patterns. *Behavior Therapy, 16,* 452–467.

Azrin, N., Flores, T., & Kaplan, S. J. (1975). Job-finding club: A group-assisted program for obtaining employment. *Behaviour Research and Therapy, 13,* 17–27.

Ballenger, J. C. (Ed.). (1984). *Biology of agoraphobia.* Washington, DC: American Psychiatric Press.

Bloom, M., & Fischer, J. (1982). *Evaluating practice.* Englewood Cliffs, NJ: Prentice-Hall.

Briscoe, R. V., Hoffman, D. B., & Bailey, J. S. (1975). Behavioral community psychology: Training a community board to problem solve. *Journal of Applied Behavior Analysis, 8,* 157–168.

Bruck, M. (1968). Behavior modification theory and practice: A reply. *Social Work, 13,* 43–55.

Butterfield, W. H., & Werkings, J. (1981). Behavioral methods in primary health care. In S. P. Schinke (Ed.), *Behavioral methods in social welfare* (pp. 287–302). New York: Aldine.

Cameron, O. G., Thyer, B. A., Nesse, R. M., & Curtis, G. C. (1986). Symptom profiles of patients with DSM-III anxiety disorders. *American Journal of Psychiatry, 143,* 1132–1137.

Carter, R. D., & Stuart, R. B. (1970). Behavior modification theory and practice: A reply. *Social Work, 15,* 37–50.

Chambless, D. L., Caputo, G. C., Jasin, S. E., Gracely, E. J., & Williams, C. (1985). The Mobility Inventory for Agoraphobia. *Behaviour Research and Therapy, 23,* 35–44.

Curtis, G. C., Thyer, B. A., & Rainey, J. M. (Eds.). (1985). *The psychiatric clinics of North America: Anxiety disorders.* Philadelphia, PA: Saunders.

Dangel, R. F., & Polster, R. A. (Eds.). (1984). *Parent training: Foundations of research and practice.* New York: Guilford.

Davison, G. C., & Stuart, R. B. (1975). Behavior therapy and civil liberties. *American Psychologist, 30,* 755–763.

Epstein, R. (1984). The principle of parsimony and some applications in psychology. *Journal of Mind and Behavior, 5,* 119–130.

Fawcett, S. B. (1977). Behavioral technology and smallpox eradication. *Journal of Applied Behavior Analysis, 10,* 558.

Fischer, J., & Gochros, H. (1975). *Planned behavior change.* New York: Free Press.

Fischer, J., & Gochros, H. (Eds.). (1977). *Handbook of behavior therapy with sexual problems* (Vols. I & II). New York: Pergamon Press.

Fischer, J., Paveza, G., Kickertz, N., Hubbard, L., & Grayston, S. (1975). The relationship between theoretical orientation and therapist's empathy, warmth, and genuineness. *Journal of Counseling Psychology, 22,* 399–403.

Gambrill, E., & Richey, C. (1975). An assertion inventory for use in assessment and research. *Behavior Therapy, 6,* 550–561.

Gripton, J., & Valentich, M. (1977). Development of a work assertiveness scale for social workers. *The Social Worker, 45,* 15–20.

Grunbaum, A. (1953). Causality and the science of human behavior. In H. Fiegl & M. Brodbeck (Eds.), *Readings in the philosophy of science* (pp. 766–777). New York: Appleton-Century-Crofts.

Haimo, S., & Blitman, F. (1985). The effects of assertive training on sex role concept in female agoraphobics. *Women & Therapy, 4,* 53–61.

Hauserman, N., Walen, S. R., & Behling, M. (1973). Reinforced racial integration in the first grade: A study in generalization. *Journal of Applied Behavior Analysis, 6,* 193–200.

Hudson, W. W. (1982). *The clinical measurement package.* Homewood, IL: Dorsey.

Hudson, W. W., & Harrison, D. F. (1986). Conceptual issues in measuring and assessing family problems. *Family Therapy, 13,* 85–94.

Hudson, W. W., & Thyer, B. A. (1986). Research measures and indices in direct practice. In A. Minahan (Ed.), *Encyclopedia of social work* (pp. 487–498). Washington, DC: NASW.

Hughes, J. R., Hatsukami, D. K., Mitchell, J. E., & Dalgren, L. A. (1986). Prevalence of smoking among psychiatric outpatients. *American Journal of Psychiatry, 143,* 993–997.

Jackson, T. R., & Smith, J. W. (1978). A comparison of two aversion treatment methods for alcoholism. *Journal of Studies on Alcohol, 39,* 187–191.

Jayaratne, S. (1978). Behavioral intervention and family decision-making. *Social Work, 23,* 20–25.

Jones, R. J., & Azrin, N. H. (1973). An experimental application of a social reinforcement approach to the problem of job finding. *Journal of Applied Behavior Analysis, 6,* 345–353.

Levitt, J. L., & Reid, W. J. (1981). Rapid-assessment instruments for practice. *Social Work Research and Abstracts, 17*(1), 13–19.

Marks, I. M. (1978). *Living with fear.* New York: McGraw-Hill.

McNees, M. P., Egli, D. S., Marshall, R. S., Schnelle, J. F., & Risley, T. R. (1976). Shoplifting prevention: Providing information through signs. *Journal of Applied Behavior Analysis, 9,* 399–405.

Nesse, R. M., Carli, T., Curtis, G. C., & Kleinman, P. D. (1980). Pre-treatment nausea in cancer chemotherapy: A conditioned response? *Psychosomatic Medicine, 47,* 320–332.

Pierce, C. H., & Risley, T. R. (1974). Improving job performance of neighborhood youth corps aides in an urban recreation center. *Journal of Applied Behavior Analysis, 7,* 207–215.

Reid, W. J., & Hanrahan, P. (1982). Recent evaluations of social work practice: Grounds for optimism. *Social Work, 27,* 328–340.

Richmond, M. (1935). *Social diagnosis.* New York: Sage. (Original work published 1917)

Rose, S. D. (1977). *Group therapy: A behavioral approach.* Englewood Cliffs, NJ: Prentice-Hall.

Rose, S. D. (1981). Assessment in groups. *Social Work Research and Abstracts, 17*(1), 29–37.

Rose, S. D., & Schinke, S. P. (1978). Assertive training. In H. Grayson & L. Loew (Eds.), *Changing approaches to psychotherapies.* New York: Spectrum.

Rothman, J., & Thyer, B. A. (1984). Behavioral social work in community and organizational settings. *Journal of Sociology and Social Welfare, 11,* 294–326.

Rubin, A. (1985). Practice effectiveness: More grounds for optimism. *Social Work, 30,* 469–476.

Schinke, S. P. (1981). Interpersonal skills training with adolescents. In M. Hersen, P. Miller, & R. Eisler (Eds.), *Progress in behavior modification* (Vol. 11). New York: Academic Press.

Schinke, S. P., & Gilchrist, L. D. (1984). *Life skills counseling for adolescents.* Baltimore, MD: University Park Press.

Shaw, M. (1972). Ethical implications of a behavioral approach. In D. Jehu, P. Hardiker, M. Yelloly, & M. Shaw (Eds.), *Behavior Modification in Social Work* (pp. 161–172). New York: Wiley.

Shelton, J. L., & Levy, R. L. (1981). *Behavioral assignments and treatment compliance.* Champaign, IL: Research Press.

Shorkey, C., & Taylor, J. (1973). Management of maladaptive behavior of a severely burned child. *Child Welfare, 52,* 543–547.

Skinner, B. F. (1953). *Science and human behavior.* New York: Free Press.

Skinner, B. F. (1957). *Verbal behavior.* Englewood Cliffs, NJ: Prentice-Hall.

Skinner, B. F. (1969). *Contingencies of reinforcement.* Englewood Cliffs, NJ: Prentice-Hall.

Skinner, B. F. (1971). *Beyond freedom and dignity.* New York: Bantam.

Skinner, B. F. (1974). *About behaviorism.* New York: Knopf.

Skinner, B. F. (1978). *Reflections on behaviorism and society.* Englewood Cliffs, NJ: Prentice-Hall.

Skinner, B. F. (1981). Selection by consequences. *Science, 213,* 501–504.

Sloan, V. L., Staples, F. R., Cristol, A. H., Yorkston, N. J., & Whipple, K. (1975). *Psychotherapy versus behavior therapy.* Cambridge, MA: Harvard University Press.

Sowers-Hoag, K. M., Thyer, B. A., & Bailey, J. S. (1987). Promoting safety belt use among young children. *Journal of Applied Behavior Analysis, 20,* 133–138.

Spielberger, C. D., Gorsuch, R. L., & Lushene, R. E. (1970). *Manual for the State-Trait Anxiety Inventory.* Palo Alto, CA: Consulting Psychologists Press.

Staats, A., & Butterfield, W. H. (1965). Treatment of nonreading in a culturally deprived juvenile delinquent: An application of reinforcement principles. *Child Development, 36,* 925–942.

Strean, H. S. (1973). Psychoanalytically-oriented casework versus behavior modification therapy. *Clinical Social Work Journal, 1,* 143–160.

Strean, H. (1981). A critique of some of the newer treatment modalities. *Clinical Social Work Journal, 9,* 143–160.

Stuart, R. B. (1967). Behavioral control of overeating. *Behaviour Research and Therapy, 5,* 357–365.

Stuart, R. B. (1978). *Act thin, stay thin.* New York: Norton.

Stuart, R. B. (1980). *Helping couples change: A social learning approach to marital therapy.* New York: Guilford.

Thomas, E. J. (Ed.). (1967). *The socio-behavioral approach and applications to social work.* New York: Council on Social Work Education.

Thomas, E. J. (1977). *Marital communication and marital decision-making.* New York: Free Press.

Thomas, E. J., Abrams, K., & Johnson, J. (1971). Self-monitoring and reciprocal inhibition in the modification of multiple tics of Gilles de la Tourette's. *Journal of Behavior Therapy and Experimental Psychiatry, 2,* 159–171.

Thomas, E. J., & Goodman, E. (1965). *Socio-behavioral theory and interpersonal helping in social work.* Ann Arbor, MI: Campus Publishers.

Thyer, B. A. (1981). Behavioral social work: A bibliography. *International Journal of Behavioral Social Work and Abstracts, 1,* 229–251.

Thyer, B. A. (1983a). Treating anxiety disorders with exposure therapy. *Social Casework, 64,* 77–82.

Thyer, B. A. (1983b). Behavior modification in social work practice. In M. Hersen, P. Miller, & R. Eisler (Eds.), *Progress in behavior modification* (Vol. 15, pp. 173–226). New York: Academic Press.

Thyer, B. A. (1985). Textbooks in behavioral social work: A bibliography. *The Behavior Therapist, 8,* 161–162.

Thyer, B. A. (1986a). Single-subject research designs in clinical social work: A practitioner's perspective. In J. Tropman, J. Rothman, & H. Johnson (Eds.), *Social work policy and practice* (pp. 292–310). Ann Arbor, MI: University of Michigan.

Thyer, B. A. (1986b). Agoraphobia: A superstitious conditioning perspective. *Psychological Reports, 58,* 95–100.

Thyer, B. A. (1987a). Contingency analysis: Toward a unified theory for social work practice. *Social Work, 32,* 150–157.

Thyer, B. A. (1987b). *Treating anxiety disorders: A guide for human service professionals.* Beverly Hills, CA: Sage.

Thyer, B. A., & Bronson, D. (1981). Behavioral training in social work education: An update and a program description. *Journal of Behavior Therapy and Experimental Psychiatry, 12,* 47–51.

Thyer, B. A., & Curtis, G. C. (1985). On the diphasic nature of vasovagal fainting associated with blood-injury-illness phobia. *Pavlovian Journal of Biological Science, 20,* 84–87.

Thyer, B. A., & Himle, J. (1985). Temporal relationship between panic attack onset and phobic avoidance in agoraphobia. *Behaviour Research and Therapy, 23,* 607–608.

Thyer, B. A., Himle, J., Curtis, G. C., Cameron, O. G., & Nesse, R. M. (1985). A comparison of panic disorder and agoraphobia with panic attacks. *Comprehensive Psychiatry, 26,* 208–214.

Thyer, B. A., Himle, J., & Santa, C. (1986). Applied behavior analysis in social and community action: A bibliography. *Behavior Analysis and Social Action, 5,* 14–16.

Thyer, B. A., Parrish, R. T., Curtis, G. C., Cameron, O. G., & Nesse, R. M. (1985). Ages of onset of DSM-III anxiety disorders. *Comprehensive Psychiatry, 26,* 113–122.

Thyer, B. A., Parrish, R. T., Himle, J., Cameron, O. G., Curtis, G. C., & Nesse, R. M. (1986). Alcohol abuse among clinically anxious patients. *Behaviour Research and Therapy, 24,* 357–359.

Watson, D. (1974). Ethical implications of behavioural approach in social work—A response. *International Social Work, 17,* 32–35.

Wodarski, J. S. (1975). The application of cognitive behavior modification techniques to social work practice. *International Social Work, 18(3),* 50–57.

Wodarski, J. S. (1981). Discussion. *Clinical Social Work Journal, 9,* 171–176.

Zung, W. W. (1971). A rating instrument for anxiety disorders. *Psychosomatics, 12,* 371–379.

# 7

# Social Group Work as a Clinical Paradigm

*Beulah Rothman, D.S.W., and*

*Catherine P. Papell, D.S.W.*

Historically, group work has not been aligned principally with the intrapsychic treatment themes in social work. The early social group workers, associated with the settlement movement and the youth-serving organizations, looked instead to the theories of Dewey (1934), Mead (1934), and Lewin (1951) for ideas that were compatible with their interpersonal perspectives about problems and with their commitment to social reform. The clinical aspects of social group work developed when it began to be practiced in treatment-oriented settings (Trecker, 1956) where it continued to be influenced by those early theorists.

This will be apparent as we set forth the method and consider how the Shore family—Nancy, Charley, Rena, and Michael—might have been helped in the past by social group work experiences. It will also be reflected in our assessments of the clinical needs of this family in the present and the contributions of the social group work paradigm to the treatment plan.

## THE CONCEPT OF THE PERSON AND THE HUMAN CONDITION

Group work shares with the profession of social work the view that the sources of behavior are not only within an individual but also in the individual's environment. Therefore, in clinically oriented group work, problematic behavior is both defined and treated in terms of an individual's interactions with other significant persons. Buber's "I-Thou" concept conveys the notion that only in partnership can any human being be perceived as an existing whole. In group work thinking, social interaction and social influence flow between the individual and the environment. Small groups are formed and sustained because of a hunger for unity and belonging. A desire to overcome the separateness that people feel between themselves and others is the essential and powerful motivating factor that moves people to search for the connectedness that is to be found in the small group.

The small group is a creative instrument for individual growth. Reciprocity in group life brings rewards, but it also requires relinquishing part of oneself to others. It generates responsibility and responsiveness to others. Feeling, thinking and behavior can be altered through its reciprocal interchange.

Within the group, individuals may become acutely aware of their aloneness. The existential appreciation of autonomy, as well as connectedness, occurs as a result of experience in a small group. In the context of reciprocity, individuals learn that they are valued for their uniqueness, and they similarly respond to others.

Action and interaction constitute the "language" of the group. Therefore, group workers espouse a nonpassive view of themselves as well as their clients. Action is necessary if growth is to occur (Middleman, 1968; Wilson & Ryland, 1948). Nonaction threatens the well-being of both the individual and the small group system. It can produce stagnation leading to dissolution of the group. Action is necessary for rational and creative problem-solving in the group. It can be either spontaneous or planned, both forms providing emotional satisfaction and change. Moreover, playful action and humor can enhance the quality of life and can produce gains in mental health. Clinical group work is as much concerned with fostering pleasurable activity as it is with ameliorating pain.

The power of the group to effect change lies in its capacity to harness motivation and social need and to take action beyond that which any individual can undertake alone. Within the small group lies the potential for mutual aid, which supports and furthers the ideal of a humanistic social order in which people help each other rather than compete with each other. In the group, the individual can become socialized to humanistic norms.

Each small group serves as a laboratory for the social processes that are found in all areas of human experience. When successful, the experience reveals the gratification to be gained from interactions with others. However, group experience also presents obstacles. The individuals and the group must overcome these in the course of their interactions with each other. The group thus exposes people not only to the problems of interaction but also to the necessity and the means for resolving them (Bernstein, 1965; Levine, 1979).

In addition to producing growth, the small group can be a source for corrective socialization or rehabilitation. Each new group experience can fill deficits or gaps that were left unattended in previous family or social group experiences. A skillful, knowledgeable group worker can contain destructive potential as well as modify earlier negative group experiences that people may have had.

In social group work, as in all of social work, there is the universal theme of process and change, of movement and development through time. In the same way that an understanding of individual development is needed, an understanding of group developmental stages is essential for the practice of group work (Garland, Jones, & Kolodny, 1965; Northen, 1969; Sarri & Galinsky, 1975). Group development is viewed epigenetically; that is, the successful resolution or incorporation of tasks in one phase will enable the group to move forward to a new set of demands and tasks (Levine, 1979).

## HISTORICAL PERSPECTIVE

The underlying assumptions of the social group work paradigm are rooted in its history. Group work, in common with all social work, had its beginnings in the effort to serve the human needs produced by the industrialization of the 19th century. Early group workers were receptive to influences from many directions. As settlement and youth workers, they were not restricted by a single functional connection with the people with whom they worked. They met their neighbors in their life space, in every aspect of their lives and around every kind of personal, community, and societal assault. They responded broadly and with a powerful commitment to the idea of developing citizenship and leadership among the newcomers to the cities and to the nation itself. A democratic ideology of an egalitarian and just society formed the basic premises out of which the methodology grew.

During the early 20th century, intellectual ideas from many disciplines created a ferment in the minds of settlement and community workers and contributed to their emerging ideas about individuals and their relationship to society. The social nature of human personality was an idea whose time had come. Early group workers turned to the social theorists and social philosophers for their insights and their intellectual guidance (Follett, 1918; Lindeman, 1924; Sheffield, 1928). For example, Follett (1924) presented the concept of circularity of human exchanges, in which each actor responded to a situation that he or she had helped create only a moment before.

The advent of new theories about the psyche (such as Freudian concepts about the internal world of the individual client) was relatively less important to the group work movement than it was to the casework movement. American intellectual life had already provided group work with relevant theoretical and philosophical perspectives.

It became clear that verbal communication was only one aspect of interaction between people. In the 1920s, Neva Boyd connected games and expressive play with the developmental and therapeutic needs of people in the playgrounds and mental hospitals (Boyd, 1919, 1938). Boyd was so opposed to reliance on verbal methods, which had been developing in social casework, that she refused to move with the other group workers into the social work profession, where new understanding of the unconscious processes of individuals was ascending and gaining priority.

In the 1930s, 1940s, and early 1950s, Coyle (1958), Kaiser (1958), Klein (1953), Phillips (1957), Trecker (1948), and Wilson and Ryland (1948) conceptualized and professionalized the theory of group work and published the early professional texts. These group work theoreticians were not only influenced by ideas rooted in sociology and social psychology but also incorporated psychodynamic theories.

Although it had traveled along a somewhat different conceptual pathway, group work began to take its place in developing a methodological group practice foundation for the profession. Group work concepts were clarified and extended in the 1960s by such authors as Hartford (1971), Konopka (1963), Northen (1969), Schwartz (1961), and Vinter (1967). Group workers were invited to take the method into settings in which previously only casework had been recognized.

Three primary models of social group work practice had emerged by the 1960s (Papell & Rothman, 1966). First was the social goals model, which focused group work practice on citizenship, social action, reform, and environmental change. Second was the remedial model, which focused on the treatment and rehabilitation of the individual in his or her environment. In this model, group practice was designed to take into account the assessed treatment needs of each member and the capacity of the group to be helpful (Glasser & Garvin, 1977; Vinter, 1967). Third was the reciprocal or interactionist model, which focused on the organismic nature of the group. It emphasized the growth potential, inherent in the group process, by which the members create their own group purposes and develop a cohesive, mutually supportive group system to meet a variety of needs. These may range widely and often simultaneously include social, educational, and clinical goals (Schwartz, 1977).

Arising out of the diversity of models that proliferated during the ensuing period (Roberts & Northen, 1976) was the call to identify the "mainstream" themes shared by all models of social work practice with groups (Lang, 1979; Tropp, 1978).

## KEY THEORETICAL CONSTRUCTS

### The Mainstream Model

The mainstream model (Papell & Rothman, 1980) is based on the interplay of five constructs: the group, the member in the group, the activities of the group, the social worker with the group, and the setting in which the group functions.

### *The mainstream group*

This is characterized by common goals, mutual aid, and nonsynthetic (natural and spontaneous as opposed to limited and prescribed) experiences. The common goal or purpose of the group is derived from the integration of the individual goals of the members with the professional goals of the worker. Sharing and yielding are experienced throughout the life of the group as decisions are made, problems are solved, and conflicts are resolved. Because a central concern is the theme of helping each other, the mainstream group may be viewed as a *mutual aid system.* Spontaneous and meaningfully evolving group processes are instruments through which group purposes are realized.

The social group work mainstream model differs from most group psychotherapies in that it emphasizes the continuation of the relationship of its members beyond the group's boundaries whenever that is helpful or satisfying. The concept of externality (the system of interacting forces that originate in, or extend into, the environment of the group) is predicated on the assumption of continuous and elaborating exchange between the external and internal realities of the group. Externality is demonstrated when the group members act collectively to influence, modify, or contribute to the environment or to assist individual members in using group-based norms with which to respond to environmental demands. The group supports the conception of itself as a frame of reference from which each member can extrapolate concepts and competencies that can be taken into his or her individual life.

Another distinctive aspect of the mainstream group is its focus upon the development of the "group-as-a-whole." This requires a high level of understanding about how groups grow and how the integration of the properties and energies in this change process relate to group purpose. A significant variable in subsequent group development is the initial composition of the group, no matter whether that composition is determined by circumstances, by the group itself, or by the professional efforts of the worker. The group creates structures, particularly those relating to increasing group autonomy, through the emergence of indigenous leadership roles. Ideally, when these roles are nurtured and expanded, both individual and group needs are fulfilled.

The factor that distinguishes the mainstream group from all others in the human services field is its flexibility of purpose and process and its availability for meeting multiple human needs.

## The member in the group

In the mainstream model, intense concern about the group is paralleled by equally intense concern about each individual member. The focus is on the individual *and* the group, rather than on one *or* the other. In the mainstream group work model there is a preference for the term *member*, rather than *client* or *patient*. Members are active rather than passive recipients of health and growth. Every member has the potential power to make a difference in the group. The exercise of this power can also generate change within the individual. In this model, therefore, individuals are viewed as social learners who expand their skills and social functioning through the group experience, regardless of the primary purpose of the group.

In the mainstream approach, concern is expressed about the individual's need to establish affiliative bonds with others and to develop the capacity for empathy and identification. This concern is the model's response to some of the problems in contemporary society (the loss of personal meaning, the malaise of alienation, and increasing anomie) that command the attention of the social work profession. In the mainstream group, members' affiliative needs are attended to, regardless of whether the group is essentially therapeutic, preventive, or developmental.

This approach also supports and encourages the members' individual differences, autonomy, and separateness. These are considered to be sources of strength in the individual as well as resources for the group. The mainstream group provides a testing ground in which the members can experience the realities and consequences of individual differences and can acquire skills in perceiving and withstanding negative as well as positive interpersonal influences.

Maintaining a balanced perspective between the needs of individual members and the needs of the group is a constant dynamic issue. Individual needs for inclusion, control, and affection (Schutz, 1958) are reflected in the group's developmental processes of affiliation, power and control, intimacy, and differentiation (Garland, Jones, & Kolodny, 1965). Negative group properties such as dysfunctional contagion, scapegoating, and exclusionary maneuvers may heighten the vulnerability of individuals in the group and may thus become a central concern with respect to the balance between individual needs and the needs of the group. In the mainstream approach, however, these and other severe hazards to individual members must be contained, resolved, or even removed, because the protection of individual members is essential in the achievement of collective goals.

## Activities in the mainstream group

Ideas about the value of nonverbal as well as verbal engagement, play as well as work, and humor as well as serious reflection are a part of the historical tradition of the mainstream model. This comprehensive and imaginative approach to group activity is one of the contributions that the mainstream approach offers to social work, as well as other helping professions.

Activity is generated out of the spontaneous interests and desires of group members and is then implemented in a purposeful, collaborative way. These two qualities—spontaneity of origin and planfulness in execution—reflect the major orientation towards group activities in the mainstream approach. Activities are developed as reality experiences in the here and now and not solely as rehearsal for future events. The new and expressive experience of the members takes place first *in vivo* and can be practiced again and again in the group as well as in future encounters outside of the group. The worker comes to the group prepared with ideas for activity, but is always ready to respond to the group's growing ability to take spontaneous and planful initiative.

## The worker with the mainstream group

The professional worker in the mainstream group has a repertoire of roles at his or her command. For example, the worker might intervene from the position of "enabler," "facilitator," or "teacher" depending upon an assessment of the needs of the group, the needs of individual members, and the situation in which the interaction is taking place.

Naturalness of group processes mandates that the professional posture should be warm, informal, and free of "remote authoritarianism" (Konopka, 1978, p. 128). The worker's style in the mainstream model is characterized by authenticity, forthrightness, and abnegation of a mystique of professionalism. Worker–member relationships have the therapeutic potential to diminish members' defensiveness, increase their trust and intimacy, and lessen the social distance between them. The informal style of the mainstream worker encourages identification with the worker. The worker takes responsibility for helping members deal with their feelings as legitimate components of the interactional process. The worker may share his or her own feelings, carefully considering the appropriateness and usefulness of such disclosures (Phillips, 1957).

A logical derivative of this conception of worker flexibility lies in the way the authority of the worker is viewed. The exercise of authority is in inverse relation to the capability of the group to manage its group life. The worker generally shares this conception of authority with the group early on, and both worker and group engage in monitoring authority transactions. In the mainstream group, challenges to the authority of the worker are generally regarded as natural and related to the growth of autonomy. However, challenges to authority may be contraindicated and the worker may want to encourage members or the group to acknowledge and accept his or her authority. The worker's ability to assess appropriately, and then accept, the increasing independence of the group is a critical factor in achieving shared authority.

## The setting of the mainstream group

The setting in which the group meets is the fifth element that plays a part in the mainstream model. Although the model may address remediation and rehabilitation, it also retains the traditional social work functions of "enhancement," "prevention," and "empowerment." The enhancement function of social work is so universalized in the practice of social group work that the content of group life always includes experiences that are pleasurable, growth-producing, and creative. Sick people take trips and go on picnics; mentally ill people hold parties and dances; adolescents create dramas and films; aging people write and share their poetry of reminiscence.

In agencies that are traditionally oriented towards dyadic service, two special concerns need to be addressed in order for a clinical group program in the mainstream model to flourish. First, the recruitment of members for a group requires the cooperation of the entire staff of professional workers, who may feel threatened if "their" clients become involved in a group. Second, the informal and more public involvement of group members has implications for loss of confidentiality and may also produce a "ripple effect" of unintended changes in the environment of the agency.

In settings in which creativity, innovation, and openness to a variety of approaches to clinical work are the norm, the mainstream model can enhance the agency's realization of its function and the client members' experience in self-growth and fulfillment. It is not surprising that social workers who use this approach with their clients often become involved in program development in their agencies, since the mainstream model is an enlarging, elaborating one that affirms growth at systemic levels as well as at the level of the group and the individual.

The mainstream group work paradigm may be one of the most effective social work methodologies for dealing with problems presented by people such as the Shores who are having difficulty relating to others. The energy and support afforded by other group members makes available experiences by which the lonely, disabled, or socially unskilled person may work towards new and restored social functioning.

## Supporting Theories

In the mainstream model, the clinical process takes place at many levels in the functioning of the individual member; therefore, no one personality theory or social-psychological theory can be considered adequate to explain this process. Some of the ideas that form the foundation for this model are drawn from ego psychology, cognitive and learning theory, object relations theory, role theory, and communication theory.

*Ego psychology* offers concepts about the organization of the internal self in relation to the external world. These concepts are necessary for the understanding of member behavior and for working clinically in groups, and therefore ego psychology is considered "congenial" to the mainstream model.

Ego psychology provides insights into how people perceive and adapt to the reality of self and others, what their defenses are in relation to threat, how they deal with external assault and internal anxiety.

Workers must recognize members' defenses (projection, rationalization, intellectualization, and displacement) that occur with frequency in the group, and they must use their skills to assist members in dealing with the underlying anxieties that call forth these defenses. With the help of the worker, the group offers members the opportunity to share anxieties and develop and test defenses that enhance flexibility and variation.

The social worker with the group must be able to recognize clinical symptoms and symptom formation. The worker should have a thorough grasp of the implications of members' unconscious and conscious drives and should also understand the concept of transference.

A member's resistance towards the worker's authority can signal strivings for resolution of dependence–independence struggles. Resistance and conflict are seen as necessary components of group life and serve as starting points for differentiation in the group as well as in the member. Resistance is not viewed solely as intrapsychic or as a member's negative response to the group situation. It may, indeed, be functional for the protective development of ongoing relationships.

In terms of ego psychology, the main thrust of the mainstream model with all groups is the support of members' healthy ego functioning, the development of a positive sense of self, and the realization of potential.

Group workers rely upon *cognitive theory* and *learning theory* to help them understand how members perceive and give meaning to their world and how they develop competencies and skills. The shaping of values, expectations, and hopefulness through group experiences is an important dimension of cognitive functioning. The internal and subjective meanings of the experience of members—and the way these are disclosed, communicated, and enlarged—are particularly salient in group life.

The shared perceptions of the group are cognitively powerful forces for altering a member's emotional response to many stressful interpersonal conditions. A person's experience of perceiving things in new ways, through the eyes of others, can lead to therapeutic gains.

*Object relations theory* is relevant to the understanding of the individual member's capacity to bond with others in the group and to maintain separateness even as group cohesion is achieved. Group life constantly creates moments in which the coexistence of involvement and separateness is challenged. These moments require each member to develop a balance between belonging and separateness, closeness and distance, participation and withdrawal.

*Role theory* links the personality of the member with accepted patterns of behavior for the roles and the functions of various roles in the group system. It provides the worker with knowledge for strengthening role performance and resolving role conflicts, thus producing growth in social functioning of the members.

*Communication theory*, which concerns the dynamic exchange of meanings, is also a basic theoretical tool. Whether the exchange is verbal or nonverbal, the intention of the communication and how it is received by others is vital to relationship among members. Communication theory guides the clinician in removing obstacles to the expression of ideas and feelings in the group.

## ASSESSMENT

Assessment and planning for the treatment of the Shore family should be undertaken in a multiple-method team approach. Ideally, a family-oriented social work model should coordinate all of the related treatment services, including group work. The assessment and planning related to group service are approached from such a perspective. Group work offers clients an array of opportunities for remediating some problems and preventing others, as well as for fulfilling some unmet needs.

### The Family

The Shore family presently functions with boundaries to the external environment that are relatively closed or impermeable. Interactions with the environment are of limited range and frequency. They are generally not sustained and are not fulfilling. In addition, the family's relationship with the outside world is nonreciprocal. Family members take what they can get from their external environment and, in return, give little that is directly related to other people's needs. The Shore family could be described as an isolated, alienated, and anomic system.

Internally, by contrast, the family members are intensely involved with each other. The involvements are principally orchestrated by Nancy, the mother, who is clearly the leader of the group in both instrumental and expressive roles. All interactions of the group seem to go through this central communication hub.

Communication patterns in this family are essentially verbal and highly intellectualized, although with a high degree of fantasy and unreality. The tendency to use psychological interpretations and insights suggests that this family has been exposed to considerable insight therapy and that members have adopted an introspective mode of communication. The family communicates through noisy and disruptive bickering, rarely engaging in physically violent behavior but also never reaching closure or making decisions. Everybody in this family is waiting for "the other shoe to drop," for the next crisis and the next failure. Frequently, the next crisis involves some kind of physical disablement or physical loss. This is a family that somaticizes by habitually associating its problems with the health of its members.

Although the family's enmeshment is essentially dysfunctional and destructive to its individual members, family members do not directly engage in hostile patterns of expression of feelings towards each other. As a matter of fact, a positive norm operating in this family is the members' genuine concern for each other. Family is of superordinate importance, including the extended family, which originally had consisted of Gram, the grandfather, aunts, and others. However, the Shores are all "hungry" people, longing to be cared for and tended. All are dependent and never feel that their needs are adequately being met, yet no member in this family is supposed to leave it.

Another positive norm in the family is that it does value the expressive arts, education, and humanistic values. Unfortunately, actualization of any competence in the area of education or in the arts is blocked by a nonwork norm in the family. "Somebody will take care of me" or "I am unable to work because of my disability" are the manifestations of the nonwork norm. Intellectualizing that therapy will provide some direction for solving the family problems is paradoxical. Therapy may be said to be almost a religion in this family, but the Shores actually have no faith that any change will occur.

In this family, decision-making is *reactive*, occurs in a crisis frame, and is carried by the mother (Nancy). Decisions made by her, however, are generally accompanied by induced guilt in other members when they do not do what she wants. The family gives lip service to preplanning,

but most of this preplanning is saturated with anxiety that is character-
istically passive and not pro-active. Family members have a variety of
different intellectual theories about what would solve family or individual
problems, but these theories are never tested.


## The Individual Members

In the individual assessment process, group workers tend not to assign
to members the DSM-III-R (American Psychiatric Association, 1987)
diagnoses. They are knowledgeable about and sensitive to issues of mental
illness. However, they focus on the present social functioning of the
individual and on social deficits in the context in which the person is
living. In the consideration of biopsychosocial aspects of personality
development, normative social skills are used as standards by which to
assess behavior.

In assessing and formulating the group work component of the treatment plan for the Shores, we will focus on the present functioning of
the individual members of the family, with some speculation about the
kinds of group experiences that might have made a difference at earlier
stages in their lives and that might have prevented some of the present
difficulties.

We will note group associations, in the past and the present, that
reinforce strengths and counter dysfunctional effects that the family
system has on its members.

Group work assessment pays considerable attention to how family
members function in their interpersonal worlds of school, work, recreation,
and the like. The developmental capacities for interpersonal effectiveness
and social competencies related to successful and meaningful extrafamilial
associations are assessed. Members of the family are also assessed in
relation to their interpersonal styles, social experiences, and social skills,
particularly those that relate to their abilities to offer, or make use of,
interpersonal support and learning in groups. We can demonstrate this
assessment process by focusing on Nancy, Charley, Rena, and Michael.

*Nancy* functions in a highly neurotic manner. Her anxieties are excessive
and immobilizing. She seeks immediate gratification in plans that require
very little investment or discipline over time. She was a child who was
abandoned by one parent, symbolically abandoned by the other, and
overprotected and indulged by an extended family that was attempting
to compensate for inadequate parental care.

Nancy is childlike, consumed by her own fears and needs. Although
she is a good problem-solver, she (like her mother) is not a nurturer.
This is disguised by the image she presents as the person who cares for
others, the nurse.

Nancy's defense as a caring person needs to be maintained and extended to her nursing profession. Could she have been enabled to carry a small part-time role in the hospital or in a nursing home, where her nursing identity could have been recognized without placing her under undue physical stress and emotional demand?

In the formal social work treatment arena, group work rather than individual counseling would be the service mode of choice for a client such as Nancy, trapped in a dependence-independence dilemma. In group experience, Nancy's problem of separation-individuation, her excessive fears and anxieties, and her rigid coping styles would be significantly challenged. The treatment group should be broad in its approach, so that the opportunities for engaging in therapeutic activities that are conceptualized in the mainstream model could be available to Nancy.

*Charley*, like many children in alcoholic families, played the role of the clown and the scapegoat in his family of origin. He says that Nancy is like his mother, but in actuality she is also like his father, in that her present role in his life seems to be an assaultive one as well as a caring one. He is incompetent in the role of father, fights with his son in sibling fashion, and flushes Rena's snails down the toilet. He not only has been unsuccessful in his family, but also has had few extrafamilial relationships—and those have been demeaning or shallow. Charley finds it more rewarding to play a scapegoat role, in which he receives negative attention, than to run the risk of being overlooked.

Despite his constant failures, however, Charley does try to move outside the family and to carry a role in which he strives towards some self-gratification. After all, even though Nancy perceives his comedy act as a failure, Charley has been allowed to return to the comedy club again and again over a five-year period. Perhaps, in that environment, he is not a failure. He might have benefited from community activity groups that would have tapped his interest in theater and clowning and at the same time would have deepened some relationships that evolve from common interests rather than common needs.

Charley has had no model for fathering. One would wonder whether a group experience preparing Charley for fatherhood during Rena's adoption process and later around Michael's birth might have modified his incompetency as a father.

*Rena's* identity as an adopted child is a major problem, which, as we would expect, moved into central importance during her adolescence. If we look at Rena developmentally, we see that she has considerable strengths. Her reality testing is less faulty than that of other members of the family. She has been able to maintain some distance from the enmeshment of the family. Her struggles for self-identity and separation-individuation are typical for a person of her age. However, we can anticipate that the process of achieving ego identity will be more complex because she is an adopted child. For example, Rena's age-appropriate efforts towards separation from her family can be turned against herself or others because there is a constant fear that she is again expendable. She can neither tolerate the enmeshment of the family, which is an obstacle to individuation, nor separate from it without excessive anxiety about her continued place in the family. Her near successes, which have inevitably culminated in failure, symbolize this struggle: She adopts the family norm of failure as a mark of family identification.

Rena's search for her natural mother may be based on her need for biological continuity and the demystification of her birth. Her recent search, "despite how painful it may be," represents strength.

It is important above all else to determine the extent to which Rena is locked into her family and its norm of failure. For example, Rena's relationships with her peers seem troublesome. She is a loner; she has no female friends, and her relationships with male friends are not gratifying. She is at a crossroads, developmentally. Her low self-esteem, her confusion, her pseudoindependence, and her definition of herself as "lazy or as something more serious" could result in her accepting a sick role in this family.

Rena could benefit from an intense therapeutic relationship with a nurturing but strong woman therapist who could be available to her during this next developmental period of her life. Therapeutic group experiences should be supplementary to individual treatment and might also include groups related to the arts and to projects in which she can use her skills to contribute in some formal way to those who may be less fortunate. It is important not only that Rena have her needs satisfied but also that she see herself as being able to contribute to others.

*Michael's* interpersonal behavior, regardless of its etiology, is a cause for considerable concern. It can be viewed as a cry for help and as symptomatic of serious pathology. Within the reality of severe symptomatology, Michael still needs group life that is responsive to his developmental struggle for peer relations, for recognition of his special abilities, and for meaningful and successful interpersonal experiences outside of the family.

His problems are not only an outgrowth of his "poor judgment" and inappropriate behavior; they are as much a function of poor placement and debilitating and inappropriate group experiences. For example, scouting is not the group or situation of choice for a youngster like Michael. High levels of coordination and self-control are required. Furthermore, a special class for learning-disabled children is not an appropriate academic solution for an emotionally disadvantaged junior high school student.

Apparently, Nancy and Charley have been unable to be advocates for Michael in the camping or school situations and to evaluate the inappropriateness of these programs for him. At this point, however, group work planners should not remove Michael from the scouting program that means so much to him, but rather they should seek ways to neutralize the demands that contribute to his loss of self-esteem.

Like the rest of his family, Michael identifies himself as a loser and a failure. Like his father, he plays the scapegoat role in social groups. In the family, he functions as the poor sick child. Michael is unhappy and lonely, unable to fend for himself in group life. His health problems appear to be chronic and severe. Asthma and seizures are central factors in his life-functioning. Aside from the medical care, the planning for Michael seems not to have been based on this reality. There are several unanswered questions about the evaluation of the side effects of the medication and asthmatic treatment that he is receiving. There are also questions about the management of his illnesses in a biopsychosocial framework. To the group worker, Michael's uncontrolled and bizarre behavior signifies that, in all groups, he would present needs for special attention and support from skilled workers.

It is possible that Michael's need for religious solace and values could be satisfied if he were to affiliate with a youth group sponsored by a humanistic religious organization such as the Ethical Culture Society or a Unitarian-Universalist Fellowship. In such a religiously oriented youth group, Michael's physical and behavioral difficulties might be more accepted.

It is imperative that Michael be safeguarded from failure and rejection at this point in his development. Special attention should be given to the form and composition of any social or therapeutic group in which he becomes involved. Michael's social experience in the next few years should not be left to chance.

## TREATMENT OF CHOICE

The mainstream model makes group work a treatment resource for the members of the Shore family, and for many people experiencing long-standing difficulties, as well as for those whose problems result from life transitions and developmental crises (e.g., adolescence, aging, and loss through death). Because the group is so ubiquitous in human experience, group treatment has a tremendous potential to be valuable for a variety of clients and problems. There are no universal criteria for determining it as a treatment of choice except as each type of group and each individual is specifically assessed in relation to the other.

The model's usefulness for various types of clients or members is made possible by the extent of the creativity of group workers in designing, organizing, and facilitating appropriate groups. The only injunction against group service is when it is determined in advance that there is a possibility of emotional or physical threat to the potential member or when a client lacks the potential for developing trust or tolerating the demands of other group members. There are also clients who are unable to share the worker's attention with others and who may insist upon being at the center of the stage in a highly narcissistic and destructive manner.

## THE THERAPEUTIC PROCESS

### Group-building Techniques

Because the group is the unit of service for group work practice, the formation and the maintenance of the group are critical concerns. Early interventions undertaken by the worker can be identified as group-building activities. These include techniques for facilitating the group formation process, recruiting suitable members, eliciting members' interest in the group, dealing with initial ambivalence towards group membership, "lending a vision" of the potential of group value to individual members (Schwartz, 1961), assisting the group in defining an acceptable and workable purpose, establishing a contract, and securing adequate facilities and support by interpreting the purpose of the group to the agency and the community.

Group-building requires the group worker to assist the group in establishing norms and procedures. As the formation process continues, the group worker strives to influence the development of conditions that contribute to mutual aid and to the acceptance of individual members. The worker underscores the commonalities among the members: common interests, common plights, similar characteristics of age, gender, culture, and ethnicity. Such factors foster group cohesion, the "interpersonal glue" that holds the group system together throughout its formative stage.

It is the responsibility of the group worker to strengthen group functioning. A major technique employed is the continuous facilitation of decision-making in and by the group, including evaluating its decision-making processes and outcomes so that it can "own" its accomplishments and acknowledge its satisfactions with increased autonomy.

Throughout the various stages of group development, the group worker focuses interventions on the processes of decision-making, communication, participation, norm formation, conflict, and control, with the goal of promoting group and individual growth. For the most part, worker influence is exerted overtly, with the members apprised of the intent of the worker's interventions. The members are thus free to reject, modify, or accept the worker's activities. In this open system, members tend to internalize the values and activities of the worker. They incorporate the worker's therapeutic posture and techniques, thus increasing their ability to assist themselves and others.

The techniques used to address obstacles to mutual aid are critical to the success of the group (Shulman, 1979). These techniques involve helping members to differentiate self-interest from the interest of others and to communicate honestly with one another. Dealing with problems as group-maintenance concerns, rather than as malfunctions of individuals, accelerates group bonding.

Methods employed by the group worker to influence or to modify group conditions, such as those outlined above, are distinguished from interventions that are directed to an individual member (Vinter, 1967). Individually focused interventions may involve, among others, enabling a member to share a problem, reframing a member's problem, or confronting limiting and inappropriate individual behavior. Therapeutic interventions reverberate in the group whether targeted for one individual or for the group-as-a-whole. Their effects rebound throughout the membership and may be beneficial for the observing members as well as the intended recipient of the intervention.

The group worker freely employs nonverbal interventions or activities, including those related to the expressive arts, games, exercises, role-plays, simulations, and fantasy. These activities are carefully chosen according to their particular attributes and potential outcomes. Several authors have classified program activities and have discussed how they can be tailored to fit the needs of the group and its members (Middleman, 1968; Vinter, 1967; Whittaker, 1985; Wilson & Ryland, 1948).

## Therapeutic Goals

The therapeutic process generally seeks to accomplish one or more of the following goals: 1) to change or modify the cognitions or perceptions of the members through learning experiences and knowledge provided in the group; 2) to change behaviors that are obstacles to problem-solving or social functioning by exposing members to new modes of behavior, practice of these behaviors, and group feedback; 3) to bring to consciousness the norms, values, and attitudes that support or prevent effective social functioning; 4) to influence or change emotional states or feelings that operate to the detriment of the individual and the group and to support and nourish those that represent strengths.

## Application of Group Work Techniques to Treatment of the Shore Family Members

In this section, we will suggest the therapeutic potential of various groups for each member of the Shore family, within the context of group work techniques and functions.

*Nancy*

Nancy may be overstating her nursing competence, but nursing is the only area, outside the home, in which she professes motivation and identity. The group workers on the team would search for ways to combine her self-proclaimed nursing and caring skills with other skills. Nancy's positive identification with a nursing work role may be reinforced through her being recruited into a volunteers' group or part-time employees' group in the hospital setting. Nancy could gain positive rewards by leading a patients' activity group that is focused on instruction in needlepoint. Leadership of the needlepoint group would take Nancy out of her home and would give her a safe environment, under social work supervision, in which she could be evaluated and held accountable for an activity based on already-proven competence. This venturing forth into group life would offer her a safe excursion with a high probability of success and status. Through such an activity, Nancy might also develop social relationships with other staff members and secure some gratification of her dependency needs.

Nancy could also be encouraged to join a group for parents of asthmatic adolescents (organized through either the school or hospital). Nancy's participation in such a group would offer her educational gains and interpersonal support. The worker in such a group would focus on the commonality associated with the difficulties and guilt in being a parent of an asthmatic child. The worker would try to draw upon feelings of universality (i.e., "We're all in the same boat"). Mutual aid would be elicited as the members deal with the specific problems presented in the varied situations that they bring to the group. Nancy's need to control her family could be discussed sympathetically, particularly since each parent may reveal some aspect of his or her mode of coping with the loss or the fear associated with parenting a child with special needs. Professional interventions in this group would be directed towards providing information about asthma and increasing parents' understanding of the normal growth needs of asthmatic children. Helping parents correct each other's misperceptions about their children's capabilities can improve their relationships with their children. The worker would also encourage and support Nancy and the other parents in advocating more directly with the schools to encourage better educational experiences for their children. Such group activity may stimulate Nancy, because she is articulate, to assume leadership in this endeavor.

Another choice for involving Nancy in group experience is a self-help obesity group. The addictive aspect of her personality might respond well to the support and demand in such a group. Like Nancy, many members of this group would have experienced social ostracism and derision. The worker in an obesity group would employ techniques that build support and challenge for the members. For example, Nancy might be encouraged to ventilate her feelings and seek group support, but in exchange she would need to accept the self-discipline and the group's weight-reduction program. Whether the obesity group is organized around self-help or is led by a professional, it symbolically represents the "maternal figure" for its members; it simultaneously nurtures and makes demands upon its dependent and childlike members. In the obesity group, the members' food addiction is explored in relation to common themes like self-hate, fear of sexuality, and damaged self-image. The demand for self-discipline, the unacceptability of defenses like denial and fantasy, and the high rewards given for positive change would contribute to Nancy's growth. For Nancy, permanent weight loss could be an unattainable goal. The invitation to return to the group whenever necessary and to depend on the friendships established through the group would anchor her in a social system with some potential for countering the downward spiral of her social functioning.

Nancy's initial motivation for group experience will undoubtedly be low. She will require considerable "reaching out" and support from the social worker during the stages of recruitment and early group participation. However, any of these group activities might serve as a springboard for promoting change and moving Nancy out of the hopeless stagnation of her family.

## Charley

For many marginally functioning people like Charley, community centers (e.g., YMCA or settlement house) offer a safe haven in which they can interact with others and enrich their relatively restrictive existence. A theater group based in a community center could provide excellent opportunities for meeting many of Charley's interpersonal needs. Participation could also include backstage activities (e.g., lighting, staging, publicity), which would help him to relate on a broader basis with other adults.

Group work services, developed in settings such as vocational rehabilitation agencies, can also help marginally functioning people develop the social skills required to secure and maintain employment. Through a connection with a vocational rehabilitation program, Charley might be offered an opportunity to join a therapeutically oriented group designed to help those with similar interpersonal needs. A vocational rehabilitation group would provide Charley with another avenue for change. It would offer him opportunities to explore his potential for employment and his unproductive fantasies that have kept him from seeking appropriate jobs. Anticipating Charley's tendency to assume the scapegoat role, the worker would deflect any group behaviors headed in this direction. Charley would be encouraged to undertake tasks within the scope of his competency. Through role-play and subsequent discussion, Charley would experience the support of the group and the worker as a "cheering section" that would offset the immobilizing and humiliating effects of Nancy's lack of belief in his abilities. The worker's strategy in the group would be to focus on strengthening the members' communication skills by encouraging their expression of needs and interpersonal responsiveness. Role-playing would be augmented by the use of structured interpersonal exercises and games, specifically designed for increasing and practicing interpersonal competencies (Pfeiffer & Jones, 1983). Moreover, the worker can encourage the group to explore possibilities for effecting change in public rehabilitation policies, thus restoring, both to the group and to its individual members such as Charley, some sense of empowerment and skills that had been diminished by past negative experiences in the community and in the family.

Another important resource could be an Adult Children of Alcoholics (ACOA) group program. The ACOA group would offer Charley an opportunity for dealing with repressed feelings from his early childhood, particularly those about his alcoholic father. This group experience would focus on helping members discover the universal pain of unfulfilled yearning commonly encountered by children of alcoholic parents. Various techniques have been developed for use in such groups. These techniques encourage members to first recognize and then deal with depressive or regressive feelings and behaviors associated with destructive past experiences. The ACOA group can offer a new dimension of self-knowledge and nurturance for Charley.

*Rena*

Developmentally focused group work in the mainstream model, including group therapy and social–recreational groups, is suggested for Rena. A clinical group worker could concentrate on Rena's relationships with her peers but should also help her acknowledge that these are echoes of her problematic relationships with her family. The group worker should try to elicit Rena's fears about enmeshment which may be made even more intense and apparent as others in the group offer her increasing affection and intimacy. The rebuffs and defensive behaviors that she may employ to distance herself from the empathic members in the group would be challenged. The worker would support Rena's attempts to experiment with other modes of response by reassuring her that she would not lose her independence by conforming to constructive demands of the group members. In the therapy group, the worker acknowledges the members' need for differentiation and separation and the tenuousness of relationships that this need may cause. The worker also emphasizes the importance of the support each member gives to the others in peeling away some of the layers of distrust and fear that obscure basic warmth and attachment. This context of mutual aid and acceptance allows members to confront and modify dysfunctional feelings and behaviors. For Rena and her young adult peers, the therapy group has particular appeal. Through its "on stage" style of discourse, it satisfies the self-centeredness of the young adults (a residual of an earlier adolescent stage), while allowing them to utilize their self-knowledge and expressions of generosity towards others as a step along the path to mature adulthood. In particular, Rena's pattern of turning away from success and engaging in self-depreciating failure would receive considerable attention in the therapy group. As the worker universalizes Rena's situation, Rena would also discover that self-doubt and self-defeating behaviors are familiar experiences in the world of the young adult.

The mainstream model of group work encourages relationships beyond the immediate therapeutic session. For example, the group worker would support members' attending cultural and social events together. These experiences would subsequently be discussed in the group, and satisfactions, achievements, and pleasures would be shared. Like many young adults who have problems, Rena needs the permission of the group and worker to enjoy such experiences. Learning about the value and joy of human companionship is a particularly critical task for Rena, so that self-indulgent isolation does not become her principal mode of functioning. In its broadest aspects, the therapy group would offer Rena a bridge to a more satisfying adulthood.

Membership in a group of adoptees and parents who have relinquished their children for adoption can also have a significant impact on Rena. Such a group might help her to further resolve her own identity. She will be able to raise her most compelling questions and discover that the child might not be the only victim in the situation. Rena's insight will be deepened by this experience. Her energies may be released so that she can make better use of individual and group therapy.

### Michael

Michael would initially present problems in any group situation. He would tend, at first, to resort to familiar acting-out behaviors, which in the past have covered his deeply felt emptiness and insecurity. The group worker should enlist the group's acceptance of Michael, pointing out that his uncertainties are shared by all. The authority of the worker, expressed with warmth and firmness, can convey a sense of security to all the members and can forestall the group's treating Michael as a scapegoat.

In a group organized around the problem of asthma, Michael would discover that he is not the only one to feel different and alone. He could share with other teenagers the hardships of their handicap, the fears of death, their physical and sexual insecurities, their apprehension about the future, and the dependence–independence struggle of growing up handicapped. The worker should strive to develop a safe atmosphere in which Michael can disclose his concerns and his fantasies. As such material comes to light, the worker may employ humor, exercises, and games to relieve tension, so that the adolescents will not be completely overwhelmed by the depressiveness of their disclosures. The worker should encourage Michael and others in the group to swap problem-solving and coping approaches. Role-plays would be useful in helping Michael develop the skills needed for appropriate self-assertion. Through positive group experiences, Michael could discover that he has strengths to cope, that he is a "person," that with supported guidance he can become part of a larger unit, and that he, too, can have friends. He may also find that he can function in a group without being "silly"— that is, that he can employ appropriate controls.

In addition, the group would provide a rich opportunity for Michael to acquire accurate information about the treatment and control of his illness and could consequently help him participate in treatment choices. The worker might also suggest difficulties that parents may have in understanding the problems of their children. Role-playing and discussion are useful in helping adolescents develop skills for communicating better with each other and with family members about the issues that are important to them.

Concerns about school are critical to these adolescents, and the worker should support discussions about conflicting values and expectations. The members should be encouraged to exchange old and new ideas about how to cope with school problems. An example might be a discussion of Michael's eventual return to his regular classroom. The worker should convey to the adolescents that resolution of difficult issues is a *process*, and that a solution arrived at in one meeting may have to be reworked or changed in another. The worker can make use of some personal experience to illustrate the idea of continuous problem-solving in life, while providing assurances about their increasing competency and re-siliency to confront problems. Worker self-disclosure (sharing meaningful personal experience with the group) presents models for more effective attitudes and behaviors.

If scapegoating of Michael should recur, the worker should deal with it as an interactional problem, and should attempt to alter the group conditions as well as Michael's behavior. Michael and the other group members would be asked to examine their roles in the scapegoating situation. The worker would require all members, including Michael, to modify their behavior in the interest of maintaining the group (Garland & Kolodny, 1973; Shulman, 1968).

Michael's home environment might also be altered somewhat if his parents were involved in a parent group related to asthmatic children. Participation in such a group might assist them to be more sensitive to Michael's developmental needs and to deemphasize his physical symptoms.

Michael's membership in a religiously oriented youth group could be used to develop his social relationships around a common ideology unrelated to asthma or to his disabling social behaviors. Recreational and social activities in the religiously oriented group are apt to be noncompetitive and unrelated to the acquisition of physical skills. Michael can be exposed to developmentally and culturally enriching experiences such as music, outings, games, and the like. These are of particular importance for Michael; he is intellectually bright and has broad cultural interests. However, because his family is isolated from the community, it does not offer him opportunities to fulfill any of his interests or use his talents.

Because Charley is limited in fulfilling the role of husband and father, he is an inadequate object of identification for Michael. In either of Michael's groups, a male group worker who is both authoritative and supportive could facilitate his socialization to the male role.

## LIMITATIONS OF THE MODEL

Organizing and forming a group present special problems for the professional. An expenditure of professional time is often necessary for developing recruitment methods specifically designed to attract people with common interests and problems within a particular area served by the agency. Because the recruitment process may be slow and unfamiliar to social workers untrained in group formation, agencies may be unwilling or unaccustomed to invest their resources. As a result, agencies and professional personnel may be easily discouraged from offering group services.

The difficulties in matching people is further exacerbated by the fact that group treatment is often viewed as being less valuable than individual treatment. Professional staff may unwittingly undermine clients' motivation for group treatment by too readily offering a substitute. If group treatment is tainted with lower status, it is understandable that clients would resist what they think of as "second-class" service.

As discussed throughout this chapter, the maintenance of the group is absolutely necessary. Group workers and members must periodically deal with factors that tend to weaken their groups. For example, some members may create disturbances of great magnitude or spread feelings of depression, hopelessness, and anger, thereby overwhelming the group and diminishing its capacity to deal with group issues and to be helpful to individual members. Should such a group condition persist despite the efforts of the group worker, members will tend to be "decathected" from the group and it will dissolve.

Finally, a major limitation in group work is that it is not always possible to find an ideal setting for group meetings. Inadequate facilities can have dire consequences for group development. The inability of an agency to provide uninterrupted meeting time under near-private conditions can often prevent a group from developing cohesion or protecting its confidentiality. Such groups generally flounder for a time, but ultimately fail to survive the encroachment of the environment on their autonomy.

Group work services rarely succeed without considerable professional planning towards reducing those conditions that are detrimental to the development and existence of a group. Most of the limitations we have mentioned can be minimized or avoided through careful planning.

## RESEARCH

Research findings from the social sciences and from social work have contributed to the scientific base of social group work. Sociology and social psychology have provided empirical information related to group dynamics, especially the patterns and processes of small group systems. Small group dynamics have long been of interest to group workers (Anderson, 1979; Balgopal & Vassil, 1983; Hartford, 1971; Toseland & Rivas, 1984). Sociological and social–psychological studies have shown group workers effective ways of dealing with the conditions that give rise to these group forces, as well as with their effects on group and individual behavior. For instance, the scientific study of the interrelationships of small group variables has spotlighted the importance of such processes as group attraction and cohesion, group structure and roles, group decision-making, leadership and influence, norm development, group conflict, and communication. Several collections about small group dynamics (Cartwright & Zander, 1968; Festinger, 1980; Hare, 1962; Maccoby, Newcomb, & Hartley, 1958; Shaw, 1981; Zander, 1977) offer a comprehensive review of major research studies and their related theories and are considered by group workers to be essential to their understanding of groups.

Psychologically or clinically oriented research from the mental health professions is a second source of empirically based findings that have been incorporated into the knowledge base of the social group worker. These studies emphasize changes—in individual clients or patients—that are associated with specific aspects of clinical group practice. This research has sought to increase understanding about group and individual factors, therapists' interventions, and therapeutic outcomes. Extensive inquiries have been devoted to such clinical issues as the differential effectiveness of directive and nondirective group therapies and time-limited group treatment. Complementary studies have focused on how group treatment is affected by therapist and patient variables (e.g., patient-therapist perceptions, expectations, satisfactions, self-disclosure, transparency, and transference). Reviews of major research within the clinical context can be found in Dies and MacKenzie (1983); Gibbard, Hartman, and Mann (1978); and Shaw (1981); as well as in the journals, *International Journal of Group Psychotherapy* and *Small Group Behavior*.

Social work research is a third source of knowledge about groups. Although this effort has been modest, it is becoming an increasingly important activity in social group work practice and in group work education (*Social Work with Groups*, 1986, 3). A three-year large-scale study of the treatment of antisocial youths in prosocial groups (Feldman, Caplinger, & Wodarski, 1983), involving 700 subjects in 60 groups, determined the effects of differential group leadership attributes, group composition, and models of group treatment on treatment outcome. The data established the efficacy of providing treatment for antisocial youths in small groups that are composed of prosocial peers. The findings also indicated that various forms of group integration bear a direct and positive relationship to the group worker's experience and capacity to promote prosocial behavior change among antisocial youths.

Landmark small group dynamics studies about the effects of different leadership styles in decision-making groups continue to be of interest to group work (Hare, 1955; White & Lippitt, 1968). These studies have supported the validity of employing a democratic mode of leadership in groups. Gero's (1985) study of "leadering" in decision-making groups in social work follows this tradition, as does a well-developed evaluation of decision-making efforts in task groups that was carried out by Toseland, Rivas, and Chapman (1984).

Group work studies that have followed the clinical path have concentrated on evaluation. The treatment problems and the group approaches examined in this genre of research are as diverse as the practice of group work itself. For example, Edwards (1982) examined the participation of spouses in the treatment of alcoholics. Shifman, Scott, Fawcett, and Orr (1986) evaluated the effectiveness of a game for both assessment and learning in sex education of adolescents who were at risk for unwanted pregnancies. Freeman and McRoy (1986) evaluated a group counseling program for unemployed black teenagers. Meadows (1982) examined the effects of pregroup preparation on group practice, and Toseland, Sherman, and Bliven (1981) compared two group approaches with the elderly.

Beyond the research carried out by individual group workers, ongoing evaluative group work research has been conducted at research centers at two schools of social work: the University of Wisconsin-Madison and the University of Washington. Research has evaluated life-skills learning for the prevention or management of such problems as teenage pregnancy, chronic stress, pain, and spouse abuse (Rose, Tallant, Tolman, & Subramanian, 1986; Schinke, Blythe, Gilchrist, & Burt, 1981).

A recent trend in group work research can be described as exploratory. Its objective has largely turned on informing group workers about patterns, practices, or problems that currently prevail in settings in which social group work is practiced. Although these exploratory studies have varied in their degree of methodological rigor, they have nevertheless provided data where none existed before, corrected misperceptions by bringing forth new information, and documented patterns and needs. For example, Galinsky and Schopler (1985) found repetitive patterns of entry and exit in their survey of open-ended groups; Paquet-Deehy, Hopmeyer, Home, and Kislowicz (1985) established a typology of social group work, based on a survey of group work practice in Montreal, and Toseland (1983) exposed myths and stereotypes about the relationships of social workers and self-help groups.

Increasingly, group workers incorporate research tools into their practices in order to clarify changes that are taking place in the groups and in individual members (Rose, 1977). Single-system designs are being used to establish baselines and to measure change at intervals during the group work process. Anderson (1986), Garvin (1987), and Toseland and Rivas (1984) describe various approaches to instrumentation that can be easily adapted to measuring changes in process and outcomes in group practice. Standardized instruments with a personal, interpersonal, and environmental focus and which are useful to group workers are described in a variety of publications (Dies & MacKenzie, 1983; Hudson, 1982; Lake, Miles, & Earle, 1973; Pfeiffer & Heslin, 1973).

Objective data about the progress of the Shore family and the groups in which they participate could become available and provide directions for the group work practitioner. Research methods, measurement, and instrumentation are now at a level of development to better inform the group work practitioner about many significant aspects of group practice.

## SUMMARY

Social group work, represented by the mainstream model, sets forth the major concepts and practice principles of the group method in the social work profession. Fashioned out of its roots in the early humanistic philosophy and social reform of the settlement movement and later incorporating psychological and interpersonal theory, the model emphasizes the use of the small group as a clinical paradigm. The model deals with the interplay of five elements: the group, the individual members, the worker in the group, the group's activities, and the setting of the group.

Major interventions in the group are directed towards releasing the forces of mutual aid, support, and group identity in clinically addressing individual and group problems.

The assessment of the Shore family and its individual members has indicated ways by which the therapeutic opportunities in groups could make a difference in the life-functioning of the family. Such experiences could rescue the family from the downward spiral of destructive relationship patterns with each other. The special contribution of social group work for Nancy, Charley, Rena, and Michael is that it offers mental health opportunities through community resources that do not taint the family with labels of illness. Instead, group work enables each member to move out, in age-appropriate and role-appropriate ways, from the enmeshment of the family, yet without loss of the familial ties that have sustained them.

## REFERENCES

American Psychiatric Association. (1987). *Diagnostic and statistical manual of mental disorders* (3rd ed., revised). Washington, DC: Author.

Anderson, J. (1979). Social work practice with groups in the generic base of social work practice. *Social Work with Groups, 2*(4), 281–293.

Anderson, J. (1986). Integrating research and practice in social work with groups. *Social Work with Groups, 9*(3), 111–124.

Balgopal, P. R., & Vassil, T. V. (1983). *Groups in social work: An ecological perspective.* New York: Macmillan.

Bernstein, S. (1965). Conflict and group work. In S. Bernstein (Ed.), *Explorations in group work* (pp. 54–80). Boston: Boston University School of Social Work.

Boyd, N. (1919). *Hospital and bedside games.* Chicago: Fitz Simons.

Boyd, N. (1938). Play as a means of social adjustment. In J. L. Lieberman (Ed.), *New trends in group work* (pp. 101–109). New York: Association Press.

Cartwright, D., & Zander, A. (Eds.). (1968). *Group dynamics: Research and theory* (3rd ed.). New York: Harper & Row.

Coyle, G. L. (1958). *Social science in professional education of social workers.* New York: Council on Social Work Education.

Dewey, J. (1934). *Art as experience.* New York: G. P. Putnam.

Dies, R. R., & MacKenzie, K. R. (Eds.). (1983). *Advances in group psychotherapy.* New York: International Universities Press.

Edwards, D. (1982). Spouse participation in the treatment of alcoholism: Completion of treatment & recidivism. *Social Work with Groups, 5*(1), 41–48.

Feldman, R. A., Caplinger, T. E., & Wodarski, J. S. (1983). The St. Louis conundrum: The effective treatment of antisocial youth. Englewood Cliffs, NJ: Prentice-Hall.

Festinger, L. (Ed.). (1980). *Retrospectives on social psychology.* New York: Oxford University Press.

Follett, M. (1918). *The new state.* New York: Longmans Green.

Follett, M. (1924). *Creative experience.* New York: Longmans Green.

Freeman, E., & McRoy, R. (1986). Group counseling program for unemployed black teenagers. *Social Work with Groups, 9*(1), 73–89.

Galinsky, M. J., & Schopler, J. H. (1985). Patterns of entry and exit in open ended groups. *Social Work with Groups, 8*(2), 67–80.

Garland, J., Jones, H., & Kolodny, R. (1965). A model of stages of group development in social work groups. In S. Bernstein (Ed.), *Explorations in group work* (pp. 12–54). Boston: Boston University School of Social Work.

Garland, J., & Kolodny, R. (1973). Characteristics and resolution of scapegoating. In S. Bernstein (Ed.), *Further explorations in group work* (pp. 46–60). Boston: Milford House.

Garvin, C. (1987). *Contemporary group work* (2nd ed.). Englewood Cliffs, NJ: Prentice-Hall.

Gero, A. (1985). Leadering in decision-making groups. In M. Parnes (Ed.), *Innovations from practice to theory* (pp. 174–189). New York: Haworth Press.

Gibbard, G. S., Hartman, J. J., & Mann, R. R. (Eds.). (1978). *Analysis of groups.* San Francisco: Jossey-Bass.

Glasser, P. H., & Garvin, C. D. (1977). Social group work: The organizational and environmental approach. In *Encyclopedia of social work II* (pp. 1338–1350). New York: National Association of Social Workers.

Hare, A. P. (1955). Small group discussions with participatory and supervisory leadership. In A. P. Hare, E. F. Borgotta, & R. F. Bales (Eds.), *Small groups: Studies in social interaction* (pp. 556–560). New York: Alfred A. Knopf.

Hare, A. P. (1962). *Handbook on small group research.* New York: Free Press.

Hartford, M. (1971). *Groups in social work.* New York: Columbia University Press.

Hudson, W. (1982). *The clinical measurement package: A field manual.* Homewood, IL: Dorsey Press.

Kaiser, C. (1958). The social group work process. *Social Work, 3*(2), 67–75.

Klein, A. F. (1953). *Society, democracy and the group.* New York: Womens Press & Wm. Morrow.

Konopka, G. (1963). *Social group work: A helping process.* Englewood Cliffs, NJ: Prentice-Hall.

Konopka, G. (1978). The significance of social group work based on ethical values. *Social Work with Groups, 1*(2), 123–131.

Lake, D. G., Miles, M. B., & Earle, R. B., Jr. (Eds.). (1973). *Measuring human behavior.* New York: Teachers College Press.

Lang, N. C. (1979). A comparative examination of therapeutic uses of groups in social work and in adjacent human services professions: Part II: The literature from 1969–1978. *Social Work with Groups, 2*(3), 197–220.

Levine, B. (1979). *Group psychotherapy: Practice and development.* Englewood Cliffs, NJ: Prentice-Hall.

Lewin, K. (1951). *Field theory in social science.* New York: Harper & Row.

Lindeman, E. (1924). *Social discovery.* New York: Republic Press.

Maccoby, E., Newcomb, T., & Hartley, E. (Eds.). (1958). *Readings in social psychology.* New York: Holt, Rinehart & Winston.

Mead, G. H. (1934). *Mind, self and society.* Chicago: University of Chicago Press.

Meadows, D. (1982). Connecting theory and practice: The effect of pre-group preparation on individual and group behavior. In N. Lang & C. Marshall (Eds.), *Patterns in the mosaic: Proceedings 1982, Fourth Annual Symposium for the Advancement of Social Work with Groups* (Vol. II, pp. 1107–1121). Toronto, Ontario, Canada: Committee for the Advancement of Social Work with Groups.

Middleman, R. R. (1968). *The non-verbal method in working with groups.* New York: Association Press.

Northen, H. (1969). *Social work with groups.* New York: Columbia University Press.

Papell, C., & Rothman, B. (1966). Social group work models: Possession and heritage. *Journal of Education for Social Work, 2*(2), 66–77.

Papell, C., & Rothman, B. (1980). Relating the mainstream model of social work with groups to group psychotherapy and the structured group approach. *Social Work with Groups, 3*(2), 5–23.

Paquet-Deehy, A., Hopmeyer, E., Home, A., & Kislowicz, L. (1985). A typology of social work practice with groups. *Social Work with Groups, 8*(1), 65–78.

Pfeiffer, J. W., & Heslin, R. (1973). *Instrumentation in human relations training.* Iowa City, IA: University Associates.

Pfeiffer, J. W., & Jones, J. E. (1983). *A handbook of structured experiences for human relations training* (Vol. I-IX). San Diego, CA: University Associates.

Phillips, H. U. (1957). *Essentials of social group work skill.* New York: Association Press.

Roberts, R. W., & Northen, H. (Eds.). (1976). *Theories of social work with groups.* New York: Columbia University Press.

Rose, S. D. (1977). *Group therapy: A behavioral approach.* Englewood Cliffs, NJ: Prentice-Hall.

Rose, S. D., Tallant, S. H., Tolman, R., & Subramanian, S. (1986). A multimethod group approach: Program development research. *Social Work with Groups, 9*(3), 71–88.

Sarri, R., & Galinsky, M. (1975). A conceptual framework for group development. In P. Glasser, R. Sarri, & R. Vinter (Eds.), *Individual change through small groups* (pp. 71–80). New York: Free Press.

Schinke, S. P., Blythe, B. J., Gilchrist, L. D., & Burt, G. A. (1981). Primary prevention of adolescent pregnancy. *Social Work with Groups, 4*(2), 121–135.

Schutz, W. C. (1958). *FIRO: A three-dimensional theory of interpersonal behavior.* New York: Holt, Rinehart & Winston.

Schwartz, W. (1961). The social worker in the group. In *The social welfare forum* (pp. 146–177). New York: Columbia University Press.

Schwartz, W. (1977). Social group work: the interactionist approach. In *Encyclopedia of social work II* (pp. 1328–1337). New York: National Association of Social Workers.

Shaw, M. (1981). *Group dynamics: The psychology of small group behavior.* New York: McGraw-Hill.

Sheffield, A. (1928). *Creative discussion.* New York: The Inquiry.

Shifman, L., Scott, C., Fawcett, N., & Orr, L. (1986). Utilizing a game for both needs assessment and learning in adolescent sexuality education. *Social Work with Groups, 9*(2), 41–56.

Shulman, L. (1968). Scapegoats, group workers, and pre-emptive intervention. *Social Work, 13,* 37–43.

Shulman, L. (1979). *The skills of helping: Individuals and groups.* Itasca, IL: F. E. Peacock.

Toseland, R. (1983). Myths and realities: Social work practice and self-help groups. In M. Goroff (Ed.), *Reaping from the field—From practice to principle. Proceedings 1981, 3rd Annual Symposium for the Advancement of Social Work with Groups* (Vol I., pp. 41–48). Hebron, CT: Practitioners Press.

Toseland, R. W., & Rivas, R. F. (1984). *An introduction to group work practice.* New York: Macmillan.

Toseland, R. W., Rivas, R. F., & Chapman, D. (1984). An evaluation of decision-making methods in task groups. *Social Work, 29,* 339–346.

Toseland, R. W., Sherman, E., & Bliven, S. (1981). The comparative effectiveness of two group work approaches for the development of mutual support groups among the elderly. *Social Work with Groups, 4*(1–2), 137–153.

Trecker, H. B. (1948). *Social group work: Principles and practices.* New York: Whiteside.

Trecker, H. B. (1956). *Group work in the psychiatric setting.* New York: Whiteside and W. Morrow & Co.

Tropp, E. (1978). Whatever happened to group work? *Social Work with Groups,* 1(1), 85–94.

Vinter, R. D. (1967). The essential components of group work practice. In R. D. Vinter (Ed.), *Readings in group work practice* (pp. 3–18). Ann Arbor, MI: Ann Arbor Publications.

White, R., & Lippitt, R. (1968). Leader behavior and member reaction in three "social climates." In D. Cartwright & A. Zander (Eds.), *Group dynamics: Research and theory* (pp. 318–335). New York: Harper & Row.

Whittaker, J. K. (1985). Program activities: Their selection and use in a therapeutic milieu. In M. Sundel, P. Glasser, R. Sarri, & R. Vinter (Eds.), *Individual change through small groups* (2nd ed., pp. 237–250). New York: Free Press.

Wilson, G., & Ryland, G. (1948). *Social group work practice.* Cambridge, MA: Houghton, Mifflin.

Zander, A. (1977). *Groups at work.* San Francisco: Jossey-Bass.

# 8

# Cognitive Therapy

## Fred D. Wright, Ed.D.

*Men are disturbed not by things but by the views which they take of them.*—Epictetus (1st Century, A.D.)

Cognitive therapy is a short-term, directive, structured, active, and collaborative form of psychotherapy that is used in the treatment of depression and a wide range of psychiatric disorders. It has also been used to help people cope with other, less "clinical" problems, such as divorce, unemployment, chronic illness, and the death of a loved one.

This treatment model is based on the hypothesis that, for the most part, people's affect and behavior are influenced by their cognitions and perceptions of the world (Beck, 1967, 1972, 1976; Beck, Rush, Shaw, & Emery, 1979). Their perceptions are derived from attitudes, beliefs, and assumptions (schemas), which are developed from past experience.

The goal of cognitive therapy is to help the client identify, examine, test, and correct cognitions and schemas that are the root of current emotional, behavioral, and coping difficulties. This is achieved by a variety of cognitive techniques that are designed to teach people to: (a) monitor their thoughts; (b) recognize the impact of their cognitions on affect and behavior; (c) evaluate the validity of their cognitions; (d) learn more objective ways of viewing the world; (e) modify dysfunctional attitudes, beliefs, and assumptions.

The original work in cognitive therapy focused on the treatment of depression, which will be the thrust of this chapter. However, many of the techniques used in treating depression have also been applied to the treatment of other disorders (Beck, Emery, & Greenberg, 1985; Emery, Hollon, & Bedrosian, 1981; Freeman & Greenwood, 1987).

## THE CONCEPT OF THE PERSON AND THE HUMAN EXPERIENCE

Human experience can be seen as being on a continuum, with normal reactions to life at one end and psychopathology (e.g., depression, which is an exaggerated reaction) at the other end. The cognitive model presumes that in addition to inherited factors, certain people have a cognitive structure that predisposes them for depression. The formation of these cognitive structures begins early in life, when children identify with significant others and base their self-perceptions on their attitudes that those significant others have towards them. Once fully developed, these structures (schemas) influence perceptions of self-image, emotional life, and behavior.

The philosophical base for cognitive therapy's view of human experience has its origins in the writings of the Stoic philosophers (in particular, Seneca, Chrysippus, Epictetus, Cicero, Marcus Aurelius, and Zeno Citium), beginning about 300 B.C. These Stoics believed that human emotions and behavior are greatly influenced by ideas (beliefs, attitudes, and assumptions). This philosophy taught that people could change their feelings and behaviors merely by changing their perceptions and ideas about events.

The essential part of Stoic philosophy that is concerned with the impact of ideas upon behavior is at the root of contemporary cognitive therapy. Cognitive therapy is built upon the belief that people can learn to be more objective in their perception of the world and can thus act in a more functional manner to achieve their goals.

Walen, DiGuiseppe, and Wessler (1980) state that people have five basic goals: survival, happiness, positive affiliation with others, intimacy, and personally fulfilling endeavors. Although people strive to achieve these ends, their perceptions and distorted ideas about the world and themselves can act as stumbling blocks.

## HISTORICAL PERSPECTIVE

Cognitive therapy began to emerge as a discrete model beginning in the early 1960s. However, as mentioned in the previous section, the impact of cognitions on emotions can actually be traced back to Greek and Roman philosophies—in particular, Stoicism. The concept that one's emotions can be influenced by one's interpretations of events can also be found in other philosophies—for example, Buddhism.

The cognitive therapy model has also drawn upon some of the ideas of the early theorists: for example, Freud's concept that cognitions form a hierarchical structure (moving from primary to secondary processes), and Adler's "individual psychology," which emphasizes the importance of understanding the patient within the context of his or her own conscious experience. The impact of Freud's and Adler's ideas can be seen in present-day assumptions about the way individuals interpret their experiences. For example, perceptions and experiences are seen as active processes that involve both inspection (observing the environment) and introspection (remembering/considering past experiences).

During the late 1940s and early 1950s, there was a shift towards thinking about experiences as being *conscious* and *subjective*. This shift is exemplified in the writings of George Kelly (1955), who is recognized as being the first to clearly define the role of beliefs in behavior change. In his "fixed role therapy," Kelly detailed very specifically how other therapists might modify cognitions and behavior in a systematic manner during psychotherapy, and how this in turn would lead to more functional behavior.

Contemporary writers—for example, Mahoney (1974), Meichenbaum (1977), and Emery (1978, 1984)—have all greatly influenced the current concepts of cognitive therapy. It is far beyond the scope of this chapter to explore all of these influences. However, at this point, it is important to briefly discuss the impact of Albert Ellis. His work (1957, 1962, 1971, 1973) provided a major change in focus in the development of the cognitive therapy model. With the development of his Rational Emotive Therapy Model (RET), Ellis helped to change the therapist's traditional, passive, "listening" role into a more active, directive, goal-oriented stance.

It is commonly accepted that the present-day cognitive therapy model was crystallized by the work of Aaron T. Beck at the University of Pennsylvania, beginning in the early 1960s. Based on his own clinical work, Beck began to question a major belief in the psychoanalytic therapy of depression—the hypothesis that depressed patients generally seek "failure." He concluded that depressed patients do not actively seek failure, but rather have difficulty recognizing their successes. He further concluded that depressed patients seem to have information-processing problems and that they become preoccupied with "negative thoughts," which often lead to distortions in perceptions and an inability to process success experiences. Beck found that patients' negative thoughts are not random, but instead appear to be persistent, situation-specific, and based on well-formulated beliefs or negative biases about the self (Beck, 1963, 1964, 1967). Additional research supported the hypothesis of the relationship between cognitions and depression (Beck, 1972, 1976). Beck's conceptualizations provided a theoretical framework for the treatment of depression.

## KEY THEORETICAL CONSTRUCTS

In order to understand cognitive interventions for treating depression, the clinician must have a clear understanding of the salient points in the cognitive therapy model. According to Beck et al. (1979), the cognitive therapy model postulates three important concepts to explain the psychological foundation of depression: (a) the "cognitive triad," (b) schemas, and (c) cognitive errors.

## The Cognitive Triad

The cognitive triad consists of three important cognitive patterns regarding the patients' view of themselves, their world, and their future. The first part of the triad centers around a negative view of self. Patients see themselves as defective and lacking in the basic attributes necessary for happiness. They feel inadequate and tend to attribute misfortune to some personal defect.

The *negative view of the self* is illustrated by some of Michael Shore's statements. Michael sees himself as "scarred" and as not being able to find the "something" that he will be good at. He says, "Sometimes I feel that I should be in another country or another time zone." Generally, Michael views himself as defective and inadequate.

*A negative view about the environment* or current situation constitutes the second component of the cognitive triad. Patients focus their attention on current negative experiences and tend to view the environment as presenting insurmountable obstacles that prevent them from achieving their goals and as making unrealistic demands upon them. Patients' problem-solving abilities also appear to be hampered. Charley is a good example. He becomes anxious when he arrives home; his thoughts center on a negative view about the home. He usually stiffens as soon as he approaches the front door of the house. Charley thinks, "Will there be a problem? Will Nancy complain about bills? Will Michael come home from school beaten up? They will want me to solve the problems. But I can't."

The third component of the cognitive triad is the patients' *negative view about the future.* Depressed patients not only see themselves as defective but also believe that their depressive suffering will be unremitting and that their current difficulties will continue into the future. For instance, Rena theorizes that because she is so accustomed to living with problems and crises, she must create them when they do not exist. She sees her future as bleak and unremitting.

## Schemas

Schemas are the basic framework by which mental activity is organized. They guide the selective attention, perception, organization, storage, and retrieval of cognitions (Beck et al., 1979; Ingram & Hollon, 1986). In any situation, people are bombarded with stimuli. It would be extremely difficult to attend to all stimuli at any one point in time. Schemas determine which stimuli people attend to, how they will organize compatible and conflicting information, and which information they will have access to at some future date.

Schemas are believed to be established in early childhood. Once they have been well-established, they are difficult to alter. New conflicting data (information that seems to contradict a belief) are denied or ignored. A schema can be dormant during a person's undepressed periods and can become activated when a depressive episode has been precipitated. Once activated, the schema causes the person to distort information. The person's thinking becomes progressively more negative with regard to perceptions about self, the future, and the environment.

In Michael's case, we can assume that one of his schemas about himself centers on a negative view about the self. He sees himself as an "underdog." This view of the self would certainly tend to distort his everyday experiences and cause him to perceive, interpret, and store information in such a way that it would be consistent with his view of himself as an underdog.

## Cognitive Errors

Through cognitive errors (distortions), depressed patients maintain their negative beliefs despite contradictory evidence. Burns (1980) has summarized many of the distortions patients use to defend their negative biases:

1. *All-or-nothing thinking* refers to people's tendency to perceive themselves and their experiences in extremes: They are either all good or all bad. Some of Nancy's views about Charley could be considered all-or-nothing thinking (e.g., funny/not funny, ambitious/not ambitious).

2. *Overgeneralization* occurs when a person takes a single negative event and concludes that it will continue to happen in a never-ending pattern. For example, Rena dropped out of high school and later dropped out of college. At this point, she probably believes not only that this will be a never-ending pattern but also that, throughout her life, she will be looking for an excuse to "mess up."

3. *Mental filtering* occurs whenever a person isolates one negative part of a situation and focuses attention solely on that detail. Say, for example, that Charley made a timing mistake with one of his jokes

during a comedy routine. He would probably focus on the mistake and ignore the fact that his overall performance was good and that he was well-accepted by the audience.

4. *Disqualifying the positive* occurs when positive experiences are seen as "not counting." The significance of an event is evaluated as trivial, even though an objective assessment does not warrant this conclusion. Rena dropped out of high school. However, she did go on to receive her GED (high school equivalency certificate) and was accepted in a pre-med program. Judging from the case reports, we can say that Rena disqualified these accomplishments, and thus she was still able to see herself "mess up."

5. *Jumping to conclusions* occurs when a person arbitrarily comes to a negative conclusion about a situation, even though there is no evidence to support that conclusion. Nancy's reservation about being interviewed grew out of her jumping to the conclusion that "After it's done, I will probably run from social worker to social worker, trying to do everything suggested."

6. *Magnification* or *minimization* occurs whenever people make mistakes and then exaggerate the importance of the error (i.e., they take commonplace negative events and catastrophize about the consequences) or they minimize their ability to cope with problems. Although it is not clear in the case study, we could assume that if Nancy has true panic attacks, she catastrophizes about the physical sensations associated with panic (racing heart, sweating, tension, dizziness, etc.) and she minimizes her ability to cope with these anxious symptoms: "Unable to leave the house, she chain-smokes and imagines the worst of all possible outcomes."

7. *Emotional reasoning* denotes the way in which people describe or interpret events according to their emotional states. (The standard example of this is a person who feels guilty, and then concludes, "I must have done something wrong.") In our case example, Charley might think that because he feels great after a performance, he must have done well. When she is outside the house, Nancy "feels" that people are making disparaging remarks about her, and therefore stays at home where she feels safe.

8. *Labeling* and *mislabeling* occur when people describe an error in behavior as a permanent human characteristic. For example, a person who does something stupid labels himself or herself "stupid," instead of recognizing that the act itself was stupid. Rena's parents labeled her lazy when she dropped out of high school, and they did not look for an alternative explanation for her behavior. Subsequently, they continued to label her as lazy whenever she failed to finish anything.

9. *Personalization* refers to a person's tendency to think that everything people do or say is some kind of reaction to him or her. The person feels unduly responsible for negative events in his or her life. When Charley comes home in the evening, it is with the anticipation that there will be a problem waiting for him. If Nancy feels angry when he arrives, we could guess that Charley would personalize this incident. Nancy might be angry at the children or at someone else, but Charley's initial response would be, "She's angry at me."

## ASSESSMENT

There are some objective tests that can be used to help patients to identify subtle beliefs about themselves. One commonly used instrument is the Dysfunctional Attitude Scale (DAS). Weissman (1979) developed this scale to assess common assumptions or beliefs that may serve as negative schemas by which individuals construe their life experiences. In clinical practice, the DAS can be used to uncover negative schemas that people may not be able to articulate in the therapy session. For example, one item from the DAS (to which the client is asked to note his or her level of agreement or disagreement) states, "I should be happy all the time." The response gives the clinician important information about the client's extreme, rigid belief structure regarding happiness. This could then be an important clue to the understanding of the depressed client's symptom of hopelessness when feeling sad.

The therapist can also ask patients direct questions about their beliefs. One technique for doing this would be to ask the patients to write down their positive and negative views about themselves.

In our assessment of patients, we would also want to know the severity of their depression. The Beck Depression Inventory (BDI) could help determine the level of the depression. The BDI (Beck et al., 1979) consists of 21 items, each composed of four statements that reflect gradations in the intensity of a particular depressive symptom. All of the members of the Shore family would score moderately high on this scale. For instance, Nancy reports that she has gained weight, is having trouble sleeping, and can't concentrate. All of these symptoms are addressed by various items on the BDI.

These instruments should only be used to supplement a thorough psychological evaluation that would also assess psychotic processes, level of intellectual functioning, and organic impairment. Standard diagnostic tests such as the Minnesota Multiphasic Personality Inventory (MMPI), the Wechsler Scales, the Rorschach, and neuropsychological test batteries would be appropriate.

## TREATMENT OF CHOICE

Under ideal conditions, clients who are entering a course of treatment in cognitive therapy should be able to accomplish five separate tasks. This is not to say that the clients *must* do these things. However, the more tasks that the clients are able to accomplish, the more the likelihood of success within the cognitive treatment model.

First, clients should be able to monitor their cognitions. They have to be able to pay attention to their own internal dialogues and images—to "think about their thinking."

Second, clients should be able to collaborate with the therapist in defining the problem areas and setting therapy goals. They should understand the rationale of the treatment model.

Third, clients should be able to work on their problem outside the therapy session. Therapeutic work should not end when clients leave the therapist's office. An important part of the cognitive treatment model is the "homework" between therapy sessions, which gives clients an opportunity to experiment with new skills.

Fourth, clients must be able to pay attention to the therapist and the activities that are happening in the therapy session. Clients should have the capacity to focus on one issue at a time. Cognitive therapy interventions would be extremely difficult if, because of psychotic processes, the client could not focus and was severely confused.

Fifth, clients should have the intellectual capacity to reason and to understand the relationship between thoughts, feelings, and behavior. At the beginning of therapy, many clients are unaware of this connection, but they come to appreciate it later in their therapy. If, after several sessions, a client still is unaware of this connection (the interaction among thoughts, feelings, and behaviors), the therapist needs to assess the efficacy of continuing to use cognitive therapy with that particular client.

It is clear that all the members of the Shore family could benefit from therapy, and they should probably be seen in family therapy. Although it appears from the case history that Nancy and Rena would be good candidates for cognitive therapy, Rena seems to be the best suited. She has a willingness to talk: "She is happy to be interviewed because she says she needs to talk about 'this stuff.' " Rena is introspective and has agreed to go to therapy. She is in the habit of monitoring her thoughts and writing them down in her journal, which is consistent with cognitive therapy techniques.

## THE THERAPEUTIC PROCESS

Therapists who are engaged in cognitive therapy for the treatment of depression must first have a good understanding of the clinical syndrome of depression.* As with the practice of any form of psychotherapy, the cognitive therapist must have the basic therapeutic skills of empathy, genuineness, positive regard, active listening, and Socratic questioning. Therapists should make every effort not to lose sight of the importance of the client-therapist relationship. Harrison and Beck (1982) contend that novice therapists often become so concerned with technique that they sometimes fail to attend to the therapeutic relationship. Even though problems such as depression are associated with a particular set of clinical signs and symptoms, therapists should look upon each client as having his or her own idiosyncratic pattern of behaviors and symptoms.

## The Course of Treatment

The following is a description of what should ideally happen during the first 20 sessions of therapy. This outline has been adapted from the research protocol for outcome studies developed at the Center for Cognitive Therapy in Philadelphia (Beck et al., 1979).

*First therapy session*

The early establishment of rapport is crucial. This process should include a discussion of the clients' expectations and their attitudes about cognitive therapy, therapists, and becoming active participants in their own treatment. For example, if Nancy were the patient, the therapist would want her to take an active part in deciding which problems will be focused on first. Early on, the therapist and the patient should identify the most urgent and accessible problems. Because of the high suicide risk among severely depressed patients, therapists should pay particular attention to signs of hopelessness, suicidal ideation, severe loss of function, and extreme unhappiness. In the first session, it is also important that the therapist use every opportunity to educate the client about the cognitive therapy model. Clarification of the relationship between cognitions, emotions, and behavior will help the patient understand the rationale for the different treatment strategies that will be introduced in later sessions. This would be an easy task for Rena. As previously mentioned, she is introspective and is in the habit of writing down her thoughts.

As part of the cognitive therapy "socialization" process, the therapist should describe the structure of the therapy sessions, the frequency and length of the sessions, the nature of homework assignments, the use of objective mood checks like the Beck Depression Inventory (Beck, Ward,

---

* Although, as noted before, this chapter primarily discusses the treatment of depression, many of the concepts can carry over into the treatment of other problems.

Mendelson, Mock, & Erbaugh, 1961) and the Beck Anxiety Checklist (Beck & Steer, 1980), and the importance of patient–therapist collaboration. It is also helpful to discuss any reading assignments that may be part of the therapy—for example, *Coping with Depression* (Beck & Greenberg, 1974), *Coping with Anxiety* (Beck & Emery, 1979), and *Feeling Good* (Burns, 1980). Finally, the therapist should summarize the first session and elicit feedback from the client in order to assess the client's understanding of the therapeutic process.

*Second therapy session*

The therapist should begin by establishing an agenda and agreeing, with the client, upon the goals for that particular session. The topics should be stated concretely and should be focused on the specific tasks and purposes of therapy. (This is especially helpful for depressed clients, who often feel overwhelmed by their problems and find it difficult to focus on one problem.) There should be a short review of the last session and an "update" about the activities between the sessions. It is also important to review the homework from the previous session and to once again review the cognitive therapy model.

At this point, the client's presenting problem should be clearly defined in behavioral terms. Therapists often hear about broad, vague problems; for example, a client says, "I am feeling depressed." It is important to understand each client's idiosyncratic meaning for "feeling depressed." A typical way of eliciting this information is to ask, "Since you have been depressed, what changes have you noticed in your behavior?" If Nancy were to be asked this, she would probably answer that she has gained weight, is having sleep problems, has trouble concentrating, and often forgets things. Rena feels lonely and confused. These symptoms need to be defined in more behavioral terms: for example, "Because I'm lonely and confused, I have withdrawn from people and spend most of my time in my room."

Once all the problems have been behaviorally defined, the focus should turn to a specific problem, and the therapist should present a rationale for an intervention. A distinction should be made between skill problems and psychological problems; depression can be attributed to a psychological problem, a skill deficit, or a combination of both. For example, Nancy's sleep problem could be psychological—she has a tendency to stay awake at night worrying about not being able to sleep. Skill problems might include her consuming too much caffeine, taking midday naps, and trying to fall asleep when she is not tired. In Rena's case her confusion could be due to her spending too much time being introspective ("[she] spends hours wondering about why she is the way she is") and not spending enough time focusing on her external environment. In most cases, there is a combination of psychological and skill problems. At the end of this session, there should be an assignment of homework and a summing up of the session.

## Third therapy session

The remaining therapy sessions should adhere to the following general format: (a) set agenda; (b) feedback about the last session; (c) mood checks since therapy session; (d) review of previous week's homework; (e) patient-therapist summary of current therapy session; and (f) discussion and assignment of homework.

Once the client has a clear understanding of the relationship between cognitions, feelings, and behavior, he or she should be helped to develop the habit of monitoring, examining, and responding to negative automatic thoughts and beliefs. This begins with the client's periodically writing down his or her negative thoughts. Nancy could be asked to write down what thoughts go through her mind when she can't sleep. Rena is already doing this, but we might want her to start noticing the feelings that are associated with certain thoughts.

Role-playing various problem situations is a powerful technique to help patients identify their automatic thoughts. For example, Charley might be asked to role-play the situation in which his lying to Nancy maintained a strain on the relationship. During the role-play, the therapist could ask, "What thoughts were going through your mind at that point, just before you lied to Nancy?" The relationship between Charley's cognitions, his feelings, and his subsequent behavior (lying) could then be pointed out.

## Fourth therapy session

The same general format should be continued. Now, however, more emphasis should be placed on examining negative automatic thoughts. If the patient has monitored his or her negative automatic thoughts correctly, the thoughts can be examined together and the therapist should point out how many of the thoughts are distortions and how they are exacerbating many of the depressive systems. Nancy's negative thought that people make disparaging remarks about her is one that the therapist would certainly want her to examine. How has she come to the conclusion that people are talking about her? Is this a fact, or is it a cognitive distortion?

## Fifth therapy session

During this session, the therapist should demonstrate the systematic method of evaluating and correcting cognitive distortions. A helpful way

of doing this is by using the Daily Record of Dysfunctional Thoughts.*
Clients use this form to record a brief description of the situation that
is causing the difficulty, the emotions that they are experiencing, and
their thoughts about the situation. Finally, these thoughts are examined
in a systematic fashion, and the cognitive errors and distortions are
identified. Rational responses are developed for coping with these negative
automatic thoughts. Is Nancy "jumping to conclusions" when she says
to herself that people are making negative remarks about her? (A detailed
method for examining these negative thoughts is outlined in the "Cognitive Therapy Techniques" section of this chapter.)

### Sixth through 12th therapy sessions

After clients have learned to monitor, examine, and respond rationally
to negative automatic thoughts, the therapist should discuss dysfunctional
attitudes, beliefs, and schemas. A hypothesis about the origin and rationale
for changing these beliefs is included in the discussion. From our case
study, it would be easy to understand the origin of Rena's belief that
she is "lazy."

### Thirteenth through 20th therapy sessions

During this period, discussion includes termination of therapy, the
continuation of homework assignments, the anticipation of potential
problems after termination, rehearsals of coping strategies, and a review
of the techniques used during the course of therapy.

## Cognitive Therapy Techniques

The following is a brief overview of the major cognitive therapy
techniques:

### Collaborative empiricism

One feature that sets cognitive therapy apart from most other clinical
forms of psychotherapy is the formal structure that allows collaboration
between patient and therapist. As Beck et al. (1979) stated, the structure
of cognitive therapy engages the patient's participation and collaboration.
This is particularly important with depressed patients who are initially
confused, preoccupied, or distracted. Although it may be difficult to do,
cognitive therapists should attempt to get the patient actively engaged

---

* This form can be obtained from the Center for Cognitive Therapy, Room 602, 133 S. 36th
Street, Philadelphia, PA 19104.

in various therapeutic operations—for example, planning treatment, setting agendas, scheduling activities, testing hypotheses, and creating homework assignments.

## Client education

Understanding the influence of cognitions is the cornerstone of this therapy. How patients learn this is dependent upon the therapist's own creativity and style. Patients can be asked to read such books as *Feeling Good: The New Mood Therapy* (Burns, 1980), or the therapist can use didactic presentations such as a brief clinical definition of cognitions. However, the use of Socratic questioning is one of the preferred methods. For example, patients can be asked how they were feeling while sitting in the waiting room prior to the session. Most patients respond that they felt anxious. Next, the therapist can ask what thoughts they were having while waiting and if there is a possible connection between those thoughts and subsequent anxious feelings.

## Monitoring automatic thoughts

After the client has an understanding of cognitions, the next step is to help him or her be more aware of the presence of automatic thoughts and images. For instance, the client learns to treat negative feelings as a cue to look for these automatic thoughts and images. The client should strive to "catch" these cognitions when they are happening and to write them down as soon as possible. If it is not practical to write them down immediately, the client should spend 15 minutes at the end of the day recording upsetting thoughts.

## Testing negative cognitions

All cognitions should be examined for accuracy. A systematic analysis of cognitions includes four basic questions about negative automatic thoughts or images: (a) What is the evidence that these thoughts or images are true? (b) Is there another way of looking at this? (In other words, do I literally mean what I am saying to myself?) (c) If these thoughts and images are true, what are the *realistic* consequences? (d) If these thoughts are true, what are the disadvantages of repeating these things to myself?

*Graded task assignments.* Depressed clients tend to avoid tasks or activities that would be emotionally rewarding. For example, Nancy, who stays at home, is often depressed and anxious. Finding a job would most likely improve her mood. Therefore, it would be helpful to get her to do some tasks that lead in the direction of accomplishing that goal, with the notion that *any* act leading in that direction would motivate her to do more. Encouraging her to get up early, get dressed, and then look through the "want ads" would be an example of a graded task assignment that might eventually lead to employment.

## LIMITATIONS OF THE MODEL

A large number of studies have demonstrated the effectiveness of cognitive therapy for the treatment of depression. Some studies have demonstrated the efficacy of cognitive therapy in the treatment of anxiety disorder, social anxiety, test anxiety, and chronic pain. Those suffering with psychotic depression and melancholia, however, have been shown to be relatively insensitive to this therapy.

Nevertheless, it appears that, in most cases, the model is only limited by the personal characteristics of the client. The client should be "psychologically minded" and have a willingness to objectively examine thoughts, feelings, and behavior. In addition, the client must be willing to test long-held beliefs and must have the motivation to change.

## RESEARCH

Rush, Beck, Kovacs, and Hollon (1977) conducted the first major study on the efficacy of cognitive therapy. They compared cognitive therapy with the use of a tricyclic antidepressant, which until that point was the accepted treatment of choice for depression. The study demonstrated that cognitive therapy could be more effective than medication in reducing the depressive symptoms. In addition, the follow-up study suggested that patients treated with cognitive therapy tended to maintain their reduction in depressive symptoms for a longer time than those who received antidepressant medication alone (Kovacs, Rush, Beck, & Hollon, 1981). In the initial outcome finding of a recent National Institute of Mental Health (NIMH) study (Elkins, 1986), cognitive therapy was shown to be just as effective as antidepressant medication (imipramine) in reducing depressive symptoms. This is a very important finding, since many depressed patients are not able to take antidepressant medications because of adverse side effects.

Emery et al. (1981) and Freeman and Greenwood (1987) have written about the clinical use of cognitive therapy with many different types of disorders and with a variety of populations of patients. However, it should be noted that controlled studies on the efficacy of cognitive therapy for treatment disorders other than depression have only started emerging in the past few years. One new area of interest is the use of cognitive therapy in treating panic; some of the preliminary findings on the efficacy of treating this disorder are already encouraging (Beck, 1986a, 1986b).

## SUMMARY

The purpose of this chapter has been to provide a brief introduction to the cognitive therapy model, particularly the cognitive therapy of depression. At this point, I shall summarize the most important basic concepts that are at the heart of the model:

1. Collaboration between therapist and client is unique and central to the therapeutic process. Together, client and therapist define the problem areas and decide on interventions that will be attempted. The client and therapist must have a clear understanding of where they are going in therapy and how they are going to get there.
2. Cognitive therapy strives to help the client become more self-exploring and more skillful in the techniques developed in therapy. The goal is for clients to become their own therapists.
3. Cognitive therapy is structured and goal-directed. Initially, its primary concern is symptom relief. Later, the focus is shifted to the modification of certain schemas to reduce the client's vulnerability to emotional and behavioral problems.
4. Activity is a valued component of cognitive therapy. Therapists encourage their clients to try new forms of behaviors and coping strategies. Although identifying and understanding problems is important, taking active steps to correct problems is primary.

The information in this chapter is only an introduction to an exciting new area of therapy. Cognitive therapy is gaining popularity at a rapid rate in the United States and overseas. In 1983, the International Congress of Cognitive Therapy was held in Philadelphia, but the Second World Congress of Cognitive Therapy, in 1986, was in Umea, Sweden. Currently, there are over 15 training centers for cognitive therapy. The largest research and training program is at the Center for Cognitive Therapy, associated with the University of Pennsylvania in Philadelphia. Two professional journals are devoted exclusively to cognitive therapy: *Cognitive Therapy and Research* and *Journal of Cognitive Psychotherapy*.

Of all the cognitive therapy models, the model described on these pages is the most systematic, conceptually well developed, and well researched.

Cognitive therapy has made a major contribution to the treatment of depression. Within the next five years we should see the same type of impact on the treatment of anxiety—in particular, the treatment of panic disorder. It is especially exciting to look even beyond the next five years where cognitive therapy holds the promise of utility for a vast array of psychological disorders and problems in living.

## REFERENCES

Beck, A. T. (1963). Thinking and depression: I. Idiosyncratic content and cognitive distortions. *Archives of General Psychiatry, 9,* 324–333.

Beck, A. T. (1964). Thinking and depression: II. Theory and therapy. *Archives of General Psychiatry, 10,* 561–571.

Beck, A. T. (1967). *Depression: Clinical, experimental, and theoretical aspects.* New York: Harper & Row.

Beck, A. T. (1972). *Depression: Causes and treatment.* Philadelphia: University of Pennsylvania Press.

Beck, A. T. (1976). *Cognitive therapy and the emotional disorders.* New York: International Universities Press.

Beck, A. T. (1986a, May). *Cognitive approaches to panic disorders.* Paper presented at the Meeting of the American Psychiatric Association, Washington, DC.

Beck, A. T. (1986b, June). *Cognitive approaches to panic disorders: Theory and therapy.* Paper presented in NIMH Conference on Cognitive Aspects of Panic Disorders, Bethesda, MD.

Beck, A. T., & Emery, G. (1979). *Coping with anxiety* (a booklet). Philadelphia: Center for Cognitive Therapy.

Beck, A. T., Emery, G., & Greenberg, R. (1985). *Anxiety disorders and phobias: A cognitive perspective.* New York: Basic Books.

Beck, A. T., & Greenberg, R. L. (1974). *Coping with depression* (a booklet). New York: Institute for Rational Living.

Beck, A. T., Rush, A. J., Shaw, B. F., & Emery, G. (1979). *Cognitive therapy of depression.* New York: Guilford Press.

Beck, A. T., & Steer, R. A. (1980). *Beck anxiety checklist.* Unpublished manuscript, Center for Cognitive Therapy, University of Pennsylvania, Philadelphia, PA.

Beck, A. T., Ward, C. H., Mendelson, M., Mock, J., & Erbaugh, J. (1961). An inventory for measuring depression. *Archives of General Psychiatry, 4,* 561–571.

Burns, D. (1980). *Feeling good: The new mood therapy.* New York: William Morris & Co.

Elkins, I. (1986, May). *NIMH Treatment of Depression Collaborative Research Program: Initial Outcome Findings.* Paper presented at the meeting of the American Psychiatric Association, Washington, DC.

Ellis, A. (1957). Outcome of employing three techniques of psychotherapy. *Journal of Clinical Psychology, 13,* 344–350.

Ellis, A. (1962). *Reason and emotion in psychotherapy.* New York: Lyle Stuart.

Ellis, A. (1971). *Growth through reason.* N. Hollywood, CA: Wilshire Books.

Ellis, A. (1973). *Humanistic psychotherapy.* New York: Crow Publishers and McGraw-Hill Paperback.

Emery, G. (1978). Cognitive vs. behavioral methods in weight reduction with college students (Doctoral dissertation, University of Pennsylvania, 1977). *Dissertation Abstracts International, 38,* 5563B-5564B. (University Microfilms No. 7806578)

Emery, G. (1984). *Own your own life.* New York: Signet.

Emery, G., Hollon, S. D., & Bedrosian, R. C. (1981). *New directions in cognitive therapy.* New York: Guilford Press.

Freeman, A., & Greenwood, V. (Eds.). (1987). *Cognitive therapy: Applications in psychiatric and medical settings.* New York: Human Sciences Press.

Harrison, R. P., & Beck, A. T. (1982). Cognitive therapy for depression: Historical development, basic concepts, and procedures. In P. A. Keller (Ed.), *Innovations in clinical practice: A sourcebook* (Vol. 1, pp. 37–52). Sarasota, FL: Professional Resource Exchange.

Ingram, R. E., & Hollon, S. D. (1986). Cognitive therapy of depression from an information processing perspective. In R. E. Ingram (Ed.), *Information processing approaches to clinical psychology* (pp. 259–281). New York: Academic Press.

Kelly, G. (1955). *The psychology of personal constructs* (Vol. 1 & 2). New York: Norton & Co.

Kovacs, M., Rush, A. J., Beck, A. T., & Hollon, S. D. (1981). Depressed patients treated with cognitive therapy or pharmacotherapy. *Archives of General Psychiatry, 38,* 33–39.

Mahoney, M. J. (1974). *Cognition and behavior modification.* Cambridge, MA: Ballinger.

Meichenbaum, D. B. (1977). *Cognitive-behavior modification: An integrative approach.* New York: Plenum.

Rush, A. J., Beck, A. T., Kovacs, M., & Hollon, S. D. (1977). Comparative efficacy of cognitive therapy and imipramine in the treatment of depressed outpatients. *Cognitive Therapy and Research, 1,* 17–37.

Walen, S. R., DiGuiseppe, R., & Wessler, R. L. (1980). *A practitioner's guide to rational-emotive therapy.* New York: Oxford University Press.

Weissman, A. W. (1979). The Dysfunctional Attitude Scale: A validation study (Doctoral dissertation, University of Pennsylvania). *Dissertation Abstracts International, 40,* 1389–1390B.

# 9

# Brief Task-Centered Treatment

*William J. Reid, D.S.W.*

The task-centered approach is one of a large variety of planned, brief forms of treatment. In presenting the model, I shall give special attention to its short-term aspects, not only because they are an important feature of the model, but also because this is one of the few chapters in this book that deals with an approach that is brief and time-limited by design. In describing the short-term features of the model, I will highlight those shared with other brief forms of therapy.

## THE CONCEPT OF THE PERSON AND THE HUMAN EXPERIENCE

The task-centered model takes the optimistic view that people can learn to cope with and solve their problems. Granted, there is much more to life than struggling with difficulties, but because our interest here is centered on the people who find themselves in such struggles, our focus will be on the way in which social organizations and their practitioners can help people who are grappling with problems. In practice, organizations can relate to only a fraction of the unending stream of problems, but that fraction is of critical importance not only to the multitude of clients who receive help but also to the rest of society.

Generally, problems that clients bring to agencies (or that the community, through its agencies, brings to the clients' doorsteps) are embedded in larger contexts—individual, family, community, or societal systems. Although it is important to understand the role that these contexts play in the formulation of problems, it is the problems themselves that the helping agencies can most *efficiently* deal with. The agencies' capacity to bring about significant contextual change is limited, even though such change may be desirable (and sometimes attainable) as a means of fostering the resolution of problems and of preventing their recurrence.

Whenever problems disrupt the adaptive equilibrium that has been achieved between clients and their environments, coping efforts become activated. These efforts are likely to diminish when the problem has been significantly managed or when an adaptation has been made to its continued presence. When these coping efforts of clients or environments are already present, or if they can be activated, the helping system can provide useful, often decisive pushes towards the resolution of the problem. In the process, the contexts of the problems may be stimulated toward corrective change.

In the task-centered model, the focus is on people in their roles as both clients and helpers—and on what happens when they come together. Although this approach does not set forth a broad philosophy of the human condition, it nevertheless provides assumptions that can undergird one's practice.

## HISTORICAL PERSPECTIVE

The task-centered model grew out of the short-term therapy movement of the 1960s. Influences that stimulated interest in short-term models included shortages of mental health professionals, long waiting lists of people who needed treatment, dissatisfaction with the accomplishments of long-term treatment, evaluations that showed promising results from brief interventions, and growing interest in crisis theory.

Although this movement first became a significant force during the 1960s, short-term practice has a much longer history. Some of Freud's earliest cases, for example, were short-term (Malan, 1963). The works of Alexander and French (1946) and Grinker and Spiegel (1944) represented further developments in the history of brief therapy in psychiatry. In social work, noteworthy contributions were made by the functional school of social work (Taft, 1933) and exponents of "short contact" casework (Lowry, 1948; Reynolds, 1932).

In the 1960s, however, developments accelerated rapidly with the emergence of short-term models that reflected a variety of different theoretical and clinical orientations: for example, psychodynamic (Malan, 1963; Sifneos, 1967; Wolberg, 1965); Rogerian (Shlien, 1966); crisis theory (Parad & Parad, 1968); and family therapy (Kaffman, 1965). Short-term adaptations for work with different client populations began to appear (Hare, 1963; Murray & Smitson, 1963; Normand, Fensterheim, & Schrenzel, 1967).

The various short-term models that emerged during this period not only developed from different parent theories but also defined "brevity" differently. Although most models limited service, at the outset, to a certain number or range of sessions, there was considerable variation in what was considered short-term. For example, Malan's (1963) short-term psychoanalytically oriented therapy was limited to 21 sessions. By contrast, several approaches used as few as six sessions. Most models fell between these extremes. Regardless of limits called for in a model, there was agreement that treatment that was limited by design should not be confused with treatment that was open-ended and designed to be long-term but that turned out to be short because of early termination by the client. In this chapter, "short-term" or "brief" will indicate treatment in which brevity was planned; "open-ended" or "long-term" will be used interchangeably to denote treatment that has no predetermined end point and which by design calls for a duration beyond the limits of most planned short-term treatment models.

The task-centered approach grew out of a psychoanalytically oriented short-term model developed at the Community Service Society (CSS) in New York City in the early 1960s. This model, which provided eight weekly sessions, was compared in a randomized experiment with long-term, open-ended treatment within the same theoretical orientation. The results actually favored the shorter service, even after the findings of a six-month follow-up were taken into account (Reid & Shyne, 1969).

In implementing the short-term service, the practitioners made use of a strategy that is common to many brief treatment approaches: They focused on key specific problems early in the case; developed shared, specific goals with clients; and actively helped clients achieve those goals. This promising short-term service model was used as a basis for developing the task-centered approach. Results of the experiment had suggested that even though the brief treatment compared favorably to longer-term service, there was still considerable room for improvement, especially in the degree of change in the client's problems. What appeared to be strengths of the model—for example, its focus on specific problems— had been more the result of an imposition of durational limits than the product of a well-articulated design. In common with other models in use at the time (and with some still being used), the short-term model tested at the Community Service Society was a truncated version of an approach that presumed that a lengthy period of assessment and treatment was needed before meaningful progress could be achieved.

Using the CSS model as a base, in the late 1960s Laura Epstein and I attempted to develop a more systematic, effective brief treatment design, one that had its own theoretical framework and was open to a broader range of interventions than those found within psychoanalytically oriented practice. Our preliminary formulation (Reid & Epstein, 1972) was particularly influenced by Perlman's (1957) view of casework as a problem-solving process, Studt's (1968) notion of the client's task as a focus of service, and the theory and techniques of crisis intervention.

Since its inception, the task-centered system has continued to grow and change. In fact, our intent was to create an approach to practice that would continue to evolve in response to continuing research and developments in knowledge and technology that were consonant with its basic principles. The model was designed to be an open, pluralistic practice system that would be able to integrate theoretical and technical contributions from diverse sources. In keeping with this feature, the model is not wedded to any particular theory of human functioning or to any fixed set of intervention methods. Rather, it provides a core of value premises, theory, and methods that can be augmented by compatible approaches.

During the past decade, the model not only has evolved in response to developments in theory and method but also has been adapted for a variety of settings and populations. Major sources for development of the model as a whole include learning theory and related behavioral techniques, cognitive theory and methods, structural family therapy, and other family therapy approaches. Variations of the model have been devised for work with groups (Fortune, 1985; Garvin, 1974; Rooney, 1977) and family units (Fortune, 1985; Reid, 1985) and as a method of agency management (Parihar, 1983). During the course of this evolution, the model has maintained a social work focus, attentive to the distinctive functions and needs of that profession.

## KEY THEORETICAL CONSTRUCTS

In this model, it is assumed that short-term modalities have a broad range of application because they provide a "good fit" to the episodic, short-lived nature of most problem change. Service that is long by design may reach a point of diminishing returns if it extends beyond these change episodes; moreover, it runs the risk of fostering complicated dependency relationships between clients and the helping system.

According to the task-centered approach, change is most likely to occur if clients and their environments are involved, or can become involved, in active "problem-coping" and problem-solving efforts. Therefore, an effective therapeutic strategy consists of helping clients clarify what they see as troubling them and then guiding and fostering the problem-solving actions of both clients and their environments.

Help is offered within a caring relationship that eschews hidden agendas on the part of the practitioner. A premium is placed on helping clients devise and implement solutions to problems as they define them.

Although practitioners provide leadership in response to clients' needs, they view clients as collaborators in a joint effort to reach mutually agreed-upon goals through explicit means. As a result, clients should benefit not only from alleviation of their problems but also from an enhancement of their problem-solving skills and capacities.


## ASSESSMENT

Assessment in the task-centered approach is problem-centered, as it is in most short-term models. The first step in assessment is explicating what is troubling the clients and what they want to do about it.


### Principles and Techniques

By focusing on the clients' own constructions of their problems, practitioners avoid imposing their own definitions of the difficulty on the clients. At the same time, the practitioners do not assume that the clients' initial complaints are automatically the problems that are troubling them. During the process of problem exploration and specification, practitioners need to be sensitive to unspoken agendas and unexpressed feelings. In response to practitioners' clarifying efforts, clients' perceptions of the difficulty may then emerge. In this process, practitioners may point out difficulties that clients have not yet acknowledged.

In some cases, the practitioner must relate to "involuntary" clients who are not seeking help but who have presented problems that are of concern to the community, such as child abuse or delinquent behavior. With such clients, the practitioner's beginning point is the "mandated problem," that is, the reason for their meeting. Although constrained to pursue this problem, the practitioner still attempts to help the client identify concerns that are in accord with the interests of both the client and the community (Rooney, 1981; Rzepnicki, 1985).

Coming to terms with the client about what problems will constitute the focus of work is the first and most essential step of assessment. Although, as the service proceeds, these problems may later be redefined, their initial "formulation" or expression provides direction for further assessment activity.

Once the initial problem formulation has been completed, a great deal will have been learned about the clients and their problems. This information is incorporated into a more systematic explanation of identified problems and their contexts. We are interested in hearing about the clients' views of when, how, and why these problems appeared and developed; we are especially interested in learning about events that caused clients to seek help in dealing with them. How have clients coped with the problems until now? What has worked, and what hasn't?

Exploration then proceeds from the problems outward into *context*. The context of a problem is made up of the causes that maintain it (i.e., obstacles to its resolution), as well as the resources that can be brought to bear in working on it. Contextual factors are organized in a multisystems framework that includes physical, cognitive, family, and community systems.

These domains are not examined comprehensively, but rather are examined in relation to the target problems. Additional data may be obtained through standardized instruments, which may be problem specific, such as the Beck Depression Inventory (Beck, 1967), or more general instruments, such as the Family Assessment Device (Epstein, Baldwin, & Bishop, 1983).

These assessment processes dominate the first session—and, in some cases, the second and third sessions as well. As the focus shifts towards intervention, the assessment process continues to be used to monitor the status of the target problems and the relevant obstacles and resources that are involved in the resolution of those problems.


## Application to the Shores

Application to the Shore family must be based on certain assumptions about the problems the family or its members might bring for help. As an example, we shall assume that the problems relate to Michael. Let us further suppose that the referral was made by the school and was occasioned by Michael's "bizarre" behavior, which, according to school officials, would need to change before he could be returned to a regular school setting. It is likely that Mrs. Shore, who devotes "80% of her worrying time" to the boy, would be receptive to the referral.

When we are dealing with a child's problems, we generally try to work with the parents and child as a unit. Consequently, Mr. and Mrs. Shore and Michael would be seen together in the first joint session. Because the presenting problem did not involve her, Rena would not be asked to attend, although, depending on the focus of treatment, she could be brought in later.

The parents' view of the problem is elicited first. In this instance, Michael's school difficulties would be taken up initially (because the referral was from the school). However, other family concerns might later be explored in a similar manner. Quite possibly, Michael's relationship with his father would be raised as an issue, probably by Mrs. Shore. Other problems discussed in the case material might be brought up as well.

After a "problem survey" has been completed, the practitioner then attempts to identify the problematic issues contained in the raw material of the discussion. In doing so, he or she tries to pull together the family members' expressed concerns in succinct statements, using concrete language the family can understand.

Without doing violence to the family's perceptions, the practitioner tries to put the problems in the most "solvable" form possible. Therefore, interactional formulations are used when family members "locate" problems in each other. For example, Michael and Mr. Shore might blame each other for things that have gone wrong in their joint activities. The practitioner might formulate their problem as their difficulty in getting along when they try to do things together.

Family members are then asked to rank the problems in terms of the order in which they would like to see them solved. With the help of interactional formulations, consensus can usually be achieved on the problems that family members regard as important to work on. Up to three problems are then selected, explored, and specified in detail. During this process, an effort is made to help clients pinpoint their difficulties. For example, what specifically does Michael do that he thinks is silly? How often does this behavior occur? What actually happens between Michael and his father?

Recent examples of the problem are elicited and examined in detail. In addition to brief histories of the problems and the clients' efforts to cope with them, data on contextual factors are gathered. In the present case, these might include a history of Michael's school adjustment and his physical condition, as well as Mr. Shore's employment situation and his psychiatric hospitalization. Some topics might be taken up with the parents alone, depending upon the parents' concern about Michael's being present. Because the parents are fairly open and expressive, a good deal of contextual information about the Shore family will likely be brought out in the course of problem exploration—perhaps as much information as is needed at this point. Like the Shores, most voluntary clients have their own ideas about what might have a bearing on their problems and will bring them out in the initial interview. These revelations (or sometimes what is not revealed) provide the practitioner with leads for further exploration.

When a problem involves the community (in this case, Michael's school), the practitioner may wish to get information from collaterals before completing problem specification. Data from school personnel (as in the present case), child-protective workers, probation officers, and the like can be important in determining the specifics of the problem.

In short-term approaches, there is usually some form of explicit agreement with the client about the duration of service and about the problems or goals to be worked on. The structure of planned brief service almost requires this kind of initial understanding, which in recent years has been referred to as a *contract*. In the task-centered model, formal contracting usually begins after the problems have been ranked and explored. The *process* of contracting—that is, conducting the intervention according to a series of explicit agreements that are subject to modification—is emphasized, rather than the contract itself.

In the usual practice of the model, the specification of the problem is followed by clarification of goals—that is, the kind of solutions that clients hope to achieve. Often these goals simply call for some degree of problem reduction. In the Shore case, for example, a goal might be that Michael and his father get along better. Sometimes, however, the goals are more specific. For instance, a possible goal might be Michael's return to a regular classroom situation, although this goal would need to be developed in conjunction with the school.

Agreement on problems and goals is followed by an understanding about service duration. Usually, the practitioner suggests a fixed number of sessions within a range of 8 to 12. A fixed number of sessions (in effect, a deadline) helps mobilize the efforts of both practitioner and client towards the achievement of goals. It is also understood that extensions are possible; I will return to this topic in *Problems and Issues* below.

## TREATMENT OF CHOICE

Adaptations of the model have been developed for most settings in which social workers practice, including child welfare (Rooney, 1981; Rzepnicki, 1985; Salmon, 1977); public social services (Goldberg & Robinson, 1977; Rooney & Wanless, 1985); school social work (Epstein, 1977; Reid, Epstein, Brown, Tolson, & Rooney, 1980); corrections (Bass, 1977; Goldberg & Stanley, 1985; Hofstad, 1977; Larsen & Mitchell, 1980); industry (Taylor, 1977; Weissman, 1977); geriatrics (Cormican, 1977; Diekring, Brown, & Fortune, 1980; Rathbone-McCuan, 1985); medicine (Wexler, 1977); family service (Hari, 1977; Reid, 1977; Wise, 1977); and mental health (Brown, 1977; Ewalt, 1977; Newcome, 1985).

Granted, the model has been applied to a broad range of problems. The real question is: For what kinds of cases is it preferable to other approaches, and for what kinds of cases is it less appropriate? This treatment-of-choice question demands evidence that is not yet available to the field. It cannot be settled simply by evidence that one model does well with one kind of case and poorly with another kind.

Well-motivated, well-functioning clients with circumscribed problems usually respond well to almost any kind of therapeutic approach. For such clients, a short-term, problem-centered model like the present one has at least one advantage over models that are longer-term and directed to more ambitious goals: the short-term model provides a better fit to what is needed and does not have to be "geared down." In addition, the planned brevity keeps the practitioner from trying to do more than is indicated, which is a helpful restraint for students and beginners. On the other hand, most approaches find the going tough with clients who are functioning poorly and who have pervasive problems. With many such clients, it may make little difference whether treatment is brief or extended, since gains will be meager in either case.

As a general rule, treatment goals are more important than diagnosis in determining the applicability of short-term models. For many low-functioning clients who have severe, chronic problems, limited goals (i.e., establishing independent living) may be all that is realistic. The task-centered model has been effective in helping mentally ill adults deal with problems of adjustment to community living (Brown, 1977; New-come, 1985). Similarly, limited-goal, brief therapy (within a psychody-namic framework) has shown promising results with hospitalized bor-derline patients (Nurnberg & Suh, 1982). When goals are more far-reaching (e.g., personality change or major modification of chronic psy-chopathology), short-term models are generally not considered as treat-ments of choice (Clarkin & Frances, 1982).

Because it is a particular type of short-term treatment that aims to stimulate, guide, and strengthen the client's problem-solving efforts, the task-centered model requires that target problems be alleviated through the client's own actions. Therefore, the model is not preferred for clients who view treatment primarily as an opportunity to sort out their goals or explore purely interior issues. By the same logic, the model does not work well if the clients are unwilling to take constructive action (as in some types of protective or correctional cases) or if no effective plan of client action can be found (as with some types of psychosomatic dis-orders).

This model would be quite appropriate for a wide range of problems that a family such as the Shores might bring to an agency. The family has multiple problems, is crisis-prone, and has a history of prior in-volvement with service agencies; however, these factors do not preclude use of this model or some other form of planned short-term treatment. In fact, it can be argued that brief service that is responsive to immediate problems might be a better plan for this family than would a long-term treatment relationship that might go on for years. Brief service, even if it is repeated as additional problems arise, might strengthen the family's own problem-solving capacity. Although a long-term treatment relation-ship might make things more comfortable for the family, it is also likely to increase their dependency on the helping system. In addition, the considerable staff time expended might not be commensurate with the gains that the family might attain after the immediate crisis had been resolved. Often, such families create their own patterns of episodic service by dropping out of open-ended treatment following abatement of the presenting problem. Putting such episodes into planned brief-treatment "packages" can provide the family with a great sense of accomplishment: The family becomes a successful terminator rather than a dropout.

## THE THERAPEUTIC PROCESS

First we will look at the intervention methods of the task-centered model as they apply to individual clients; then we will consider variations for work with families.

### Task Development and Implementation

The treatment process begins with the selection of the problem, usually the one that the client has ranked as most important. The initial role of the practitioner is to help the client generate and evaluate alternative courses of action. The immediate objective is to help the client develop a plan of action or a task that can be carried out before the next session. Emphasis is placed on stimulating the client's problem-solving capacities, although the practitioner may suggest task possibilities—or even assign tasks, if the client is unable to propose any. Often the best tasks are those that are produced through close client-practitioner collaboration.

The task is spelled out with whatever degree of detail is appropriate to the problem, the situation, and the client's problem-solving style. In some cases, a very detailed plan is called for (who does what, when, how, etc.); in others, the task plan is best left open and flexible. Regardless of the degree of structure, it is important that the client understands the nature of the plan and its rationale and expresses a commitment to carry it out. The practitioner tries to avoid making unilateral directives, such as setting tasks in which the client has had little input or that the client is skeptical about attempting. When tasks involve unfamiliar or anxiety-provoking behaviors, guided practice or rehearsals (e.g., through role-plays) may be employed. Anticipating likely obstacles and planning ways of avoiding them is also a useful device. For example, clients may be asked to think of ways that a task might fail (Birchler & Spinks, 1981). If substantial obstacles appear, techniques of contextual analysis (described below) can be used. Alternatively, the task can be modified, or another can be developed.

The same principles are applied to planning of *practitioner tasks* or actions that the practitioner will take outside the session in an attempt to bring about desired changes in the client's social system. Although such actions may not be planned in detail with the client, the knowledge that they are being considered as tasks not only enables the client to understand and perhaps help shape the practitioner's environmental interventions, but also makes the practitioner as accountable for task performance as the client is.

## Problem and Task Review

The client's progress on problems and tasks is routinely reviewed at the beginning of each session. The review covers developments in the problem and the client's progress in accomplishing the tasks to resolve it. Practitioner tasks are reviewed in a similar manner.

What the practitioner does next depends on the results of the review. If the task has been substantially accomplished or completed, the practitioner may formulate another task with the client for either the same problem or a different problem. If the task has not been carried out, or if it has been only partially achieved, the practitioner and client may discuss the obstacles, devise a different plan for carrying out the task, or apply other implementation activities. Moreover, the task may be revised or even replaced by another, or the problem itself may be reformulated.

## Contextual Analysis

During the course of the review of tasks and problems, the practitioner identifies obstacles to task achievement and problem change that clients have encountered in their life situations. The essential difference between a target problem and an obstacle is that the former is a difficulty that the client and practitioner have contracted to change, and the latter is a difficulty that stands in the way of progress towards resolution of a target problem.

Obstacles block progress; resources facilitate it. Resources are usually found in the strengths and competencies of individual clients, in the ties of loyalty and affection that hold families together, and in the supports— both tangible and intangible—that are provided by external systems. However, a given characteristic may serve as either an obstacle or a resource, depending on its function in relation to the problem.

In contextual analysis, the practitioner helps clients to identify and resolve obstacles as well as to locate and utilize resources. The discussion is led by the practitioner, who relies on focused exploration, explanations, and other methods designed to increase the client's understanding. The process may overlap with the problem-and-task reviews, during which obstacles and resources may emerge and be explored. The practitioner may help clients modify distorted perceptions or unrealistic expectations and may point out dysfunctional interactions or patterns of behavior. Obstacles that involve the external system (such as interactions between a child and school personnel, or the workings of a recalcitrant welfare bureaucracy) may be clarified, or resources within these systems may be searched for.

We can illustrate this facet of the task-centered approach by looking at Rena. The model might not be the most appropriate for her if she is interested primarily in self-exploration; indeed, as the case material suggests, she may have a need to look into "why she is the way she is"— more specifically, to examine her pattern of creating crises. In that case, short-term psychodynamic treatment that is centered on focal issues (such as models developed by Sifneos, 1972, Mann, 1973, and Malan, 1976) would be quite appropriate.

Suppose, however, that Rena requested help for her problems of loneliness and her inability to become involved in meaningful activity. We might expect that task development with her would be a slow and complicated process, because she is confused and conflicted. However, an optimistic view of people's capacities is often rewarded: If she is helped to clarify what she wants and what she has already tried, she may find some directions that would enable her to move ahead more rapidly than might be expected.

For the purpose of this illustration, let us assume that Rena's initial search for direction has come up empty; for example, she has opportunities to develop a social life but cannot take the first step. Perhaps she has failed to accomplish an initial task, such as contacting an old friend. The practitioner would then shift to contextual analysis, with an emphasis on identifying and working through obstacles that prevent action. Although traditional techniques such as exploration of feelings or interpretation might be brought into play, they would be focused on helping her achieve a particular action goal.

Contextual analysis may not in itself prove sufficient to resolve obstacles, but it may point to actions that can. For example, fear of rejection may be found to be an obstacle. A task might then be developed that would require Rena to make a social contact in a situation in which a rebuff would be unlikely (e.g., joining an informal group for coffee following her "adoptees" meeting) and being responsive to overtures to additional contacts that might grow out of this.

## Work with Families

The strategy that has been outlined for treatment of individuals may be applied, with certain modifications, to work with families. In most cases, family members are seen together, and when possible, problems are defined in interactional terms. In addition to the tasks carried out by individual family members and the practitioner, as in the general model, joint tasks are undertaken by family members (either in the session or at home). Tasks within the session generally involve family members in face-to-face problem-solving efforts that are structured by the practitioner; in addition, the practitioner may help family members improve their skills in problem-solving communication. Additional kinds of session tasks involve role-playing and "live" enactments of family interactions.

Possible solutions devised by family members in their problem-solving work in the session are also used as the basis for tasks that are to be carried out at home; the theme of collaborative effort extends to these home tasks. *Shared tasks* (which family members perform together) provide a means for continuing the problem-solving and communication tasks worked on in the session or for implementing solutions that have been devised in the session tasks. *Reciprocal tasks* involve exchanges between family members. For instance, Charley Shore may agree to earn extra money; in exchange, Nancy agrees to stop complaining about their bills. Similarly, parents may provide rewards to their children in exchange for constructive behavior; we will see an example of this later when we discuss the Shores in more detail.

Whatever their form, reciprocal tasks require that participants express a willingness to cooperate and that they regard the exchange as equitable. Although it is important to work out the details of the exchange in the session, it is also essential that participants have a "collaborative set." This ensures that they are prepared to accept reasonable approximations or equivalents of expected behavior, rather than letter-of-the-law performance, and are willing to adjust expectations in the light of unanticipated circumstances (Jacobson & Margolin, 1979). All of this suggests that, in the session, work towards clarifying and negotiating conflicts around particular issues should precede the setting up of reciprocal tasks to deal with the issues at home. If reciprocal tasks are "tacked on" at the end of the session without sufficient preparatory work, they are likely to fail.

In addition to resolving target problems, session tasks and home tasks may bring about contextual change. Frequently, such change is necessary to resolve obstacles in family interaction that may be blocking solutions to problems. For example, a coalition between Mrs. Shore and Michael may be undermining Mr. Shore's attempts at discipline. Session and home tasks may be designed to weaken the mother-son coalition and to strengthen the parental alliance. In this way, the model draws on the strategies of systems-based (especially structural) family therapy (Minuchin & Fishman, 1981).

Contextual change is important, but target problems are the first priority. A fundamental principle of the task-centered approach is to concentrate on alleviating target problems through relatively simple, straightforward tasks. Any contextual change that occurs is an incidental, added benefit. Moreover, structural dysfunctions, underlying pathologies, and the like are left alone unless they intrude as obstacles. To the extent that they do, practitioners can then shift the clients towards tasks that are more directed at contextual change—tasks (including paradoxical varieties) that may be aimed at structural modifications. This progression from the simple to the not-so-simple fits the needs of practitioners who deal with a wide range of problems and family types (from normal to highly disturbed) in a wide variety of settings, and who may not be expert in family therapy. Many families do not want a change in structure; many problems do not require it; and many practitioners lack the skill to effect it.

The family treatment variation is viewed as part of a more comprehensive system of task-centered practice. Although work with the family as a unit is generally seen as the treatment of choice when target problems consist of difficulties in family relationships, this method must be evaluated against other options when the target problem involves behavior outside the family context—for example, a child's difficulty at school. In such a case, family treatment may be indicated if the problem is reactive to family processes or if the family can be used as a resource for solving it. However, work focused on the individual and the setting in which his or her difficulty occurs may prove to be a more effective alternative. By incorporating methods for work with individuals, family units, and the environment within a single framework, the task-centered model facilitates flexible, combined approaches to helping client systems resolve problems.

The task-centered approach to family practice can be illustrated by our example about Michael Shore and his parents, in which the target problems concerned his behavior at school and his relationship with his father. We shall assume that the family considers the school problem more important; consequently, it will receive the most emphasis, at least initially. Although the task-centered model has been used successfully with school problems of this kind in individual work with the child in collaboration with school personnel (Reid, 1978; Reid et al., 1980), family involvement is preferred. In this case, family sessions might be used to help Michael develop tasks to attempt at school, tasks that would decrease his "silly" behavior. The teacher might be asked to evaluate his task performance on a daily behavioral report card or home note, which would be used as a basis for the parents to reward his task accomplishment; this is an example of a reciprocal task. In the session, Michael might rehearse his task through role-plays involving his parents, who might take roles of other children or the teacher.

While working on the school problem, the practitioner would also be alert to ways of strengthening the relationship between Michael and his father. For example, Michael's reward might involve an activity with his father—a shared task that might be structured to avoid the conflicts that disrupted their previous attempts to do things together. Alternatively, they might be involved in a session task in which Charley might be asked to recount how he, as a child, successfully handled a problem that Michael is facing—for example, being picked on by older boys. Among other benefits, the task might provide much needed reinforcement for Charley's parental role vis-à-vis Michael.

Additional (and more direct) work on the father-son relationship problem might involve session tasks addressed to improving communication; for instance, Michael and Charley might reenact a recent conflict at home or on an outing. Carefully structured activities at home might also provide a way of facilitating the generalization of communication skills to other settings.

An obstacle to improving their relationship may arise from Nancy's tendency to "take over" when father and son fight. As the case record states, she finds herself "storming in, breaking them up, and scolding them both." Whether this reflects her need for control or her perception that "each one fights for her attention," the result is that father and son are prevented from working out their differences. Moreover, Nancy's treatment of them both as siblings probably reinforces their tendency to relate to one another that way. To counteract these tendencies, Nancy might be instructed to refrain from interrupting Michael's and Charley's attempts to work out a conflict during the session. Home tasks around this issue might involve a shared task for Charley and Michael (e.g., father helping son with homework) and an individual task for Nancy (to refrain from interfering but to support Charley if he asks for her help). In keeping with the collaborative spirit of the model, the rationale for the tasks would be made clear. In particular, we would want Nancy to see the possible value of "not trying so hard" with Charley and Michael.

The immediate purpose of this contextual intervention would be to resolve an obstacle to resolution of the agreed-upon target problem. At the same time, the structural change that might ensue would be expected to strengthen family functioning in other respects as well.

## LIMITATIONS OF THE MODEL

Although the task-centered approach has been successfully applied to a broad range of problems and clients, there are still some questions that have been raised about its use with certain types of case situations and about its short-term features. I will share some of our current struggles with one type of case and will discuss some of the dilemmas associated with the use of a brief-service design. The first example addresses distinctive aspects of the task-centered model; the second is relevant to brief treatment approaches in general.

## Adolescents in Trouble

The task-centered model has not been particularly successful in cases in which the presenting problem has concerned serious chronic acting-out behavior of an adolescent, especially when the problems include antisocial behavior in the community and overt conflict between the adolescent and parent—or, as is often the case, between the parents themselves. To put the above statement into perspective, I note that no other therapy approach has consistently demonstrated outstanding success with this type of case either, although the task-centered model, probably in common with most others, has shown some degree of success in some cases involving such adolescents. In any event, there is considerable need for improvement, which is the focus of our current efforts.

A number of specific difficulties have been encountered in attempting to apply the model to cases in this category. These adolescents, who are often unwilling participants in treatment, may not comply with home tasks, even if the tasks are agreed upon in the session. Rewards and other incentives administered by parents often prove ineffective since they may not be able to compete with more powerful reinforcers that are available to the adolescents in their peer relationships or in other contexts outside the home. Family conflicts (parents versus adolescent and parent versus parent) and cross-generational coalitions (one parent and the adolescent versus the other parent) may disrupt or distort problem-solving efforts in the session and may often undermine tasks at home.

Recent work in such cases has combined task-centered methods in the session and home with attempts to bring about contextual change by using techniques of structural family therapy. At the same time, considerable attention is still given to the target problems, not only when working with the family but also when working with school personnel and others in the community. How much energy should go to direct work on the target problem and how much to bringing about structural change is perhaps the most pressing unresolved issue, at this point, in work with this type of case.

## The Dilemmas of Durational Limits

The most important questions concerning the service duration of the model have to do with determining projected length of service, flexibility in use of limits, and criteria for extensions. Although there are issues relating to whether clients should be referred to brief or open-ended service, they have been of secondary importance in development of the task-centered model. We have taken the position that almost all clients can first receive short-term service, with options for longer-term work if such is indicated at the end of the brief service period. In this way, "initial referral" issues have been recast as issues concerning conversion of short-term service into longer-term service.

Of course, this issue has ramifications beyond short-term designs, since it involves the question of practitioner responsibility for termination. Should practitioners determine when the end should occur, which has the advantages of stopping treatment at the "right" time with an appropriately structured terminal session but which carries the risk of a wrong judgment? Or should they allow the case to end when the client has "had enough," which has the attendant risks of excessively prolonged treatment, "no show" termination, and the like?

For most clients who seek help for personal and family problems, a range of 6 to 12 sessions may be sufficient, but there is a need for tested criteria to decide where within this range to set the limits. Some practitioners who prefer to keep their options open as long as possible may delay fixing a specific number of sessions, at the cost of introducing uncertainties and of sacrificing advantages that may be gained from working against fixed limits. Usually a figure is reached on the basis of some judgment about the client's motivation and about the length of service needed to achieve what might be achievable in the case. However, this kind of judgment needs refinement, at least to permit one to distinguish between "short" (6–8 sessions) and "long" (10–12 or more) brief treatment cases.

Decisions about length of treatment usually are made on the basis of a one-session-per-week service model. Increases in the frequency of sessions (e.g., to 2 sessions a week) within a limited period of time (e.g., 6 weeks) will also fit well with the strategy used in the task-centered approach; tasks can then be tried out, reviewed, and corrected more quickly. (An illustration is provided in Reid et al., 1980.) Experimentation with different variations, not only in session frequency but also in session length, with different types of case situations would help create a richer array of options than the standard 6-to-12 50-minute sessions once a week.

Setting durational limits in terms of sessions within a given time period works well for problems of voluntary clients; these problems can be satisfactorily treated within such time frames. Other standards need to be developed for cases in the following situations: 1) when service duration may be connected to events over which neither practitioner nor client has control (e.g., discharge from a hospital); 2) when the practitioner has to abide by mandated protective or correctional functions (e.g., when a court has set a length of time for treatment); 3) when the practitioner and client are part of a long-term care system (e.g., a residential institution); 4) when the target problem is expressed in terms of a specific goal that may require more time to accomplish than has been provided by the short-term design (e.g., securing the return of a child from foster care). In some of these cases, it makes sense to move to open-ended or goal-related service designs, whereas in others a short-term contract can be used to work on immediate problems, with the option for additional short-term work later if it is needed. We have not yet developed good criteria for making such differentiations or for deciding on the optimum length of service in these situations.

Suppose, for example, that the practitioner in the Shore case is a school social worker with responsibility for students in learning-disabled classes, and that Michael has been referred for a behavior problem. (Mainstreaming, we will assume, is a long-term goal.) Would it be better for the practitioner to work with Michael and perhaps the Shore family on a continuing basis, with the eventual goal of returning Michael to a regular classroom, or to deal with immediate problems with the hope that a limited amount of focused help would enable the family to move effectively towards that goal on its own? If the practitioner had time to spare, and the family was committed to doing whatever was necessary to achieve the goal, it would make sense to use an open-ended service plan. If the goal were related to some point in time that was not too far removed—say, for example, the end of the school year five months hence—the service duration could be fitted to that period. However, if the practitioner's time is at a premium, if the family commitment is less clear, and if there are uncertainties about when or whether the goal could be achieved, the case for short-term design becomes more convincing.

Regardless of the setting or circumstances in which short-term service is used, a perennial issue concerns extensions of service after the agreed-upon limit has been reached. The task-centered model favors flexibility on this point, although it is often difficult to distinguish judicious flexibility from either indiscriminate looseness, at one extreme, or overzealous adherence to the original service limits, at the other. If extensions are made or "recontracting" is done routinely as long as clients appear willing to continue, the model becomes short-term in name only. On the other hand, if little allowance is made for their needs for additional time or sessions, clients may become resentful or frustrated, as has been shown by client-satisfaction questionnaires (O'Connor & Reid, 1986). The issue becomes more subtle when practitioners follow the advice of experts in brief treatment and remind clients of agreed-upon time limits during the course of service. When the last scheduled interview comes, the client may feel that termination is expected and be reluctant to voice needs for additional services, even when he or she is asked about those needs by the practitioner. The client may then complain in a postservice follow-up that service ended prematurely. In other situations, clients who might be content to terminate on time will respond positively to the practitioner's expectations that more service is needed.

For task-centered practitioners, the recommendation has been to consider extensions 1) when the clients explicitly express an interest in continuing, 2) when there are unrealized but reachable goals, and 3) when the clients have been making progress towards those goals. As noted, the clients' responses to the expectation that service will be brief may mask their wishes with respect to the first of these criteria. The other two criteria are always difficult to evaluate, since some unfinished business can almost always be found, as well as some signs of progress.

In our experience, it is often the case that shows marginal progress at the scheduled time of termination that receives the extension. Either cases that have gone nowhere do not survive to that point, or everyone is happy to quit when termination time does arrive. Of course, cases in which presenting problems have been largely alleviated are also likely to exit at this point. Consequently, criteria that are hard to specify must be applied to cases that are seldom clear-cut. Although the seriousness of the problem may justify continuing the treatment effort in certain cases, frequently the additional service adds little to the outcome, as, for example, with adolescents in trouble. We need to find ways to identify those "marginal gain" cases that appear to have the potential for sustained progress beyond the limits of short-term service.

## RESEARCH

The evidence from research that has been conducted over the past quarter-century has suggested that brief, time-limited treatment is at least as effective as open-ended treatment of longer duration (Gurman & Kniskern, 1981; Wells, 1981). The best support for this generalization is derived from studies in which similar groups of clients were assigned to brief or open-ended service patterns and the results were compared (e.g., Fisher, 1980, 1984; Gelso & Johnson, 1983; Reid & Shyne, 1969; Wattie, 1973). Comparisons between the two modalities are complicated, however, by differences in their time spans and by the possibility of differences in the outcome expectations of practitioners and clients. Clients generally appear satisfied with the *results* of brief treatment, but their dissatisfaction with its *brevity* appears to be a problem for some (O'Connor & Reid, 1986; Woodward et al., 1981).

Studies of client change in treatment and how clients utilize treatment provide a better understanding of the relative effects of brief and extended forms of service. In their meta-analysis of studies of outcomes at different time points in treatment, Howard, Kopta, Krause, and Orlinsky (1986) demonstrated that gains tend to accumulate at a diminishing rate as treatment progresses; planned short-term treatment, then, may capture most of the progress that is likely to occur in most cases. Their analysis also suggests, however, that some clients will continue to make progress over a long-term course of treatment, which justifies its use for selected clients.

The slight advantage that long-term treatment acquires overall from such clients is probably offset by dropout problems. As Garfield's (1986) careful review of a large number of continuance studies has shown, the average duration of treatment, whether short-term or long-term *by design*, is relatively brief—on the order of 5 to 8 sessions. There is also evidence that planned short-term treatment, perhaps because it offers a fixed, limited number of sessions, has a lower dropout rate than long-term treatment (Parad & Parad, 1968; Reid & Shyne, 1969). If this is so, short-term treatment probably gains an advantage by holding some clients longer, as well as profiting from goal-gradient (deadline) effects. In the final analysis, both forms of treatment may then show equivalent outcomes in head-to-head comparisons.

The effectiveness of the task-centered model as a means of resolving specific problems of living has been demonstrated in a variety of experiments in which control groups or multiple baselines have been used to rule out the influence of extraneous variables (Gibbons, Butler, & Bow, 1979; Larsen & Mitchell, 1980; Newcome, 1985; Reid, 1975, 1978; Reid et al., 1980; Rzepnicki, 1985; Tolson, 1977; Wodarski, Saffir, & Frazer, 1982). Populations in these studies have included psychiatric patients, families in which a member has attempted suicide, distressed marital couples, school children with academic and behavioral problems, and delinquents in a residential center. A larger number of studies in which controls were not used have provided additional support for the effectiveness of the model with these and other populations (see, e.g., Ewalt, 1977; Goldberg, Gibbons, & Sinclair, 1985; Goldberg & Robinson, 1977; Reid, 1977; Rooney, 1981; Segal, 1983). Other studies have concerned the process of intervention used in the model (Fortune, 1979a, 1979b; Reid, in press; Reid & Helmer, 1986) and educational and training aspects (Epstein, Tolson, & Reid, 1978; Reid & Beard, 1980; Rooney, 1985).

The questions answered by this body of research are dwarfed by those still to be investigated, including many raised by the studies themselves. Although the model has been proven to be an effective means of intervention for a range of specific problems, little is known about its impact on the overall functioning of client systems. Despite evidence that problem change that has been produced by the model is durable (Gibbons, Butler, & Gibbons, 1978; Reid, 1978), most studies have lacked systematic long-term follow-ups. Although there is considerable evidence that client and practitioner tasks are instrumental in bringing about problem change, there is much to be learned about what kinds of tasks work best for what kinds of problems and clients. Finally, there is a need for continuing research and development to improve the effectiveness of the model with such populations as adolescents in trouble and to find better ways of adjusting service limits to client need.

## SUMMARY

In common with most planned short-term treatment approaches, the task-centered model is designed to help clients achieve limited, explicit goals through structured and active intervention that is carried out within a limited, predetermined number of sessions. Distinctive features of the model include its problem-solving focus, its emphasis on practitioner and client collaboration, its social work orientation, and, of course, its stress on straightforward client tasks as a major means of achieving change. The model is integrative in the sense of drawing on a range of theories and methods from other approaches, including psychodynamic, cognitive, behavioral, and structural models. Its basic concepts and techniques can be applied to work with individuals, families, and groups.

The processes and effectiveness of the task-centered approach have been investigated in a large number of studies, including several controlled experiments. This research, carried out in a wide variety of settings and by numerous investigators, has demonstrated the usefulness of the model as a basic mode of service for most of the types of clients and problems that are dealt with by social workers.

## REFERENCES

Alexander, F., & French, T. M. (1946). *Psychoanalytic therapy.* New York: Ronald Press.

Bass, M. (1977). Toward a model of treatment for runaway girls in detention. In W. J. Reid & L. Epstein (Eds.), *Task-centered practice* (pp. 183–194). New York: Columbia University Press.

Beck, A. (1967). *Depression: Clinical, experimental, and theoretical aspects.* New York: Harper & Row.

Birchler, G. R., & Spinks, S. H. (1981). Behavioral-systems marital and family therapy: Integration and clinical application. *The American Journal of Family Therapy, 8,* 6–28.

Brown, L. B. (1977). Treating problems of psychiatric outpatients. In W. J. Reid & L. Epstein (Eds.), *Task-centered practice* (pp. 208–227). New York: Columbia University Press.

Clarkin, J. F., & Frances, A. (1982). Selection criteria for the brief psychotherapies. *American Journal of Psychotherapy, 36,* 8–18.

Cormican, E. (1977). Task-centered model for work with the aged. *Social Casework, 58,* 490–494.

Diekring, B., Brown, M., & Fortune, A. (1980). Task-centered treatment in a residential facility for the elderly, a clinical trial. *Journal of Gerontological Social Work, 2,* 225–240.

Epstein, L. (1977). A project in school social work. In W. J. Reid & L. Epstein (Eds.), *Task-centered practice* (pp. 130–146). New York: Columbia University Press.

Epstein, L., Tolson, E., & Reid, W. J. (1978). Dissemination. In W. J. Reid, *The task-centered system* (pp. 294–308). New York: Columbia University Press.

Epstein, N. B., Baldwin, L. M., & Bishop, D. S. (1983). The McMaster family assessment device. *Journal of Marital and Family Therapy, 9,* 171–180.

Ewalt, P. L. (1977). A psychoanalytically oriented child guidance setting. In W. J. Reid & L. Epstein (Eds.), *Task-centered practice* (pp. 19–26). New York: Columbia University Press.

Fisher, S. G. (1980). The use of time-limits in brief psychotherapy: A comparison of six-session, twelve-session, and unlimited treatment with families. *Family Process, 19,* 377–392.

Fisher, S. G. (1984). Time-limited brief therapy with families: A one-year follow-up study. *Family Process, 23,* 101–106.

Fortune, A. E. (1979a). Communication in task-centered treatment. *Social Work, 24,* 5–25.

Fortune, A. E. (1979b). Problem-solving processes in task-centered treatment with adults and children. *Journal of Social Service Research, 2,* 357–371.

Fortune, A. E. (1985). *Task-centered practice with families and groups.* New York: Springer.

Garfield, S. L. (1986). Research on client variables in psychotherapy. In S. L. Garfield & A. E. Bergin (Eds.), *Handbook of psychotherapy and behavior change* (3rd ed., pp. 213–256). New York: John Wiley and Sons.

Garvin, C. D. (1974). Task-centered group work. *Social Service Review, 48,* 494–507.

Gelso, C., & Johnson, D. (1983). *Explorations in time-limited counseling and psychotherapy.* New York: Teachers College Press.

Gibbons, J., Butler, J., & Bow, I. (1979). Task-centered casework with marital problems. *British Journal of Social Work, 8,* 393–409.

Gibbons, J. S., Butler, P. U., & Gibbons, J. L. (1978). Evaluation of a social work service for self-poisoning patients. *British Journal of Psychiatry, 133,* 111–118.

Goldberg, E. M., Gibbons, J., & Sinclair, I. (Eds.). (1985). *Problems, tasks, and outcomes.* London: George Allen and Unwin.

Goldberg, E. M., & Robinson, J. (1977). An area office of an English social service department. In W. J. Reid & L. Epstein (Eds.), *Task-centered practice* (pp. 242–269). New York: Columbia University Press.

Goldberg, E. M., & Stanley, S. J. (1985). Task-centered casework in a probation setting. In E. M. Goldberg, J. Gibbons, & I. Sinclair (Eds.), *Problems, tasks, and outcomes* (pp. 111–118). London: George Allen and Unwin.

Grinker, R. R., & Spiegel, J. P. (1944). Brief psychotherapy in neuroses. *Psychosomatic Medicine, 6,* 123–131.

Gurman, A. S., & Kniskern, D. P. (1981). *Handbook of family therapy.* New York: Brunner/Mazel.

Hare, M. (1963). Shortened treatment in a child guidance clinic: The results of 119 cases. *British Journal of Psychiatry, 112,* 613–616.

Hari, V. (1977). Instituting short-term casework in a "long-term" agency. In W. J. Reid & L. Epstein (Eds.), *Task-centered practice* (pp. 89–99). New York: Columbia University Press.

Hofstad, M. O. (1977). Treatment in a juvenile court setting. In W. J. Reid & L. Epstein (Eds.), *Task-centered practice* (pp. 195–202). New York: Columbia University Press.

Howard, K. I., Kopta, S. M., Krause, M. S., & Orlinsky, D. E. (1986). The dose-effect relationship in psychotherapy. *American Psychologist, 41,* 159–164.

Jacobson, N. S., & Margolin, G. (1979). *Marital therapy: Strategies based on social learning and behavior exchange principles.* New York: Brunner/Mazel.

Johnson, D. H., & Gelso, O. J. (1980). The effectiveness of time limits in counseling and psychotherapy: A critical review. *The Counseling Psychologist, 9,* 70–83.

Kaffman, M. (1965). Short-term family therapy. In H. J. Parad (Ed.), *Crisis intervention: Selected readings* (pp. 202–219). New York: Family Service Association of America.

Koss, M., & Butcher, J. N. (1986). Research on brief psychotherapy. In S. L. Garfield & H. E. Bergin (Eds.), *Handbook of psychotherapy and behavior change* (3rd ed., pp. 627–670).

Larsen, J., & Mitchell, C. (1980). Task-centered strength-oriented group work with delinquents. *Social Casework, 61*, 154–163.

Lowry, F. (1948). Casework principles for guiding the worker in contacts of short duration. *Social Service Review, 22*, 234–239.

Malan, D. H. (1963). *A study of brief psychotherapy*. Springfield, IL: Charles C Thomas.

Malan, D. H. (1976). *The frontier of brief psychotherapy: An example of the convergence of research & clinical practice*. New York: Plenum.

Mann, J. (1973). *Time-limited psychotherapy*. Cambridge, MA: Harvard University Press.

Minuchin, S. N., & Fishman, C. H. (1981). *Family therapy techniques*. Cambridge, MA: Harvard University Press.

Murray, E., & Smitson, W. (1963). Brief treatment of parents in a military setting. *Social Work, 8*, 55–61.

Newcome, K. (1985). Task-centered group work with the chronically mentally ill in day treatment. In A. E. Fortune (Ed.), *Task-centered practice with families and groups* (pp. 78–91). New York: Springer.

Normand, W. C., Fensterheim, H., & Schrenzel, S. (1967). A systematic approach to brief therapy for patients from a low socio-economic community. *Community Mental Health Journal, 3*, 394–454.

Nurnberg, H. G., & Suh, R. (1982). Time-limited psychotherapy of the hospitalized borderline patients. *American Journal of Psychotherapy, 36*, 19–26.

O'Connor, R., & Reid, W. J. (1986). Client dissatisfaction with brief treatment. *Social Service Review, 60*, 526–537.

Parad, H. J., & Parad, L. G. (1968). Study of crisis-oriented planned short-term treatment. Part I. *Social Casework, 46*, 346–355.

Parihar, B. (1983). *Task-centered management in human services*. Springfield, IL: Charles C Thomas.

Perlman, H. H. (1957). *Social casework: A problem-solving process*. Chicago: University of Chicago Press.

Rathbone-McCuan, E. (1985). Intergenerational family practice with older families. In A. E. Fortune (Ed.), *Task-centered practice with families and groups* (pp. 149–160). New York: Springer.

Reid, W. J. (1975). A test of the task-centered approach. *Social Work, 20*, 3–9.

Reid, W. J. (1977). Process and outcome in the treatment of family problems. In W. J. Reid & L. Epstein (Eds.), *Task-centered practice* (pp. 58–77). New York: Columbia University Press.

Reid, W. J. (1978). *The task-centered system*. New York: Columbia University Press.

Reid, W. J. (1985). *Family problem solving*. New York: Columbia University Press.

Reid, W. J. (in press). Evaluating an intervention in developmental research. *Journal of Social Service Research*.

Reid, W. J., & Beard, C. (1980, Spring). An evaluation of in-service training in a public welfare setting. *Administration in Social Work, 4*, 71–85.

Reid, W. J., & Epstein, L. (1972). *Task-centered casework*. New York: Columbia University Press.

Reid, W. J., Epstein, L., Brown, L., Tolson, E., & Rooney, R. (1980). Task-centered school social work. *Social Work in Education, 2*, 7–24.

Reid, W., & Helmer, K. (1986). Session tasks in family treatment. *Family Therapy, 8*, 177–185.

Reid, W. J., & Shyne, A. W. (1969). *Brief and extended casework*. New York: Columbia University Press.

Reynolds, B. (1932). An experiment in short-contact interviewing. *Smith College Studies in Social Work, 3*, 3–107.

Rooney, R. H. (1977). Adolescent groups in public schools. In W. J. Reid & L. Epstein (Eds.), *Task-centered practice* (pp. 168–182). New York: Columbia University Press.

Rooney, R. H. (1981). A task-centered reunification model for foster care. In A. Mallucio & P. Sinanoglu (Eds.), *Working with biological parents of children in foster care.* New York: Child Welfare League of America.

Rooney, R. H. (1985). Does in-service training make a difference? *Journal of Social Service Research, 8,* 33–50.

Rooney, R. H., & Wanless, M. (1985). A model for caseload management based on task-centered casework. In A. E. Fortune (Ed.), *Task-centered practice with families and groups* (pp. 187–199). New York: Springer.

Rzepnicki, T. L. (1985). Task-centered intervention in foster care services: Working with families who have children in placement. In A. E. Fortune (Ed.), *Task-centered practice with families and groups* (pp. 172–184). New York: Springer.

Salmon, W. (1977). Service program in a state public welfare agency. In W. J. Reid & L. Epstein (Eds.), *Task-centered practice* (pp. 113–122). New York: Columbia University Press.

Segal, C. A. (1983). *Parent enrichment project: A community based preventative service to families.* Montreal: Allied Jewish Community Services & Ville Marie Social Service Centre.

Shlien, J. M. (1966). Comparison of results with different forms of psychotherapy. In G. E. Stollak, B. G. Guerney, & M. Rothberg (Eds.), *Psychotherapy research* (pp. 156–162). Chicago: Rand McNally.

Sifneos, P. (1972). *Short-term psychotherapy and emotional crisis.* Cambridge, MA: Harvard University Press.

Sifneos, P. (1967). Two different kinds of psychotherapy of short duration. *American Journal of Psychiatry, 123,* 1069–1074.

Studt, E. (1968). Social work theory and implications for the practice of methods. *Social Work Education Reports, 16,* 22–46.

Taft, J. (1933). *The dynamics of therapy in a controlled relationship.* New York: Macmillan.

Taylor, C. (1977). Counseling in a service industry. In W. J. Reid & L. Epstein (Eds.), *Task-centered practice* (pp. 228–234). New York: Columbia University Press.

Tolson, E. (1977). Alleviating marital communication problems. In W. J. Reid & L. Epstein (Eds.), *Task-centered practice* (pp. 100–112). New York: Columbia University Press.

Videka-Sherman, L. (1985). *Harriet M. Bartlett practice effectiveness project: Final report to NASW board of directors.* Unpublished manuscript.

Wattie, B. (1973). Evaluating short-term casework in a family agency. *Social Casework, 54,* 609–616.

Weissman, A. (1977). In the steel industry. In W. J. Reid & L. Epstein (Eds.), *Task-centered practice* (pp. 235–241). New York: Columbia University Press.

Wells, R. A. (1981). The empirical base of family therapy: Practice implications. In E. R. Tolson & W. J. Reid (Eds.), *Models of family treatment* (pp. 248–305). New York: Columbia University Press.

Wexler, P. (1977). A case from a medical setting. In W. J. Reid & L. Epstein (Eds.), *Task-centered practice* (pp. 50–57). New York: Columbia University Press.

Wise, F. (1977). Conjoint marital treatment. In W. J. Reid & L. Epstein (Eds.), *Task-centered practice* (pp. 78–87). New York: Columbia University Press.

Wodarski, J. S., Saffir, M., & Frazer, M. (1982). Using research to evaluate the effectiveness of task-centered casework. *Journal of Applied Social Sciences, 7,* 70–82.

Wolberg, L. R. (1965). *Short-term psychotherapy.* New York: Grune & Stratton.

Woodward, C. A., Santa-Barbara, J., Streiner, D. L., Goodman, J. T., Levin, S., & Epstein, N. B. (1981). Client treatment and therapist variables related to outcome in brief, systems oriented family therapy. *Family Process, 209,* 189–197.

# 10

# Family Therapy: A Structural Approach

*Jay Lappin, M.S.W.*

It is hard to describe family therapy without also thinking about social work. Both share common ground at the conceptual and practice levels. Each encompasses a way of looking at the individual in context, scrutinizing the relationship between behavior and environment, between part and whole. Family theory and social work reject a passive problem-solving stance and instead support active empowerment of people by tapping their existing resources, uncovering new ones, and creating a viable context for change.

This chapter will describe some of the central concepts of this perspective, using structural family therapy as a model. The structural approach is but one of many "schools" of family therapy.* In the same way that the individual reflects only a part of the family, this model represents just a partial image of family theory. Structural family therapy was chosen to represent family therapy because, as Hoffman (1981) points out, "Minuchin has a clear method and a theory consistent with that method" (p. 262). The effectiveness of the structural approach has been investigated with a number of clinical populations, particularly psychosomatics and substance abusers (Minuchin, Rosman, & Baker, 1978; Stanton, Todd, et al., 1982). I believe that these measurable results support

The author wishes to thank Mary Eno, Ph.D., for her encouragement and editorial clarity, Bruce Buchanan, M.A., M.S., Jorge Colapinto, Lic., and Patrick McCarthy, Ph.D., for their suggestions and clinical wisdom, and my wife, Joyce, and two sons, Jeffrey and Timothy, for their patience and love. This chapter was written in honor of Salvador Minuchin, M.D., and Charles Fishman, M.D.

* The "schools" of family therapy are well represented in Gurman and Kniskern's (1981) *Handbook of Family Therapy* and in Piercy & Sprenkle's (1986) *Family Therapy Sourcebook*.

and explain the clinical relevance of a family therapy perspective. In addition, it is the approach that I know best, and I have remained comfortable with my bias in favor of it.

## THE CONCEPT OF THE PERSON AND THE HUMAN EXPERIENCE

Without a doubt, Western society, more than any other in the world, emphasizes the importance of the individual. Our cultural stereotypes are rich with images that seem to call for individualism at any cost. The context of human drama becomes a mere backdrop to highlight the triumph of the person over circumstance, a view constantly reinforced by virtually every medium. Yet even the Lone Ranger had Tonto—and without the bad guys, there would be no good guys.

From a family therapist's perspective, individual behavior can only be understood within its relational context. Man and his fellow creatures are "looked upon as inseparable from their environments" (Haley, 1971, p. 1). Although this premise may sound simple and even obvious, it is by no means easy to apply. Co-responsibility—the idea that all parties in a social system contribute to a shared reality—is a difficult concept to grasp. The following story illustrates how foreign this perspective is to the Western mind, or at least to the Western tourist:

> An American woman was driving her car in China. While stopped at a corner, she was suddenly struck by a man on a bicycle, causing both man and bike to go tumbling. Fortunately, the man was unhurt, but the car and bicycle each sustained damages. A policeman was summoned to assess the damages. After carefully looking over the vehicles and hearing the story, he proceeded to write out two tickets: One ticket was issued to the hapless bike rider for being "90% at fault." The second went to the woman who had been sitting, stopped in her car, for being "10% at fault." The American was furious and demanded to know how she could be found "at fault" since 1) she was at a complete stop and 2) the bike rider had run into her. The policeman heard her complaint and then patiently explained that had she not been in China, there would have been no accident at all.*

When watching and listening to each person's story, family therapists borrow the eyes and ears of the Chinese policeman. Power in a system, or the "relative influence of each member on the outcome of an activity" (Aponte, 1976b, p. 434), is shared, but not in equal proportions. This is particularly true in cases of abuse, rape, or incest, in which power is

---

* My thanks to Jorge Colapinto for relating this story.

unevenly distributed and is supported in this arrangement by a larger social and political context (Taggert, 1985). This concept is a departure from traditional reductionistic positions. Speculating about internal forces is one thing; accounting for contextual organizers, particularly if they include the observer, is another. Examining events in context changes how we think about aberrant behavior—and what we do about it.

Although family therapists understand that people are part of increasingly larger systems, they do not believe that individuals are reduced to being helpless cogs in the machine of life. A key to the systems position is in recognizing that individuals and their larger social system counterparts are nonsummative (Speer, 1970). It is the human equivalent of two plus two equaling nine. People are viewed as active participants of a mutually constructed reality and are always more than what they seem.

The emotions of pain, sorrow, love, and joy are still very much a part of the human experience. It is not only people's "internal" system that determines emotions and behaviors, but also—and largely—the dynamic interplay of their responses to other people and situations. This is vividly true for children, who are born with specific genetic and temperamental predispositions; this "raw material" is shaped by and shapes the lives and forces around them. The longitudinal research of Thomas and Chess (1984) makes the cumulative impact of these forces clear. If the "fit" between individuals, their capacities, their motivations, and their styles of behaving are consonant with the environment, "optimal development is possible" (Thomas & Chess, 1984, p. 8).

Context affects everyone, even therapists. As the process of change begins, the therapist is inexorably pulled to "fit" the family and its context.

## The Therapist as System Member

*Principle of Least Effort . . . a system will try to adapt to its environment or will try to change the environment to suit its needs, whichever is easier.*—Stuart Umpleby (1984, p. 32)

Like Schweitzer treating the sick, therapists like to believe they are immune. Edgar Levenson, a psychiatrist who applied structuralism to psychoanalysis, points out, "It is an epistemological fallacy to think that we can stand outside of what we observe, or observe without distortion what is alien to our own experience" (Levenson, 1972, p. 8).

Levenson's point makes apparent the difficulty of embracing a systemic view of human beings, namely, we cannot look at others without also looking at ourselves. If clients are acting crazy when they are with us, then, from this perspective, there is a reasonable chance that we might have something to do with it. Likewise, if someone is "acting out" in a family, one can safely assume that it is part of a larger drama of which we, the family, and other systems are a part. Ernst von Glasersfeld (1980), a radical constructivist, points to the universal aspect of this interactive process between environment and organism—namely, survival:

> In order to remain among the survivors, an organism has to get by the constraints which the environment poses. It has to squeeze by the bars of constraints. . . . The environment does not determine *how* that may be achieved. Anyone who by any means manages to get by the constraints, survives. (p. 90)

Family therapists agree that the business of surviving changes the organism. In social environments, this change is circular. That is, as a person changes to meet contextual demands, the context also changes to absorb new input. Each affects the other in always subtle and sometimes dramatic fashion as the dance of reciprocity shapes its participants in the mutual struggle for survival.

Over 30 years ago, this discovery—that we all contribute to interpersonal problems—provided a sobering yet hopeful beacon to family therapy's early pioneers. In the knowledge of our contribution, also lies the hope that we can likewise participate in the resolution of problems. Either way, we are touched by the process.

## HISTORICAL PERSPECTIVE

The early years of family therapy have been described as every thing from a "kaleidoscope" (Kaslow, 1980) to a "guerrilla war" (Guerin, 1976). It was most likely a little of both, and much more.

Broderick and Schrader's (1981) historical account of marriage and family therapy is the most comprehensive. Of particular note for social workers is the authors' recognition of the social work movement and their comment that although social work has been "inextricably woven" with the history of marriage and family therapy, social workers have been, in turns, "the most daring pioneers and the most passive Johnny come lately's in the whole parade of professionals" (p. 6).

The idea of looking at behavior in the context of the family began sometime in the late 1940s and early 1950s. According to Guerin (1976), the impetus for the movement stemmed from those who were frustrated by the limitations of traditional psychiatry with schizophrenics and their families and with the problems of juvenile delinquency. According to Guerin, research provided the umbrella under which new theories could be tested. Ironically, "for unexplained reasons a number of therapists began to deal with whole families in the 1950s, often without knowing that anyone else was doing so" (Haley, 1971, p. 2). This isolation may have contributed to the delay of family therapy's acceptance and to the formation of "schools" that were formed around some of the early pioneers.

Throughout the 1960s and 1970s, these schools did little to promote dialogue and cross-fertilization. However, as Bill Vaughn once said: "It's never safe to be nostalgic about something until you're absolutely certain there's no chance of its coming back" (Gardner & Gardner-Reese, 1975, p. 191). Perhaps that is why family therapy is now showing hopeful signs that it is ready for both nostalgia concerning its origins and dialogue about its future.*

Despite these diverse beginnings, however, the field of family therapy began to jell by the early 1960s, about the time Salvador Minuchin began writing about his work at the Wiltwyck School for Boys in New York, a school for delinquent boys from poor, disorganized, multiproblem families (Colapinto, 1982).

## The Development of Structural Family Therapy

During the 1950s and early 1960s, therapists had found that certain clinical populations seemed to repel traditional psychotherapy methods with unnerving consistency. Inner-city delinquent children, like those who filled the halls of the Wiltwyck school, were particularly troublesome. It was there Minuchin found that he needed a model of change that worked.

In 1966, when Minuchin's work was first published, political and social forces also seemed ripe for change (Malcolm, 1978). The "Great Society" became national testimony to the end of Social Darwinism. People were ready to experiment, to try new things. Medicare was introduced; communes were started; long hair, short skirts, drugs, and strange music were "in." There was a prevailing belief that changing the environment could, in fact, change people. Money, programs, and politicians poured into "the community." It was empowerment on a grand scale. Social workers were delighted. President Kennedy's "If you are not part of the solution, you are part of the problem" speech became the guiding principle of social policy. Systems thinking was everywhere, or so it seemed.

In the case of structural family therapy, however, Colapinto (1982) has noted the confluence of three factors: the difficult population with which Minuchin was working; timing; and the collaboration with Braulio Montalvo, a man whom Minuchin said "has the rare capacity to receive an idea and then give it back enlarged" (Minuchin, 1974, p. vii), that

---

* See Olson (1970) for another historical account of the family therapy movement.

set the stage for the evolution of structural family therapy. Commenting on his own family therapy work, Minuchin said:

> We must be doing something wrong, I thought. At this point I read an article by Don Jackson or Virginia Satir or somebody, and I said to my colleagues, "Let's begin to see families," and we did. It was a great adventure. We didn't know anything. And since we didn't know anything, we invented everything. We broke through a wall in our treatment room and put in a one-way mirror and began to observe one another and to build a theory out of nothing. (Malcolm, 1978, p. 84)

The one-way mirror was to become a symbol of the new therapy's brazenness. Theory and therapist were pushed to unify the abstract with the concrete. In fact, Minuchin's early works and those of the other founding parents could have easily been dismissed as yet another "fad." However, the times were right and research results eventually supported the new theory. A move to Philadelphia and the challenge of working with psychosomatic children presented an opportunity to make structural family therapy and family theory more legitimate.

## The Child Guidance Years

In 1965, Minuchin was appointed Director of the Philadelphia Child Guidance Clinic. Montalvo followed Minuchin to Philadelphia and was later joined by Bernice Rosman, another Wiltwyck colleague. In 1967, Jay Haley (a communications expert) came from California, where he had worked with Gregory Bateson and the team from the Mental Research Institute.*

The 1960s also were a time for a commitment to the community, and in 1969 the Clinic received a grant to train members of Philadelphia minority groups (who had no formal education or experience as psychotherapists) to become family therapists. The two-year program used innovative teaching methods, including the use of one-way mirrors, videotapes, and intensive live supervision of family sessions, to create highly competent therapists (Montalvo, 1973). All 24 of the program graduates returned to work within the community. (However, the graduates never had the opportunity to share their expertise with successive

---

* The work of Gregory Bateson and his colleagues at the Mental Research Institute (MRI) was a seminal contribution to the field. A comprehensive overview of the MRI group can be found in Bodin (1981). Further readings by members of the present and former MRI staff are suggested as excellent sourcebooks. For example, see Bateson (1972); Bateson, Jackson, Haley, & Weakland (1956); Haley (1963, 1973); Jackson, (1957); Satir (1967); Watzlawick, Beavin, & Jackson (1967); Watzlawick, Weakland, & Fisch (1974).

trainees: Economic policies changed and there were fewer grants for this type of program. The model had to prove successful in other applications to remain credible.)

## Structural Theory Comes of Age

Research for the model was provided by the clinic's affiliation with Children's Hospital of Philadelphia. Diabetic children who had an unusually high number of hospitalizations for acidosis (a stress-related condition) were not improving with traditional forms of therapy. Minuchin and his team began to see a correlation between certain family characteristics (such as enmeshment, overprotectiveness, rigidity, and lack of conflict resolution) and the reasons for recurrent hospitalization (Baker, Minuchin, Milman, Liebman, & Todd, 1975).

This study also provided the key to working with another challenging patient group—anorectics. Unlike other disorders that bring children to hospitals (such as diabetes or asthma), anorexia has no physical etiology, and therefore the effectiveness of therapy (as opposed to medical treatment) can be more readily measured in terms of a "cure."*

As the application of the theory grew, so did the Child Guidance Clinic. It stretched the boundaries of traditional outpatient and inpatient work by incorporating the structural approach into all facets of programming, including the construction of two residential apartments, fully equipped to hospitalize entire families.

## KEY THEORETICAL CONCEPTS

*There is no such thing as an individual, there are only fragments of families.*—Carl Whitaker**

One can say that a person's problems are a result of present relationships, or past relationships, or both. Regardless of the source of the difficulties, one must still decide what to do about them.

For example, a therapist can believe that the source of Charley Shore's Bipolar depression is genetic, predisposed, and historic. If interventions are designed to address these sources, the therapist will talk to Charley individually, attempt to resolve intrapsychic conflicts, and perhaps prescribe medication. If, on the other hand, the therapist can make a

---

* The most complete record of the research and clinical work on anorexia from a structural approach can be found in Minuchin, Rosman, and Baker (1978).
** (Carl Whitaker, staff seminar, Philadelphia Child Guidance Clinic, March, 1983.) Whitaker's work has had a tremendous impact on the field of family therapy. An excellent overview of his work can be found in Neill & Kniskern (1982).

distinction between the source of the problem and the source of the solution, he or she greatly increases problem-solving possibilities. In our example, this means recognizing that Charley's depression occurs in a context that affects not only him, but his wife, his daughter, his son, and so on. It follows that if the depression affects them, they can also affect the depression. It is possible to challenge Charley's illness by helping him change, but the probability of success is lowered by ignoring the roles of the rest of the family.

A systems position does not ignore the individual, the past, or even the need for medication. It simply puts these issues into a useful, nonblaming therapeutic context, in which all the opportunities for change can be incorporated. Critics of family therapy have charged that biological issues are overlooked or often discounted by the model. A family systems based paradigm does not preclude components in the genetic or physical substrata. One cannot cure mental retardation or other disabling or limiting aspects of certain diseases. From a systems perspective, these are all part of the "fit" between the individual and his or her environment. Family therapists who ignore these "givens" are simply doing bad family therapy. The family and present circumstances are, however, always looked to first, as a primary context in which behaviors are manifested, maintained, and changed.

## The Family as a System

A family is a living, open system composed of individuals who are connected in specific ways that mutually affect one another.* Families evolve patterns of transacting that are both economical and effective for that particular group of people (Minuchin, 1972). These accustomed ways of relating are interdependent and complementary and are necessary for carrying out system functions. The rules that regulate family interactions are known as the family's *structure* (Colapinto, 1982, p. 116).

These rules can be either explicit or implicit. Explicit rules—bedtimes, curfews, no stray socks in the living room—come to mind when one is thinking of how families work. Implicit rules, on the other hand, can only be observed in action. In other words, in order to know that there is a rule in a particular family about who is responsible for nurturance, one must repeatedly observe that in that family, when the child cries, it is the mother who picks it up. These rules or structures emerge over time and are content-specific for each family but universal at the level

---

* Jane Jorgenson (1986) has researched how families define the concept of "family." Definitions ranged from strictly blood relatives to inclusion of non-blood-related people who were treated as if they were related. Also see Minuchin, P. (1985) for an excellent integration of the individual development from a systems perspective.

of family functioning. Other universals of family functioning are growth, change, and maintenance of stability.

## Growth

Because the family is a living, open system, it influences and is influenced by a myriad of circumstances both inside and outside of its membership. From the viewpoint of structural family therapy, this means that the family's continuous evolution as a system and its members' evolution as individuals will tend to move in the direction of growth and increased complexity. We know, for example, from sensory deprivation experiments, that people's inner stability depends on stimulation (Allport, 1960). In families, these necessary stimuli come not only from internal sources (e.g., the developmental changes that each member experiences), but also from external forces such as community, culture, work, and attitudes about sex roles and race. Each factor impacts the family in different degrees at different times. The family absorbs societal change as it percolates down and then in time returns the favor, changing itself and society in the process.

## Regulation, rules, and change

In the same way that permeable membranes allow organisms to regulate the constant in-and-out flow of energy between themselves and their surroundings, semipermeable boundaries between the family and the outside world modulate changes (i.e., "stimuli," such as births, deaths, marriages, divorce, and death) imposed by the exigencies of life (Katz & Kahn, 1966/1969). Through a process of feedback, this in-and-out flow of information alters family structure, rules, and roles as the system adapts to change.

*Homeostasis,* which in the context of family therapy means the tendency for social systems to "seek a steady state" (Dell, 1982, p. 27), ensures the stability of the system over time (Jackson, 1957; 1965). If the family were to change with every new bit of information, it would cease to be a system and would instead be a jumble of disconnected parts. On the other hand, not responding to new information would result in *entropy*— that is, undifferentiation or "a gray, random sameness without movement or change" (Hoffman, 1981, p. 340). Without change, growth cannot occur, and without growth the system will cease to be functional or, in the case of families, will have an increased probability of becoming symptomatic.

Change and homeostasis become interchangeable forces—figure and ground in dynamic balance—pushing and protecting the family throughout the life cycle. Health of the family members is measured by their ability to successfully adapt to their environment. To the extent that people can choose how and when to respond and not simply "react," they will experience greater mastery over their circumstances. Health and choice, then, are inseparable (Dubos, 1978).

*Complementarity* of functioning in patterns and roles ensures the internal stability of the system and helps to counterbalance the stress associated with change. That is, the component parts co-evolve an "organized coherent system," in which all parts of the system fit together (Dell, 1982, p. 31). To the degree that Charley is distant and underresponsible, Nancy is proximate and overresponsible.* This complementary unity unfolds in sequences of behavior and thinking that can range from seconds to generations (Breunlin & Schwartz, 1986). Put together, these sequences "reveal a fundamental pattern of oscillation, or cyclical change, among the various parts as the influence of each element temporarily moves into ascendancy in response to inputs from the larger environment and then is overcome by the opposite" (Jordan, 1985, p. 167).

Here again, "the ability to respond fluidly to changing conditions by temporarily drawing on one side of a polarity within the system is the key to successful adaptation of that system" (Jordan, 1985, p. 167). In the Shore family, for example, Nancy's proximity to Michael as an infant was appropriate and necessary: Michael was sick; she was a nurse as well as a mother; Rena was busy with the extended family; and Charley was at work. As Michael grew older, this arrangement needed to shift, and a different complementarity was called for.

When a system must change structurally to meet new needs, the system becomes stressed and temporarily loses its equilibrium. However, such disequilibrium ideally leads to a healthier adjustment and further development—in other words, greater differentiation and complexity. Some people may feel disloyal to their families at these transition points; moreover, as family members attempt to differentiate themselves, some may be pressured to resume old roles as the uncertainty of change calls for the familiarity of old patterns (Boszormenyi-Nagy & Spark, 1973).

According to the structural approach, subsystems are the way in which "the family system differentiates and carries out its functions" (Minuchin, 1974, p. 52). One can begin at any transition point in the life cycle to illustrate the shift in family roles and rules. Birth, marriage, death, and adolescence, as well as unemployment, divorce, or a move, all embody these changes. However, we most clearly see subsystem development when a child is born and husband and wife also become mother and father. According to Minuchin (1974):

Subsystems can be formed by generation, by sex, by interest, or by function. Each individual belongs to different subsystems, in which he has different levels of power and where he learns differentiated

---

* The concepts of overresponsibility and underresponsibility have been diligently explored and developed in work with alcoholics and their families by Bepko and Krestan (1985).

skills. A man can be a son, nephew, older brother, younger brother, husband, father and so on. In different subsystems, he enters into different complementary relationships. (p. 52)

The composition of the subsystem is not as important as the clarity of the boundaries. For example, Rena could only be parented effectively by Charley and Nancy to the degree that they worked together and to the extent that Gram and Aunt Flo did not interfere with parental decisions.

## Boundaries

Boundaries are the subsystem rules that determine who participates in which situations, when, and how (Minuchin, 1974). Expanding on Minuchin's work, Wood and Talmon (1983; Wood, 1985) distinguish two types of boundaries: 1) interpersonal boundaries, or "proximity" (Wood & Talmon, 1983, p. 351); 2) boundaries that reflect who participates in certain subsystem roles—that is, intergenerational boundaries or "generational hierarchy" (Wood, 1985, p. 489).* Each of these boundaries has affective consequences for family members as they negotiate subsystem membership. Examples of such negotiations include one parent's telling a child to be quiet while the other parent is on the phone, an older sibling's increased privileges, or an injunction to the children to stop interfering with husband-wife time. These kinds of boundaries affect family members' internal experience and their experience of others. Just as specialized cells in the body have to be free from interference to function effectively, so, too, do familial subsystems need clear boundaries (Kerr, 1981).

Boundaries can be conceptualized along a continuum of permeability, ranging from *enmeshed* (diffuse) at the one end to *disengaged* (rigid) at the other. Most families fall somewhere in the middle of the continuum and may, at different points in the life cycle, temporarily operate near either end (see Figure 1).

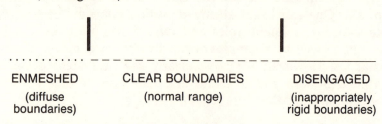

| ENMESHED | CLEAR BOUNDARIES | DISENGAGED |
|----------|------------------|------------|
| (diffuse boundaries) | (normal range) | (inappropriately rigid boundaries) |

**Figure 1.** Diagram from *Families and Family Therapy* (p. 54) by S. Minuchin, 1974, Cambridge, MA: Harvard University Press. Copyright 1974 by S. Minuchin. Adapted by permission.

---

* My thanks to Betsy Wood for clarification of this point.

"Enmeshed" and "disengaged" are not family types that connote either health or pathology; instead, they are styles of interaction for a particular family group, at a particular time, mitigated by culture and context. For example, if one listened to a family's interactions shortly after the birth of a new child, one would hear sounds that reflected a healthy over-involvement in the baby's life. Later, when the children leave home, interactions would reflect more distance.*

As the family attempts to cope with internal or environmental change, boundaries may collapse, leading to greater proximity among family members, or they may become underorganized as the family attempts to find problem-solving pathways within the existing family structure (Aponte, 1976b).

Problems can occur when boundaries remain unclear or when a family consistently operates at either extreme of the boundary continuum. Repeatedly enmeshed interactions will heighten a family member's sense of belonging. However, this is often paired with a reduced sense of independence and differentiation.** For example, children who grow up in an enmeshed subsystem can be discouraged from risk-taking and from pursuing peer membership outside the family. Conversely, members in a disengaged system may have an exaggerated sense of independence, but do not experience adequate nurturance. Michael's "loner" status at school can be seen as a byproduct of both an enmeshed mother–son dyad and a disengaged father–son dyad. Not only is he physically and emotionally close to his mother and distant from his father, but also, because his parents cannot operate as an effective unit, he is denied the systemic permission needed for him to move beyond the family limits. Within and between the various systems, a cycle of self-fulfilling prophecies develops. For example, to the extent that Michael is marked as "different," he remains wired to the family. Likewise, to the degree he orbits in close proximity to his family, he will remain "different."

In order for Michael to successfully move out into his peer group, two things would need to change. First, there would need to be more proximity and agreement between Nancy and Charley. Second, there would need to be more distance between Nancy and Michael and more proximity between father and son.

## Symptoms

What is it about the Shores that prevents their growth and development? The Shores' family development has been arrested. Despite the

---

* Two primary sourcebooks on family development from a systems perspective are Carter and McGoldrick (1980) and Walsh (1982).

** Murray Bowen's work at the National Institute of Mental Health during the mid-1950s with schizophrenics and their families led to his development of family systems theory and concepts that are now a part of the family therapy vocabulary. Kerr (1981) provides an informative historical and theoretical overview of Bowen's work. (Also see Bowen, 1966.)

constant pressure of new circumstances, the Shores have clung to a structural artifact—adaptive at an earlier stage of family life, outdated in its current one. When Thomas and Chess (1984) refer to a poor fit or "dissonance between the individual and the environment" (p. 8), they could be referring to the Shores' current inability to find an organizational shape that will get them out of the developmental woods. In family therapy terms, this is what is known as being "stuck."

Another way to examine why families get stuck is to explore the consequences of change. For example, Nancy's continuous TV-watching and her overconcern for Michael begin to make sense when we remember that she has no other family members to support her at home and has a disability that limits her activities. If Michael and his father were to get closer, Nancy's isolation would increase. Although she and Rena might be able to renegotiate their relationship, the change would mean entering into dimly charted waters with few markers to guide them.

When family members are faced with such stress, it is not uncommon for triangular patterns to appear. *Cross-generational coalitions* can form when one child and parent become pitted against the other, undermining generational hierarchy. When it is chronic, this dysfunctional arrangement can result in symptoms ranging from psychosomatic illness to addiction (Minuchin, Rosman, & Baker, 1978; Stanton, Todd, et al., 1982). Conflict avoidance is a way for the system to maintain a level of stability and prevent the possible dissolution of the family. It does so at the cost of individual differentiation and growth, which are the result of conflict resolution (Colapinto, 1982).

Michael's poor social judgment, inappropriate laughter, and rejection from camp are poignant tributes to the status quo. The Shores—and all families—must struggle to walk the narrow path between the predictable and the unknown. To follow their route is to understand how families work and how they change.

## ASSESSMENT

In structural family therapy, assessment and intervention are an inseparably woven fabric, tailored by the system's feedback. The therapist is included in this weaving process at the experiential level and at the intellectual level (i.e., he or she knows that the mere observation of a system affects both it and the observer). Assessment is both ongoing and inseparable from each stage of treatment and every intervention. From a structural family therapy standpoint, assessment is also less concerned with the etiology of symptoms and more concerned with current symptom maintenance. Sorting out past from present, and what factors are maintaining dysfunction, is no easy task. Therefore, the therapist must be an editor, choosing, from all the available data about the family, the information that best illuminates patterns and thus enhances therapeutic leverage.

Families create and maintain an idiosyncratic world view by punctuating some aspects of reality with greater emphasis and minimizing others. The therapist must come to understand the family's world view and the way in which it supports dysfunction. (For example, to the degree that Michael's frailties are accentuated, his strengths are overlooked.)

When families come to treatment, they have a world view that is at the level of *content*—their story is usually about one member, the identified patient. (In this case, the Shores might attribute their problems—Michael's lack of friends, Nancy's depression, and Charley's joblessness—to individual frailties or circumstance.) The structural therapist must have a competing *interactional* perspective that involves all the family members and their larger context.

Assessment becomes the ongoing process of the therapist's refining his or her world view while attempting to modify the family's world view (Lappin, 1984b). The therapist begins with an initial hypothesis about what structure(s) might be maintaining the symptom. This is done against a developmental backdrop based on universals of healthy family and individual functioning. In families, these universals would include clear boundaries, a clear and effective hierarchy, nurturance, and conflict negotiation (Lewis, Beavers, Gossett, & Phillips, 1976). These universals are both generic and specific; different families will fit into different subsets—that is, families with young children versus families with older children, single-parent families versus two-parent families, and so on for each family form.

In the session, what happens among family members and between members and the therapist is called *process*. Does the father sit looking absently away from the family? Does the mother do most of the talking? What happens when the therapist attempts to contact the son? Does he speak for himself or does someone interrupt? Who? and how often? During what content? By enacting familial patterns, the therapist tests for flexibility. How permeable are the boundaries? Through what channels does the family permit the therapist to have access? How does the family attempt to organize the therapist's behavior? Who is the most concerned about the problem, and the least? What happens when the problem surfaces? Who handles it and how?*

---

* Selvini Palazzoli and her associates in Milan, Italy, developed a method for working with severely disturbed families that uses a team of therapists. One therapist is in the room with the family, while the rest of the team observes from behind a one-way mirror. The interviewer asks questions that are "circular" (i.e., questions made on the basis of the feedback from answers to his or her questions to family members about the relationships between members). After the team meets and consults as a unit, it prescribes a task for the family. The task is designed to dislodge dysfunctional patterns so that the family can begin to generate new, more functional sequences of its own. (See Selvini Palazzoli, Boscolo, Cecchin, & Prata, 1978; Selvini Palazzoli, Boscolo, Cecchin, & Prata, 1980a.)

What family members *say*—their world view, their story—is the content. (In this instance, Michael might describe his life as having a "scar" on it, and Rena might offer her "continual crises" theory.) All of a family's stories relate to the level of systemic rules and functioning, but since the family members are so much a part of their own story, the level of process and pattern is, for the most part, unconscious and unavailable to them. However, because the therapist has greater distance from the system and is thus not as constrained by the rules organizing the family, he or she can begin to use this information in the service of change.

## TREATMENT OF CHOICE

Structural family therapy has been applied to a wide range of presenting problems in almost every kind of treatment setting. As previously noted, psychosomatic families and drug abusers have been studied and written about extensively. Other areas described in the literature include adolescent substance abuse (Fishman, Stanton, & Rosman, 1982); school problems (Aponte, 1976a; Berger, 1974; Eno, 1985; Moskowitz, 1976); mental retardation (Fishman, Scott, & Betof, 1977); elective mutism (Rosenberg & Lindblad, 1978); encopresis (Andolfi, 1978); cross-cultural work (Lappin, 1983; Lappin & Scott, 1982; Montalvo & Guiterrez, 1983); and low-income and single-parent families (Aponte, 1976b; Lindblad-Goldberg & Dukes, 1985; Minuchin & Montalvo, 1966, 1967; Minuchin, Montalvo, Guerney, Rosman, & Schumer, 1967). Instructional videotapes (with commentary) have also been made about a broad range of presenting problems and issues, including fire-setting, anorexia, depression, blended families, delinquency, and single parents.*

## THE THERAPEUTIC PROCESS

As we look at the Shores, we are overwhelmed with data. What is important and what is not? Whose story are we to believe, and to what degree? Is Nancy telling the "truth" when she says, "I worry and Charley doesn't give a damn"; or is Charley sacrificing himself so that his wife can feel better by being the familial nurse?

As we study this case, we need to keep in mind that reality, from a systems perspective, is an interlocking construction. The Shore family

---

* A brochure about Philadelphia Child Guidance Clinic videotape rentals is available through Videotape Library, Philadelphia Child Guidance Clinic, Two Children's Center, 34th St. & Civic Center Blvd., Philadelphia PA 19104.

story, as presented in the case report, is merely one version of reality. Another therapist, in another book, at another time, would present another reality equally as valid: "Reality is what we take to be true. What we take to be true is what we believe" (Zukav, 1979, p. 310). However, if *everything* can be "true," where does one intervene, and how? Ultimately, the answer lies in the therapist's theory of change and how he or she uses it (Colapinto, 1979).

## Maps: Blueprints for Change

The therapist is guided in the change process by the construction of a family map. Maps statically depict the family's current transactional patterns, much as blueprints statically represent the evolving process of building a home. During the assessment phase—and refined throughout treatment—maps serve the twofold purpose of concretizing a structural hypothesis and assisting in the formulation of treatment goals. Minuchin writes that a person who constructs a family map is like an anthropologist who joins the family's "culture," experiencing their system, connecting and disconnecting, constantly "making deductions that enable him to transform his experience into a family map from which he derives the therapeutic goals" (Minuchin, 1974, p. 124). With the Shores, for example, an attempt to contact Michael might result in Nancy's talking for him, while Charley and Rena might seem distant and uninterested. It is the nature of systems that these sequences of interactions will be repeated and that "regardless of their ultimate origin, symptoms (conflicts of any sort included) can only persist if they are maintained by ongoing inter-actional patterns" (Sluzki, 1981, p. 275). The presenting problem then provides a metaphor for the structure's maintenance of the symptom. Mapping simply provides the therapist with a heuristic device that aids in identifying family structures and helps to maintain the therapist's focus on the present.

The therapist's job is to organize the family so that its members can begin to restructure their relationship in the here and now. The Shores' current map would show great proximity (or overinvolvement) between Nancy and Michael, reflecting a diffuse subsystem boundary (Figure 2-a).

The subsystem of Charley and Michael, on the other hand, would have much greater distance between the two, indicating a more rigid or disengaged boundary between father and son (Figure 2-b). The executive subsystem of Charley and Nancy would reveal unresolved stress, or conflict, between husband and wife (Figure 2-c). These subsystem structures fit together like the complementary pieces of a jigsaw puzzle, presenting a partial picture of the Shore family (Figure 2-d).

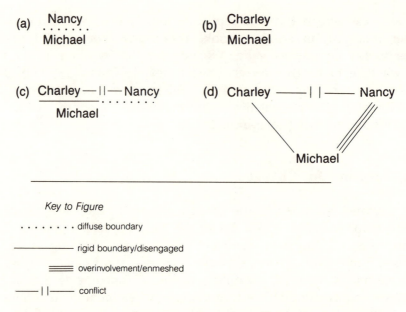

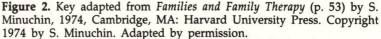

*Key to Figure*

· · · · · · · · diffuse boundary

————————— rigid boundary/disengaged

≡≡≡ overinvolvement/enmeshed

——— | | ——— conflict

**Figure 2.** Key adapted from *Families and Family Therapy* (p. 53) by S. Minuchin, 1974, Cambridge, MA: Harvard University Press. Copyright 1974 by S. Minuchin. Adapted by permission.

Other aspects of the system that would need to be explored as treatment progressed would be Rena's connection to the family system and a possible cross-generational coalition between Nancy and Michael against Charley.

An examination of the evolution of the Shores' current structure will illuminate how adhering to an adaptive organization that "fits" one context can cause problems if the structure is not flexible enough to accommodate itself to new conditions. As I indicated earlier, family structure is embedded in larger societal forces. Prevailing attitudes and policies concerning gender roles pulled the father out of the home to work and left the mother home with the daughter. However, when Nancy returned to work, the structure shifted to meet the family's new circumstances. Gram, Greatgrandfather, and Aunt Flo became more proximate and powerful. Gram, in particular, openly violated parental boundaries through her criticism of Nancy and Charley. To the extent that Rena was Gram's "angel from heaven," she was not her parent's daughter. Conversely, neither Charley nor Nancy attempted to retain control of Rena or retrieve her from Gram's overinvolvement. However, at that point, the fit between the family structure and its ecological and idiosyncratic requirements was "good enough."

When Michael was born, the family had to restructure itself again. This time, Michael's physical condition demanded even greater proximity from his parents than his sister's arrival had called for. Within a few years, the family's structure began to crystallize into the shape it would retain for years to come. Michael's developmental and physical needs, Nancy's disability, Charley's unavailability, and Rena's proximity to the greatgrandparents resulted in a structure that seemed to be the most effective for everyone at the time. It fit the constraints imposed by the environment of its day.

Ordinarily, restructuring would take place in a family when a child enters school. Proximity between mother and child is attenuated by the child's move to the world of peers and school, and greater proximity between mother and father is facilitated by their mutual support for each other and their child's move outward. Moreover, as the child becomes drawn into the subsystem of peers, he or she learns important social skills. This kind of restructuring did not occur in the Shore family. Instead, Michael's "problematic" behavior in kindergarten contributed to the distance between Nancy and Charley, which in turn contributed to the enmeshment between Nancy and Michael and to the distance between Charley and his son. Michael's symptoms maintained, and were being maintained by an outdated structure.

## Therapeutic Attitude

Like all therapists, a structural family therapist is never neutral. Structural assumptions form the basis of all operations (Aponte & VanDeusen, 1981). The principal goal of therapy is to change the family's transactional rules that maintain the symptom. Once those rules have been modified, family members experience an expanded sense of "self" and "other," and the system's viability is improved through increased flexibility and problem-solving choices. Following change, homeostasis, which originally embedded the symptom, now works in the service of incorporating and maintaining some of the very role and rule changes that the system previously rejected or nullified.

The therapist must be both a challenger and an accommodator. Change cannot occur unless the therapist risks challenging the dysfunctional rules of the family. At the same time, the therapist must respect the family's culture, or the family will not return. An answer to this dilemma is for the therapist to adopt an attitude that balances elements of risk and respect (Lappin, 1983). The therapist challenges people's problem-solving methods, never their motives. That way, it is easier to remember that the therapist and the family have a common enemy—the rules that bind the system—which makes them colleagues in a shared endeavor. In order to understand this endeavor and what to do about it, treatment is divided into a series of stages.

## Stages of Treatment

All family therapists agree that the road to symptom resolution is through system reorganization, but not all agree upon its route (Breunlin, 1985). One need only survey a pile of training brochures to get the feeling that the roads to change are indeed clogged (Lappin, 1987). Even though each stage has its own goals, techniques, and hazards, stages are not seen as discrete entities; rather, they are conceptualized as nesting interdependently, each one containing some proportions of all. Just as a cake tastes different depending upon when you sample the mix, so technique varies for each stage. The nature of the blend depends on the stage of treatment, its concomitant goals, the stage of the particular session, the techniques being used, and the idiosyncratic mixture between the therapist and the family—the point at which the therapeutic context is shared. Therefore, all five stages unfold over the course of treatment, but the stages can also be used as guidelines in the initial interview and in subsequent sessions.* I will discuss some of the techniques employed in this context as I describe the stages of treatment with which they are most commonly associated.**

The techniques of the structural approach can be classified into two categories: 1) those that help to form the therapeutic system and maintain the family's sense of self; 2) those that challenge the sense of self, disequilibrate the system, and promote change (Silver, 1983; Colapinto, 1982).

### Stage One

The goal of the first stage is to form the therapeutic system. The technique that is most often used at this stage is *joining*. Therapists must come to know the families they treat and join their particular "culture" without compromising themselves or their goals. Guided by feedback, the therapist strikes a dynamic balance between proximity and distance, establishing leadership by following the clients through the aspects of joining known as *maintenance, mimesis* (mimicry), and *tracking*. Preliminary hypotheses are formed, tested, confirmed, modified, or refuted, and are then woven into the process of change. Any initial discomfort that the therapist and the family experience is only the momentary lapse of a context in transition, the rules of which are being established "in vivo." Such discomforts actually present a unique opportunity to connect with the families and to "read" and experience their structure.

---

* These treatment stages were originally developed (with the assistance of Braulio Montalvo) for a training manual as part of a grant application for research with adolescent substance abusers (Lappin, 1984a).

** See Haley (1976, Chapter 1) for a clear model of the stages in an initial family interview.

Joining is the temporary coupling of two systems (family and therapist), which occurs in order to create a workable treatment context. This in turn requires the therapist to have a "therapeutic attitude" (a belief that the problem is solvable and that she or he can help) that necessarily involves an element of challenge (Colapinto & Lappin, 1982). This attitude is not an absolute quality attached to certain behaviors and absent from others, but rather is the automatic result of the therapist's correct assessment of what it takes to gain a position of influence with each family (Colapinto & Lappin, 1982). This assessment is highly idiosyncratic and is based upon the style of the therapist, the "culture" of the family, the presenting problem, and the context of treatment.

Although joining is primarily present in the early stages of treatment, it is essential to every session. It is the "glue" that binds the therapeutic system (Minuchin & Fishman, 1981). Good joining stems from the therapist's conviction that the family is its own greatest resource. Family members should have the experience of being listened to and understood, but not necessarily agreed with. Nonverbal responses or mimesis on the part of the therapist can facilitate reciprocal cues such as a confirmatory head-nod, a smile, or a look of understanding as signs that joining is occurring. Other processes (such as positive responses to therapeutic directives and acceptance of co-responsibility for problems and change) also signal that the therapist and the family have joined.

*Maintenance* is a joining technique by which the therapist confirms and validates the reality of family members, reinforcing their strengths and highlighting proximity. The therapist, too, is proximate. Trust takes time, yet trust must be established between the therapist and the family in order for treatment to begin. The therapist uses questions and statements that compress time, which increases the family members' sense that the therapeutic system has been together longer than it actually has. The therapist must be accepted as the leader; leadership is contingent upon the ability to forge connections and convey a genuine sense of interest. At the same time, the therapist must balance this interest with respect by not being oversolicitous.

Maintenance operations emphasize accommodation. However, that does not mean that the therapist needs to accommodate to system rules that may be at the expense of an individual family member. For example, if Nancy Shore talked for her husband during an interview, the therapist could say, "Mrs. Shore, you already know your husband so well that I am sure it is tempting to answer for him, but I need a chance to get to know him myself. Perhaps you can fill me in on some of the details later." In this way, the family rule is gently challenged, the father is contacted, the therapist is in charge, and the mother knows that she, too, will be heard.

*Tracking* is the joining technique that the therapist uses to follow the content of what family members say, as well as the process of what is happening. Tracking is done from a median range of proximity. From this vantage point, the therapist can both participate and observe. The flexibility of modulating distance relative to family patterns is a luxury denied the family. They, after all, cannot see something of which they are so much a part. The median position helps guard the therapist from becoming "inducted"—that is, overly proximate or too distant. It is a calculated compromise between becoming either another family member or "the phone company." Either extreme offers little hope to the family. By asking clarifying questions and encouraging members to speak, the therapist watches familial metaphors and idiosyncratic aspects of family life unfold. Correct tracking means not only that the therapist knows the language of the family, but also that he or she knows how to use it contextually, as in a phrase or metaphor, which can be a transitional bridge between ideas or members.

For example, tracking Michael's Boy Scout experience could create opportunities for him to speak competently: "Why did you want to be a Boy Scout? Is it hard not to tell lies? Who is the proudest about your scouting? The most nervous when you go on trips? Does your Dad ever go? Would you like him to?" This line of questioning increases Michael's sense of self, begins to draw boundaries between him and his mother, and starts the process of testing the system's ability to tolerate more proximity between father and son.

### Stage Two

This stage combines three operations: 1) identifying the problem; 2) identifying the structure; and 3) setting goals and planning.

Identifying the problem would be done with the family in a concrete, explicit fashion, focusing on why they are in treatment and on specific behaviors they want changed.

Identifying the structure occurs at the conceptual level within the mind of the therapist, who begins to form a map of the family, determining the constellation of interactions that maintain the symptom. This conceptualizing produces an "interactional diagnosis" (Minuchin, 1974, p. 131) about who speaks to whom and when; it also includes the therapist's sense of his or her impact on the system. Hypotheses about other relevant systems such as school, work, or extended kin also need to be incorporated in the tentative map that is being plotted.

The third component is both cognitive and operational: The therapist's world view and the family's are combined to create a workable reality (Minuchin & Fishman, 1981). This means establishing a shared paradigm between the family and the therapist so that individual causality is replaced by co-responsibility. This transformation is an important signal because "the beginning stage of family therapy ends when a problem has been redefined and the redefinition has been accepted by the family" (Cimmarusti & Lappin, 1985, p. 17).

The techniques employed with greatest frequency in Stages Two through Four are aimed at restructuring and maintaining change. These goals can be achieved in two ways: by creating different behavioral sequences through *boundary-making* and *enactment,* and by fostering an alternative world view through *reframing, punctuation,* and *unbalancing* (Colapinto, 1982).

During reframing, family myths about the symptom-bearer, the symptom, or the family itself are challenged and recast into forms that are more workable. Such alternative perspectives offer members a face-saving opportunity to see things differently. For example, Charley's joblessness and hassles with employers could be framed not as stemming from depression but from his being "too honest." Similarly, Michael could be reframed as a son who is honoring his father's values by being a good scout, and his strange behaviors can be viewed as part of that tradition (they keep him home, protecting his mother from any more painful losses).

Such reframings "relocate" the problem from *within* people to *between* them. In this way, therapeutic goals become a natural outgrowth of reframing. In the Shores' case, Nancy could choose whether or not she wanted Michael's protection, perhaps reallocating it to a more productive and age-appropriate area. She and Charley could jointly help Michael to be less "scoutlike" (i.e., protective of others at the expense of himself) by encouraging peer relations and enforcing generational boundaries. It might not even be too optimistic to suggest that Charley and Nancy could begin to engage in a dialogue about how he could become *less* "honest" with employers and how they could become more honest with each other as a couple.

*Complementarity,* the systems principle of mutuality and reciprocity of functioning, takes concrete form as a technique for facilitating change and reframing. Remembering this principle can help the therapist avoid linear thinking (e.g., "Rena is immature") in favor of more circular thinking ("Who keeps her young?"). It is important, therefore, for the therapist to maintain a median position, always keeping in mind that the meaning of behavior is determined by its context and that context is shared (by the family and by the therapist). This posture allows the therapist to track sequences and content that are enacted in the session and offer reframings that are constructed with the family's raw material (as opposed to the therapist's agenda). The more systemic a family's view becomes, the closer the family moves to healthier functioning (Lewis, Beavers, Gossett, & Phillips, 1976).

*Enactment* (which can be either spontaneous or planned) refers to the actualization of family transactional patterns. This technique, which can occur in all stages, serves the dual purpose of diagnosis and restructuring. Minuchin and Fishman (1981) have characterized enactments in three movements. In its first movement, the therapist watches the family's spontaneous interactions, allowing the unfolding of sequences that may suggest structural hypotheses. For example, does the mother rush to take the coat off of her 12-year-old son? Who talks the most, and to whom? The therapist then decides which aspects to highlight in the second movement (eliciting transactions). Here the therapist is more active; he or she has seen possible clues to dysfunctional sequences and now needs to test the hypotheses. If we directed Charley to talk with Michael, for example, the following interactions might take place:

*Charley:* Well, son . . . uh, how is school?
*Michael:* Not so good, Dad. The kids pick on me.
*Charley:* How come?
*Michael:* They just don't like me—they say I'm weird.
*Charley:* Who? Who calls you weird?!
*Nancy:* Now Charley, calm down, you know how excited you get. Besides, it's not Michael's fault—he's just sensitive.
*Charley:* Oh, but . . .
*Nancy:* Michael, why don't you tell the nice man about how you think God is putting a "scar" on you?

Even though this brief enactment is hypothetical, it is based on what we know about the family from the case report. Enactments such as this reveal the structure of the family. They also offer therapeutic potential by giving each family member an opportunity to experience themselves and one another differently. This is done through blocking accustomed transactional pathways.

In the third enactment movement, the therapist can begin to suggest alternatives. Ideally, these new alternatives "take" (i.e., are adopted by the family), but many times they do not. In either case, the feedback yields additional diagnostic data about the family. The more rigid and resistant to change the family is, the greater the need for impactful and precise interventions.

For example, the therapist in the example above would quickly see that father and son have difficulty maintaining a dyad, and he could alter the family's experience simply by asking Nancy to stay out of the conversation and by preventing Charley and Michael from inviting her in:

*Therapist:* Nancy, I know that you are eager for Michael to tell his story, but he really needs to talk to his Dad now.
*Nancy:* But I was only trying to help.

*Therapist:* Yes, I know, but the more you help Michael, the less he learns to help himself, and I know you want him to be independent. [Complementarity/Reframing]

*Nancy:* Oh, well, OK. . . .

*Therapist:* Go ahead, Mr. Shore.

*Charley:* Uh . . . OK, Michael, tell me about these kids in school.

*Michael:* They pick on me, Dad, and I don't like it. *(He starts to cry.)*

*Charley: (Confused, he looks to therapist and Nancy. The therapist nods and points for Charley to move near his son.)* Don't feel bad, son. Kids used to pick on me, too.

This is a small step towards a larger goal. By creating an enactment and altering the "rule" that father and son have to "bicker and fight like small boys," the therapist has given the mother, the father, and the son an opportunity to experience family life from a different perspective. One can not expect families to change unless they have begun to experience change as a possibility.

## Stage Three

Stage Three consists primarily of restructuring operations. The therapist now actively moves to incorporate the stated treatment and structural goals by attempting to introduce and strengthen appropriate boundaries, dissolve coalitions, reinforce the parental subsystem, and correct dysfunctional arrangements between the individual family members (as well as between the family and their larger context). Such dysfunctional arrangements would include those instances in which an institution (or other systems) becomes part of the symptom-maintaining structure. For example, in the Shore case, this might be the nightclub manager who encourages Charley, or a school or agency person who too readily agrees with Nancy that Michael should not be taxed and that Charley is no good.

Interventions should be consistent with structural goals and empowerment of appropriate hierarchies within the family. For instance, in the Shore case, assigning both the mother and the father to attend child-study team meetings would be congruent with therapeutic goals. Task assignment at this stage is both diagnostic and therapeutic; it can reinforce treatment goals and experiences from within the session and couple them with the family's natural environment. The tasks that are assigned, however, are only as good as the therapist's grasp of the family forces.*

---

* Proponents of the "strategic" school of family therapy attempt to solve presenting problems through indirect methods and through the assignment of tasks. These tasks and indirect suggestions interrupt family members' dysfunctional sequences of behavior that maintain the problem. The strategic school's roots can be traced to the pioneering work at the MRI. The "Milan group," along with Jay Haley and Cloé Madanes, has continued in this innovative tradition. (See Haley, 1976, 1984; Madanes, 1981, 1984.)

Like enactments, tasks may or may not go well, but they always provide essential information. The fishing trips between Michael and his father provided the feedback that this dyad needed more than a prescription to be successful; it needed systemic permission, that is, a clear and full sanction of the trip, negotiated within the parental subsystem and between the parents and Michael. For example, Nancy and Charley would need to agree that the trip was supposed to happen, Nancy would need to tell Michael that she wanted him to go, and Charley would need to tell Michael that he wanted it to succeed.

*Boundary-making,* another enactment technique, alters the psychological distance between family members by controlling who interacts with whom, about what, and for how long. In the enactment between Charley and Michael, for instance, the therapist enforced a boundary by temporarily excluding Nancy. Boundary-making is a powerful technique because it forces members to reach into the unfamiliar, to tap little-used aspects of self. In fact, it is possible to alter a person's experience of self and other simply by altering his or her subsystem membership. Different aspects of self are reflected by changes in context. Like when we stand in front of the different mirrors in a funhouse, the changes can both amuse and alarm, depending on where we stand. Through boundary-making, families with an enmeshed transactional style can become disentangled from overproximity, and families who are disengaged can reduce interpersonal distance.

*Unbalancing* is the name given to all techniques that destabilize the system. Boundary-making changes subsystem membership, whereas unbalancing changes hierarchical relations (Minuchin & Fishman, 1981). Because the goal is to create a crisis, unbalancing is the technique that requires the most therapist involvement.

Crisis challenges the family's stability and fosters a "discontinuous change" to new levels of organization (Hoffman, 1981, p. 102). Such reorganizations occur naturally in the life of the family following the birth of a child or a death (Combrinck-Graham, 1985). In treatment, the planned process of generating stress and providing support helps the family reach a new level of organization. The therapist is required to generate enough intensity, through effective use of self, to activate the family. The therapist may enter into a temporary coalition with one member against another, which serves to unblock stalemated transactions. For example, joining with Nancy against Charley would destabilize the couple's homeostatic "dance."

At first blush, unbalancing seems to be a technique of unfairness, yet unfairness of the moment is balanced by the greater needs of the system. This technique also requires careful monitoring of feedback. If resistance is too great, the therapist may have to retrench, rejoin, and try again at another time, temporarily putting the crisis on the "back burner" until another opportunity is afforded.*

Unbalancing can tax therapists as well; they should have adequate institutional and personal supports. The effectiveness of unbalancing does not simply rely on technical virtuosity, but rather on the strategic use of the therapists' own interpersonal resources. Warmth, humor, authority, and nurturance are all qualities therapists call forth as they join the family in the process of change.

## Stage Four

Stage Four focuses on maintaining change. The self-reinforcing gains made during previous stages need to be consolidated as the family struggles with the stress of change (Karrer & Schartzman, 1985). New rules and relationships, although more functional, are still subject to the pull of their preferred patterns. This is a critical transition point in the therapeutic process. These middle stages of treatment are long and arduous. The therapeutic context can be lulled into complacency, "now that the crisis is over." Frequently, some changes have occurred, and symptoms will have diminished or perhaps disappeared. At this point, both family and therapist tend to be tired of their struggle, as well as somewhat pleased with their progress. However, as Yogi Berra said, "It ain't over till it's over."

From a systems perspective, the consequences of change may be just as forceful as the dynamics maintaining the symptom—and, in fact, they are opposite sides of the same coin.** The Holmes and Rahe Social Readjustment Scale (1967), for example, lists "positive" events alongside their negative counterparts. Both positive and negative events are considered to be stressors. Consequently, the apparent benefits of symptom resolution are often thought to more than compensate for the loss of dysfunction. The point, however, is that at some level, the symptom(s) represented an attempt at survival. Any successful attempt, however flawed it may ultimately prove to have been, is one that was, for a time, "good enough." Relinquishing such powerful coping mechanisms does not come easily.

Keeping this in mind will help the therapist appreciate that all change is stressful and that we are always a part of the systems we treat. Because of the time spent together and due to the emotional nature of that time,

---

* I am indebted to Paul Riley for his development of this effective therapeutic technique.

** Karrer and Schwartzman (1985), in their chapter on the stages of structural family therapy, note that the strategic therapists often use paradoxical prescriptions at this stage to anticipate and counter the consequences of change.

both therapist and family are now even more subject to all of the same regulatory principles that apply to any social system. Therefore, as termination approaches, the therapist will need to carefully monitor both the family system and the therapeutic system for signs of reluctance to end.

*Stage Five*

Stage Five is the termination phase. Although it is often overlooked, it is no less important than the other stages. There is no "optimum" number of sessions in the structural family therapy model. However, treatment is usually brief, modulated by the family, their cultural background, and the presenting problem. For example, during the years in which the theoretical emphasis at the Philadelphia Child Guidance Clinic was most structural, outpatient cases averaged between 6 to 10 sessions (Aponte & VanDeusen, 1981). Psychosomatic cases, which, because of their more serious nature, sometimes involve both outpatient and inpatient work, averaged about seven months (Minuchin, Rosman, & Baker, 1978).

At this stage, the clear statement of goals that was developed in Stage One can help determine when treatment can be terminated. Other indicators, such as increased social time, more joking, or requests to schedule appointments further apart, can also signal that treatment is nearing its end. Structural reorganization provides useful and concrete markers for change and termination. For example, has the family's map changed? Is there increased variety and flexibility in the family? Are boundaries clear? Is there an absence of harmful coalitions? Are people developmentally on track? Can members speak and act in differentiated ways?

Again, these are therapeutic ideals, and one must always put any treatment goals into context. In the Shore case, it is not reasonable to expect that all the members will achieve interpersonal perfection (even if it existed). However, it is reasonable to expect that, within a therapeutic framework, the limits of their abilities can be tested, and that, in the testing, the family will be transformed.

In Stage Five, the therapist needs to begin the process of distancing from the family. The therapist should make it easy for the family to leave treatment, so that if the need arises, they can return more easily. He or she needs to punctuate the family's changes by supporting new behaviors and minimizing remnants of the past. For instance, if Michael raises concerns about school, the therapist could say, "That's to be expected. What does your father think?" Indications for ending would include Michael's report about his father's views (indicating that they had talked), Nancy's respect of the father-son dyad, and perhaps the parents' report that they had decided to take a specific course of action.

At the end of the course of treatment, the therapist has to trust the family's natural ability to heal itself and to understand that his or her brief journey into the family's system is coming to an end.

## LIMITATIONS OF THE MODEL

One inherent bias in the structural approach is that its principal development and applications have been in families in which the minor child is the identified patient. Exceptions have been Stanton, Todd, et al.'s (1982) work with heroin addicts and their families and Stanton's (1981) work with couples.

Hoffman, in her book *Foundations of Family Therapy* (1981), states:

> Although Minuchin's theory is most eloquent about family systems and family structure, it does not contain a comprehensive theory of change to cover the area misnamed "resistance," and the moves which deal most successfully with it, especially in cases of what Minuchin would call "enmeshed" families. (p. 270)

Later that same year, Minuchin and Fishman published *Family Therapy Techniques*, and although they do not devote themselves to specific populations, their "how-to" approach provides useful treatment possibilities guidelines and strategies for change.

Structural family therapy has not yet been dismissed as ineffective with any specific client population or in any setting. This is not to say that it can work equally well with all people in all situations. As a theory, however, it is a useful starting point whose limits need continual testing so that growth and complexity of both clinician and theory are ensured.

## RESEARCH

Some have argued, from a systems perspective, that all research is only relative to its cultural context (Colapinto, 1979). However, the attempt still needs to be made to discover effective therapeutic models and methods. The question of "what works and with whom" is central to the evaluation of any treatment paradigm. In the case of structural family therapy, it is a question that can be reasonably assessed.

In Gurman and Kniskern's *The Handbook of Family Therapy*, Aponte and VanDeusen (1981) present a comprehensive overview of 20 separate studies, cover both family functioning and treatment, and provide background information (both conceptual and historical) about the relationship between research and the evolution of structural family therapy. In another chapter, Gurman and Kniskern (1981) review research on marital and family therapy and conclude that structural family therapy has "thus far received very encouraging empirical support for the treatment of certain childhood and adolescent psychosomatic symptoms" (p. 749). They go on to specify that structural family therapy "should be considered the family therapy treatment of choice for these childhood psychosomatic conditions and, to our knowledge, it is the most empirically supported psychotherapy approach of any sort for these conditions" (p. 750).

Stanton's excellent work with adult heroin addicts is highly respected and provides further validation of the model (Gurman & Kniskern, 1981; Stanton, Todd, et al., 1982). The structural approach has also proven effective when practiced by family therapy trainees (who have had little or no prior formal training in family therapy), which indicates that it can be taught successfully to people from diverse backgrounds (Flomen-haft & Carter, 1974, 1977). The areas of adult symptomatology and treatment of couples need to be fully investigated to test the model's applicability to these groups and to provide new ground for research and the evolution of the theory.

## SUMMARY

The principal goal of structural family therapy is to restructure dys-functional family organization. In this approach, the family and its members are conceptualized as systems that nest interdependently within larger systems, each influencing the other. The therapist is an active change agent, responsible for forming the therapeutic system and creating a context for transformation through restructuring.

The theory was developed in the 1960s by its main proponent, Salvador Minuchin. Although it was initially used as a treatment model for delinquent boys from low-income families, its reputation as an effective paradigm was made through research into treating families with psy-chosomatic members and later with heroin addicts and their families.

In the structural approach, systems thinking and normal developmental processes are woven together to form the basis for treatment. The ecosystem, or the larger sociocultural context, is considered to be an important aspect of family functioning. In order to meet the demands from this larger context (as well as adapt to the members' individual changes), a change is required in the family's organizational structure. Greater complexity and growth are counterbalanced by the need for protection and stability. Families that are "stuck" at a developmental plateau are unable to negotiate the stress of restructuring and instead adhere to preferred rules and roles. Through a dynamic balance of techniques of accommodation and disequilibrium, the therapist is re-sponsible for organizing a therapeutic context with the family. This shared treatment paradigm presents family members with the opportunity of discovering untapped aspects of themselves and transforms the family into a more flexible, developmentally appropriate structure.

## REFERENCES

Allport, G. (1960). The open system in personality theory. In W. Buckley (Ed.), *Modern systems research for the behavioral sciences* (pp. 343–350). Chicago: Aldine Publishers.

Andolfi, M. (1978). A structural approach to a family with an encopretic child. *Journal of Marriage and Family Counseling, 4*, 25–29.

Aponte, H. J. (1976a). The family-school interview. *Family Process, 15*, 303–310.

Aponte, H. J. (1976b). Underorganization in the poor family. In P. J. Guerin (Ed.), *Family therapy: Theory and practice* (pp. 432–448). New York: Gardner.

Aponte, H. J., & VanDeusen, J. M. (1981). Structural family therapy. In A. S. Gurman & D. P. Kniskern (Eds.), *Handbook of family therapy* (pp. 310–360). New York: Brunner/ Mazel.

Baker, L., Minuchin, S., Milman, L., Liebman, R., & Todd, T. C. (1975). Psychosomatic aspects of juvenile diabetes mellitus: A progress report. In *Modern problems in pediatrics. 12*. Basel: S. Karger.

Bateson, G. (1972). *Steps to an ecology of mind.* New York: Ballantine Books.

Bateson, G., Jackson, D. D., Haley, J., & Weakland, J. (1956). Toward a theory of schizophrenia. *Behavioral Science, 1*, 251–264.

Bepko, C., & Krestan, J. (1985). *The responsibility trap: A blueprint for treating the alcoholic family.* New York: The Free Press, A Division of Macmillan, Inc.

Berger, H. (1974). Somatic pain and school avoidance. *Clinical Pediatrics, 13*, 819–826.

Bodin, A. M. (1981). The interactional view: Family therapy approaches of the Mental Research Institute. In A. S. Gurman & D. P. Kniskern (Eds.), *Handbook of family therapy* (pp. 267–309). New York: Brunner/Mazel.

Boszormenyi-Nagy, I., & Spark, G. (1973). *Invisible loyalties.* New York: Harper & Row. (Reprinted by Brunner/Mazel, New York, 1984.)

Bowen, M. (1966). The use of family theory in clinical practice. *Comprehensive Psychiatry, 7*, 345–374.

Breunlin, D. C. (1985). *Stages: Patterns of change over time.* Rockville, MD: Aspen.

Breunlin, D. C., & Schwartz, R. C. (1986). Sequences: Toward a common denominator of family therapy. *Family Process, 25*, 67–87.

Broderick, C. B., & Schrader, S. S. (1981). The history of professional marriage and family therapy. In A. S. Gurman & D. P. Kniskern (Eds.), *Handbook of family therapy* (pp. 3–35). New York: Brunner/Mazel.

Carter, E. A., & McGoldrick, M. (1980). *The family life cycle: A framework for family therapy.* New York: Gardner.

Cimmarusti, R. A., & Lappin, J. (1985). Beginning family therapy. In D. C. Breunlin (Ed.), *Stages: Patterns of change over time* (pp. 16–25). Rockville, MD: Aspen.

Colapinto, J. (1979). The relative value of empirical evidence. *Family Process, 18*, 427–442.

Colapinto, J. (1982). Structural family therapy. In A. M. Horne & M. M. Ohlsen (Eds.), *Family counseling and therapy* (pp. 112–140). Itasca, IL: F. E. Peacock.

Colapinto, J., & Lappin, J. (1982). *Joining revisited.* Unpublished manuscript.

Combrinck-Graham, L. (1985). A developmental model for family systems. *Family Process, 24*, 139–150.

Dell, P. F. (1982). Beyond homeostasis: Toward a concept of coherence. *Family Process, 21*, 21–41.

Dubos, R. (1978, January). Health and creative adaptation. *Quest*, pp. 74–82.

Eno, M. M. (1985). Children with school problems: A family therapy perspective. In R. L. Ziffer (Ed.), *Adjunctive techniques in family therapy* (pp. 151–180). Orlando, FL: Grune & Stratton.

Fishman, H. C., Scott, S., & Betof, N. (1977). A hall of mirrors: A structural approach to the problems of the mentally retarded. *Mental Retardation, 15,* 24.

Fishman, H. C., Stanton, M. D., & Rosman, B. L. (1982). Treating families of adolescent drug abusers. In M. D. Stanton, T. C. Todd & Associates (Eds.), *The family therapy of drug abuse and addiction* (pp. 335–357). New York: The Guilford Press.

Flomenhaft, K., & Carter, R. (1974). Family therapy training: A statewide program for mental health centers. *Hospital and Community Psychiatry, 25,* 789–791.

Flomenhaft, K., & Carter, R. (1977). Family therapy training: Program and outcome. *Family Process, 16,* 211–218.

Gardner, J. W., & Gardner-Reese, F. (1975). *Quotations of wit and wisdom: Know or listen to those who know.* New York: W. W. Norton.

Guerin, P. J. (1976). Family therapy: The first twenty-five years. In P. J. Guerin (Ed.), *Family therapy: Theory & practice* (pp. 1–22). New York: Gardner Press.

Gurman, A. S., & Kniskern, D. P. (1981). Family therapy outcome research: Knowns and unknowns. In A. S. Gurman & D. P. Kniskern (Eds.), *Handbook of family therapy* (pp. 742–775). New York: Brunner/Mazel.

Haley, J. (1963). *Strategies of psychotherapy.* New York: Grune & Stratton.

Haley, J. (1971). A review of the family therapy field. In J. Haley (Ed.), *Changing families* (pp. 1–12). New York: Grune & Stratton.

Haley, J. (1973). *Uncommon therapy: The psychiatric techniques of Milton H. Erickson, M.D.* New York: Ballantine Books.

Haley, J. (1976). *Problem solving therapy.* San Francisco: Jossey-Bass.

Haley, J. (1984). *Ordeal therapy.* San Francisco: Jossey-Bass.

Hoffman, L. (1981). *Foundations of family therapy.* New York: Basic Books.

Holmes, T. H., & Rahe, R. H. (1967). Social Readjustment Scale. *Journal of Psychosomatic Research, 11,* 213–218.

Jackson, D. D. (1957). The question of family homeostasis. *Psychiatric Quarterly Supplement, 31,* 79–90.

Jackson, D. D. (1965). The study of the family. *Family Process, 4,* 1–20.

Jordan, J. (1985). Paradox and polarity: The tao of family therapy. *Family Process, 24,* 165–187.

Jorgenson, J. (1986). *The family's construction of the concept of "family."* Unpublished doctoral dissertation, University of Pennsylvania, Philadelphia, PA.

Karrer, B. M., & Schwartzman, J. (1985). The stages of structural family therapy. In D. Breunlin (Ed.), *Stages: Patterns of change over time* (pp. 41–50). Rockville, MD: Aspen.

Kaslow, F. W. (1980). The history of family therapy: A kaleidoscopic overview. *Marriage and Family Review, 3,* 77–112.

Katz, D., & Kahn, R. L. (1969). Common characteristics of open systems. In F. E. Emery (Ed.), *Systems thinking* (pp. 86–104). New York: Penguin. [Reprinted from D. Katz & R. L. Kahn. (1966). The social psychology of organizations (pp. 14–29). New York: Wiley.]

Kerr, M. E. (1981). Family systems theory and therapy. In A. S. Gurman & D. P. Kniskern (Eds.), *Handbook of family therapy* (pp. 226–264). New York: Brunner/Mazel.

Lappin, J. (1983). On becoming a culturally conscious family therapist. In C. Jaes-Falicov (Ed.), *Cultural perspectives in family therapy.* Rockville, MD: Aspen.

Lappin, J. (1984a). *A structural family therapy training manual for working with adolescent substance abusers.* Unpublished manuscript. ’

Lappin, J. (1984b). *The therapeutic weave: A guideline for structural family therapy.* Unpublished manuscript.

Lappin, J. (1987, May-June). Pile therapy. *The Family Therapy Networker,* 45–48.

Lappin, J., & Scott, S. (1982). Interventions in a Vietnamese refugee family. In M. McGoldrick, J. K. Pearce, & J. Giordano (Eds.), *Ethnicity and family therapy* (pp. 483–491). New York: Guilford.

Levenson, E. (1972). *The fallacy of understanding.* New York: Basic.

Lewis, J. M., Beavers, W. R., Gossett, J. T., & Phillips, V. A. (1976). *No single thread: Psychological health in family systems.* New York: Brunner/Mazel.

Lindblad-Goldberg, M., & Dukes, J. L. (1985). Social support in black, low-income, single-parent families: Normative and dysfunctional patterns. *American Journal of Orthopsychiatry, 55,* 42–58.

Madanes, C. (1981). *Strategic family therapy.* San Francisco: Jossey-Bass.

Madanes, C. (1984). *Behind the one-way mirror: Advances in the practice of strategic therapy.* San Francisco: Jossey-Bass.

Malcolm, J. (1978, May 15). A reporter at large: The one-way mirror. *The New Yorker,* pp. 39–114.

Minuchin, S. (1972). Structural family therapy. In G. Caplan (Ed.), *American handbook of psychiatry* (2nd ed., pp. 178–192). New York: Basic.

Minuchin, S. (1974). *Families and family therapy.* Cambridge, MA: Harvard University Press.

Minuchin, P. (1985). Families and individual development: Provocations from the field of family therapy. *Child Development, 56,* 289–302.

Minuchin, S., & Fishman, H. C. (1981). *Family therapy techniques.* Cambridge, MA: Harvard University Press.

Minuchin, S., & Montalvo, B. (1966). An approach for diagnosis of the low socioeconomic family. *American Psychiatric Research Report, 20,* 163–174.

Minuchin, S., & Montalvo, B. (1967). Techniques for working with disorganized low socioeconomic families. *American Journal of Orthopsychiatry, 37,* 380–387.

Minuchin, S., Montalvo, B., Guerney, B. G., Rosman, B. L., & Schumer, F. (1967). *Families of the slums.* New York: Basic.

Minuchin, S., Rosman, B. L., & Baker, L. (1978). *Psychosomatic families: Anorexia nervosa in context.* Cambridge, MA: Harvard University Press.

Montalvo, B. (1973). Aspects of live supervision. *Family Process, 12*(4), 343–359.

Montalvo, B., & Guiterrez, M. (1983). A perspective for the use of the cultural dimension in family therapy. In C. Jaes-Falicov (Ed.), *Cultural perspectives in family therapy* (pp. 15–32). Rockville, MD: Aspen.

Moskowitz, L. (1976). Treatment of the child with school-related problems. *Philadelphia Child Guidance Clinic Digest, 5,* 1.

Neill, J. R., & Kniskern, D. P. (1982). *From psyche to system: The evolving theory of Carl Whitaker.* New York: Guilford Press.

Olson, D. H. (1970). Marital & family therapy: Integrative review critique. *Journal of Marriage and the Family, 32,* 501–538.

Piercy, F., & Sprenkle, D. (1986). *Family therapy sourcebook.* New York: Guilford Press.

Rosenberg, J. B., & Lindblad, M. (1978). Behavior therapy in a family context: Treating elective mutism. *Family Process, 17,* 77–82.

Satir, V. (1967). *Conjoint family therapy: A guide to theory and technique* (rev. ed.). Palo Alto, CA: Science & Behavior Books.

Selvini Palazzoli, M., Boscolo, L., Cecchin, G., & Prata, G. (1978). *Paradox and counterparadox: A new model in the therapy of the family in schizophrenic transaction.* New York: Jason Aronson.

Selvini Palazzoli, M., Boscolo, L., Cecchin, G., & Prata, G. (1980a). Hypothesizing-circularity-neutrality: Three guidelines for the conductor of the session. *Family Process, 19,* 2–18.

Selvini Palazzoli, M., Boscolo, L., Cecchin, G., & Prata, G. (1980b). The problem of the referring person. *Journal of Marital and Family Therapy, 6,* 3–9.

Silver, W. (1983). Techniques of structural family therapy. In P. Keller (Ed.), *Innovations in clinical practice* (pp. 101–112). Sarasota, FL: Professional Resource Exchange.

Sluzki, C. E. (1981). Process of symptom production and patterns of symptom maintenance. *Journal of Marital and Family Therapy, 7,* 273–280.

Speer, D. C. (1970). Family systems: Morphostasis and morphogenesis, or "is homeostasis enough?" *Family Process, 9,* 259–278.

Stanton, M. D. (1981). Marital therapy from a structural/strategic viewpoint. In G. P. Sholevar (Ed.), *The handbook of marriage and marital therapy* (pp. 303–334). Jamaica, NY: S. P. Medical & Scientific Books (division of Spectrum publications).

Stanton, M. D., Todd, T. C., & Associates (1982). *The family therapy of drug abuse and addiction*. New York: Guilford Press.

Taggert, M. (1985). The feminist critique in epistemological perspective: Questions of context in family therapy. *Journal of Marital and Family Therapy, 11*, 113–126.

Thomas, A., & Chess, S. (1984). Genesis and evolution of behavioral disorders: From infancy to early adult life. *American Journal of Psychiatry, 141*, 1–9.

Umpleby, S. (1984). *Glossary on cybernetics and systems theory*. Washington, DC: Department of Management Science, George Washington University.

von Glasersfeld, E. (1980). The concepts of adaptation and viability in a radical constructivist theory of knowledge. In I. Sigel, R. Golinkoff, & D. Brodzinsky (Eds.), *New directions in Piagetian theory and their application to education* (pp. 87–95). Hillsdale, NJ: Erlbaum.

Walsh, F. (1982). *Normal family processes*. New York: Guilford Press.

Watzlawick, P., Beavin, J. H., & Jackson, D. D. (1967). *Pragmatics of human communication*. New York: W. W. Norton & Co.

Watzlawick, P., Weakland, J., & Fisch, R. (1974). *Change: Principles of problem formation and problem resolution*. New York: W. W. Norton & Co.

Wood, B. (1985). Proximity and hierarchy: Orthogonal dimensions of family interconnectedness. *Family Process, 24*, 487–507.

Wood, B., & Talmon, M. (1983). Family boundaries in transition: A search for alternatives. *Family Process, 22*, 347–357.

Zukav, G. (1979). *The dancing Wu Li masters: An overview of the new physics*. New York: Bantam.

# 11

# The Psychosocial Rehabilitation Model: An Ideology of Social Functioning

*Terry Eisenberg Carrilio, Ph.D.*

Psychosocial rehabilitation concepts have gained much attention in the public health arena in recent years, especially in the development of policies and programs for the chronically mentally ill. I was introduced to this approach when, after many years of training and clinical practice based on traditional psychodynamic and object relations theory, I found myself working in a policy and planning capacity for a large urban mental health system. As I have learned more about psychosocial rehabilitation, I have come to realize two things: first, that much of its basic practice wisdom sounds very much like good "old-fashioned" social casework principles; second, that psychosocial rehabilitation is an ideological movement as much as it is a treatment approach.

In a recent article, Wintersteen (1986) explores some important parallels between social casework and methods of rehabilitating the severely mentally ill. He makes a strong case for the appropriateness of using social work principles in working with this population. My own experience suggests that he is correct in encouraging social workers to provide leadership in programs whose goal is to rehabilitate severely mentally ill individuals. Certainly the principles of psychosocial rehabilitation are consistent with well-accepted social work concepts such as "starting with where the client is" and "working with the person-in-situation" gestalt.

Some readers may be surprised at the idea of calling a treatment approach an "ideology." Nevertheless, it appears to me, after some consideration of the tenets of psychosocial rehabilitation, that it contains the basic characteristics of an ideology: it presents a set of integrated assertions and goals and establishes a sociopolitical agenda. Psychosocial rehabilitation represents a movement in that many of its luminaries see themselves as social reformers whose aim it is to improve the lot of the mentally ill through direct program intervention, community education, and social policy initiatives (Baron, Rutman, & Klaczynska, 1980).

A key issue in the relationship between clinical social work and the psychosocial rehabilitation approach is the presumed dialectic between case management and psychotherapy. Recently, some of the difficulties involved in reaching chronically mentally ill individuals and keeping them in treatment have been addressed by introducing case management as a function separate from therapy or medication management. Case management is a generic service that helps the client to identify and then maintain a financial, social, and personal support system in the community. Ideally, the case manager coordinates a client's treatment plan, refers to and coordinates needed services, and serves as the single point of responsibility for the client. (That is, rather than depending upon multiple service providers to coordinate their efforts and take responsibility for a case, the case manager is responsible for the plan and its implementation.) Sometimes, assertive case management and creative use of existing treatment resources have been effectively combined to maintain chronically mentally ill individuals in the community for long periods (Berzon & Lowenstein, 1984; Pepper & Rygelwicz, 1984; Stein & Test, 1984). However, case management with the chronically mentally ill is often considered to be merely a concrete "brokerage and advocacy" task, rather than something that requires high levels of clinical skill.

The appropriate use of case management in psychotherapy is a serious issue that needs to be addressed in the training of clinical social workers. Many clinical social workers appear to find the concrete issues involved in case management demeaning and feel that such mundane tasks ought to be left to paraprofessionals, while the trained clinical professionals deal with "more important" therapeutic matters. However, the history of casework is filled with discussions of the importance of using both the therapeutic relationship and the therapist's clinical understanding in working with clients at a very concrete level (Hollis & Woods, 1981;[*] Turner, 1974; Wintersteen, 1986).

---

[*] See particularly Chapter 2, "The psychosocial frame of reference."

## THE CONCEPT OF THE PERSON AND THE HUMAN EXPERIENCE

True to its roots in rehabilitation, the psychosocial rehabilitation model takes an optimistic view about human potential: Even the most impaired individual is seen as having strengths and worthwhile qualities that can be built upon. One goal of psychosocial rehabilitation is to enable highly impaired people to develop and maintain the skills necessary to function in the community. There is a strong emphasis upon "normalization," that is, creating an atmosphere in which people feel "normal" and are treated "normally." Such normalization reduces the stigma of diagnostic labels and "difference." Moreover, empowering disenfranchised mental patients through egalitarian program structures and providing them with experiential social learning opportunities is seen as a prerequisite to enhancing their capacity to cope and to contribute to society. The focus is upon improving the fit between clients and their social surroundings; less attention is paid to the cultural dysfunctions and stresses that may be affecting them (Finch, McGowan, & White, 1984; Hatfield, 1984).

In psychosocial rehabilitation programs, staff and "members" (as participants are often called) are partners in the rehabilitation process. Facility-based programs offer a wide range of activities that emphasize wellness and taking responsibility for one's own treatment goals. The tone is upbeat; the focus is on the tangible, here-and-now issues of everyday life.

The rather unorthodox role relationships between members and staff are a reflection of another characteristic of psychosocial rehabilitation treatment: its sometimes anti-"labeling," anticlinical bias. Many psychosocial rehabilitation programs are so concerned with fostering a philosophy of acceptance, empowerment, and normalcy that they tend to reject discussions of diagnosis and psychodynamics. In a review of psychosocial rehabilitation programs, Glasscote and his colleagues (Glasscote, Cumming, Rutman, Sussex, & Glassman, 1971) found that "All eleven programs agreed that they seem to have very little capacity to predict which applicants will do well and which will not after they have entered the program. There was considerable impatience with the diagnostic labels that the referring agents had attached to their members" (p. 188). Psychosocial rehabilitation programs are intensely and minutely practical, expending a great deal of program resources on teaching individuals the practical skills needed to function in the community. Insight is seen as less useful than behavioral change and skill development. Glasscote et al. (1971) reported that "In each program, there is a deliberate de-emphasis of symptoms and of thought disorder, amounting in many cases almost to a denial that the client is or has been sick" (p. 18). Even though the Glasscote study was conducted many years ago, its conclusions are still valid.

## HISTORICAL PERSPECTIVE

In 1947, a group of formerly hospitalized individuals met in New York and formed a self-help group called We Are Not Alone Anymore. Out of that initial effort, with the help of the League of Jewish Women, the first psychosocial "club house" program at Fountain House was developed. The new program was directed by John Beard, a social worker.

In the early 1950s, Marcella Schmoeger, a teacher, developed a Fountain House type program in Philadelphia. Schmoeger, who herself had been briefly hospitalized, recognized that many individuals were languishing in the hospital because there was no place in the community for them (M. Schmoeger, personal communication, April 19, 1987). Fountain House became Horizon House, and a psychologist, Irvin Rutman, became the executive director.

Early on, the inherent tension between the professionalization of psychosocial programs and a "sense of mission" emerged. In 1957, Schmoeger left Horizon House and founded Tricounty Fountain Center. Horizon House went on to become a leader in the emerging psychosocial movement, while Tricounty Fountain Center remained a small, homey, community-based program with few ties to a larger "movement" (Schmoeger, 1981; personal communication, April 19, 1987).

The initial model was one of a "social club" in which members mutually supported each other in the community. During the 1950s and 1960s, new programs developed in rapid succession. Multiple services and staffing patterns emerged. In 1963, Rutman reviewed existing programs and identified wide variability in programs in the budding psychosocial movement. He observed:

1. Funding sources and services were highly variable.
2. The programs tended to be flexible and experiential.
3. Programs were community-oriented and transitional (i.e., it was intended that clients would "graduate" to independent living).
4. Programs were ambivalent about the role of psychiatrists.
5. Systematic theory and a body of practice methods had not yet developed. (Rutman, 1963)

Psychiatric rehabilitation, a relatively new "school" within psychosocial rehabilitation, developed out of the psychology focus pioneered by Horizon House. Psychiatric rehabilitation attempts to develop highly technical interventions utilizing professional practitioners, in addition to relying on self-help and milieu approaches. Much of the underlying philosophy of empowerment remains, but there is an attempt to develop more precise, measurable interventions (Anthony, 1980). However, the proponents of psychiatric rehabilitation consider themselves to be members of the psychosocial rehabilitation movement.

As public funding and national recognition for psychosocial rehabilitation programs have increased, there has been a trend towards a more professional approach to psychosocial rehabilitation. However, this calls attention to an underlying debate about increasing professional authority (which may decrease the clients' sense of involvement in the rehabilitation process). The current tension within the movement—between those professionals who were trained in the Fountain House model and those trained in the Boston University (psychiatric rehabilitation) model—is actually the continuation of tensions that emerged early in the psychosocial rehabilitation movement. The former model focuses upon milieu, resocialization, and social learning approaches, and the latter approach focuses upon sequential skill development in *practitioners.*

The current popularity of general psychosocial rehabilitation concepts within the public policy arena is relatively recent and is directly linked to the massive deinstitutionalization of mental patients over the past 25 years. Because the psychosocial rehabilitation model provides a concrete, pragmatic approach to complex social problems such as those presented by the deinstitutionalized mental patient, it has often been incorporated into public policy—for example, through initiatives such as the federal-state Community Support Program.

As I have noted, the psychosocial approach has its roots in the field of rehabilitation (Glasscote et al., 1971; Rutman, 1963; Rutman, in press). Many programs began as attempts to provide vocational rehabilitation to former mental hospital patients. Over time, they expanded their services in response to clients' needs for additional support. Although it continues to emphasize the qualities of pragmatism and social adaptation that carried over from the rehabilitation philosophy, the psychosocial rehabilitation movement has expanded considerably over the past two decades. Because of this broadening of scope, the term *psychosocial rehabilitation* has taken on several meanings; it may refer to services for the chronically mentally ill, to particular kinds of interventions, to a philosophy of treatment, or to a professional movement (Rutman, in press).

Although the psychosocial rehabilitation approach embraces an ideology of pragmatism and social melioration, it does not attempt to either criticize or address the social forces that may themselves lead to mental illness. Instead, the perspective is inherently *conservative:* it focuses on vocational rehabilitation, education, and adaptation. Clients are rewarded for "buying in" to the values of the larger society and are encouraged to keep both their symptoms and their social criticisms to themselves.

The psychosocial rehabilitation movement has historically been associated with the treatment of the most chronically mentally ill, especially those who have had long periods of incarceration in mental hospitals.

Currently, however, practitioners are involved with a variety of clients in a number of settings. One of the groups more recently addressed is the population often referred to as "young chronics." Young chronics are highly resistant to treatment, are frequently aggressive, often abuse drugs and alcohol, and strongly resist being identified with the mentally ill. These "post-deinstitutionalization era" clients frequently maintain unrealistically high expectations for themselves and are highly volatile in their dealings with a service system set up for more compliant, formerly institutionalized individuals (Goldfinger, Hopkin, & Surber, 1984; Pepper & Rygelwicz, 1984).

The psychosocial rehabilitation movement currently encompasses both types of clients. Theoretically, psychosocial rehabilitation should be able to work with a fairly heterogeneous population of severely psychiatrically disabled individuals; in practice, however, many programs have had to separate the two groups, because the young chronics intimidate the older, more placid clients. Nevertheless, for both populations, the focus is on solving here-and-now problems, resolving difficulties with material resources such as food, shelter, and medical care, reducing dependent behavior, increasing coping skills, and developing community resources. Taken as a whole, this approach provides a highly effective combination of individual and environmental interventions. The goal for these clients is not "cure" but rather the acquisition and maintenance of the basic skills needed to survive in a community setting. The individuals best served by psychosocial rehabilitation programs are those whose ability to function in society is so highly impaired that they are at risk of institutionalization or homelessness.

## KEY THEORETICAL CONSTRUCTS

One of the psychosocial movement's criticisms of traditional psychotherapy has to do with the implicit expectation (in most therapies) that the skills and insights developed in the treatment setting will seep into the individual's day-to-day functioning. Psychosocial rehabilitation deals with the person in his or her current situation and attempts to work with both the environment and the client in reaching goals and maintaining functioning.

Practitioners of *psychiatric* rehabilitation take into account the clinical characteristics of the chronically mentally ill population by recognizing that adequate functioning in one environment does not guarantee success if the client moves into a new situation (Anthony, 1980). For example, the client who does well in a sheltered workshop may require assistance in making the transition from the workshop to a job situation. The specific skills developed to cope in one setting do not necessarily generalize to all others. There is a strong behavioral component to this approach (in that clients are taught to adjust to the minute factors of a specific environment), and it is expected that any change in the gestalt will require teaching them additional skills. The advantage to such an approach is that it recognizes that clients cannot simply transfer skills from therapy or job training into other areas of life without assistance.

In the psychosocial rehabilitation approach, individual change is considered to be mediated by change in the social environment.* For example, Rubin (1980), in discussing the ideological underpinnings of the psychosocial rehabilitation movement, noted its similarities with the early settlement houses. As he demonstrated, psychosocial rehabilitation programs provide many of the same functions for their clients that the settlements provided for immigrant communities. He stated, "The settlement house gave direct help with housing, food, job development, language skills, assisted in getting medical and legal services and organized their members . . . to advocate around [the] social issues [they] faced" (p. 88). An ongoing debate within the psychosocial movement, therefore, involves the focus of intervention: Ideologically, many psychosocial rehabilitation programs stand "up and against" the established system; yet in order to "normalize" their members, they must convince the members to become a part of that system, through personal change. Although the "up and against" flavor of the movement is invigorating, in practice it seems that rather than addressing the structural defects in society, it instead provides a valve for the anger that can be released when an individual is asked to make basic and deep changes to please the majority.

This somewhat anti-intellectual trend has given the psychosocial rehabilitation movement the flavor of an ideological crusade. In fact, however, psychosocial rehabilitation, like most theories of treatment, rests on a foundation of development and learning that suggests the importance of developing a sense of a secure, cohesive context before an individual is capable of risking change. To ask clients for changes in behavior, or to insist upon "autonomy" without first assuring some continuity and stability upon which they can rely, is to invite increased disorganization and deterioration in functioning.

The kinds of activities involved in helping clients meet the demands of living must take place within the context of a trusting relationship with the therapist. Developing such a relationship, in the face of the intensity of the clients' needs, is an extremely difficult task. An hour of talking on a weekly basis will not be sufficient; these clients require "doing" on the part of the therapist. Once their living and working contexts have been stabilized, some clients may then choose to establish more traditional therapeutic relationships. Even with the most impaired

---

* For a further discussion of this topic, see Paul and Lantz (1977).

individuals, however, there is still a place for clinical skills and understanding and rich opportunities for therapeutic interaction.

Related to the recognition of therapeutic potential in even the most concrete issues is the need to approach this population with humility. For many severely mentally ill individuals, just functioning in the community *at all* is a major accomplishment; they may have no interest whatsoever in going beyond what is necessary for them to simply get through each day. Even if one understands something of a client's dynamics and wants to improve that client's functioning, it does not follow that the client shares the same goal. A valuable contribution of the psychosocial approach is the recognition that seemingly small accomplishments for some clients would be major successes for clients who are severely mentally ill.

## ASSESSMENT

Putting aside the "why" and even some of the "how" of a client's current functioning, psychosocial rehabilitation practitioners begin by looking at the ways in which their clients are currently functioning and the ways in which the clients' skills and deficits help or hinder the accomplishment of their goals. Assessment starts with a look at what the clients want for themselves and what is needed to realistically accomplish these goals.

A psychosocial rehabilitation practitioner who evaluated members of the Shore family might find that they would agree to the following goals for themselves (although they would probably phrase things somewhat differently):

Nancy would probably be interested in reducing her anxiety attacks, losing weight, finding a better way to structure her time, improving the family finances, and enhancing her marital relationship.

Charley would want to seek and obtain a job, reduce his lying, learn to be a better parent to Michael, feel better about being a husband to Nancy, and find an activity in which he could feel that he was doing well and was gaining approval from his family and society. Although the comedy club provides him with some notice and sense of mastery, it is not well-integrated into his goals and stands in marked contrast to his presentation as a failure in other areas. A psychosocial rehabilitation practitioner might help Charley to build upon the comedy club to set a clearer direction for himself. Moving it from "child's play" into an adult hobby might be a goal.

Rena would increase her social interaction (particularly with people her own age), identify a job or make a career choice, follow through on training, and continue to search for her birth mother.

Michael would improve his relationships with children his own age, reduce his bizarre and "silly" behaviors, improve his school performance, and find a hobby or activity in which he can excel.

Although the psychosocial rehabilitation movement promotes family involvement as a way of providing support to psychiatrically impaired individuals, it tends to focus on intervention with individual clients rather than with the family system. That is, the family is seen as both a potential resource for the individual client and as deserving of support and encouragement as it attempts to engage the mentally ill individual, but the psychosocial approach stops short of intervening in family dynamics to help achieve improvements in the client. Therefore, a psychosocial rehabilitation approach to the Shores would look at the family system only to see how it enhanced or impinged upon the individual goals of its members.

Because the psychosocial approach begins "where the client is," typically the first step in working with a family is to identify *who* the client is. However, in the Shore family, it would be difficult to identify the client because of the complex interplay of problems within the family system. Although the problems are quite intense and intractable, they are less severe than those usually addressed by psychosocial rehabilitation, and, except for Charley (who had a brief psychotic episode), no one in the family has been labeled severely mentally ill. The psychosocial intervention most likely to be applied to this family (if one were to be applied at all) would probably be intensive case management, but additional services might be required for some family members.

Nevertheless, I will consider Nancy's functioning for the purpose of presenting a psychosocial rehabilitation practitioner's viewpoint of assessment.

The practitioner would begin by noting Nancy's skills—her intelligence and her ability to act in a crisis. Despite her disability, she has been able to maintain a home, and she serves as the organizer for family life. She is able to function at fairly high levels under crisis circumstances, but she deteriorates and loses some of her skills during the gaps between crises. Her anxiety attacks and lack of confidence in other family members are problematic both for herself and for them. Although the case report describes the dynamics between Nancy and other family members, there is little mention about the details of their interactions or the observed quality of their relationships. These specific observations about Nancy's interpersonal skills would be an important part of the assessment.

I have carefully avoided delving into the "why's" of Nancy's behavior but have instead presented a *descriptive* accounting (the "what's") of her strengths and weaknesses. Psychosocial rehabilitation can be seen as building ego strength by focusing on current adaptation. The complex feelings behind many of Nancy's difficulties are not ignored; they are merely cast in a different light. She has experienced loss and a lack of control throughout her life. The psychosocial rehabilitation approach would concentrate on helping Nancy take responsibility for her life by setting reachable goals and on supporting her as she tries to meet these goals.

Because of her "investment" in her disabling condition, loss, and lack of control, Nancy may not experience clear goals or initially show interest in changing any of these things. For this reason, a psychosocial rehabilitation practitioner might spend a substantial period of time in the assessment and goal-setting process.

One of Nancy's chief difficulties seems to be the lack of structure in her life. Despite her injury, she is capable of doing more than she does now; a psychosocial rehabilitation approach might identify activities or hobbies for her to pursue. She is socially isolated and has not developed supportive relationships with peers; a psychosocial rehabilitation program would include having her become involved in a group or club, or in some other way interacting with others outside the family. She might be encouraged to join a weight-loss group or to develop a diet program for herself. The strength of the psychosocial rehabilitation approach lies in helping clients like Nancy to set such goals. However, because the approach avoids psychodynamic interventions, it would lose effectiveness as her inner resistances to these "improvements" began to express themselves.

Overall, a psychosocial rehabilitation program for Nancy would build upon her intelligence and capacity to organize and would encourage her to become a more involved participant in the world. Even though Nancy has a history filled with "good" reasons for isolation and depression, the psychosocial rehabilitation approach would not focus on the "reasons behind the madness" but would emphasize current functional deficits and would propose solutions that would alleviate them.

## TREATMENT OF CHOICE

My attempt to apply the psychosocial rehabilitation model to the Shore family has required a bit of a stretch, and my attempts to connect elements of the approach to this family's needs do not depict actual practice. The Shores are not really a good illustration of the effective use of the approach because, although the family members present multiple problems, they are not "sick enough." The psychosocial rehabilitation approach seems to be best applied in cases in which the main problem is one of reality testing, and in which the individual's social skills are seriously impaired.

Nevertheless, I will draw upon the Shores to illustrate some interventions that might be possible under the rubric of psychosocial rehabilitation, even though in all likelihood this family would not be seen by a psychosocial practitioner.

## THE THERAPEUTIC PROCESS

Psychosocial rehabilitation currently encompasses a number of models that represent different means to the same end: the maintenance of chronically mentally ill individuals in community settings in ways that maximize their potentials and minimize their deficits. Despite the differences in program components, the common denominator is the recognition that the target population is extremely vulnerable and requires substantial assistance in order to simply carry on everyday activities. This recognition rings true at a "gut" level for anyone who has ever worked with seriously mentally ill individuals; but beyond this, there needs to be a sense of *why* this feels so true and why specific interventions make sense with this population. In this respect, the psychosocial rehabilitation movement has fallen short of its potential; although it suggests a set of interventions, it has not yet provided a strong theoretical basis for the appropriate uses of these interventions (Crystal, 1978; Glasscote et al., 1971).

Within the Shore family, for instance, Michael seems at considerable risk for lifelong dependency and inadequate functioning. A psychosocial rehabilitation intervention might involve reviewing his goals with him and exploring the consequences of his disturbed behavior vis-à-vis his goals. A psychosocial rehabilitation practitioner would focus attention on hope for the future rather than on his rage about "being different." Michael might do well in a child or adolescent partial-hospitalization program as part of a larger plan to reduce his bizarre behaviors and increase his social skills. A strong case management approach in such a setting would stress engaging him in activities and working with him while he is there to model and teach more appropriate behaviors. Although some of his feelings of deep narcissistic injustice and injury would not be addressed by the psychosocial rehabilitation approach, Michael would be taught specific, concrete behaviors and skills, in the hope that active mastery would lead to an improved sense of self-esteem. There are good reasons to believe that such an experience of mastery would be extremely helpful to Michael, but the theoretical and dynamic implications of these interventions would not be addressed. In fact, such attempts at "insight" would be ridiculed as irrelevant in many psychosocial rehabilitation programs.

## Techniques and Methods

The International Association of Psychosocial Rehabilitation Services (IAPSRS), an organization representing agencies that consider themselves to be a part of the psychosocial rehabilitation movement, has recently defined psychosocial rehabilitation services as follows:

> [Those services that involve] the process of facilitating an individual's restoration to an optimal level of independent functioning in the community . . . while the nature of the process and the methods used differ in different settings, psychosocial rehabilitation programs invariably encourage persons to participate actively with others in the attainment of mental health and social competence goals. In many settings, participants are called members. The process emphasizes the wholeness and wellness of the individual and seeks a comprehensive approach to the provision of vocational, residential, social/recreational, educational, and personal adjustment services. (IAPSRS, 1985)

Rutman (in press) has summarized the nine categories of psychosocial rehabilitation services that are described in the IAPSRS statement: vocational; residential; social-recreational; educational; personal adjustment; services to natural support systems; client outreach and linkage; basic need-oriented services (e.g., food, clothing, shelter); and larger system-oriented services (e.g., advocacy, planning).

In a recent report that looked at current information about psychosocial programs (Carrilio, 1985), I noted that all psychosocial rehabilitation programs incorporate the following principles:

1. Respect and attention are given to the client's perspective and goals.
2. Adequate supports are provided for clients in areas of functioning in which they may be deficient.
3. Individualized plans address the "whole client"; that is, although symptoms and diagnosis are taken into account, a client's ability to function independently on multiple dimensions is bolstered through a program of training and support that takes into account many of the environmental and contextual variables that impinge upon the client.
4. Interventions are coordinated, and fixed responsibility for a client is clearly identified. In other words, responsibility for the client remains with the same case manager; it does not shift as the client moves around in the service system.
5. Programs are intended to enhance an individual's skills and are expected to encourage and accommodate a client's growth.

Additionally, I noted that, in a psychosocial rehabilitation program:

The primary consideration should be that of developing an approach which meets the needs of clients. At a minimum, the following goals need to be considered: (a) improving the quality of life for clients; (b) enabling clients to experience success and movement from one level to another; (c) developing programs which take into account self-defined client goals; (d) enabling clients to maintain their highest functioning through a system of supports; (e) improving the client's functioning whenever possible; (f) preventing deterioration in functioning through the development of strong networks for clients; (g) developing pre-vocational and vocational skills. (Carrilio, 1985, p. 2)

Much of the literature in the field of psychosocial rehabilitation is devoted to explicating service structures and program models that can meet the needs of a highly impaired client population. Three major approaches within psychosocial rehabilitation are the intensive case management model, the club house model, and the high expectancy model. Each differs significantly with regard to auspices, goals, and program structure.

## Intensive case management model

This model, which is highly effective with noncompliant "young chronics" (Berzon & Lowenstein, 1984; Goldfinger et al., 1984; Pepper & Rygelwicz, 1984; Stein & Test, 1980), involves a case management team that carries fixed responsibility for a case, regardless of the client's movement between programs and from one residential situation to the next.

Team members work with the client's own situation (Stein & Test, 1980), which can mean in the client's home, at work, at the local welfare office, or anywhere else in the community at large. The team provides 24-hour support and crisis availability; the goal is preventing regression or hospitalization. Team members model appropriate behaviors and teach the client the skills needed to function independently within the community. Interventions are highly individualized and the intensity varies with client need (Test, 1979).

## Club house model

This model represents the traditional psychosocial rehabilitation approach as embodied in the original Fountain House concept. Programs that follow this model have a very accepting attitude towards members and support them over an indefinite period of time. Most of the club house programs place a great deal of emphasis on the value of work in improving a member's self-esteem and status and in maintaining gains in social functioning. Much attention is paid to developing vocational skills and job placements. Programs that follow the club house model usually stress the need for housing, which is as normalized as possible, frequently in specially supervised apartment settings. These programs also utilize the program milieu itself as a therapeutic tool; members actively participate in the program, from assisting at the phones to helping with the agency's bookkeeping. The milieu is highly interactive and fosters mutuality and responsibility for oneself.

Charley, more than the other Shore family members, might benefit from a club house approach, in which he would be accepted and in which he could make a positive contribution that others would appreciate. He appears to be more functionally disabled than Nancy; his role functioning as a husband, father, and worker is quite impaired. He dreams about who he might be, instead of focusing on who he actually is. He has a hard time sticking to the mundane tasks that are required to maintain himself in the community, and he is quite dependent upon his wife. In assessing his functional deficits, a psychosocial rehabilitation practitioner would attempt to examine with Charley the things he realistically is capable of doing. Charley's inability to maintain himself as an adult in the community might be addressed through both the vocational rehabilitation program and a structured day program. Like Nancy, Charley is isolated from his peers, and the lack of feedback from others exacerbates his deficits. In a structured program, he might participate in groups, training, and recreational activities that would involve him with others.

*High expectancy model*

This model consists of a continuum of program components along which the client moves. Often, program elements are time-limited, and clients are expected to "graduate" from one level to the next. This approach stresses goal-setting as well as planning between the staff person and the client. Progress is frequently reviewed, and there is a clear expectation that the individual will follow the program that he or she has developed with the staff. Careful assessment of a client's skills and deficits with respect to independent living is an important part of this approach.

Because of her difficulty in sustaining effort and her tendency to lapse into inertia, Rena might do quite well with a high-expectancy approach, especially if she could move into an intensive case management situation after she had graduated from a high-demand program.

No one psychosocial rehabilitation program follows one of these models precisely; instead, programs combine elements of these models to varying extents. The psychosocial approach has been developed not only to address a population with severe disabilities but also to establish a supportive network which provides "continuity of care." Psychosocial rehabilitation programs work quite effectively with clients who are extremely vulnerable and who have had repeated experiences of failure, decompensation, and hospitalization (Bachrach, 1979, 1984a, 1984b; Stein & Test, 1984; Test & Stein, 1980).

## LIMITATIONS OF THE MODEL

In previous sections of this chapter, I have hinted at some limitations of the psychosocial rehabilitation approach. Some limitations seem to be particularly relevant for clinical social workers who attempt to utilize its principles in their practices:

### 1. Population

At present, the approach targets a small subgroup of the mental health population—the severely mentally ill. The benefits of "normalizing," mutuality, and sharing of responsibility for treatment goals, and a focus on adaptive skills, could very well be helpful to other populations. However, the psychosocial rehabilitation movement tends to consider those people who are not severely disabled to be among the "worried well"; they are therefore not seen as needing psychosocial rehabilitation intervention.

### 2. Conceptual development

The psychosocial rehabilitation approach is pragmatic and concrete. For clients whose functioning in daily tasks shows marked impairment, there are often "easy" successes—that is, small concrete goals are reached and can be built upon. However, this concrete, problem-solving approach often leads to an avoidance of theory development and a conceptual understanding of why particular interventions may or may not be successful. The tendency is to attribute success to ideology and program structure rather than to acknowledge a connection between psychodynamic and developmental theory and the logic of a particular program approach. For example, the director of one psychosocial rehabilitation program told Glasscote and his colleagues:

All of the existing efforts are well-intentioned but intuitive efforts to make people more comfortable in the community. If there is a process or sequence of some unique combination of services, so far no one has adequately identified or documented it. . . . We have put a new program together out of experience and common sense, not from a formulated theory. (Glasscote et al., 1971, p. 197)

## 3. Ideology

The psychosocial rehabilitation movement sees itself as championing the most downtrodden populations, but within the movement there is little questioning of the larger social forces that lead to the problems of mental illness. There seems to be an acceptance that there is a "norm" from which the psychosocial rehabilitation client deviates; treatment involves convincing the client to follow the rules better. Although this may prove to be an effective way to reduce social deviance, there is a disturbing lack of self-consciousness about imposing normative behavior upon clients.

Because of its equalitarian "social treatment" position, the psychosocial rehabilitation approach seems to have a great deal of potential. However, that potential is often unrealized, because techniques and concepts have been arrived at in a somewhat trial-and-error fashion and need further development.

## RESEARCH

As an ideological movement, psychosocial rehabilitation does not generate research into clinical theory as much as it generates policy research into program models (see, for instance, Pepper & Rygelwicz, 1984; Stein & Ganser, 1983; Stein & Test, 1976, 1980; Talbott, 1978; Weisbrod, Test, & Stein, 1980). The evidence thus far indicates that with highly impaired mentally ill individuals, psychosocial rehabilitation is quite effective, as long as the intervention is maintained; the challenge is to develop strategies for long-term community support for this population. Although it is clear from the research (see especially Pepper & Rygelwicz, 1984; Test & Stein, 1980) that highly impaired individuals can be maintained in the community, it is not clear who is to be responsible for the costs and sponsorship of such programs; these questions continue to be debated.

The psychosocial rehabilitation model tends to focus on field research that explores the efficacy of one or another policy objective. The attempts to develop clinical concepts (see, for example, Anthony, 1980) are just beginning and a great deal more research is needed.

## SUMMARY

I have presented an overview of the psychosocial rehabilitation model and have demonstrated some of the issues that this approach raises for clinical social workers. Although the psychosocial rehabilitation approach has many similarities to social casework's traditional person-in-situation approach, it is also an ideological movement. Psychosocial rehabilitation focuses heavily on program structure and on creating a treatment milieu within which clients and staff actively *work* together on the clients' problems, rather than on first trying to *understand* the individual or social roots of the problem.

Psychosocial rehabilitation nobly addresses ameliorative issues of social policy and funding, but it tends to give little attention to clinical theory and social critique (see, for example, Crystal, 1978; Finch et al., 1984; Talbott, 1983). Most psychosocial rehabilitation practitioners know what will work and what will get favorable responses from their clients. What is missing is a clinical understanding of why an intervention is effective, and how the approach can be expanded so that it can be useful for a broader population. It is here that the trained clinical social worker who embraces the ideals of the psychosocial rehabilitation movement can have the most effect.

Psychosocial rehabilitation as a movement and as social policy has the potential to generate an important resurgence of interest in both the environmental and individual sources of pathology. The challenge now is to add depth to the approach by developing a better understanding not only of the ways in which traditional psychosocial interventions reflect sound clinical theory but also of the ways in which psychosocial rehabilitation, as an ideological movement, can move from a status-quo, conservative movement into a force for true social change.

## REFERENCES

Anthony, W. (1980). *Principles of psychiatric rehabilitation.* Baltimore, MD: University Park Press.

Bachrach, L. (1979). Planning mental health services for chronic patients. *Hospital and Community Psychiatry, 30,* 387–392.

Bachrach, L. (1984a). Asylum and chronically ill psychiatric patients. *American Journal of Psychiatry, 141,* 975–978.

Bachrach, L. (1984b, December). *Planning services for chronic mental patients.* Speech given to a seminar of agency executives, Philadelphia, PA.

Baron, R., Rutman, I., & Klaczynska, B. (Eds.). (1980). *The community imperative.* Proceedings of a National Conference on Overcoming Public Opposition to Community Care for the Mentally Ill. Philadelphia, PA: Horizon House Institute for Research and Development.

Berzon, P., & Lowenstein, B. (1984). A flexible model of case management. In B. Pepper & H. Rygelwicz (Eds.), *Advances in treating the young adult chronic patient. New Directions in Mental Health Series* (No. 21, pp. 49–57). San Francisco: Jossey-Bass.

Carrilio, T. (1985, August). *Report on psychosocial rehabilitation.* Paper presented to Philadelphia County Office of Mental Health and Mental Retardation, Philadelphia, PA.

Crystal, R. (1978). A survey of the current status and program evaluation needs in the state-federal rehabilitation program. D. K. Harrison & J. V. Miller (Eds.), *Michigan Studies in Rehabilitation* (Series 1, Monograph 2). Ann Arbor: University of Michigan.

Finch, E., McGowan, S. A., & White, K. M. (1984, November). *Developing psychosocial rehabilitation services* (Kansas Community Support Project monograph). Topeka, KA: Kansas State OMH/MR.

Glasscote, R., Cumming, R., Rutman, R., Sussex, J., & Glassman, S. (1971). *Rehabilitating the mentally ill in the community: A study of psychosocial rehabilitation centers.* Washington, DC: American Psychiatric Association.

Goldfinger, S. M., Hopkin, J., & Surber, R. (1984). Treatment resisters or system resisters? Toward a better service system for acute care recidivists. In B. Pepper & H. Rygelwicz (Eds.), *Advances in treating the young adult chronic patient. New Directions in Mental Health Series* (No. 21, pp. 17–27). San Francisco: Jossey-Bass.

Hatfield, A. (1984). The family consumer movement: A new force in service delivery. In B. Pepper & H. Rygelwicz (Eds.), *Advances in treating the young adult chronic patient. New Directions in Mental Health Series* (No. 21, pp. 71–79). San Francisco: Jossey-Bass.

Hollis, F., & Woods, M. (1981). *Casework: A psychosocial therapy* (3rd ed.). New York: Random House.

International Association of Psychosocial Rehabilitation Services. (1985). *Organizations providing psychosocial rehabilitation and related community support services in the United States: 1985* (p. iii). McLean, VA: Author.

Pepper, B., & Rygelwicz, H. (Eds.). (1984). *Advances in treating the young adult chronic patient. New Directions in Mental Health Series* (No. 21). San Francisco: Jossey-Bass.

Paul, G. L., & Lantz, R. G. (1977). *Psychosocial treatment of chronic mental patients: Milieu versus social learning programs.* Cambridge, MA: Harvard University Press.

Rubin, M. (1980). Reducing disincentives and fostering the rehabilitative process: An existing model program. In L. Perlman (Ed.), *A report of the fourth Mary Switzer Memorial Seminar* (pp. 87–110). Washington, DC: National Rehabilitation Association.

Rutman, I. (1963, December). *The historical origins, dimensions, and present status of psychiatric rehabilitation.* Presented at the National Institute of Psychiatric Rehabilitation Centers, Chicago, IL.

Rutman, I. (in press). The psychosocial rehabilitation movement in the United States. In A. Myerson & T. Fine (Eds.), *Psychiatric disability: Clinical, administrative and legal dimensions.* Washington, DC: American Psychiatric Press.

Schmoeger, M. (1981). *An interpretation of the theme: Community mental health—pendulum or synthesis?* 21st Annual Contributing Membership/Community Meeting, Lansdale, PA.

Schmoeger, M. Personal interview, April, 1987.

Stein, L., & Test, M. A. (1976). Retraining hospital staff for work in a community program in Wisconsin. *Hospital and Community Psychiatry, 27,* 266–268.

Stein, L., & Test, M. A. (1980). Alternative to mental hospital treatment. Part I. Conceptual model. *Archives of General Psychiatry, 37,* 392–397.

Stein, L., & Ganser, L. (1983). The dollar follows the patient. In J. Talbott (Ed.), *Unified mental health systems: Utopia unrealized. New Directions in Mental Health Series* (No. 18, pp. 25–32). San Francisco: Jossey-Bass.

Stein, L., & Test, M. A. (1984). Community treatment of the young adult patient. In B. Pepper & H. Rygelwicz (Eds.), *Advances in treating the young adult chronic patient. New Directions in Mental Health Series* (No. 21, pp. 57–67). San Francisco: Jossey-Bass.

Talbott, J. (1978). *The chronic mental patient: Problems, solutions, and recommendations for a public policy.* Washington, DC: The American Psychiatric Association.

Talbott, J. (Ed.). (1983). *Unified mental health systems: Utopia unrealized. New Directions in Mental Health Series* (No. 18). San Francisco: Jossey-Bass.

Test, M.A. (1979, Spring). Continuity of care in community treatment. *New Directions for Mental Health Services, 1,* 15–23.

Test, M. A., & Stein, L. (1980). Alternatives to mental hospital treatment. Part III. Social cost. *Archives of General Psychiatry, 37,* 409–412.

Turner, F. (1974). Psychosocial therapy. In F. Turner (Ed.), *Social work treatment* (pp. 84–111). New York: The Free Press.

Weisbrod, B., Test, M. A., & Stein, L. (1980). Alternatives to mental hospital treatment. Part II. *Archives of General Psychiatry, 37,* 400–405.

Wintersteen, R. (1986). Rehabilitating the chronically mentally ill: Social work's claim to leadership. *Social Work, 31,* 332–337.

# Part III
# Metaparadigms

# 12

# The Eco-Systems Perspective

## *Carol H. Meyer, D.S.W.*

The eco-systems perspective is unlike the other treatment approaches discussed in this book. It is not a model, with prescriptions for addressing cases; it does not draw from a particular theory of personality; it does not specify outcomes. It is often misunderstood as being a treatment model, however. When it fails to live up to people's false expectations, it is denigrated as being "too abstract for practitioners to use," "too nonspecific for the case at hand," and "nonclinical in its orientation." The most common misuse of the eco-systems idea occurs when it is confused with theories of social systems (Parsons, 1969), a substantive (nonclinical) theory of the way social systems function. This confusion probably has to do with the similarity in language, as does the confusion of the eco-systems perspective with the ecological *Life Model of Practice* (Germain & Gitterman, 1980), which *is* a practice model.

Given its reputation (which is based upon these confusions and criticisms), the eco-systems perspective has only slowly found its way into the social work treatment repertoire, and has had no empirical tests of effectiveness. Its inclusion in this book of paradigms indicates that the misunderstandings are fading away, because the perspective *is* a paradigm, a "metamodel" for use in social work practice.

Its major claim is that it is a model for assessment, and because it can encompass *any* treatment model, it has the potential for serving as a unifying perspective in social work practice (Meyer, 1983). Given the proliferation of disparate treatment models, this unifying idea seems vital for the future coherence of practice in social work.

The eco-systems perspective, which is drawn from ecological ideas and General Systems Theory, is specifically concerned with providing a broad context for clinical social work practice. As a complement to the linear perspective of most clinical approaches, it allows the clinician to view cases (individuals, families, and groups) holistically, that is, to recognize the interrelatedness of each person to his or her environment. When making an assessment, the clinician who employs this perspective can "step back" from the client, in order to gauge his or her representativeness of a particular population, problem-type, community, or other unit of analysis. The resultant view of the client stimulates the clinician to use a broad repertoire of interventions that are suitable for the varying needs of a particular case.

## THE CONCEPT OF THE PERSON AND THE HUMAN EXPERIENCE

The underlying philosophical position of the eco-systems perspective is that the person is connected to others, as well as to the social institutions, cultural forces, and the physical space that make up his or her environment. Although there is no explicit assumption about the substantive nature of things or people, there is, in this perspective, heavy reliance upon the person's *connectedness*.

The clinician's sense of the interrelatedness of components in a case—the people, ideas, problems, functioning, history—derives from empirical observation, clinical evidence, and philosophical conviction. The idea is that once we have decided what the boundaries of a system are in a particular client's case, we can demonstrate that all of the components are tied together by virtue of sharing psychological, ideological, social and/or physical space. Given this primary assumption from General Systems Theory (von Bertalanffy, 1968), there is always a systemic explanation for behavior and events in the life of a case.

The ecological metaphor of mutual adaptation suggests that the connectedness referred to is reciprocal—that is, a certain adaptiveness takes place between the person and others in the environment they share. Adaptation, as discussed by biologists such as Dubos (1965) and psychoanalysts such as Hartmann (1958), is the key to human survival. In modern clinical practice, it is becoming viewed as the most practical and humane goal of treatment. To manage one's life through coping and mastery—the two major instrumentalities of adaptation—seems to be the closest one can come in treatment to the reality of life. We all must adapt in order to grow and develop, to love and to work. When we fail, the therapeutic process is most successful and least costly when it follows what happens naturally in life. Thus, the constructs of ecology and General Systems Theory offer scientific grounding for a philosophy of persons in their environments, which, after all, describes the human experience.

## HISTORICAL PERSPECTIVE

The eco-systems perspective had its origins in the two theoretical streams of General Systems Theory and ecological theory. Its application to social work occurred in the late 1960s (Germain, 1968; Hartman, 1970; Janchill, 1969; Meyer, 1970), partially in response to the social turmoil of that era, and partially in response to a half-century-long pursuit of a single holistic framework to support social work practice theory.

Although Lutz (1956) and Hearn (1969) had introduced important monographs concerning General Systems Theory and its implications for social work, for a long time there was only academic interest in developing this line of thought. However, when Gordon (1965) and Bartlett (1970) wrote about restructuring the way in which practice should be thought about, their efforts made the next step (the development of the eco-systems perspective) possible. Bartlett and Gordon argued that it was dysfunctional for social work to continue to view methodology as the central feature of practice. They promoted, instead, the idea that *knowledge* was the common core. Up to then, methods such as casework and group work had generated their own methodological knowledge, because cases had not been viewed as complex phenomena that generated differential tasks to be worked with. Social workers approached their cases with fixed methodological commitments, and in a sense they shaped their view of cases to their predetermined technologies (Nelsen, 1975). This made it difficult to encompass the yet unknown or unrecognized events that were not addressed by those technologies. Thus, many potential clients with problems that were unresponsive to particular methods were simply left out of social work's purview and services.

The pressures felt by all professions during the years of social turmoil in the 1960s and 1970s were of particular concern to many social workers, who felt that they were obliged to address the broadest scope of client need and to develop the knowledge base required to do this.

The eco-systems perspective evolved through the collegial efforts of faculty at the Columbia University School of Social Work, as an effort to carry forth the work of Bartlett and Gordon. The goal was to restructure the prevailing orientation to practice—to begin to view cases holistically, to educate students as social workers (rather than as caseworkers or group workers or family therapists), and to give them a range of methodological skills that would prepare them to "do what was needed" in their own practice. The perspective simply enlarged their view of cases, and attuned them to actors and events that might have been lost to view had they approached those cases from a linear practice orientation.

The path of the eco-systems perspective has been uphill since its inception. When faced with criticisms of its "abstractness," its nonprescriptive, open-treatment repertoire, and its focus on the environment, proponents have often felt it necessary to defend it against what they feel to be an unjustified claim that it is "nonclinical." Conscious application of the perspective has been slow in developing in the profession, but there is presently evidence that the perspective is gradually becoming known and is being found to be useful, particularly as a unifying framework for the full repertoire of clinical practice approaches.

## KEY THEORETICAL CONSTRUCTS

### Explanation of Problems

The eco-systems perspective has the ability to order the complex and fluid data that make up all clinical cases. This ordering is accomplished through the use of *structural* features of General Systems Theory, which serve as a framework for case assessment.

The Shore case, for example, is a family "system" by definition. First, it exists *separately* from other families and the community. Second, it has *boundaries* that are more or less permeable, but which clearly delineate the family as both a unit and as subgroups of individuals within it. In fact, the decision as to where to locate the boundary involving the daughter, Rena, is a significant clinical decision. Is she part of the family, even though she has left the home? Are there others in the family's life space who ought to be included in their "system" even though they are not present?

A third structural feature that identifies this family as a system is their *commonality*, their having a shared history, culture, daily life experience. The problems the family cite are not extraneous to their past and present lives, and it has to be assumed that their crises, problem behaviors, dysfunctioning, and views of the world are not new to them. Rather, the ways in which they conduct their individual and family lives represent *patterned behavior*, which is part of the definition of a living system.

Finally, the hallmark of systems thinking, *interconnectedness*, is self-evident in the Shore family. The *reciprocity* or mutuality in their relationships is like a thread being pulled through fabric; it shapes the garment all the way through; even the distortions it creates are organic to the material of which it is a part. Mrs. Shore's lifelong quest for unconditional love and for control of events contributes to her demands upon her husband, who in turn requires the controls she places upon him to restrain him in his manic behavior. The children, as so often happens in enmeshed families, carry out the parents' struggle with each other, and undoubtedly serve as safety valves, scapegoats, or displacements so that the marriage can stay intact. Everyone "needs" everyone else, and that is a recognizable feature of all intimate systems such as families. The consequence of the Shores' mutuality—a kind of emotional seesaw and crisis-ridden life—constitutes their individual family thumbprint, their particular version of interconnectedness.

This perspective, using principles of General Systems Theory and ecology, not only provides a structure for ordering the case data, but also allows for inclusion of *contextual variables*. Every case has actors, processes that flow between them, and environments, which are all too easy to overlook when the clinician is preoccupied with features of personality. In the case of the Shore family, the environments are institutional, concrete, and cultural. They include their economic situation (his unemployment and her disability payments), the agencies with which they have been involved, the medical and psychiatric care they have received, their housing arrangements, and schools. Issues of gender, mental illness, personality disorder, and the legacy of adoption also feature prominently in this case. All of these environmental factors, when salient and relevant (Germain, 1968), impinge upon the family members to some degree or other, influence them, and are influenced *by* them, in regard to feelings, attitudes, and behaviors. The eco-systems perspective induces the clinician to pay attention to these environments, to include them in the case assessment, and to consider them as vital components of the case, no matter which practice approach is selected.

Apart from the structural framework and contextual underpinnings that are provided for in the eco-systems framework, the idea of *hierarchical relations* is a vital feature of General Systems Theory that is crucial in clinical practice. Systems theorists describe the existence of subsystems, which are always interacting with the larger systems—for example, the individual in the family, the family in the community, and so on.

An element that is often overlooked in some family treatment approaches and other practice models (Johnson, 1986) is the biological and psychological "system" within people that gives substance and definition to their individuality. Thus, in the Shore case, Mrs. Shore's obesity and the back pain that has disabled her, Mr. Shore's mental illness that has shaped his behavior, and Michael's asthma that has created a "sick role" for him have to be seen as problems in their own right, but also as problems with systemic repercussions. Once they are involved in an intimate family network, family members cannot suffer psychological or physical problems without repercussions.

Finally, the perspective allows for inclusion of those characteristics of the family and its members that belong simply because they are part of the case "story." They are elaborations to be found nowhere else but in the client's *history*. Clinicians know that the past is always expressed in the present, and it is the *use* made of the past that is often a forceful part of the family's problems. We shall view the Shores' significant history in our assessment.

This way of looking at cases may require of some clinicians a kind of cognitive restructuring, because we are so accustomed to thinking in a linear way. Here, however, we are required to think in circles, not lines. The eco-map (Hartman, 1978; Meyer, 1970) is a model for this thinking style; it is a structure for ensuring that the familiar social work psychosocial focus is carried out. The context of cases (Rein & White, 1981)—whether it is institutional, sociocultural, economic, or political— is as integral to fathoming meanings as are the individuals and their relationships. In systems terms, interconnectedness applies to all of the components of the case.

## Theory of Change

In this perspective, change occurs partially as a consequence of *imbalance* within the system. Living systems normally survive when their boundaries are sufficiently permeable to allow for exchange with the outside environment. The subsequent events affect the balance of the variables within the system, so that too little stimulation can result in a winding down of the system (this is called *entropy*), and too much of an intrusion can result in overextending the resources of the system. In the case of the Shores, they appear to be enmeshed as a family, and in great need of improved ego functioning as individuals. They are ripe for being overwhelmed by events. Systems survive when they can maintain *equilibrium*—taking in and giving out "energy," always *changing within tolerable limits*, and theoretically regenerating themselves to move on to a higher level of functioning. Examples are everywhere in life: schooling, illness, new jobs, moving to a new location; if the family can absorb the influence of these events, as they usually can, life can improve for them. If, on the other hand, there are idiosyncratic features of their individual or collective lives that are threatened by these life events, or if the event itself is stressful, then loss of equilibrium can take place, and the family may become flooded with influences, energy, information, or experiences that they cannot absorb into their way of living. This seems to be the case with the Shores: Their imbalance, or loss of equilibrium, could account for their state of chronic crisis. The imbalance, and the anxiety it creates, can also be a force to induce them to change. One wonders what it did to them, or for them, to have read the narrative of their case.

As we have seen, the Shore case comprises relationships, contextual variables, internal physical and psychological features among its individual members, and the psychosocial history (both individual and collective) of the family members. Thus, one seeks multiple and complex "parts" of the case. Here, we can go into the vast repertoire of practice approaches as represented in this book and elsewhere (Meyer, 1983), and even the "invention of interventions" (Rosenfeld, 1983), in the effort to "fit" the treatment to the individualized needs of the clients involved. Psychosocial, problem-solving, behaviorist, and cognitive theorists propose distinct views of the world, and the eco-systems perspective provides for these ideas to be applied where there are substantive problems to be addressed.

What the eco-systems perspective demands is that whatever change is induced through clinical measures be managed with *systemic implications* in mind. So a change in feeling, attitude, or behavior in one family member would, through timing, depth, and direction of treatment, have to be tolerable to the other family members *if* the intention is to maintain that family system. The aim is to avoid overwhelming the capacities of the family for absorption of change, to match, if possible, the shift in one member's behavior with that of another, so that an adaptive fit between them would remain. In the natural, ongoing life of a family, each member manages changes that might occur in the family (or in himself or herself, for that matter) in accordance with what he or she can tolerate. Thus, we observe defenses of all kinds to block out or avoid the recognition or impact of some changes. When left to their own devices, and when ego structures are in place, people stay in balance within their own personality system, and in relationship with others. When they cannot—when adaptations fail—they often become clients, and then it is up to the clinician to keep a close watch on the adaptive propensities of the individuals involved. Maintaining or re-righting the equilibrium of a family system is a major treatment goal, but the paths to that end are multiple.

Systems theorists use the concept of *equifinality* to describe the phenomenon of similar outcomes deriving from different entry points. This can occur in a given system because of the connectedness of case variables, which in turn engender *reciprocity*. Equifinality in the Shore case means that there is no à priori entry point, that one can introduce treatment measures in a number of alternative places so as to induce change. This will be illustrated concretely in the section on the therapeutic process.

Finally, note that there has been no mention of the idea of "cure" in this discussion. Treatment in a systemic view is normally addressed to adaptations—the capacity of people to master their life tasks and to cope with their problems. There are at least two reasons for this discounting of cure as an outcome of treatment. First, there are limitations in clinicians' knowledge, skills, and resources. Can the clinician "cure" Michael's asthma? Mr. Shore's Bipolar mental illness? Mrs. Shore's disabling back condition or gross obesity? Rena's adoption history? Second, we should recall the systemic goal of re-righting the balance; there is some parsimony involved in helping the individuals in this family to cope better with the reality of their lives.

## Personality Theory

Just as there is no particular treatment approach that is integral to the eco-systems perspective, there is no particular personality theory that supports it. As a viewing and assessment tool, the perspective allows for ideas from other theories, for example, psychoanalytic, behavioral, or cognitive.

Since I have been trained in psychosocial practice and psychoanalytically oriented ego psychology, I will discuss the Shore case with this commitment in mind, making some excursions into developmental and cognitive theories as well. The adaptive view of ego psychology is particularly fitting to the eco-systems perspective (Goldstein, 1984).

## ASSESSMENT

The Shore family appears to be an exemplar for the use of an eco-systems perspective. Their family story can only be described systemically, because their personalities and behaviors are locked into each other. At the same time, their individual histories and problems introduce different dimensions to the family story, adding to the complexity of the case assessment.

This is a case of an enmeshed family (Minuchin, 1974), whose general functioning is probably on a level lower than it might be, given the internal resources of the members. The mother is the linchpin that determines the directions in which the father, daughter, and son move in their lives, yet each of the family members carries a personal compass by which he or she struggles to keep from being overwhelmed by the mother's control. The father and son are having difficulty in maintaining their integrity—or personal boundaries—while Rena has tried to escape from the family altogether.

## Some Unanswered Questions

There are some features of this family that are bizarre, but answers to some important questions might alter this judgment. For example, what exactly *is* Mrs. Shore's medical diagnosis? The fact that she can on some occasions do nursing duty, and at other times is disabled and unemployable, suggests that some clarification of her back problem could throw some light upon the central problem in this case. Had this mother been able to work at what she loved, her need to control might well have been sublimated, and her family might have been spared her continuing vigil. Is further medical treatment out of the question? Is there work she can do in her field that would not be painful for her? Would her back pain be less debilitating if she were not so obese?

Michael is another person for whom health information is incomplete. Has he ever had a neurological examination? His behavioral problems and his asthma do not seem to qualify him for a learning-disabled class. His symptomatology suggests an organic source of his behavioral problems; he seems to be bright and, to a degree, self-aware, but is unable to control the "silly" and provocative behavior he describes so well.

Mr. Shore's belated psychiatric diagnosis of Bipolar illness does not seem to be integrated into the family's understanding or its behavior towards him. Nor is there any suggestion that his vocational rehabilitation program is adapting his job training to his interests or capabilities. Why should he be a janitor, when he is bright and interested in the theater and nonphysical work? If becoming a janitor is the only goal under consideration, could he at least be placed as a janitor in a theater?

Rena's situation is very unclear. When, how, and under what circumstances did she learn of her adoption? What were the parents thinking of when they allowed a 13-year-old girl to live by herself? How is she supporting herself?

## The Family Balance

Mrs. Shore, once a "princess" in her family, was doted upon by parents and relatives until she was 11, when her father, a gambler and possible ne'er-do-well, left the family. Given her view of life as a small child, and then her fall from grace, it is a testament to Mrs. Shore's courage and competence that she studied and became a successful nurse. Her disability carries not only the back pain, but also the equally significant severe disappointment in the loss of her career. This loss of career also has a secondary impact, in that she has lost an arena in which she can exercise control of events, express aggression, and be in charge of others.

Mr. Shore appears to be the perfect foil for Mrs. Shore's psychological needs. He describes his wife as "the same as my mother," whom he says he remembers fondly—although one explicit memory was of her knocking his father out. (His father, like Mrs. Shore's, was a gambler.)

His propensity to talk expansively about his dreams (probably an early sign of his manic-depressive illness) caught the imagination of his wife-to-be, who had her own "little princess" fantasies. In their early marriage, his frequent job changes were not stressful, probably because they provided concrete justification for Mrs. Shore to rely upon herself as the chief wage earner. She was only 20 when they married (he was 27). During their first few years of marriage, his fantasies about his own career were understandable. That he was perceived of as a perpetual kid who did not mature was not an issue until the Shores decided to raise a family, and his sporadic employment was not a problem until Mrs. Shore stopped working. Up to that time, the unreality of their lives didn't make a difference; there was time enough and space enough for the couple to share a romanticized life. Mr. Shore's plaintive cry that "all I ever wanted was to be somebody" is reminiscent of Willy Loman's in *Death of a Salesman.* As in the play, there is a wife who unconsciously supports her husband's fantasies while overtly patronizing him.

The adoption of Rena—and six years later the birth of Michael—introduced realistic responsibilities and undoubtedly placed greater demands upon Mr. Shore to work steadily and to bring money into the household. He, of course, could not meet such worldly requirements. Soon after Michael's birth, Mrs. Shore developed her back problem and began to receive disability checks. With Mrs. Shore at home, treating her husband as if he were a child and demeaning his expressed wishes to assume a more responsible role in the household, it was only a matter of time before he began to fail at his odd jobs, to become virtually unemployed, and subsequently to have his psychotic episode.

The children appear to play roles imitative alternately of their mother and father. When Rena describes her "little princess" childhood, it is as if she is describing her mother's description of her own childhood. When Michael talks about his dreams and wishes, he says, "I just want to be good at something," echoing his father's hopeless affect. Because of what appears to be uncontrollable, impulsive behavior, Michael cannot fit in anywhere that is age-appropriate for him, especially at school, in the Boy Scouts, or among friends. What is left to him is to be oppressed by the attention of his mother and the competition of his father. With his sister out of the home, he is locked into a dangerous enmeshment that could create permanent psychological and physical damage for him.

Rena, on the other hand, appears to have escaped this nonnutritive environment, although under circumstances that are not serving her too well. She has theatrical interests like her father and appears to share the competence of her mother. But, on her own, without the means to support herself, she has an uncertain future. She appears to still be part of the family, and they seem to "need" her to maintain their equilibrium, but without her they have regrouped and turned their attention intensively to Michael.

## The Contextual Variables

The story of this case begins with the frustration felt by the community agencies because of the Shores' unending demand for services. This is a serious issue in service delivery: the assumption that services should be proffered and used towards the goal of closing cases, preferably through resolution, if not "cure," of problems. In truth, psychosocial and health services are not like public school education; often there is no graduation at the end. In cases like the Shores', where family conflict is at the center of their difficulties, many agencies would not offer ongoing clinical help, because the family members are not actively motivated to change, their relationships seem to be so intractable, and their problems are so longstanding.

It is a significant context that we are describing, for not only does the community view the family as incompetent, but also this perception cannot help but support the family members' view of *themselves* as incompetent. They have worn out the school, the health-care facilities, and probably the social agencies. Even if there were a cure for the ill-defined maladaptations of people like the Shores, it is unlikely that they would get to the source of help, or that the helpers would look kindly upon a family who seemed to be "unreachable" and apparently so hell-bent on their own destruction. Although this family might place severe demands upon a community's resource system, the fact is that it does *not* contain particularly unusual problems. Perhaps it is their quantity, as well as their complexity, that confounds us.

## The Presenting Problem

It was Mrs. Shore who expressed the family's problem as being in a state of perpetual crisis. From her own point of view, she seems to be a person who anticipates the worst; if it doesn't happen, she may even precipitate a crisis. Why? Perhaps to generate situations in which she can repetitively establish her role as the controlling force in the family. Does she need to do this because she has lost her ability to affirm herself in her own nuclear family, where she felt so loved, or in a work situation where she had proven herself to be so competent? If this hypothesis proves to be true, then there are treatment implications (to be discussed in the following section) that derive from this description of Mrs. Shore's needs.

Having almost worn out the effects of his "charm" and infectious fantasies, Mr. Shore possibly has become defeated by his diagnosis of Bipolar mental illness. In the first place, he is on medication that diminishes the very behaviors which he (and clearly his wife, as well as others) found attractive in the past. Second, he may well be playing a "sick role": "If they feel I'm sick, then I'll *be* sick, unemployed, and moody." To this Willy Loman, "attention must be paid," but the demeaning attention paid by his wife is not really helping him to develop self-esteem or a sense of competence. A clinical focus that is family-centered (actually, in this instance, wife-and-husband-centered) could be of significant help to Mr. Shore.

Michael clearly appears to be identified with his father in many respects; after all, Mr. Shore is his model as an adult male. In school, he is a loser; he has no friends, and his behavior may be provocative in order to gain attention. On the other hand, as has been mentioned before, there is a real question about the nature of his medical and behavioral problems. Is he brain-damaged? Is there medical, chemical, or rehabilitative treatment for him? As far as his role in the family is concerned, it would appear that Michael is scapegoated in order to mitigate parental tensions. For his part, Michael plays out the victim role to perfection. Only clinical help can interrupt this dysfunctional arrangement.

Rena, of course, is trying to escape this unhealthy family situation. She has identified with the potential capacities of both her mother and her father. She is bright and has demonstrated competence in school, and at times in work. She has the flair that is a feature of her father's character, even though in his case he has failed so miserably to put it to constructive use. Rena needs to have help in defining her own boundaries and achieving her own goals before she can safely reenter this family, so that she does not become engulfed by their crises. Perhaps, down the road, Rena can become a supportive influence in the family; it is unlikely that they can offer her the autonomy she needs at this time.

In summary, this family is engaged in a macabre dance, each member futilely seeking sustenance from the others through crisis behavior. What is needed is some kind of reconstitution for each of them, based on the others' ability to tolerate those changes. Treatment for this family would have to be sensitive to timing and balance. As each individual achieves a greater sense of self-esteem and competence, his or her hopeless demands upon the others will diminish. The Shores should then be better able to live as separate people together in their family.

## TREATMENT OF CHOICE

Treatment of choice is one of the many elements that make up the multilayered approach of the eco-systems perspective. In the spirit of true eclecticism, it would be possible to employ any number of practice models, just as long as the focus of treatment did not stray appreciably from the focus defined in the assessment. So, for example, one might use psychosocial, cognitive, or behavioral schemes with each family member, towards the goal of helping each one separate from the others and find his or her own ego boundary and life pursuit. Additionally, however, Mr. and Mrs. Shore would probably profit from couples' treatment (subsequent to their individual treatment) to help them find a more functional way of living together. Moreover, the children might have to be included in family treatment sessions, with the goal of reinforcing their separateness and redefining their mutual roles. Michael might find helpful peer support in a group experience; at the least, it would provide a counteraction to the excessive pull of his family. Throughout all of these sequences of treatment, concrete information about themselves and each other would go a long way towards helping these family members deal more realistically with their self-regard and their distorted views of each other.

What is always interesting in any examination of practice approaches in social work is the awareness that no intervention approach in the repertoire is directed totally towards the environment. In some models, some sort of environmental intervention is built in, or is at least subsumed under a psychosocial focus. Yet no approach spells out the protocol for environmental intervention under particular circumstances in the same way that all approaches address the individuals in a case. The eco-systems perspective considers environmental variables as interrelated and reciprocal with the person variables, and therefore environmental intervention must be included among the treatments of choice.

The Shores are dependent upon many public institutions for their survival and are probably being extremely demanding of these agencies as well. They are going to require professional help in interpreting their behaviors and needs so that they can continue to receive services in as beneficent a way as possible. Some imagination is definitely called for in planning employment for Mr. Shore and a weight-reducing plan for Mrs. Shore. Michael's school should be engaged on his behalf. Because Rena has the potential for advancing herself through higher education, she might receive academic counseling from her local college. Since Mr. Shore is taking medications, it would seem that the dispensing psychiatrist could be asked to explain his illness to Mr. Shore and his family, so that all of their expectations of him would become more realistic. Finally, if it is true that Mrs. Shore was as competent in nursing as has been described, exploration of modified employment for her in a less arduous role might be fruitful. According to our assessment, her loss of a work role has proved to be devastating to the family's equanimity.

## THE THERAPEUTIC PROCESS

On the presumption that the Shore family suffers from victimization from themselves, and undoubtedly from the community, it would be important to approach them as if they were competent. Appealing to their individual strengths and family ties, the opening strategy would be one that reviews their predicaments, what they have (and have not) done up to then, and the ways in which each of them sees the problem. This should be a family meeting, since it would entail developing a treatment agenda for each and for all, and would provide them with a cognitive mapping of their situation. The fact that they have already read their case summary would serve as a perfect entry point: What did they think of it? Of themselves? Of their future? And so on. Separate treatment plans might be structured for each family member, depending upon how each one views his or her problems, wishes, complaints, and readiness.

For example, *Mrs. Shore* has to be helped, through supportive and confronting techniques, to recognize her mourning for the loss of her prior status as "princess," successful career woman, healthy person in control of her life, and contented wife and mother. In addition, she will have to be helped to recognize her anger at these losses. It may be a difficult process for her to understand why she needs to control her family so closely and how she attempts to do it. In particular, she needs to examine why she demeans her husband. Along with this clarification of her feelings, she would undoubtedly find it helpful and reassuring to have information about her husband's illness and Michael's physical and behavioral problems. In order to throw light upon her own condition and her potential for working and socializing outside of the home, it will be necessary to obtain medical information and an evaluation of her physical capacities.

When she is able to absorb these emotions and accept her reality, then she will be better able to view her relationships with her husband and children from their point of view. Further, if it should turn out that she *can* work at something and can entertain the idea of finding gratification outside of her family, then she might need help in making a reentry to extrafamily life. At that point, if the other family members have undergone parallel changes, a series of family treatment sessions could cement those changes and offer the family the opportunity to redraw their boundaries, coming together as separate individuals.

*Mr. Shore's* mental illness appears to be kept under some control through the use of medication. Given the importance of this treatment, there should be explicit attention paid to his grasp of his illness and the medication he uses. Engaging the psychiatrist and Mrs. Shore in this psychoeducational process would appear to be the first order of business, because unless his affect can be modified in its extremes, all other interventions will be for naught. Mr. Shore, in his boyish and charming manner, functions almost like a child to his wife and a brother to his children. Although it may be impossible for him to relinquish this behavior, clinical intervention can help him find more appropriate ways to perform his most comfortable roles. The record describes an effort to join Mr. Shore and Michael in a father–son subsystem of the family and to encourage their joint activity. This is probably a good idea, but one would have to adjust one's expectations here: the outcome would more likely be a successful expression of Mr. Shore's immature interests than establishment of "father–son" patterns of relationship. But so what? Michael will have fun with his father, and his father will be relieved of some of the tensions involved in having to act like a grown-up father.

The employment situation, about which we have commented earlier, has to be attended to for practical economic reasons, as well as for Mr. Shore's improved self-esteem. Whatever his rationale for believing himself to be a theatrical person, Mr. Shore now has this vision as part of his self-image, and it should be treated as his reality wherever possible and within reasonable boundaries. He has probably listened to (but not heard) endless arguments—from his wife, friends, family, employment counselors, social workers, and psychiatrists—that he is not a comedian and that he ought to give it up to find "honest work." But if this fantasy is by now part of him, perhaps a defense constructed against his depression, then he cannot give it up without risking the failure of his functioning ego. This is why we suggest that he be helped to find a job in a setting that will give him at least the semblance of theatricality. Given his ability to distort his roles so as to accommodate to his fantasies about himself, Mr. Shore might find that even a laboring job in a theater could support his image of himself as "being in the theater." But this dynamic cannot be played out unless there is careful intervention with the employment service.

Mr. Shore's treatment, based upon our knowledge of his Bipolar illness and his general immaturity, would be supportive and directive towards life goals that he can tolerate. As he finds greater gratification (and income) through work that is meaningful for him, he will be less of a burden to the rest of the family. To the degree that he achieves even a modicum of competence, he will assume a role that is more self-defined. Mr. Shore's separateness should then allow him, like his wife, to participate in the later family treatment sessions, without his becoming swallowed up by demands for achieving and relating that he is probably incapable of meeting.

*Michael*, of course, has to be helped to become a 12-year-old boy. This will entail some disillusionments for him, because his continuing identification with his father and the consequent overprotective attention paid by his mother will have to be faced and surrendered as a way of life. Michael appears to be bright and self-aware, and it might be possible to lead him towards significant understanding of the way he perpetuates his scapegoat role in life. Michael needs help in finding his own place, his own interests, his own persona. He is on the threshold of adolescence and soon will have to "age out" of his family. He cannot do this while he is caught in the entanglements of his parents' mutual struggle, so it is high time for him to enter the world of his peers. Certainly his participation in a group would be of first importance—a group in which he can learn what 12-year-olds are like and in which the others can confront his provocative behaviors.

Michael will not readily give up his family role as a baby son and a foil for his parents, so he will have to have individual treatment to help him in the transition from family child to individuated person. His resistance to growing up will be fierce, and the clinician who works with him will have to deal sensitively and firmly with his anger and fear, always pointing out to him the enticements involved in becoming a successful adolescent. As noted earlier, serious work has to be done in Michael's case to ferret out information about his physical condition. The question of organicity should be resolved, and if medical treatment is warranted, it should be explored. As Michael finds his own place outside his parents' boundaries, as he is helped to negotiate his independence, family treatment will be useful to him, just as it will be for his parents when they reach a similar stage. Of course, if his parents are successful in achieving their own self-definitions, then Michael will be released; it is hard to imagine that he will find his freedom unless his parents find theirs simultaneously.

*Rena* is quite unknown to us from the available record. On the face of it, it would appear that she has tried to escape the entanglements that Michael remains caught in. Yet she is not functioning up to her capacity, and at the age of 18 is probably still emotionally involved in her family's life, even though she has moved away. Rena needs clinical help in finding her way. We do not know her goals, but her prior interest in the theater and in pursuing her education are strong entry points to engaging her. The facts about her adoption, and when and how she learned about it, are of immediate concern and should be cleared up through straight information. Rena's living situation is unclear, and where she lives and how she pays her way needs clarification. We do not know, but might guess, that her interruption of her education might be a consequence of acting out the family's persistent scenarios of failure. This possibility might be explored in order to help Rena find a more satisfactory way to live her life. If she and the other members of her family are finally able to achieve separateness from each other, then Rena could well find family treatment helpful as a way of finally resolving her unfinished business. That she lives away from her family in no way signifies that she has left them emotionally. Family treatment can help her, as it might the others, to find closure and to restructure her life.

The worker–client relationship implied in all of these contacts that we have described would be honed to the nature of the work, the individual personalities and needs, and the purposes of each intervention. In the eco-systems perspective, in which cases are viewed within circles, the clinician becomes part of the circle, a significant dynamic actor in the lives of the clients. The traditional hierarchical arrangements of therapist to client cannot apply in this depiction, so the roles of the clinician may range from therapist to psychoeducator to advocate, where some degree of reciprocity between clinician and clients is to be expected. In any event, the influence of the clinician will be felt *because* he or she is part of the life space of the family, so it behooves the clinician to always be aware of the direction his or her influence is taking. In this case, a relationship would be a means to a therapeutic purpose, but not an end in itself. The intention here is to ultimately relate the family members to each other as expeditiously as possible. Transference manifestations would be handled and not promoted, so that progressive forces of the client's ego would remain in control, and the therapeutic task would always be in the forefront of attention.

## Outcome and Follow-up

As mentioned earlier, we would expect that the Shores would find their individuality and then come to some resolution of their enmeshment. We cannot know ahead of time whether Mrs. Shore will find gratification through work and/or socialization outside of her family, or if Mr. Shore will be able to work at something gratifying for him. Nor can we know if Michael and Rena will be able to escape the family net. A feature of systems-oriented practice is its unpredictability, because it is not possible to control interwoven, simultaneously occurring events. There is no linear connection sought between beginnings and endings; causality is viewed as interactive, with people and events playing off one another. Nevertheless, follow-up to see how this family is doing would be expected as part of the course of treatment. In fact, periodic check-ups might well be desirable throughout clinical social work practice.

## LIMITATIONS OF THE MODEL

Because the eco-systems perspective is not a practice model, it need not be judged for its effectiveness; it is not supposed to *do* anything, although its use anticipates a certain intellectual performance on the part of the clinician. Its limitations lie more in the area of the expectations its use holds out. Since the intent of this perspective is to capture the complexity of cases in their real-life contexts, its use and application require two things of clinicians that are antithetical in the traditional ways of practice: "cognitive restructuring" to allow for a nonlinear view of cases and for multiple clinical interventions, and explicit awareness of contextual variables that might escape notice in a linear perspective. The use of the eco-systems perspective thus tends to alienate practitioners who become frustrated when they see the complexity and are often unable to attend to the perceived needs. The perspective demands a wider practice repertoire, often a wider knowledge base, and almost always involves confrontation with irresolute problems whose recognition often can be avoided when cases are viewed through a more narrow, linear type of lens.

## RESEARCH

No research has been published on the use of the eco-systems perspective, because of the reasons we have cited above as limitations. There is limited experience with the perspective, and as it is essentially suggestive of a way of thinking, it is hardly the stuff of research. Yet there must be empirical evidence for its utility, so a comment about research possibilities is indicated.

Although it is always possible to quantify events, and even the recurrent patterns of reciprocal processes, it is not always necessary or desirable to do so. The current ideological debate in the field concerning the empiricist "quest" versus the heuristic mode (Heineman-Piper, 1985) can be applied to research concerning the eco-systems perspective. Because of the lack of predictability *by design* in this perspective and because of the ever-changing directions of treatment, it would be inconceivable to attempt to quantify changes brought about by this form of practice. Furthermore, there is reasonable doubt that one would gain much in a quantitative study. On the other hand, there are "what if" and "then" questions (Maas, 1964) in need of answers. Given the myriad of transactions occurring in the Shore case, can we learn what *might* happen *if* we attempted to work with one or the other, in this way or that? This kind of investigation, in which the research methodology follows the practice mode, seems to be the appropriate approach, rather than the construction of statistical models within which practice would have to take place in order to demonstrate effectiveness. The very nature of eco-systems thinking is heuristic: given $x$, what does this suggest for $y$ and $z$? The answers would be useful for practice, but they would not fit any statistical model yet known. A perfect adaptive fit between the eco-systems perspective and the research model might be naturalistic research, in which the researcher/practitioner could literally be in the life space of the family being studied (as in the circle drawn by the eco-systems perspective) in order to observe and record events.

## SUMMARY

We have introduced the eco-systems perspective as a thinking style and as a framework for capturing the complexity and reality of clinical cases. Its concepts are abstract, and the thinking style is not in keeping with the traditional linear modes in social work practice. However, we have attempted to demonstrate its utility. The eco-systems perspective requires that the clinician have an open mind, one that can allow for the unexpected and for unpredictable events. Each clinical intervention in a case could generate movement that might not have been anticipated and that might well be beyond the control of the clinician. So it takes a professionally secure and courageous clinician to undertake practice in this perspective.

It also takes a knowledgeable clinician, one who can address the substantive issues in the case. In the Shore case, one needs to know about mental illness, behavior problems, separation-individuation, adoption, ego functioning, marital conflict, family and group dynamics, and environmental interventions. The flexibility to move among clinical modalities and various kinds and levels of problems is at issue here. We have assigned no priority to any of the problems or modalities cited; one does what is needed when the need arises.

The Shores themselves have not been assigned hierarchical positions in the treatment scenario. Since, in this view, they are interrelated and interactive, what happens (clinically or otherwise) to each of them will have an impact on the others; it is not essential to establish a hierarchy of need beforehand. We have suggested the use of clinical modalities with individual family members, with the Shores as a couple, and with the family, and have proposed at least one group for Michael. In viewing this family as enmeshed, we have used the psychosocial clinical model for our work with individual family members. This approach is also peppered, in our use, with techniques borrowed from the cognitive approach and from task-centered practice. In addition, we have used some concepts from ego theory and systems theory.

Finally, we have explicitly addressed the service structure the Shores have to cope with, and some of the policies that govern the functioning of those agencies. But most of all, we have implicitly acted upon our strong commitment to social work values: to regard the client's self-determination and confidentiality, to not prejudge behavior, and to be committed to the client's welfare, even when he or she makes this difficult.

# REFERENCES

Bartlett, H. (1970). *The common base of social work knowledge.* New York: National Association of Social Workers.

Dubos, R. (1965). *Man adapting.* New Haven: Yale University Press.

Germain, C. (1968). Social study: Past and future. *Social Casework, 7,* 403–409.

Germain, C., & Gitterman, A. (1980). *The life model of social work practice.* New York: Columbia University Press.

Goldstein, E. (1984). *Ego psychology and social work practice.* New York: Free Press.

Gordon, W. E. (1965, Fall). Toward a social work frame of reference. *Journal of Education for Social Work, 1*(2), 19–26.

Hartman, A. (1970). To think about the unthinkable. *Social Casework, 8,* 467–474.

Hartman, A. (1978). Diagrammatic assessment of family relationships. *Social Casework, 8,* 465–476.

Hartmann, H. (1958). *Ego psychology and the problem of adaptation.* New York: International Universities Press.

Hearn, G. (Ed.) (1969). *The general systems approach: Contributions toward an holistic conception of social work.* New York: Council on Social Work Education.

Heineman-Piper, M. (1985). The future of social work research. *Social Work Research and Abstracts, 4,* 3–10.

Janchill, Sr. M. P. (1969). Systems concepts in casework theory and practice. *Social Casework, 2,* 74–82.

Johnson, H. C. (1986). Emerging concerns in family therapy. *Social Work, 4,* 299–306.

Lutz, W. (1956). Concepts and principles underlying casework practice. In *Social work practice: Medical care and rehabilitation settings.* Monograph III. Washington, DC: National Association of Social Workers, Medical Social Work Section.

Maas, H. (1964). Developing theories of social work practice. In *Building social work knowledge.* Washington, DC: National Association of Social Workers.

Meyer, C. H. (1970). *Social work practice: The urban crisis.* New York: Free Press.

Meyer, C. H. (1983). *Clinical social work in the eco-systems perspective.* New York: Columbia University Press.

Minuchin, S. (1974). *Families and family therapy.* Cambridge, MA: Harvard University Press.

Nelsen, J. (1975). Social work's fields of practice, methods and models: The choice to act. *Social Service Review, 2,* 264–270.

Parsons, T. (1969). *Politics and social structure.* New York: Free Press.

Rein, M., & White, S. (1981). Knowledge for practice. *Social Service Review, 1,* 1–41.

Rosenfeld, J. (1983). The domain and expertise of social work: A conceptualization. *Social Work, 3,* 186–191.

von Bertalanffy, L. (1968). *General systems theory: Foundations, development, applications.* New York: George Braziller.

# 13

# Existential Social Work

## Donald F. Krill, M.S.W.

Amid the myriad of problems and historical complexities in the Shore family's case study, we see a theme of hopes that have been diminished by failures and despair. The family's inspiration stems not from successes and clarity of purposes, but rather from the courage to endure. Like Steinbeck's Joad family in *The Grapes of Wrath*, the Shores somehow maintain their family cohesion through multiple plights. Although the family is plagued by forces that seem to be more "inner and among" than "outer," family members also appear to be partial victims of the "therapeutic state" mentality of helping professionals with whom they have rubbed shoulders.

Nancy, the mother and central hub of the family, appears to have learned well the notion of "mental illness," probably from her professional nurses' training (and the continued culture of nursing), as well as from her numerous past therapists. She concluded early that her son had "learning deficiencies," and more recently that her husband is "psychotic." Now she seeks to convince her daughter of her "serious disturbance." Nancy is a woman whose primary meaning in life appears to be that of deriving a sense of personal strength and control as a "helper" in times of crisis; these pathological conclusions are most useful to her own self-concept or "world design." She is so central and powerful in this family's self-definition and functioning that all members seem to cooperate by escalating their problems in order to maintain family unity. Had Nancy not found ready supports in the world of professional helpers, she might have found it a shade easier to own up to her personal self-deceits a long time ago.

In true systemic fashion, however, we might also wish that Charley, the father, had found it within himself to be something other than a dreamer, a distractor for the family, a sort of innocent fool. Had he put more of his energy into the marriage and countered Nancy's controlling maneuvers with some lasting strength of his own, Nancy might not have had to remain a victim of her helping image and its societal reinforcements. But Charley seemed to prefer being the overgrown child, even to the point of competing with his son, Michael, for Nancy's motherly attentions.

Admittedly, this picture is overdrawn; we have exaggerated both the idealization of the family and the "demonization" of the professional helpers. Neither is warranted from the known data of the case description. I have taken such liberties in order to introduce the existential perspective and to give you some of its flavor.

## THE CONCEPT OF THE PERSON AND THE HUMAN EXPERIENCE

Existentialism offers neither a formal theory of personality development nor a prescribed methodology of treatment. It is a philosophical stance that has implications for social workers' views of themselves and their clients, and the interactions between them. It also helps them to understand what is happening in the clients' daily lives. As a critical posture, it could be termed anti-"guru," anticategorization, antitechnical, antirescuer. From this existential vantage point, the worker looks at the interplay of the person and societal forces as an effort to find a satisfying match. The person wants some secure "hideout" and the system needs to have its members take predictable, conforming roles. This wedding of security needs is often accompanied by alienation, loss of personal meaning, and the evaporation of choice awareness and responsibility.

The above speculation suggests that Nancy's needs as a controlling-knowing helper are a welcome fit with her professional culture and role. She is naturally responsive to similar attitudes of other helping professionals she encounters. Existential alienation might be seen as the courting of a secured image of self-adequacy through a process of self-deception and manipulation of others. Societal forces, both outside and within the family, are readily responsive and willing to provide value and image reinforcements in order to maintain some harmony and homeostasis.

A positive way of characterizing the existential stance is to stress its emphasis upon those attributes, especially strengths, that distinguish human beings from other life forms. As a human being, Nancy is able to know that she is alienated, and at some level of awareness has a sense of herself as a deceiver and manipulator. She knows her need for meaning, personal integrity, and commitment—from the very lack of their existence in her life. There is a vitality, a willingness to dream, a yearning for what is still elusive, a readiness to risk. At the very moment of her deepest despair, when she sees herself as a determined robot—helpless, hopeless—she can also glimpse some point of awareness wherein she is amused by this whole melodramatic spectacle. Humor, beauty, awe, rhythm, interpersonal intensity reveal another realm of life experience called hope, and sometimes faith. Nancy's fantasy about returning to nursing and Michael's belief that God will reveal a unique purpose for him may not simply be unrealistic wishes. Charley's and Rena's bids for audience appreciation, despite the risks of public scrutiny, may not be merely grandiose longings. The creative spirit is evident even in its distorted disguises of defensive maneuvering and self-deceptions. Human beings always struggle with the unsettling paradox of being totally determined while at the same time being free spirits.

An existential worker will seek ways to activate hope, vitality, spontaneity, humor, personal meaning, and openness to both joys and obligations in the client's current life situation. Out of his or her own need for intensity, such a therapist will engage clients and press for a response from them, a response that is alive and real in that very moment of conversation. This is the initial step towards enabling clients to infuse their life situations with some renewed vitality and hope. Symptoms, complaints, and pain become signposts for new directions. This is an important difference from the therapeutic expectation of some long-term, heavy, "uncovering" process of intricate historical complexities. It is also quite the opposite of presenting some bland, objective scheme of behavioral reinforcement.

## HISTORICAL PERSPECTIVE

The historical origins of existential thought include the works of both religious and nonreligious philosophers: Kierkegaard and Nietzsche, Berdaev and Sartre, Buber and Camus, Kazantzakis and de Beauvoir, Tillich and Heidegger, Weil and Bergson. Existential thinking is not unique to what we think of as European culture; we find its themes associated with Zen Buddhism, with the Black conception of "soul," with Castenada's rendition of Native American truth quests. In psychiatry and psychology, we have the voices of Rollo May, Frankl, Maslow, Allport, Whitaker, Yalom, and Offman. Social workers have also emphasized the interpersonal linkage with the search for individual authenticity. (See Bradford, 1969; Curry, 1967; Krill, 1978; Sinsheimer, 1969; Stretch, 1967; and Weiss, 1975.) Ernest Becker, an anthropologist, accomplished an important integration of personality theories (Freud and Rank) that had eluded the conflicting social work schools (Dynamic and Functional) of the 1950s. He did this in his Pulitzer-Prize-winning work *The Denial of Death* (1975), utilizing an existential perspective grounded in Kierkegaard.

Although Szasz, the controversial psychiatrist of "myth of mental illness" fame, claims no particular linkage to existential thought, his incisive moral critique of the helping professions is fully in line with existential value concerns (Szasz, 1970). His insights apply as much to the professional hypocrisies and control maneuvers of the social work profession as they do to psychiatry.

Existential thought is part of a wider movement called "humanistic" or "third force" thinking. This third force is the appreciation of human potentials, of the creative–integrative forces at work within human beings apart from traumas and pathological categorizations. Such writers as Jung, Angyal, Fromm, Horney, Rogers, and, more recently, Erickson are associated with this positive emphasis (Moustakas, 1956). Clients may be "pulled" towards change by the creative forces within themselves and their situations, rather than "unraveled" or "remolded."

## KEY THEORETICAL CONSTRUCTS

Existential thinking is, of course, not theoryless, despite its common protests against formal theories of personality and social systems. Its knowledge base is drawn from a variety of speculations, assumptions, insights, and models related to many theoretical orientations. The special emphasis of the existentialist, however, is that theory does not *explain* a client or family. Rather, theory provides a variety of options for understanding the unique world design of each person or system. To an existentialist social worker, the effort to fit the person into an existing scheme of diagnostic categories is a backward, limiting, and erroneous way of thinking. Such categorization may aid students in appreciating the variety and complexity of human problems, and it serves a function in bureaucratic record-keeping, insurance verification, statistics, and research designs. However, it tends to do more harm than good in actual work with clients.

Concepts are found useful as they enhance client understanding and facilitate change, and as they integrate with underlying philosophical beliefs. The existentialists see human beings as meaning-making forces in the scheme of nature. Each person creates his or her own meaning in a given situation; this is his or her given freedom. Associated with this meaning-making process are two human requirements: the need for *individuation,* or self-differentiation; and the need for *belonging,* for being a necessary part of others' lives (Yalom, 1980).

Individuation involves awareness of oneself as the maker or creator of meanings as one deals with other life forms, whether human or nonhuman. One is a responsible self, in this sense, whether one likes it or not.

Belonging means the never-ending yearning for relation, for engagement, for being needed and valued. One's personal meanings must be worth something to others and must provide some direction for engaging situations of one's unique world. If not connected to life engagement, meaning is useless—hence, meaningless. Meanings are reformulated through a continuing interaction with life's realities.

Freedom of choice, as emphasized by existentialists, does not refer to unlimited opportunities. Its stress, in fact, is more upon life's limits and boundaries than upon opportunities. Freedom centers upon the meaning-creating process I have described. However, prior to becoming aware of themselves as meaning-makers, individuals first experience a more primitive life drive; the will to survive. All human tragedy stems from the conflicted interplay of the will to survive and the search for meaning.

Becker elaborates this theme when he proposes that the basic threat to human awareness does not come from sexual, aggressive, power, or conformity drives, but rather from the awareness of death (Becker, 1975). Death awareness challenges survival, not only physical survival, but also the survival of human consciousness, of the self as builder of a unique world view in which one finds a needed role in the overall scheme of life. One is limited and dependent upon forces beyond oneself in a world that combines awe and beauty with terror and misery. The anxieties of guilt and death and meaninglessness (Tillich, 1952) are overwhelming. Each human being must seek protected hideouts by developing illusory notions as to who one is and how this self is best secured. The outer world of societal values—whether coming from political, cultural, or institutional sources, or from one's own family and support groups—is a ready and waiting partner for building and reinforcing these hideouts. In this sense, Sartre's comment, "Hell is other people," rings true (Sartre, 1955, p. 47).

Any of a variety of conceptualizations of defensive process may be found useful by the existential worker; it matters little whether one enumerates defenses, systemic triangulation, persona and shadow, irrational beliefs, character, or habit patterns. What *is* important to understand is that the security images of clients consist of those aspects of their world design that are involved with seeking protection, reducing threat, acquiring comfort (with its attendant sense of self-adequacy), and finding ways to be cared about (or at least attended to) by others. The security process is based upon memory; clients seek to reexperience certain pleasures or again avoid specific discomforts. Clients can reinforce certain conclusions about themselves and the world through relationships and activities, by using their own bodies, even by controlling their own awareness. We can gain access to these conclusions about "how one must be" by learning about the beliefs and attitudes of a client; we call such conclusions *demands*. These beliefs and their related memories are tied to emotions. The emotional energy generates engagement with the world; it also maintains the beliefs, which are often experienced as grandiose "needs." Problematic emotions might be said to express the passionate yearning for individuation and belonging, which has been distorted into directions of isolation or ego-fusing conformity. (These latter concepts have their counterpart in the family systems theory ideas of *disengagement* and *enmeshment*.)

In Charley Shore's world design, he is a nonthreatening "big kid" who never grows up. It is easy for others to blame him for his lack of responsibility, his grandiose and ineffectual schemes, and his tiresome jokes, especially when he accomplishes little over time. Charley sees life as a perpetual teenager might see it: He is wide-eyed, confused, and innocent, yet scheming; and he spends endless hours in the world of his imagination. He still hopes to be "discovered," but we can see that this hope is now in vain. Charley believes that such a discovery will depend on luck, not on anything *he* can do. Charley's stance has tended towards increased isolation, until finally he has found a solution in psychosis. His fantasies have been intensified and have become more gratifying emotionally than his real life of continuing failures. Moreover, his wife has begun to see him as another disturbed patient to be nursed and is therefore more ambivalent in her complaints about his being little more than a financial drain on the family. He has effectively sidestepped her attempts to provoke his guilty feelings. Charley's world design leads him towards isolation, whereas the other family members' strivings for identity tie them closer together.

In the same way that an individual pursues some stabilized, secured identity, so too does the family (or support group) seek predictability and role conformity to assure its preservation of group identity. Mutual stroking, mutual valuing, mutual myths, and mutually agreed-upon rules of communication maintain a consistent system. This system can change in a positive way. For example, an individual can further differentiate himself or herself and maintain that new stance while remaining engaged with the group. Alternatively, several members can change how they deal with one member by differentiating themselves more clearly and maintaining *that* change, while still remaining involved with the single resistant member. System defense patterns commonly persist from one generation to another, along with the justifying attitudes that support them.

Rena is a good example of an individual who is maintaining old family patterns. Many of her parents' ways of dealing with the world are also expressed in *her* life. Rena and her mother both grew up as the "princess" in a family of adults who doted upon them; Nancy was an only child, and Rena was an only child for six years. Now Rena shares her mother's grandiosity and need to control. Both mother and daughter also describe a similar life expectation: They will feel relief when the expected crisis hits. At present, both seem to have a dearth of relationships with their peers. In the past, both had substituted the relationship with Gram for peer relationships. Rena's difference from Nancy is evident in her self-expectation of being a star performer, an expectation not unlike Charley's unfulfilled ambitions. Other parallels with the family history exist; as an attractive young woman, Rena seems alarmingly like Nancy's own mother. The competition between Nancy and her daughter has precipitated arguments, physical fights, Rena's running away, and finally a power struggle about Rena's truancy, her removal from the play, her dropping out of high school and college, and her remaining dependent on her parents' support. Nancy had strongly disliked her own mother, whom she perceived as uncaring and as a rival for her boyfriends. Now Nancy competes with Rena for Charley's allegiance and seems bent on convincing Rena that she is inferior—either "bad" or "mad."

These repetitive, habitual, and addictive defensive patterns of individuals or groups may sometimes change as a result of other factors. Beliefs and "awareness experiences" may be altered by *unexpected events* that occur in the environment and that require some new response. A death, loss of a job, sudden illness, or a relocation may be the impetus to unbalance habitual mind-sets. To understand this concept, we must accept that individuals have varying access to undeveloped parts of their own personalities. The establishment of personal identity is based upon the development of specific aspects of the self; this process requires a suppression of, or at least inattentiveness to, some opposing characteristic. For example, a person who is consistently aggressive is unlikely to develop a passive, tender side, and may even feel threatened at the very notion that he or she has such attributes. (The dynamic of opposites is recognized in both gestalt and Jungian psychologies.)

In Michael, the opposing sides of weakness and strength are at the level of his awareness. This is not true for Nancy. She is aware of her identity as a strong, controlling, righteous helper and is unaware of her helpless, dependent side. Even though she claims that she is willing to follow therapeutic suggestions, her history shows no evidence of compliance. Nancy either blocks her needs for love and dependency from her awareness, or else acknowledges them but does not integrate them into her identity. Her ailments, her smoking, and her overeating may satisfy those needs enough so that she continues to see herself as independent.

Charley's opposing sides are fairly obvious—the grandiose dreams and the ineffectual performance. In the past, he supplied the marriage with vitality; now he can only experience his dreams by withdrawing into silence and perhaps occasionally slipping into psychotic fantasies. One indicator of strength in this man, however, is his honesty: He says that because he doesn't know what to do about the family's problems, he simply doesn't talk about them.

The opposites in Rena have recently appeared. She no longer sees herself as a successful young actress at center stage; she speaks of feeling tired, old, confused, and unloved, and she is unable to support herself.

Suppressed or ignored opposites may at any time be dramatically brought to the surface by dreams, bodily ailments, or new social feedback from significant others (those people whose opinions shape one's identity), as well as by unexpected events. A person may even go through a profound reversal of his or her belief system by encountering another belief system that is experienced emotionally as far more true and meaningful; a good example of this is religious conversion experiences. This sort of sudden world-design transformation frequently accompanies a new response to personal suffering that is different from a person's usual defensive maneuvers. In such cases, the pain of that suffering is experienced keenly, rather than disrupted by a defensive response. One's fearful attitudes are exposed as unreal or unnecessary, and growth may spontaneously begin. Psychological insight is commonly experienced in this way.

Michael has experienced this kind of insight. At first glance, Michael seems to view himself as sickly, fragile, and confused. Like his father, he seems to succeed at nothing except being the object of laughter and ridicule; and, like his father, he is willing to play the fool in exchange for attention. Michael's health problem and "learning deficiency" fulfill his mother's need for a constant source of worry. Both his body and his learning problems seem to prevent his comfortable adaptation to the world. Despite his role as baby of the family, he has an uncanny, adult-like perception of his situation. Recognizing his need of peer relationships, he persists in his efforts to make friends. He maintains a hope that he will be able to differentiate himself by some day discovering what God wants him to do and how He wants him to be. He holds to this faith, despite repeated failures and negative reactions from others. Moreover, he senses some connection between his personal suffering and the eventual likelihood of finding himself.

For the existentialist, it is important to understand, in detail, the recent past. What we know about a person's current world design (beliefs and reinforcement methods) enables us to understand the meaning of symptoms and offers options for change. The world design of a client 10 years ago, or in early childhood, will undoubtedly have connecting linkages with his or her present world design. Although the distant past may enrich our understanding, it may also distort it, because the world design of the person may have undergone certain shifts, even in recent years.

This recent present should certainly go back to the onset of the problem or symptoms and should include some comparative details of how life had been before the onset of the problem. For instance, we note that, until six years ago, the only apparent problem in the Shore family was Michael's asthma. However, within approximately one year (between five and six years ago), several crises occurred: Nancy sustained her back injury (the nature of which we do not know from the case description) and had two subsequent operations. After that, she concluded that she had to give up her beloved nursing career and depend upon Charley as the sole support of the family. This was a role reversal for them both, and they must have been plagued with much anxiety and doubt. During that same year, Gram, the powerful matriarch, died. Rena moved downstairs to stay with her great-grandfather, who died a year later. By this time, Rena had retreated from peer relationships and never resumed them. Michael, who had experienced severe asthma attacks, was attending first grade, where he was placed in a special class for children with learning problems. At about the end of that year, Charley performed what he believed to be a successful comedy act at an amateur night, so he had taken a risk and had accomplished something new. Within a single year, we see a compounding of stress and a reshuffling of roles.

In subsequent years, additional important changes of world view occurred. Nancy slowly concluded that she might never work again as a nurse. Rena moved from being the young, talented, independent hope of the family to believing that she was lost, tired, and unloved; she began to withdraw into a preoccupation with her own inner complexities and origins. Charley was hospitalized for a psychotic break, was labeled manic and grandiose, and is now viewed as crazy and a pathological liar instead of childlike and unpredictably charming.

The symptoms that are displayed by the Shores may be seen as protective, helpful, reactive, or revealing in nature—or they may simply be expressions of problem-solving efforts that have been ineffectively or incorrectly applied. However, symptoms are most usefully understood as a natural expression of the person's world design or life stance. The only exception would be a symptom that is physiological in origin, and even then the person's response to it will be compatible with his or her world design. As discussed above, the symptoms of the Shore family members are easily understood, given their individual world designs and the roles they play out with each other.

## ASSESSMENT

A traditional framework for social work assessment is "the situation—the problem—the person (with attention to the uniqueness of individuals)." Existentialism has something to say about each of these domains.

The *situation* is seen from the dual focus of social work. The dual focus differentiates social work treatment from psychotherapy by locating, understanding, and treating the problems as existing between the person and his or her environment, especially issues involving significant others (Gordon & Schutz, 1977). Social work students are taught to explore the recent present in detail: family members, extended family, friendships and support groups, job functioning, hobbies and recreational activities, health and illness, and social forces affecting the life of the individual. Such an account not only supplies the framework for understanding the meaning of specific symptoms and problems, it also provides potential possibilities for problem-solving.

When we look at the Shores, we notice that some information is missing; important details need to be clarified before we can proceed with treatment. For example, as I mentioned earlier, we do not know the nature of Nancy's back injury, or the doctor's prognosis for her recovery. We know nothing about Nancy's mother, who apparently dropped out of the picture even before Nancy's marriage. Aunt Flo had been an important parenting figure of the past, but we know little about her now. Charley has two younger sisters, about whom we know nothing. The rehabilitation work program that Charley is involved in appears to be working at cross-purposes with what Charley thinks he is capable of doing. His rehabilitation counselor needs to be contacted to see if this is really the case. Michael's teachers have viewed his behavior as bizarre and thereby reinforced his mother's stereotype of him as a troubled, fragile youngster. However, one wonders if the school ever appreciated what was happening in this family at the very time Michael began school. Although the school personnel must be credited with having realized that Michael does not have a learning disability, they may need help in recognizing his behavior as a meaningful personal struggle to find a place among his peers. We know that other therapists have worked with this family; it will be important to know when this occurred, which family members were involved, and what the goals, methods of treatment, durations of therapy, and outcomes were. It is possible that the church may prove to be an important support, in light of Michael's references to his own religious assumptions. Who else in the family takes religion seriously? Has the family been involved with a church group?

By exploring all of these unknown areas, we may uncover potential resources for this family. Despite the client's willingness and efforts to change, change usually requires the nurturing support of others besides the social worker, whose involvement must be of limited duration.

As mentioned before, existentialists consider that the primary causal context for study is the recent past. We do not need to seek out details of early personal or family traumas. It is useful to view problems as indications of interruption, distortion, and avoidance of current growth tasks, or as the failure to complete individual or family life stages. The Shores are facing family life stages of emancipation, along with a corresponding reexamination of the marriage. Problems represent the manner by which individuals and the family engage themselves with each other and their environment. These problematic patterns also express the individual world-design assumptions of each family member. Activities, habitual behaviors, and relationship managements reveal much about these individual world designs.

The *problem* needs to be assessed in detail. We need to look at its onset, the previous attempts to solve it, the effects of symptoms on one another, how the symptoms affect (and are affected by) the world at large, and details about behavioral sequences and timing that are related to the occurrence of symptoms. Equally important are such factors as: meanings that have been ascribed to the problem, including guilt (realistic and unrealistic) and utopian or pessimistic expectations; the degree to which the symptom can be controlled; emotions and physiological conditions that accompany the problem; and any past issues that the problem brings to mind. Families such as the Shores often appear to be overwhelmed by their problems and despairing about being able to handle their chaotic crises. In instances like these, the social worker may want to prioritize the problems (decide which ones need the most immediate attention).

Existentialists are client-centered, rather than theory-centered. During assessment, the social worker and client *together* attempt to understand the client's unique world view and the way in which his or her problem expresses that view; similarly, goal-setting must also stem from the client's understanding of the problem.

The principle of client-centeredness stresses the importance of mutuality. A social worker must be careful not to impose his or her own goals upon the client, but rather seek to develop the *client's* hopes and expectations in detail. The worker may suggest alternative or expanded possibilities but must be most cautious about having the client accept these ideas out of a conforming stance. (Nancy Shore warned the social worker in advance that she would probably do this.)

There are schemes of goal categories that fit common views of clients (Reid, 1978; Simons & Aigner, 1979). My own scheme (Krill, 1978) includes the following goal possibilities:

*Provocative contact*—the client does not want help.
*Sustaining relationship*—the only help of interest to the client is a supportive, affirming relationship with no expectations of change.
*Specific symptom change*—a troubling symptom is to be eliminated without focusing upon its meaning, either systematically or intrapsychically.
*Environmental change*—the client or family seeks help in dealing with social forces, institutions (job, school, housing, medical care, social agencies) *outside* the family.

> *Relationship change*—family members want help in relating to one another or to significant others because of recurring interactional conflicts and frustrations.
>
> *Directional change*—an individual is in a state of confusion about his or her personal identity (world design) and seeks clarity of personal direction or differentiation of self (Krill, 1978).

Each person in the family represents a unique world view that is compatible with but not wholly dependent upon his or her role in the family. In assessment, it is not necessary to understand all the intricacies of a client's world design. Those elements of the picture that are tied in with the problems of concern are sufficient for elaboration. Nancy, the mother in the Shore family, describes herself as being a worrier. Her anxiety mounts towards panic and is finally relieved when some crisis breaks forth. At such times, she can feel strong, in control, and able to take over. In her teenage years, she had concluded that her most desired goal was to be helpful to others. One aspect of Nancy's control (as we learn from her daughter) is her skill at provoking guilt in others. She apparently needs to be surrounded by people suffering from pain, trouble, or guilt. Because she has such a world view of herself as a helper, does she have the ability to have an adult-to-adult, mutually affirming, caring relationship? One wonders, too, how an only child, doted upon by adults, concludes as a teenager that she will be a helper to others, rather than pursue more direct pleasures for herself. This decision seemed to arise at about the same time that her weight increased, her parents divorced, and she experienced her father's rejection. Her early decisions and later independent manner of functioning suggest an "unloved" world view.

Although categorization was emphasized in selecting among the goal categories mentioned previously, the worker's way of thinking about individual persons seeks to avoid categorization. It is what is unique or special about a person that is emphasized in describing his or her world view, not what he or she has in common "pathologically" with many others. One might say that the *problem* is diagnosed, not the *person*. The person is actually "normalized" in relation to his or her problem; one might tell a client, "Since this is the way you look at the world, it's no wonder you have a problem like this." As described earlier, problems are a natural expression of people's stance towards life—who they are, how they view their relationships with others, their assessment of their potentials and limits, and their hopes and prized meanings or assumptions about their lives.

This connection of problem and world view can often be usefully shared with a client, who may find it reassuring to know that there are no "problem-free" world views. Changing the problem will inevitably have an effect upon the client's sense of identity (Offman, 1976). Perhaps the client is better off *with* the problem, considering the consequences of a shifted world view. Although the worker may remain neutral about whether change is wise, he or she may point out the consequences of not changing, of allowing the problem to continue or worsen.

As I have noted, an individual's world design is based on his or her beliefs, emotional responses (and related memories), roles with others, use of the body, use of activities, goals, and personal commitments. Such world designs will usually become apparent in treatment. The way in which I characterized the Shore family members' world designs was speculative, because I depended upon the written case material, rather than upon personal contact with the Shores. In actual practice, any such conclusions need to be shared with the client, in order to discover whether the assessment "fits" or whether some of the assumptions are inaccurate.

The special importance of world design differentiates the existential emphasis from that of the behaviorist. For the behaviorist, problems will be clarified, goals set, and symptoms diminished with little attention to world design, other than the cognitive-behavioral connections involved with the symptom. For the existential worker, on the other hand, problems are frequently signposts of distress related to the person's life style or value assumptions.

Existential psychotherapy can also be a humanizing process (Krill, 1986a). Through "problem engagement," clients can come to a heightened understanding of themselves as human beings. The worker needs to be aware of specific value perspectives that may be introduced within the treatment process. Therapists will work towards helping clients see their symptoms as revealing forces. When the symptoms are understood in this way, clients may penetrate some of their self-deceptions and the maneuvers by which they have pursued certain illusions of security or judgments that have proven false. In addition, therapists will generate clients' awareness of choices and the value of developing some clarity of personal commitment or direction. Furthermore, the clinician should suggest that the strengthening of personal identity is interwoven with the quality of one's relationship with others. In effect, the worker attempts to make the client aware of, and desirous of, the goals of relationship and directional change, regardless of the initial goal agreed upon. Of course, a client may reject such a shift; this in turn is resolved by working on a goal both can agree upon.

## TREATMENT OF CHOICE

For whom is the existentialist approach best suited? Sophisticated literary sorts and artist types? Intellectuals mired down in their own narcissistic emptiness? People in search of some spiritual meaning in their lives? Although these groups might make for the most interesting conversationalists on existentialism in late-evening coffee-houses, they certainly do not define target client groups for the social worker. As a matter of fact, I have had little luck with these groups. I have found that their opposites are much more reachable, on an emotional level, with an existential stance. These opposites are people who see themselves as marginal in role performance or on the fringe of society, or who, until a recent troubling crisis, have been rather unreflective about their own values and directions. The existential worker is soon bored by intellectual conversations about meaning and soul-searching.

Nor does the conflict of concern have to focus upon confusion about self-identity. Since the existentialists are attuned to loneliness, alienation, and failure at honesty and intimacy in relationships, existential workers will especially be aware that interpersonal problems underlie most symptoms. Where there is a lack of relationships, workers will seek ways to help the client build or fit into new relationship possibilities. Because of the existentialists' view about hopeful potential in all human beings, they will not be inclined to accept pessimistic diagnoses. Existentialist workers will tend to see "chronic clients" as challenges rather than as a dull caseload.

On the other hand, because of existentialist social workers' zeal about choice and hope, they may tend to err with clients whose problem involves realistically limiting chemical or physiological conditions that impair awareness and motivation. Workers should be careful not to let their idealized hopes about human potentials blind them to a client's need for medication or hospitalization.

## THE THERAPEUTIC PROCESS

Each psychological theory defines "problems" in a specific way, and these ways of understanding the nature of problems naturally lead towards planned interventions. Depending upon our allegiance to a particular theory, however, we may end up treating our own theoretical concepts instead of treating the people in front of us. This is the reason that existentialists view theory in a relative, secondary way, as opposed to an absolute and primary base for treatment. Theory is a tool to help us understand a complex, elusive, shifting situation. We need "handles," a sort of first-draft map, even though we know that much knowledge will elude us because of distortions and errors in judgment, and we know that our intuitive capacities will often tell us far more, over the long run, than will our cognitive speculations.

This manner of thinking about theory disturbs those who hold to a view of the scientific method that is rooted in the laws of mathematics and physics. To an existentialist, it seems that such thinking emphasizes the impersonal over the personal, the species or class over the individual, and the general over the singular. The existential perspective reverses these points of emphasis, without dismissing scientific concern.

With this in mind, let us gingerly approach some treatment possibilities for the Shore family. We need to begin by thinking about what specific goals might be attainable and by selecting the therapeutic modality: individual, couple, family, or group.

There are a number of potential goals that a therapist might raise with the members of the Shore family; I have explained a little about these goals earlier in the chapter. For example, for Nancy, the goal might be *provocative contact*, because she does not appear sincere about having problems of her own. In Charley's case, *directional change* might be appropriate, because of his confused sense of self and personal direction. Rena and Michael might benefit from *directional change* and *relationship change* (especially with peers). For the marriage separately, and for the family as a total group, *relationship change* seems to be needed. But such speculations are of little help without hearing problems and hopes defined and reacted to by the actual people involved. Additionally, of course, the worker would want to check their responsiveness to each of these goals as it is posed.

A further consideration would be to determine how the family prioritizes their problem now and what occurred in previous counseling efforts. The answers to these questions would also indicate what combinations to work with—individuals, dyads, family—and whether to press for short-term or longer-term treatment expectations. I would guess that a short-term plan would be best, given this family's past counseling experiences and apparent tendency to depend on a social worker to handle their numerous problems.

Considering the goal possibilities for the Shores, and viewing this as an overly enmeshed family (too emotionally entangled with each other for satisfactory differentiation of separate identities), a therapist might choose to do family therapy that would involve work in various combinations: the family together, parents without children, children without parents, and occasional individual sessions with each family member. The whole family should be available for each session, if possible, and the therapist could use whatever combinations seemed indicated by the content and plans of the previous session as well as the evolving content of the current session. Sometimes using a co-therapist is an option; in this case a co-therapist would speed up the process of helping the family accomplish more differentiation of selves, because he or she would be able to see separate combinations simultaneously and could support and empower individual members in the family sessions. It might also be useful to work with the different combinations during the assessment phase, in order to determine motivations, fears, powers of influence, and the power of self-esteem of individual members, as well as dyad potentials and limitations.

The key treatment consideration for this family seems to be the arousal of both hope and a willingness to cooperate in doing something different in their life management. Despair, helplessness, and desperation seem to characterize the mood of this family, and these states need to be quickly and surprisingly countered.

In choosing techniques, the existential worker should first of all consider those treatment methods that have been indicated as effective by research studies: mutual liking of client and worker, use of power of suggestion, core conditions of warmth-empathy-genuiness, behavioral tasks, attitude change that includes emotional arousal, and the involvement of significant others wherever possible. However, the worker would also respect the idiosyncratic differences among both clients and workers, which sometimes accounts for effective therapeutic work being achieved through other, often unorthodox, techniques. (Incidentally, the therapist should also remember that a family that has had as much exposure to past treatment as the Shores have had will be quick to recognize therapeutic techniques that they have already deemed ineffective.)

Again, the possible goals for the Shores are based upon both their problems and our sense of their individual world views. The description of each goal suggests related techniques. Nancy, for instance, presents a position of questionable treatment motivation. Although she appears cooperative and invested in a treatment experience for the family, she also seems interested in having other family members change. We know, also, that she is in a position of control in this family and that other treatment experiences have apparently been of little consequence. An initial goal with Nancy would therefore be a gentle provocation concerning her view of herself. For example, one could highlight her doubts about the effectiveness of her own control maneuvers with family members. This might need to be done without other family members present, so as not to threaten her position of being the center of power in the family. Similarly, the directional change efforts with Charley, Rena, and Michael would call for techniques that seek to draw out and differentiate personal attitudes and related hopes, doubts, and fears about who they think they are as individuals and what they want for themselves. This effort would be facilitated by individual sessions for each person. Such differentiation of self, along with efforts at relationship change (especially with peers) could also constructively occur in dyad sessions with Rena and Michael, who share the common problem and task of eventual emancipation. Relationship change issues focus not only upon self-expression but also upon communication skills; both of these could be addressed with the parents in dyadic sessions that focused upon a reassessment of their marriage. This is yet another aspect of the emancipation tasks related to the children's growing up and leaving home.

In addition to these family and individual goals, the worker would need to appreciate the limitations of this family. Such a highly enmeshed "island" of relationships, in which family members are so interdependent upon each other's fears and apparent inadequacies, will no doubt require assistance from outside the family system itself. The worker would want to activate supportive contacts available to the family by looking at such possibilities as the school teachers and counselor for Michael; the rehabilitation counselor for Charley; a church for whoever may already have religious interests; relatives such as Aunt Flo, the maternal grandmother, and father's two sisters; potential peer friendships for both Michael and Rena (especially a drama group for Rena); and former peer friendships from mother's culture of nursing. We are considering, in these efforts, avenues for opening this family to the world of other potential significant relationships.

The social worker also needs to appreciate the uniqueness of each therapeutic contact. This includes three factors: the person of the client today; the content focused upon in the discussion; and the person of the worker today. The worker's task is to enliven the contact by creatively integrating these three factors so that the client experiences a level of intensity that conveys the sense that something special is happening. It is this vitalization of a session that inspires hope and a willingness to engage the world in some different way. Aliveness tends to stir aliveness, rather like a "contact high." Similarly, repetitive dullness tends to increase mutual boredom and alienation.

This brings up the very delicate process of managing the motivations of family members. As we know, clients are not the only ones with needs; therapists, too, want to feel fully awake and engaged, rather than dull and disappointed. The many problems presented by the Shore family could overwhelm and discourage the most energetic helper. By being overly eager in his or her expectations for change, the worker could cause the family to become discouraged and to begin to doubt the worker's ability to help them. On the other hand, if the therapist delays change efforts by dwelling too long upon acquiring assessment data and achieving catharsis, the family may also react in a negative manner.

In order to stimulate hope and cooperation, the worker should neither concentrate too much on the presenting problems nor be too intent upon trying to find out all the multiple causes of the many problems. We already have sufficient information to understand this family and proceed with a change process.

The worker should begin by normalizing the problems (as opposed to pathologizing them), appreciating and congratulating the family on what they are doing that is useful and effective, exploring how the family members behave when they are feeling good or when they are not preoccupied with problems, and helping them define how their family will behave when they are no longer beset by problems.

Any early change efforts should be based upon ideas that arise from this affirming, appreciative approach. Family members should be assigned tasks that would require them to use their available skills, attitudes, and coping efforts. Such an approach would stir hope in the family as they sense the therapist's appreciation of their present skills, instead of feeling weakened by dependency upon the therapist's direction, insights, and solutions. This would be far more useful than attempting to teach them new coping skills or reflecting upon different ways of understanding their motives, intentions, and behaviors.

By this normalizing stance, the worker expresses that he or she values the unique potentialities and capacity for choice inherent among family members. Such a stance also conveys the belief that suffering and pain are educative because they reveal to people what they already have learned about coping with life, even though this wisdom may, at the moment, have been forgotten or have been obliterated by a focus of attention upon ineffective problem-solving efforts. Because directions for change are discovered within the family's own frame of reference, the sense of family mutuality and cohesion is also enhanced.

As counseling continues, these same value perspectives are also conveyed in other ways. The sense of choice and personal commitment are an outgrowth of the directional change goal. As family members are helped to differentiate themselves, their individual needs and wants are clarified, along with possibilities for activating choices in relation to affirmed directions. A focus on relationship change conveys the importance of dialogue and intimacy, both for the marriage and for the individual members as they attempt to expand and enrich their peer relationships. Suffering also becomes a vehicle for clarifying erroneous problem-solving assumptions; at the same time, it invites consideration of new hopes and plans. Matters of guilt are clarified when clients are led to examine the ways in which they are impairing their own growth and how they disrupt the possibility of trust, understanding, and intimacy with each other.

At first, the worker will need to be the one to promote caring, understanding, and an appreciation of intimacy. Later, he or she should try to encourage the family members to use these attributes when dealing with others, both within the family and outside it. A plan for short-term work would thwart the family's desire to depend upon the counselor as "the only one who understands us." It may be necessary to specify the number of sessions—perhaps 6 to 10—from the outset and plan to evaluate progress and termination-readiness in the final session.

## LIMITATIONS OF THE MODEL

The existential model stresses the personal, unique, and creative aspects of the therapeutic *process*, as well as of client understanding. In some ways, it represents a swing to the opposite pole from that of valuing and using theory with precision. In so doing, there is a tendency to diminish and sometimes even ignore such deterministic variables as chemical and physiological causative conditions. In shunning clinical diagnostic categories, the existentialist worker may at times also be less interested in the accumulation of professional knowledge that suggests certain specific techniques considered useful with particular problem configurations. When so much emphasis is given to the personal qualities of the worker—qualities such as creativity, vitality, openness, and transparency—the existential approach may seem elusive, even unattainable, for many workers whose personalities move them in different directions from these attributes.

The existential model also poses a dilemma for teaching students about client complexities and about rules for assessment, prognosis, and the devising of a careful treatment plan. The idea of "world design" will often appear vague and confusing to students who prefer the safety of fixed categories. So, too, the emphasis on the here-and-now, active process (managing motivations, use of self, incorporating value perspectives, etc.) is often frightening to students who fear this "artistic looseness" and worry about triggering unexpected psychic decompensation in their clients. Students, who inevitably come to training with their own needs to be rescuers and protectors, are put off by the existentialist emphasis upon choice, normalization, and the valuing of pain, and its view of guilt as usually based on reality.

To counter these impediments to learning, I have required my students to pursue a process of self-examination and understanding, using exercises both within and outside the classroom. Some of the results of their personal-awareness searches are shared with other students and with the teacher. The primary emphasis here is that students must come to know their clients as people very much like themselves, so that they need not fear them as alien and pathological beings.

Anxious students too often use theory as a protective barrier between themselves and their clients. Theory can be constructively used to help students integrate their own personal self-awareness; it can also be a source for learning, when students find blind spots within themselves or imagine clients' "pathology" to be completely beyond their own experience (Krill, 1986a).

## RESEARCH

Because existentialists emphasize the unique, creative, intuitive, artistic aspects of knowing and helping people, they follow a path that often eludes evaluation by scientific research. Historically, the existentialist philosophers have argued, in an age of scientific rationalism, that man is beyond theories that seek to analyze and explain him.

On the other hand, existentialists are eager to have research expose the myths, faulty assumptions, and ineffective work of dogmatic psychology models. They rather enjoy the sense of freedom that comes from seeing that psychotherapy research repeatedly concludes that no single theory of personality (and related psychotherapy) has proved itself superior to any other single theory (see Luborsky, Singer, & Luborsky, 1975).* This notion fits well with their belief that the critical factor in therapeutic success is not the theory, but the person using it. By this, existentialists mean that such success results from the type of human sensitivity developed over time that enables workers to see themselves in every one of their clients.

Existentialists tend to align themselves with the fringe and marginal groups in society; they are generally considered (by themselves and others) to be rebels in relationship to the mainstream of societal values. They are therefore concerned about theoretical debates regarding the cause of schizophrenia, for example. They are highly interested in supporting research that evaluates the interplay of such factors as belief systems and identity issues, chemical and physiological influences, and roles in significant-other systems. When professionals are overly concerned with choosing sides around these issues, the client tends to be the loser. In this regard, research could be viewed as protective of client rights and might eventually provide far more accurate assessments and subsequent treatments.

## SUMMARY

Niebuhr (1951) defined existentialist decision-making as "decisions that cannot be reached by speculative inquiry, but must be made in freedom by a responsible subject acting in the present moment on the basis of what is true for him" (p. 241). I hope that the spirit of this case discussion

---

* For a summation of psychotherapy and casework research, see Krill (1986a).

has conveyed that such decision-making is not only an ideal for client growth but also—even more—for the mature functioning of the worker.

I would hazard a guess that each chapter in this book will present a different explanation of why this family has these problems, and a different description of the sorts of individuals who make up the Shore family. However, when it comes to treatment methods, there will be much in common among the authors' suggestions as to how this family might be helped. These family members present themselves with a vivid humanness; it is our personal human response to them, as well as the awareness of our therapeutic limitations, that produces the common themes in the various treatment approaches. The theoretical differences will simply be our varied efforts to explain and conceptualize this human melodrama called "the Shore family." We sense deeply what is true for us, seek to explain this conceptually in order to illustrate a framework, and then proceed to respond out of what again seems true for us. Perhaps most of us are existentialists at heart.

Maintaining that theory should be of secondary importance—an occasionally useful tool and interesting area for speculative consideration—the existentialists elevate the "personal" to the primary level of concern. This "personal" is apparent in the very human way in which workers utilize themselves to stir vitality, intensity, creativity, and dialogue. It is also apparent in the client-centeredness of world-design understanding, diagnostic and prognostic thinking, and goal-setting (Krill, 1986b). The personal is stressed again in the process of training social workers by requiring them to come to grips with themselves as persons, so as to better understand their clients. Finally, the personal is validated by the interpersonal emphasis I have stressed in this chapter. Clients' relationships with their own special circle of significant others are considered in the long run to be far more important than their relationship with the worker. Whenever possible, personal resources are to be preferred over professional assistance.

## REFERENCES

Becker, E. (1975). *The denial of death*. New York: Free Press.

Bradford, K. (1969). *Existentialism and casework*. Jericho, NY: Exposition Press.

Curry, A. (1967). Toward a phenomenological study of the family. *Existential Psychiatry, 6*(21), 35–44.

Gordon, W. E., & Schutz, M. L. (1977). A natural basis for social work specializations. *Social Work, 22,* 422–426.

Krill, D. F. (1978). *Existential social work*. New York: Free Press.

Krill, D. F. (1986a). *The beat worker: Humanizing social work and psychotherapy practice*. Lanham, MD: University Press of America.

Krill, D. F. (1986b). Existential social work. In F. Turner (Ed.), *Social work treatment* (pp. 181–217). New York: Free Press.

Luborsky, L., Singer, B., & Luborsky, L. (1975). Comparative studies of psychotherapies. *Archives of General Psychiatry, 32,* 995–1008.

Moustakas, C. E. (1956). *The self: Exploration in personal growth.* New York: Harper & Row.

Niebuhr, H. R. (1951). *Christ and culture.* New York: Harper Torchlights.

Offman, W. (1976). *Affirmation and reality.* Los Angeles: Western Psychological Services.

Reid, W. (1978). *The task-centered system.* New York: Columbia University Press.

Sartre, J. P. (1955). *No exit and three other plays.* New York: Vintage Books.

Simons, R. L., & Aigner, S. M. (1979). Facilitating an eclectic use of practice theory. *Social Casework, 60,* 201–208.

Sinsheimer, R. (1969). The existential casework relationship. *Social Casework, 50*(2), 67–73.

Stretch, J. (1967). Existentialism: A proposed philosophical orientation for social work. *Social Work, 12*(4), 97–102.

Szasz, T. (1970). *Ideology and insanity.* New York: Anchor Books.

Tillich, P. (1952). *The courage to be.* New Haven, CT: Yale University Press.

Weiss, D. (1975). *Existential human relations.* Montreal: Dawson College Press.

Yalom, I. (1980). *Existential psychotherapy.* New York: Basic Books.

# 14

# The Constructivist–
# Developmental Paradigm

## *Hugh Rosen, D.S.W.*

The constructivist paradigm, which is based on the cognitive–structural approach to human development, offers a metatheoretical frame of reference that cuts across all schools of clinical social work practice. It is not a comprehensive system of psychotherapy, but a well-documented formulation of developing ways of knowing-in-the-world that enables one to generate therapeutic guidelines and interventions. The paradigm need not be adopted to the exclusion of other approaches, but may be considered for integration with them. What it illuminates about the way in which individuals develop and organize knowledge—the way in which they make meaning out of the world—has the potential for increasing the practitioner's therapeutic efficacy.*

The constructivist–developmental paradigm is complex and involves many distinct but interrelated strands. It delineates human development in a way that respects the autonomy of the growing person, while at the same time offering a vision of "what ought to be" for optimum functioning. Its emphasis upon creative adaptation maintains a focus on the relationship between the person and the environment; the bridge between the *psychic* and the *social* is inherent in the paradigm's very structure. It does not embrace a medical or sickness model, but instead construes psychological and behavioral problems from the perspective of developmental lags, blocks, needs, and potentials. Finally, although it takes a longitudinal view of the stages the growing person passes through, its implications for practice are present-centered and future-oriented.

---

* An elaboration of the many ways in which it is compatible with social work philosophy and practice, beyond what is described in this chapter, has been presented at length elsewhere (Rosen, 1979).

## THE CONCEPT OF THE PERSON AND THE HUMAN EXPERIENCE

Vital to the way people think, feel, and act in the world is their *construction* of knowledge about self, others, and physical reality. This brings us directly into the realm of genetic epistemology, a study of the nature of knowledge and the process of its acquisition (Piaget, 1968/ 1970, 1970/1972). All growing individuals have a "need to know"—an intrinsic motivation—that propels them forward into an active exploration of the environment, particularly of those things that arouse their curiosity. As a human organism actively interacts with the environment, it develops an increasingly more complex and adaptive construction of knowledge structures. That construction is neither random nor idiosyncratic, but instead constitutes a developmental sequence of universal cognitive-structural stages, each of which is characterized by a progressively greater approximation to "objective reality."

Paradoxically, however, objective reality has a significantly relativistic component to it. Individuals gradually decenter from their own points of view and acquire the capacity to take into account the alternative points of view of other people. Over time, they develop a sense of the relational character of such concepts as friend, foreigner, sibling, and left, right, and middle. Although culture influences the content of what one comes to know, there are categories of knowing that constitute the essences of universal structures and are to be found in all cultures. In the physical world, these are time, space, causality, object permanence, and means-end behavior. In the sociomoral domain, these universals include social concepts, the justice structure, and the coordination of self–other relations.

Stage development follows an invariant sequence. A stage is never skipped and its order of appearance is never reversed. The process of development is one of differentiation and integration, with each subsequent stage comprising a hierarchical reorganization of old and new cognitive structures. Each newly emerging stage constitutes a transformation from the old way of knowing and provides the individual with a qualitatively different and more adequate way of knowing. An advance in stage offers the person wider perspectives, greater problem-solving effectiveness across a greater range of domains, and liberation from the constraints of the former stage.

Critical to understanding the nature of human behavior within the constructivist-developmental paradigm is a grasp of the concept that knowledge is not *inherent* in either the individual (the knowing or epistemic subject) or in the known object or environment. Knowledge is essentially a *relation* between subject and object, between knower and known. The critical dimension here is the construction of meaning. The object that is known does not directly communicate its own meaning, yet it does exist in the real world as contributing something to be known. Nevertheless, the epistemic subject will come to know the object variously as he or she progresses developmentally through different stages. This cognitive–structural orientation illuminates the understanding of what is known, while at the same time it delimits how it can be known. A ball, for example, at an early stage is known merely as something to be thrown. Later, it can be comprehended and classified as one of a variety of geometric forms. Finally, it can be understood as an object that is governed by laws pertaining to its mathematical and physical properties. This same analysis applies equally to one's comprehension of self, others, social institutions, and moral judgment. As individuals move through stages of development, their strategies of reasoning across physical, social, and moral domains are transformed and become increasingly more efficient.

When we talk about cognitive–structural evolution as *creative adaptation*, we need to look at the twin concepts of assimilation and accommodation that comprise it. A cognitive structure is a relatively enduring generic form that provides a way of knowing and organizing knowledge regardless of content. For example, a classification structure enables an individual to classify or organize knowledge of any kind, be it of minerals, foods, nations, emotions, friendships, or family relations. Implicit in these structures are operating rules for processing information. To illustrate, if X is a brother to Y, and Y is the son of Z, then Z is a parent to X. (One must be careful, however, when extrapolating such rules into the realm of emotion. If X loves Y and Y loves Z, it does not necessarily follow that Z loves X—or even Y, for that matter.) *Adaptation* signifies an equilibrium or balance between assimilating and accommodating activities.* When something is known, it is *assimilated* to a cognitive structure, while at the same time that structure *accommodates* the particular features of what is known.

For instance, children reading books assimilate the story line to their cognitive–structural understanding of action and plot. Specifically, however, they must attend to, or accommodate, what the authors are depicting, or the children's fantasies will lead to gross distortion of the material. (Furthermore, the actual print itself must be accommodated before it can be transformed into meaning through assimilation.) As a child, an in-

---

* Structural modifications and stage transitions are brought about through disequilibrating experiences. When a cognitive structure comes across a moderately novel object or problem situation which it cannot adequately assimilate, then a state of disequilibrium is induced. This triggers an auto-regulative process, referred to as equilibration, in which accommodation plays a major role. The structure is either modified sufficiently to meet the challenge, or a new structure is invented to resolve the conflict. For example, at an advanced stage of development, individuals may construct a concept of the unconscious to explain otherwise puzzling behavior in which they persist in performing self-defeating actions that run counter to their conscious intentions and rational self-interests (Selman, 1980).

dividual may have been able to construe a story of political adventure and intrigue only in terms of concrete actions and explicit dialogue. At more advanced stages of development, however, the same individual can assimilate the story into a new cognitive–structural paradigm that enables him or her to grasp the characters as symbols or embodiments of political orientations and to discern that varying sociopolitical ideologies are implicit in the dialogue.

Similarly, an individual may be familiar with a given word throughout his or her development, but the depth and complexity of his or her comprehension of that word will alter with development. In the child's developing conception of personality, the word "change" is first understood only in very physical terms, such as changing geographical locations or a change in clothing, whereas later it is comprehended as a modification of one's traits, intentions, feelings, and values (Selman, 1980). In the case of the Shore family, for example, it would be important to explore with Michael the developmental level of his understanding of such existentially experienced concepts as "sickness," "asthma," and "God," each of which enters into his theorizing about himself and his life. It would also be significant to determine how Rena's current sociocognitive stage affected her understanding of "adoption."

Philosophically what has been depicted here is a portrait of the human being as an epistemological creature, a seeker of meaning and an active constructor of the knowledge structures generating that meaning. Each higher stage is viewed as a paradigmatic or interpretive framework, with accompanying strategies of reasoning that are "better" and "more adequate" than preceding stages. Therefore, it cannot be said that a constructivist approach to clinical practice is value-free. What can be asserted, however, is that the client moving in the direction under discussion here will achieve a greater sense of personal competence and autonomy in meeting life's challenges.

## HISTORICAL PERSPECTIVE

The work of Jean Piaget (1896–1980) constitutes the foundation and framework of the constructivist-developmental paradigm. A student of the natural sciences, Piaget received his doctorate in 1918. The biological emphasis of his formal education remained a cornerstone of his theoretical formulations on human cognitive development. Early in his career, Piaget took a job administering standardized intelligence tests to Parisian grade-school children. He became absorbed with the wrong answers that children were offering, and realized that they revealed a pattern of qualitative transformations with age progression.

Upon leaving France, where he had gone to study at the Sorbonne, Piaget returned to his homeland, Switzerland, and settled in Geneva. There he embarked upon a life-long study of the nature and acquisition of knowledge in the individual from infancy to adulthood, thus founding what is now known as "genetic epistemology."

In his early work, Piaget (1923/1955, 1926/1960, 1932/1965, 1924/1969a, 1927/1969b) used a clinical interviewing method to explore children's evolving conceptions of the physical and natural world, as well as their moral judgment. In the second period of his work, he developed his theories about infant cognition through direct observation, primarily of his own three infants (Piaget, 1936/1963, 1936/1971). In the third period of his research, he introduced a more experimental method, which involved attempts at problem-solving by children of varying ages who were provided with certain materials and assigned to carry out specified tasks. Out of these later endeavors, Piaget (Inhelder & Piaget, 1955/1958, 1959/1969) constructed highly complex models to describe the character of natural thought as it evolved in middle childhood and adolescence. In the final period of his work, Piaget (1974/1976, 1975/1977, 1974/1978, 1974/1980) gave less emphasis to the description of cognitive–developmental stages and focused more attention upon strengthening his theoretical model of equilibration, which accounts for stage transition and transformation.

Throughout his career, Piaget wrote prolifically on these and other topics, covering children's construction of knowledge in areas such as space, number, time, movement and speed, causality, memory, perception, chance, affect, and imagery. His work was largely introduced to professionals in the United States with the publication of an excellent volume by Flavell (1963). Recent expositions of Piaget's theory and research that would be of special interest to clinicians are those by Cowan (1978) and Rosen (1985).

There are ongoing attempts to incorporate Piaget's work into other areas of psychology and psychotherapy. The earliest attempts to integrate Piaget's constructivist paradigm with psychoanalysis were by Anthony (1956, 1957, 1976) and Wolff (1960). They were followed by others, most notably Basch (1977), Greenspan (1979), and Fast (1985). Piaget himself had suggested in a lecture to the American Society of Psychoanalysis that consideration be given to synthesizing genetic epistemology and psychoanalysis (Piaget, 1973). Another approach has been to examine the potential for combining Piaget's theories with contemporary information-processing models (Siegler, 1986).

Social–cognitive development, based on a Piagetian constructivist viewpoint, is a rapidly growing and promising field (Shantz, 1975, 1983). Selman (1980) has elaborated upon a model of social perspective-taking that contributes significantly to our comprehension of the ways in which social reasoning and interpersonal understanding develop in children and adolescents. This model has its roots in the work of Baldwin (1906), Mead (1934), and Piaget (1932/1965). Selman has also drawn upon the work of Feffer (1959) and Flavell, Botkin, Fry, Wright and Jarvis (1968), which focuses on evolving sequences of role-taking capabilities.

A major domain within the field of social–cognitive development is that of moral judgment. Influenced by Dewey (1930) and Piaget (1932/1965), Kohlberg (1981, 1984) has organized a systematic formulation of moral reasoning as it develops from childhood through adulthood. His work is based on a longitudinal study that began in the 1950s and is still in progress. It is further supported by a considerable body of cross-cultural research. A complementary perspective to Kohlberg's work on moral reasoning is to be found in the current research by Gilligan (1982), who specifically addresses the "feminine voice" in resolving moral dilemmas.*

While the Genevan School, which represents the orthodox Piagetian approach, continues to be vigorously productive, we are also witnessing the emergence of neo-Piagetian models (Case, 1978; Fischer, 1980; Kegan, 1982). In addition, Piaget's work is being applied in the areas of developmental psychopathology (Cicchetti, 1984) and clinical intervention (Gholson & Rosenthal, 1984; Hickey & Scharf, 1980; Rosen, 1985; Selman, 1980; Weiner, 1985).

### KEY THEORETICAL CONSTRUCTS

This section will introduce several interrelated constructivist–developmental models, particularly those of Piaget, Selman, Kohlberg, and Kegan, and examine some of their implications for intervention.

Several points should be kept in mind during this discussion. First, when we talk about individuals from the standpoint of stages, we are not evaluating the individuals themselves, but the worth and adequacy of the *type of reasoning pattern* that typifies the stage. The worth of an individual in any ultimate sense is not determined or compromised by the stage he or she may be in. Second, when we suggest that someone is at a particular stage, we do not imply that all of his or her reasoning is at that stage. A variety of circumstances, including the situation, the impact of affect, and the process of stage transition, can influence the stage of reasoning in use. Last, it is important to distinguish between competence and performance. Saying that someone has the competence for a certain mode of reasoning—be it logical, social, or moral reasoning— implies that the undergirding cognitive–structural development has been

---

* See Rosen (1980) for a full-length treatment of Kohlberg's work.

achieved. However, this does *not* mean that the competence will always be employed functionally. For these reasons, therefore, intervention may aim either to promote development or to activate or strengthen structures that have already developed.

### Egocentrism and Decentration

The concept of egocentrism threads its way throughout all of Piaget's work (see Table 1, p. 326). In his usage, it is not a pejorative label and does not connote selfishness. It is a cognitive limitation that is conquered with the emergence of each new stage, only to reappear in a different form; indeed, Flavell (1985) has suggested that we are at risk for egocentrism all of our lives. Egocentrism is defined as an inability to differentiate between subject and object, internal and external, knower and known. The specific aspect of egocentrism that will be emphasized here is the inability to decenter from one's own point of view in order to assume another's perspective, especially when that alternative perspective is different from one's own.

At birth, infants are in a state of radical egocentrism, unable to differentiate between themselves and the world. Objects in the world, as they are acted upon by the infant's sensory and motor capabilities, are known only as extensions of self (of which, of course, there is no awareness). Moreover, objects are not "believed" to have any existence outside of the infants' sensorimotor range.

Gradually, however, through interaction with the environment, infants begin to differentiate between themselves and their world. By the end of the sensorimotor period (at around 18 to 24 months), children have developed a structure of objective permanence, "re-cognizing" that objects have an enduring existence independent of their actions upon them. At this stage, children have attained a symbolic capacity to "re-present" absent objects to their minds through imagery. In Piaget's view, the toddler has undergone a "miniature Copernican Revolution," demonstrating by its behavior that it appreciates the fact that it is but one object amidst a multiplicity of many, none being the center around which the others revolve. Throughout ontogenesis, this is a realization that the individual must come to again and again, at increasingly more complex levels of conceptualization.

During the preoperational period (2 to 7 years), children's thinking is perceptually grounded. They center on salient perceptual cues, which leads to incorrect judgments. For example, when shown a ball of clay which is then reshaped into an elongated "sausage," children will say that there is more clay in the sausage shape, because of its length. Children in this stage are easily misled by appearances and are not able to draw inferences that go beyond the sensory data before them. These children center not only on salient perceptual cues, but on their own point of view as well. This is manifest in their speech pattern, which is largely egocentric because it is not adapted to the listener's informational needs, an achievement that would require taking the perspective of the listener. It is in the arena of social interaction that children begin to develop sociocentric speech, which is adapted to the listener's needs. Argumentation, rebuttals, and demands for clarification, proof, and verification all combine to challenge the egocentric speaker. Accommodation to these natural confrontations leads to much of the decline of egocentrism in preoperational thought.

The concrete operational period (7 to 12 years) ushers in systematic rational thought. The child can now make inferences that go beyond the information given. For example, in the experiment involving conservation of the amount of clay, the middle-childhood youngster reasons that while the sausage-shaped clay appears longer, what was gained in length was lost in width, hence the amount remains the same. The child is now taking into account simultaneously both length and width to coordinate them. This same capacity for decentering is occurring in the interpersonal realm, where the child is beginning to decenter from his or her own point of view and to see things from the other's perspective, eventually going on to coordinate multiple perspectives.

Concrete operational thought promotes quantitative judgment and enables children to classify, as well as seriate, objects. Conceptual reasoning transcends the perceptual, so that appearances are no longer taken for reality. Children can now think in propositional terms about reality. However, they are still egocentric in the sense that their thought is restricted to what is known and familiar to them. Hypotheses about that which is *not* known to the youngsters will be rejected as simply impossible; the "what-if-it-were-true" mentality has not yet developed. In brief, youngsters cannot decenter from known reality to hypothesize about imagined possibilities.

In the formal operational period, which begins at about 12 years of age, reality becomes the subset of the total range of possibilities in the adolescents' thought. They are now capable of hypothetico-deductive reasoning, as opposed to the empirico-deductive reasoning of the concrete operational thinker (Flavell, 1977). Their thinking can deal with the form of an argument irrespective of its content, and it is interpropositional insofar as it can draw conclusions from statements on a logical basis without direct reference to reality. For example, given the statement, "If *x*, then *y*; it follows that if *not y*, then *not x*," adolescents can conclude that it is true by logical inference, without *x* and *y* actually having to represent anything concrete (Flavell, 1977). They now develop a scientific mind that facilitates their capacity to design an experiment in which they can test out hypotheses systematically, holding all variables constant but one, while that one is tested for its effect.

At this stage, however, there is still another mode of egocentrism to contend with. Adolescents who have constructed a formal operational thought system become enamored of the power of their newly found cognitive capacities. They generate ideas about communal utopias, social reforms, and political ideologies, only to become intolerant of those who preceded them for not having implemented such ideas. It is as if they do not recognize the force of resistance from reality and others; they believe that somehow their own ideas and ideologies are so potent and forceful that they will by their own virtue transform society (Inhelder & Piaget, 1955/1958). Piaget once again cites social interaction as a major medium through which this egocentrism will decline, as peers discuss, challenge, debate, and confront each other's cherished theories and ideas. Elkind (1974) advances the notion that while adolescents are able to take the point of view of another, they tend to assume that other people share the same preoccupation that they do. Hence, adolescents who are preoccupied with themselves will assume that others are concentrating upon them as well. Elkind labels this the "imaginary audience." According to him, by about age 15 the adolescent has tested out this assumption and, upon disconfirming it, has revised it to conform with reality.

## Cognition and Affect

The constructivist–developmental paradigm views cognition and affect as conceptually distinct but experientially inseparable (Piaget, 1962, 1954/1981). Emotion supplies the "energetics" or motivational component of every act of cognition. There must be sufficient interest or curiosity to initiate and sustain cognitive activity, which can also be accompanied by such emotions as excitement, frustration, anxiety, or satisfaction. Affect can influence the pace of an individual's development, but not the sequence of stages or the structure of cognition. There is an inherent and unalterable logic to the order of stage development. As for structure, if $A = B$ and $B = C$, then $A$ will always equal $C$, regardless of how the individual feels about it.

Emotions do not exist independently of cognition, but are structured by the individual's stage of cognitive development. During the *preoperational period,* emotions tend to be unstable—in keeping with the growing child's lack of conservation structures, specifically, and lack of a systematic organization of cognitive structuration, generally. Emotions during the *concrete operational period* are confined to the known and familiar from one's immediate environment, such as friends, family, neighborhood,

Table 1
Piagetian Stages of Cognitive Development

| | |
|---|---|
| 1. *Sensorimotor*<br>(Birth-2 years) | Infants gradually differentiate between their physical selves and the world. They manifest increasingly more complex intelligence on an overt behavioral plane. Object permanence is constructed throughout this stage. |
| 2. *Preoperational*<br>(2–7 years) | Representational thought emerges. Thinking is unsystematic and is perceptually rooted. Children tend to center on their own point of view and use a large amount of egocentric speech. They cannot coordinate two points of view or take into account more than one dimension of an object at a time. |
| 3. *Concrete operational*<br>(7–12 years) | Systematic rational thought emerges. Children can now make inferences that go beyond the information given. They can take alternative perspectives into account simultaneously and can coordinate them. They achieve competence at conservation, classification, and seriation. Reasoning is limited to what is familiar and known to the child. |
| 4. *Formal operational*<br>(12 years and above) | Adolescents conceive of reality as a subset of the possible. They can design scientific experiments to test hypotheses that they have devised. Their thinking is interpropositional and hypothetico-deductive. |

and local church. With the advent of *formal thought*, however, the range of emotional life expands considerably to encompass such abstract areas as humanity, sisterhood, the Mother Church, philosophical systems, and political ideologies. In the case description of the Shore family, there is no evidence that any of its members experience an emotional life that extends beyond the concrete range of what is directly known to them. Nevertheless, we cannot be sure of this until an appropriate exploration of the question is conducted with the family.

From another perspective, the same emotion can be experienced differentially in accord with one's position in the developmental hierarchy. At each of the six stages in Kohlberg's cognitive–structural theory of moral reasoning, for example, anxiety will be construed differently (depending upon the subject's evolving conception of justice) and hence will hold a different meaning. Upon committing a moral transgression, an individual who is at Stage 1 will experience anxiety in terms of anticipated physical harm or punishment. An individual at Stage 4, however, will think of that anxiety in terms of not having adequately fulfilled his or her duty or obligations.

The clinical implication of this is that merely knowing *what* emotion the client is experiencing is not sufficient. One must further explore *how* it is being experienced to more fully understand the client and to convey that he or she is understood. Towards this end, a constructivist-developmental paradigm offers a useful conceptual framework. In the case of the Shore family, the therapist would do well to realize that the multiple crises that arise within it, and the feelings aroused by the crises, will have various meanings to its members, depending upon which stage each one is in and how events are construed in that stage.

## Social Perspective-Taking

Based on research in both the laboratory and in natural settings, Selman (1971, 1976a, 1980; Selman & Byrne, 1974) has articulated a model that describes the ontogenesis of social perspective-taking (see Table 2). For Selman (1980), "Social perspective taking includes a developing understanding of how human points of view are *related* and *coordinated* with one another and not simply what social or psychological information may appear to be like from an alternative individual's perspective as in the construct of role taking" (p. 22). It also entails an evolving in-depth comprehension of the internal psychic characteristics and capabilities within individuals. It is derived from, and predicated upon, a Piagetian orientation, in the sense that it is concerned with both the *mode* of reasoning involved and the *relationship* of evolving concepts to deep cognitive structures, as posited in Piaget's theory. The deepest underlying structure in Selman's model is social perspective-taking itself. This is held to be a logically prior structure to four major *domains of social concepts*, each of which can be studied in detail ontogenetically from a stage theory perspective. These domains are *individuals, friendship, peer groups,* and *parent-child relations*. Each of these, in turn, is examined from the standpoint of a variety of related issues. For example, the domain of individuals is divided into four issues: subjectivity, self-awareness, personality, and personality change. There is a combined total of 22 issues across domains, and each issue is viewed as developing through five stages. In essence, Selman's position is that structural advances in social perspective-taking parallel and promote development in "personality, motivation, and other elements of social relations" (Selman, 1976a, p. 301).

Table 2
Selman's Social Perspective-Taking Levels

| | |
|---|---|
| 0. *Undifferentiated and egocentric* (3–6 years) | Children resort to physical remedies to resolve personal problems. They confuse their own perceptions with the perspectives of others. |
| 1. *Differentiated and subjective* (5–9 years) | Children make a clear differentiation between the perspectives of themselves and others. They realize that other people may feel differently in a given situation. They also realize that the same behavior in two different people may arise from different motives. |
| 2. *Self-reflective and reciprocal* (7–12 years) | Children can view themselves through another's eyes and can recognize that others have the same capability. This enables them to take into account another person's intentions. |
| 3. *Third-person and mutual* (10–15 years) | Children can assume the perspective of a hypothetical observer who coordinates the perspectives of both the children and the persons they are interacting with. They also realize that others can do the same. |
| 4. *Social and conventional system* (12 years and above) | Adolescents have the ability to assume the viewpoint of an abstract-generalized other. They transcend their immediate environment to adopt a societal or national perspective, which embodies conventional, moral, and legal codes. |

The capability for decentering and coordinating multiple perspectives is crucial to interpersonal effectiveness and social reasoning because of its vast influence upon the following: sympathy, empathy, prosocial behavior, communication, negotiation, conflict resolution, persuasion, problem-solving, self-control, cooperation, competition, and moral reasoning. The capacity to appreciate another, from the viewpoint of that other's feelings, intentions, motives, thoughts, and aspirations, depends largely on one's own ability for social perspective-taking. Similarly, skill in modifying one's own behavior in response to inferring how it would look when viewed from another's perspective requires the ability to engage in social perspective-taking.

Observe, in our case example, how neither Michael nor his father seems aware of how his behavior appears from a perspective other than his own. Actions that are seen as only "silly" by Michael are interpreted as "bizarre" by others. Mr. Shore seems to believe that his attempts at comedy are genuinely humorous, while from Mrs. Shore's point of view, those attempts are an embarrassment; if we can accept her account, the audience laughs not at humor in Mr. Shore's performances but at Mr. Shore himself. Efforts to achieve conflict-resolutions in the family are at a very low level of social perspective-taking, often at what Selman would designate as Level 0. Such attempts tend to be physical in nature and exhibit no evidence of taking another's point of view, much less of coordinating it with one's own to arrive at a balanced or equilibrated resolution. For example, Mr. Shore uses physical force: he beats his daughter. Both parents agree that when Rena is old enough, they will simply insist that she remove herself from the household. The relationship between Michael and his father is like two young boys at loggerheads with one another; neither perceives the subjectivity of the other nor recognizes the other as a psychological being.

Each member of the Shore family appears to be locked into his or her own egocentric prison, and the world is seen through that centered vantage point. From a constructivist–developmental perspective, the task would be to help each individual achieve a glimpse into his or her self and the selves of the other family members, and to help them all to apply what they see towards the aim of more effective living in interpersonal and social contexts. As things stand, the family members' needs and goals keep bumping into one another, without understanding, empathy, negotiations, or cooperation; and, as a result, the members are continually being badly bruised.

The development of social perspective-taking deals with the *structure* of social reasoning and not with the *content* of individuals' minds (Selman, 1976b). Children do not differentiate between their own perspective and another's before Level 0, which is predominant from ages 3 to 6. Upon the emergence of Level 0, they do make such a differentiation, but confuse their own perspective with that of the other person. Although they recognize that others may feel differently from them at times, children at this level assume that, given the same situation, other people would feel what *they* would feel.

At Level 1, which generally ranges from ages 5 to 9, a clear differentiation between self and other is made. Children realize now that even in the same situation, others may not have the same feelings that they do. Further, they have become aware that the same behavior in two people may arise from different reasons or motivations. A new recognition and appreciation regarding the distinctiveness of each individual's inner life emerges.

Level 2, which ranges from ages 7 to 12, is often referred to as self-reflective perspective-taking. It is characterized by children's ability to take a "second-person" perspective—that is, to decenter from their own perspective and view themselves through the eyes of another person. Simultaneously, they realize that others also have that capability. At this time a capacity for recursive thought ("I think that he thinks that I think . . .") is emerging (Flavell, 1985).

With the advent of Level 3, which develops largely between ages 10 to 15, youngsters have acquired the capacity for *third*-person perspective-taking. This enables them to view the interpersonal exchange in dyadic relationships from the perspective of an abstract, generalized other person who observes subject and object mutually interacting. In Selman's words, "Subjects thinking at this level see the need to coordinate reciprocal perspectives, and believe social satisfaction, understanding, or resolution must be mutual and coordinated to be genuine and effective. Relations are viewed more as ongoing systems in which thoughts and experiences are mutually shared" (1980, p. 39).

At Level 4, which becomes manifest at about age 12 and continues throughout adulthood, an even more abstract generalized–other perspective is adopted. It is one that transcends the immediate environment of the interacting participants to encompass broad systems—for example, the symbolic perspective of a society or nation, with its conventional, legal, and moral codes.

The ages cited above are approximations and will vary with individuals and across cultures. The ages also overlap; the growing person, as well as the adult, will rarely perform consistently at the same level at all times and in all domains. Moreover, not everyone will reach the higher levels of the developmental hierarchy. *Developmental lags in this area contribute significantly to psychological and behavioral disorders.* In addition, problems in psychosocial functioning arise when a person has the competence for perspective-taking at any particular level, but does not activate it under appropriate circumstances. Moreover, an individual (child *or* adult) is vulnerable to problems in communication and interpersonal relations when there is a *mismatch* between that individual's predominant level of perspective-taking and the level of his or her peer reference group.

### Moral Reasoning

Kohlberg (1984) has succinctly applied the concept of constructivism to his well-researched theory of cognitive–structural moral development, stating, "The assumption of constructivism implies that moral judgments or principles are human constructions generated in social interaction. They are neither innate propositions known a priori nor empirical generalizations of facts in the world" (p. 216). His theory posits six stages, each of which constitutes a more complex and adaptive reconstruction of evolving conceptions of fairness and justice (see Table 3). These conceptions, or moral meanings, shape the growing person's view of the way human relations ought to be.

The first two stages are concrete and individualistic. They are characterized by a "concrete–individual" perspective; there is no understanding of society's rules or expectations. Personal interests reign supreme. What is right is defined by behavior that will avoid harm or punishment and will provide pleasure or reward. The third and fourth stages embrace a "member-of-society" perspective. The majority of adolescents and adults in all societies are at this level, in which personal interests are subordinated to the welfare of the group. Rules and laws are internalized and are increasingly recognized as necessary to the maintenance of social order, as individuals develop from loyalty to the small group or family (Stage 3) to loyalty to the wider societal or national system (Stage 4). Whereas previously individuals obeyed laws to avoid punishment (Stage 1) or reap rewards (Stage 2), they now obey them to preserve relationships (Stage 3) or the social order (Stage 4).

Relatively few people achieve a postconventional level of moral development (Stages 5 and 6). This level generally does not make its appearance before age 20; when it *does* emerge, it continues developing throughout adulthood. The postconventional level, a "prior-to-society" perspective, transcends society, recognizing moral principle as the proper source of law. The principled moral thinker conceives of laws as protective of individual rights and the general welfare, not as merely maintaining the status quo (as in the case of conventional moral thought). A "bad" law, one not based upon moral principle, should be changed by the democratic process (Stage 5) or even disobeyed by civil disobedience (Stage 6). At Stage 5 there is an emphasis upon the sanctity of voluntary social contracts and just procedural mechanisms for resolving conflicts. Stage 6, predicated upon universal ethical principles of justice which all rational people would agree upon, is the only stage which Kohlberg does not claim to have empirical support for.

The role-taking abilities of Selman's model serve as a necessary but not sufficient condition for reaching the stages of moral development in Kohlberg's theory; each moral stage depends upon the prior emergence of a corresponding level of role-taking. The provision of role-taking opportunities in the social environment is, therefore, critical in laying the groundwork for maximum moral development. Cultures in which families and peer groups encourage and value the growing person's role-

Table 3
Kohlberg's Moral Stages

I. *Individual-concrete perspective*

Stage 1     Punishment and obedience orientation: Rules and laws are externally imposed. They are obeyed to avoid punishment.

Stage 2     Instrumental relativist orientation: Rules and laws are externally imposed. People obey them to reap rewards and satisfy their own needs.

II. *Member-of-society perspective*

Stage 3     Interpersonal concordance: People obey laws and rules out of loyalty to their families and reference groups and to preserve relationships. Rules and laws are construed as more of an intrinsic part of people's own outlooks.

Stage 4     Law and order orientation: People obey laws and rules to maintain the social order of the societal and national system. Duty and responsibility are paramount.

III. *Prior-to-society perspective*

Stage 5     Social contract orientation: People have a commitment to the democratic process for making and changing laws, as well as to voluntary social contracts and individual rights.

Stage 6     Universal ethical principle orientation: People advocate civil disobedience to protest unjust laws that violate universal ethical principles. Acting upon principles takes precedence over following laws that do not embody them.

taking activities are likely to produce individuals who attain higher stages of moral development; cultures in which such activities are not supported are less likely to produce such individuals. Role-taking enables the moral reasoner to take into account each person's point of view—or claim—in a conflict situation. However, the actual resolution to the conflict brings into play the evolving justice structure, which leads to a fair, coordinated balancing of the disequilibrium introduced by the conflict. It is not accidental that the figure of Justice is depicted holding scales, and that her eyes are covered to ensure impartiality.

Kohlberg identifies role-taking as a bridge between cognitive development and moral development. In a broader sense, logical stages also serve as necessary conditions for the corresponding stages of moral reasoning. For example, it is not possible to exercise conventional moral reasoning (Stages 3 and 4) if one has not attained at least the early phase of formal operational thought. Similarly, principled moral thought requires the prior attainment of advanced formal thought.

The achievement of a particular logical stage, however, merely makes possible the corresponding moral stage, but does not necessitate it (Walker, 1980). Thus, while the constructivist–developmental paradigm depicts a *vertical* hierarchy of invariant stage sequences in the development of logical processes, perspective-taking abilities, and moral judgments, it also addresses a *horizontal* interlocking network across these same dimensions. A final link in the horizontal chain is that of moral *action*. Is there a relationship between moral judgment and behavior? The answer is a qualified "yes." Blasi (1980) concluded from a comprehensive review of the research that a positive correlation between moral judgment and action *does* exist. Yet there is not a one-to-one correspondence between the two, since other variables such as personality, motivation, affect, situation, and peer pressure are all contributing factors. It is essential to bear in mind that two individuals can be at the same moral stage while proposing opposing resolutions to an ethical dilemma or engaging in contrary behavior. This is because the *structure* of the moral reasoning determines the stage, not the *content*.

For example, one person at Stage 3 may think that it is right for a husband to steal a drug, whose cost is prohibitive, in order to save his wife's life, while another person at the same stage may think that it is wrong. What links them to the same stage is that both would base their definition of what is "right" on the extent to which it would maintain significant relationships or win approval from significant others (Kohlberg, 1984). Furthermore, two people at different stages may recommend the same resolution or engage in the same behavior. Given the above dilemma, a Stage 2 response might be that it would be right for the husband to steal the drug, because if the wife were to die, there would be no one around to perform the household duties for him. A Stage 5 or 6 response would also hold that stealing the drug would be right, reasoning that the wife's claim to life is greater than the druggist's claim to his property—the drug.

A missing component in Kohlberg's theory has been that of the role of *care* and *responsibility*. Gilligan (1982) has articulated a model that emphasizes those elements as central ethical concerns. Her research suggests that this ethical orientation, which emphasizes personal relationships, communication, and the avoidance of harm to others, is more distinctively that of women, whereas Kohlberg's formulation, which is more characteristic of men, construes ethical dilemmas in terms of fairness, justice, and laws. These conclusions are controversial, but Gilligan and Kohlberg do agree that ultimate moral maturity in men and women reflects both points of view. Davis (1985) has addressed some implications of Gilligan's model for social work ethics; Rhodes (1985) has done the same for social work education.

## The Ontogenesis of Self

The work of Piaget, Selman, and Kohlberg has been synthesized and elaborated upon to form a constructivist-developmental model of personality (Kegan, 1982; Kegan, Noam, & Rogers, 1982). In the view of Kegan and his colleagues (1982), "The experience of self refers to both the contents of experience, which we call object, and the experiences of holding or organizing those contents in a coherent form or structure, which we call subject. Development is the ongoing transformation of the subject-object balance in experience, the transformation of the psychologic of self" (p. 119). The evolutionary construction and reconstruction of meaning is constitutive of qualitatively different self-object balances at each newly emerging stage. Each stage is embedded in a self structure that cannot know itself, but which can take its former self as an object of knowledge. As development occurs, that which was subject—the self structure—at one stage will shift to being object—the known —at the next stage (see Table 4). Each newly reconstructed or transformed self provides a broader, deeper, and more powerful way of knowing-and-being-in-the-world. The former self that is replaced is not completely lost, but is re-placed on the object side of the self-object balance.

Stage 0 is simply the undifferentiated state of the infant, in which everything is incorporated into a state of oneness and there is no separate object or other to be known. Infants are embedded in their own reflexes, sensations, and motoric activities. With the advent of object permanence and representational thought, toddlers can take these elements as objects

### Table 4
#### Stages of Self-Other Development in Kegan's Paradigm

|         | *Self (Structure)* | *Other (Content)* |
|---------|--------------------|--------------------|
| Stage 0 | Undifferentiated state of oneness | None |
| Stage 1 | Impulses and perceptions | Reflexes, sensations, and motoric activities |
| Stage 2 | Personal needs and desires | Impulses and perceptions |
| Stage 3 | Interpersonal relationships | Personal needs and desires |
| Stage 4 | Autonomy, self-governance and ideological commitment | Interpersonal relationships |
| Stage 5 | Interdependence, interindividuality, and a multisystems perspective | Autonomy, self-governance and ideological commitment |

of knowledge and begin to coordinate them, for they are no longer embedded in them. At Stage 1, children have become embedded in their perceptions and impulses, which they equate with self. They *are* their own impulses and perceptions, but can now experience themselves as having reflexes and sensations. Subject to their own impulses, they cannot take them as object; they cannot coordinate or control them. While they are subject to their own impulses and to how those impulses are expressed, children cannot take the point of view of another. In addition, children at this stage are extensively engaged in fantasy, especially fantasy that has little likelihood of materializing.

By Stage 2, children have become subject to their needs, which now are taken to be the essential structure of self, while their impulses and perceptions have shifted to object and have become content that can be coordinated and organized. Impulse control is now possible. Although individuals at Stage 2 realize that others have needs and interests, they do not take these needs and interests into account unless it is to manipulate them to get their *own* needs met.

Adolescence is a period of development during which youngsters are emerging from embeddedness in their own needs. The self structure is no longer defined as *being* those needs: at Stage 3, needs are simply "that which one possesses," not "that which possesses one." Now relationships have become the defining feature of the growing person's self structure. An increasing capacity to take others' points of view and coordinate them with one's own is a part of this development. It is at this stage that a concept of other has become an integral part of one's emotional life. Anticipating and experiencing concern over another's reaction to one's own behavior becomes of singular importance. Individuals at this stage will often inhibit the expression of anger, to avoid the disruption of significant relationships.

In the shift to Stage 4, the individual does not so much think, "I *am* my relationships," but rather, "I *have* relationships." Relationships are no longer conceived of as the totality of the self structure, but have become only a *part* of the totality; they can now be reflected upon as content that is apart from the essential self. Once an individual is no longer embedded in an interpersonal self structure, a new sense of identity—of being in charge of one's own self—emerges. Personal autonomy and self-governance are now paramount characteristics in defining the self structure. Being in command of one's feelings and being concerned with the proper discharging of duty preoccupy Stage 4 development. Accompanying this stage is an ideological commitment to one's reference group, be it ethnic, religious, political, or national.

Finally, in the evolution to Stage 5, the self is no longer equated with maintaining one's career, performing work roles, and discharging responsibilities. Having moved apart from the self structure to become only a part of the total personality, these concerns now occupy a position as object in the self-object balance. No longer embedded in the institutional self of Stage 4, as Kegan refers to it, the person's self is now essentially interindividual; it is embedded in a multisystems perspective. The interdependence between institutions and individuals is recognized. Personal autonomy need no longer be defended against a threat to it, as though a successful assault would signify the annihilation of self. It is at this stage that the individual is capable of genuine intimacy and adult love.

In Kegan's formulation of human development, each stage consists of a special organization of meaning that imparts a particular stability to the self and its experience. However, these unique ways of dealing with meaning at each stage also make the self vulnerable to specific types of events that seem to signify an attack upon the very existence of the self. For example, a Stage 3 organization of self is especially vulnerable when a significant relationship is in jeopardy or has been discontinued. Such an event would be less threatening to a Stage 4 self, which would be similarly threatened, however, by the loss of work, autonomy, or competence. During times of stage transition, there is always a heightened vulnerability as an old self is being lost, or at least "re-placed," and before the evolving person is aware of the self that will later take its place.

Kegan's model is an attempt to account for emotion and its indissociability from cognition within a constructivist-developmental paradigm. Kegan, Noam, and Rogers (1982) state, "With respect to process, the experience of transformation at any stage involves emotions of disequilibrium and loss (anxiety, grief, depression, conflict, confusion), each time colored by the shape of the particular psychological transformation under way" (p. 110).*

To see how this model can be applied in practice, consider the behavior of the father in the Shore family. Based on the information available, it appears that Mr. Shore exhibits features of both Stage 1 and Stage 2; it is possible that he is stuck in transition between the two. He is certainly not in control of his impulses, since he has resorted to physical violence in the critical contexts of family and work. He does not demonstrate the perspective-taking characteristics of either Stage 2 or Stage 3; he fails to take into account the intentions of others and does not modify his own behavior based on how others might perceive him. The reason he gives for his compulsive lying is that he doesn't want to upset Mrs. Shore. Yet, in reasoning this way, he confuses his own point of view with hers regarding his truth-telling. It is likely that in many cases his lying is

---

* For a more detailed explanation of Kegan's comprehensive neo-Piagetian model of personality, consult *The Evolving Self* (Kegan, 1982).

designed to avoid unpleasant situations. Note that when he enters the house he routinely becomes apprehensive that he will not be able to meet the expectations that he anticipates will be placed upon him. Mr. Shore fantasizes a great deal; he still daydreams about Hollywood, starlets, and autograph-seekers. However, as is typical in Stage 1, these fantasies do not appear realistic for him. They are not the forerunners to accomplishment; such fantasies are more likely to keep him separated and isolated than to help him build an interpersonal bridge to others.

Mrs. Shore would like her husband to be more of a father to their son, and Mr. Shore states that he would like this, too. To truly be able to participate in the role of father, however, he would have to evolve *beyond* Stage 2. However, it may be that he has not yet *arrived* at this stage. He continues to impulsively fight and bicker with Michael. He not only does not recognize his *son's* needs, but he also is not fully at the point (Stage 2) where he would be subject to his *own* needs. When and if he successfully makes that transition, he will be in a better position to take his impulses as an object of knowledge, to coordinate and control them. His relationship with his son and others will have improved when he reaches a Stage 2 orientation, but not until he evolves beyond being embedded in his own needs (when he attains at least a Stage 3 orientation) will he truly be able to begin performing in the role of father to Michael. In the meantime, he is dependent upon an external control, his wife, who serves as a mother surrogate.

## The Process of Change

We have previously examined the adaptive functions of assimilation and accommodation in the constructivist–developmental paradigm. Recall that assimilation is a *conservative* element; it means that experience is interpreted in terms of the way cognitive structures are presently organized. Accommodation, on the other hand, is a *progressive* element. It refers to structural modification, or the invention of new structures, when the current cognitive structures prove to be inadequate for solving a problem or comprehending an object or event. To some extent, accommodation is present in all acts of cognition, even when change is not involved.

A more precise hypothesis regarding developmental change within the assimilation-accommodation framework invokes the role of cognitive conflict. The premise here is that contradiction, incongruence, or discrepancy induces disequilibrium, which triggers heightened curiosity, interest, interaction, and ultimately a cognitive–structural reorganization which provides a new and higher form of understanding. This applies equally across the realms of logico-mathematical knowledge, perspective-taking, social concepts, and moral judgments (Furth, 1980; Inhelder, Sinclair, & Bovet, 1974; Kuhn, 1972; Piaget, 1975/1977; Turiel, 1974, 1977).

The equilibration process depicted by Piaget describes the change mechanism. Piaget identified two major sources of conflict: those instances in which two subsystems of the individual's knowledge organization are perceived to be in opposition to one another and, alternatively, those situations in which a cognitive scheme or structure predicts a certain outcome in the real world, which experience disconfirms. It is essential that the contradiction or discrepancy be perceived as such; otherwise, it will not have the effect of inducing conflict. Reasons why it may not be perceived range from lack of attention to not being at a relevant stage in the developmental hierarchy.

Michael believes that God gives everyone a special talent but also gives everyone a scar. Michael's scar is his asthma, and he cannot discover his talent, he believes, until he overcomes his illness, which isn't happening. In some sense, Michael's two premises collide. Clearly, God's will is not materializing fully. Since Michael is not improving medically, he might find it more beneficial, once he is helped to perceive this dilemma, to "re-cognize" his illness as the grain of sand in the oyster shell around which the pearl of his talent can grow. Hence, his asthma can become the impetus to his adopting the goal of treating others with asthma by becoming a physician or nurse, or by working in some other health-related capacity. (Obviously, whatever the goal, it must be assessed in relation to his capability.)

When two beliefs within the same cognitive system are discrepant or in contradiction, the less adaptive of the two can be eliminated in favor of retaining the more adaptive one, or the two beliefs can be synthesized into a single adaptive belief, as in the above example. Note that what is illustrated is not just a simple reframing of the situation. In this case, accentuation of the conflict between two existing beliefs is followed by a *conceptual reorganization* and synthesis of them. It is quite likely that Michael holds a tacit belief that anyone who suffers from asthma, as he does, cannot be socially and vocationally successful. If he were to make this belief explicit, he might logically predict that it would not be possible to find anyone with asthma who meets the criteria of success. If Michael were to be confronted with people with asthma who *were* socially active and vocationally productive, his prediction would be disconfirmed, and he would be forced to reexamine his premise.*

The illustrations provided here may strike the reader as being similar to what is practiced in cognitive therapy. Elsewhere (Rosen, 1985), I

---

* Of course, the history of science is replete with illustrations of scientists who have not modified or abandoned their theories in the face of contrary evidence (Kuhn, 1972). On the other hand, when we look at the natural progression of development, we find that eventually many clients will shift in a more adaptive direction (Inhelder, Sinclair, & Bovet, 1974; Piaget, 1974/1980; Selman, 1980; Turiel, 1966).

have tried to show that the cognitive therapy model can be further enriched on both theoretical and practical grounds by adopting a cognitive–developmental perspective. Some of its major strategies and techniques, in my opinion, derive their effectiveness from inducing cognitive conflict in exactly the way described by Piaget's equilibration model.

## Conceptualizing Psychopathology

There are a variety of perspectives from which psychopathology can be understood within a constructivist–developmental paradigm. To some extent they are overlapping and not mutually exclusive. Piaget, himself, was interested in only normal development, not in what he termed "the tricks of the unconscious." Nevertheless, he predicted the eventual emergence of an interdisciplinary science of developmental psychopathology that would incorporate genetic epistemology. Many theoreticians and researchers working in the Piagetian tradition have in fact been actively pursuing studies on cognitive–developmental psychopathology.*

The most obvious major way to approach psychopathology within this paradigm is to view a problem from the standpoint of stage arrest or developmental lag. Most other approaches would be subsumed by this one. The impact of a developmental lag is related to the physical environment and peer reference group. Some problems, for example, can be adequately solved with Piagetian concrete operations or a Stage 3 capability in Kegan's model of the evolving self. Trouble ensues when one's developmental level proves inadequate, and one is confronted with the need to either progress further in the hierarchy of stages, strategies of reasoning, and meaning construction, or remain stagnant, conflicted, and disorganized. In other cases, the stage competence necessary for higher level functioning or the resolution of conflict may be present, but the individual may lack the judgment to recognize the need for it (Flavell, 1985).

Preoperational thought, with its precausal understanding of the world, as well as its global and absolutistic character, is especially prevalent in the thinking of many disturbed individuals, children and adults alike (Anthony, 1956; Beck, Rush, Shaw, & Emery, 1979; Serban, 1982). Beck and his colleagues (1979) have pointed out that maladaptive cognitions tend to have their origins in the primitive thought of the preoperational period, which contributes to depression and dysfunctional anxiety.

Assimilation that is excessive, unchecked by a proper balance of accommodation, will lead to gross distortion and maladaptive fantasy. Schizophrenic patients will often exhibit this in its extreme form. Accommodation, in excess, can lead to an inhibited, overly conforming, robot-like human being.

---

* See Rosen (1985) for a review of the literature on this topic.

In the interpersonal and social realms, it is essential that the conquest of egocentrism occur at each new level of development. Without the appropriate capacity for decentration, in order to coordinate multiple perspectives, adaptive social functioning will be severely curtailed, often with painful consequences. Individuals who are locked into centering on their own perspective, understanding neither what life is like for other people nor why other people "behave so badly" towards them, will inevitably have dysfunctional relationships.

Juvenile delinquents generally function at Stages 1 and 2 in their moral reasoning. They frequently have the sociocognitive capacity to reason morally at a higher level, yet fail to do so. In other cases, they appear not to have even progressed to a level of competence beyond Stage 2. Some may actually reason at moral Stages 3 and 4, yet fail to exhibit behavior consistent with that conventional level of reasoning (Jurkovic, 1980). In any event, the moral meanings they construct are obviously relevant to their plight in society.

Based on his research with psychiatric patients, Kegan (1977) has elaborated a theory of depression within a constructivist–developmental framework. He found that, to the patients, the meaning of their depression varied according to the stage or transitional point in development at which they happened to be. Thus, while depression may have certain common characteristics in a number of patients, it can be best understood for *each* patient in relation to his or her position and progress along a developmental hierarchy. The patients in Kegan's sample all suffered from depression, but cut across several categories of psychiatric diagnosis. Kegan found that there were three subgroups in his sample and that members of each group construed their depression, and the world, in a similar manner, one that was distinctly different from the constructions of those in the other two groups. Further, there was a positive correlation between membership in a group and each member's "score" in respect to a particular Kohlbergian moral stage.

Depressed people, in Kegan's view, are concerned about the possible annihilation of self as they experience it. Stage 2 individuals are preoccupied, for example, with not having their needs gratified, fearful that, should this occur, they would simply cease to be. Further, radical doubt is cast upon the validity of their self's "meaning-making" at *any* given stage. For example, depressed individuals at Stage 4 have acquired a fear that their primary source of meaning, which has been derived from life's roles, fulfilled duties, and career achievements, is without foundation. The coherence of their present way of meaning-making is challenged and undermined. Moreover, depressed individuals in transition from one stage to the next are disturbed over the loss of their own selves, while unaware that a new one—a new and better way of meaning-making—will evolve. As Kegan (1980) states, "In surrendering the balance between self and other through which I have 'known' the world, I may experience this as a loss of myself, my fundamental relatedness to the world, and meaning itself" (p. 374).

## ASSESSMENT

The overriding consideration in assessing individuals' developmental stages is the structure or form of the reasons they provide for what they do or state. In assessing for pure Piagetian stages, it is commonplace to provide subjects with materials and tasks. They are observed while they are solving the problem and are asked a series of probing questions along the way and at the end. The nature of their explanations and reasoning reveal the structure of their thought, and this is what guides the assessment procedure.*

The open-ended clinical interview is a major tool of sociocognitive developmentalists. Piaget initiated the use of this method, combined with close observation, and it continues to be of paramount importance in bringing to light the data needed for assessment. Both Selman and Kohlberg have proceeded along similar lines. They have designed a series of vignettes that reflect the domains they wish to explore; these are presented to subjects, who are asked to solve the social or moral dilemmas inherent in each vignette. As the subjects respond, they are asked a semistructured set of probing questions that are intended to elicit the highest mode of social or moral reasoning they are capable of. Their responses are then scored according to a manual designed in conjunction with the test. The scoring manual is more likely to be used in a research setting, whereas in a clinical setting therapists would make an assessment based upon their own familiarity with the forms of reasoning involved. In either event, the emphasis is not on standardized interviews or statistical calculations, but on *qualitative* evaluation.

Age is a poor criterion for assessment, since the pace of development varies between individuals and across cultures; and arriving at adulthood does not automatically signify achievement of higher levels of sociocognitive thought. It is essential in assessment to consider the distinction between *competence* and *function*. For example, as we have mentioned before, sometimes a person has the structural ability to use a particular stage of interpersonal reasoning or moral judgment, but does not recognize the need to do so (Flavell, 1985). In such a case, the treatment goal is not stage advance, but teaching the individual when to use the competence he or she possesses.

---

* Voyat (1982) has provided a volume solely devoted to assisting in the diagnosis and evaluation of cognitive stages in developing children and adolescents. Flavell (1985) has some cogent comments to make regarding the theoretical subtleties and complexities of cognitive diagnosis.

Knowledge about a client's predominant sociocognitive level of development can in turn influence treatment design and intervention selection. From a constructivist perspective, assessment is aimed at identifying the client's capabilities and limitations. From that information, the therapist can proceed to craft an intervention that can be optimally utilized by the client, according to his or her developmental stage.

## TREATMENT OF CHOICE

The constructivist–developmental paradigm is not a competitor in the therapeutic marketplace. A good deal of what it has to offer is on a metatheoretical level and can be readily incorporated, in the form of guidelines, within existing clinical approaches. This will be made clearer in the following section on therapeutic processes. However, when a sociocognitive assessment reveals a developmental lag, then strategies and techniques specifically designed to compensate or correct for those lags are indicated. Even so, this does not necessarily preclude the use of methods drawn from other systems.

It is not necessary to confine the use of this paradigm to children and adolescents. Indeed, to do so would be an unnecessary restriction of its range and power. It has applicability in any setting or situation in which communication is occurring between therapist and client or patient, and where understanding the client's way of making meaning out of his or her experience is important. Variations of the paradigm have been applied in such diverse settings as mental health clinics, psychiatric wards, public schools, residential settings, correctional institutions, and private practice.

## THE THERAPEUTIC PROCESS

A constructivist–developmental orientation does not generate a single and monolithic practice model. Instead, it offers a multiperspective framework from which to view clinical interventions. Therefore, we shall explore the therapeutic implications of the orientation from several different viewpoints.

### Implications for Traditional Psychotherapy

When communicating verbally in psychotherapy, it is essential that the therapist take into account the client's level of sociocognitive development. The meaning of the therapist's communication will be assimilated to the client's cognitive–structural stage organization. For example, in discussing friendship, the therapist cannot assume that the client shares his or her complex and subtle understanding of the concept. At the most primitive stage, friendship is conceived of in purely physical terms: A friend is one who lets you use his or her possessions. People's worth is determined by what they own and the amount of money they have. At subsequent stages, the increasing complexity of mutuality and reciprocal interaction in friendship is grasped. We are not discussing here personal or idiosyncratic differences in meaning, but a change governed by a universal developmental hierarchy that applies to the client's comprehension abilities regarding any concept or theme being discussed in therapy. Similarly, a therapist who is discussing a fairness issue in relationships must keep in mind that the client's concept of what constitutes fairness will vary with the predominant stage undergirding the client's reasoning. This has special implications in the treatment of juvenile delinquents (Hickey & Scharf, 1980).

If the therapist attempts to get ideas across by speaking on a hypothetical plane, citing illustrations that run counter to the client's empirical reality, the therapist's meaning will not be understood unless the client is capable of formal operational thought. The effectiveness of poetically using extended metaphors, as advocated in some therapeutic quarters (Barker, 1985; Gordon, 1978), will be reduced when one is working with concrete operational thinkers. The implication here is not that only formal operational thinkers are suitable for traditional psychotherapy, but that the communication should be adapted to whatever cognitive level the client seems to be functioning at.

It is often the case that clients are labeled resistant, sometimes not without a trace of irritation or frustration on the part of the therapist. The realization that the client may not be understanding or getting the "insight" because of a mismatch between the therapist's formulation and the client's cognitive–structural abilities offers an alternative explanation to the hypothesis of resistance—and may soften the therapist's reaction. It also provides direction for a constructive response.

Very often therapy seems to get bogged down because, it is said, the client lacks "psychological mindedness." While there is truth to this, the term is a rather grossly undifferentiated one and is not particularly useful. Selman (1980) has described the ontogenesis of self-awareness and self-reflection. Therapists who are familiar with the evolutionary stages of these related capacities will have greater leverage for understanding their clients and for making contact within the framework of the clients' capabilities.

For maximum effectiveness of therapeutic intervention, it is important to achieve maintenance and generalization of gains. Otherwise, improvement is of limited value. Goldstein, Lopez, and Greenleaf (1979) report that such an achievement is not common, regardless of which model of therapy is being practiced. Training studies in cognitive development have demonstrated that the most durable and transferable gains are those that induce structural transformation—a reorganization of knowledge structures (Smedslund, 1961). Conditioning and cathartic methods, while having a place in the therapeutic repertoire, are not sufficient to maximize the desired degree of generalization and permanence of gains. It appears that therapists can most likely assure maintenance and generalization either by strengthening their clients' present-stage capabilities (by showing them how to make better or wider use of their cognitive abilities) or by furthering clients' development (by facilitating stage advance).

Another Piagetian-related approach to heightening the possibility of maintenance and generalization is based on focusing upon metacognition. Metacognition involves the ability to think about one's own reasoning strategies and other cognitive processes. Although the ability to think about one's own thinking reaches its apex in formal thought, its origins can be traced to earlier stages (Wellman, 1985). By concentrating upon metacognition, therapists can help their clients to modify and correct faulty reasoning patterns (Beck et al., 1979), as well as to craft general rules that transcend specific situations and can therefore be applied to a variety of contexts (Cohen & Schleser, 1984). The demands made upon the clients for metacognizing, however, must be correlated to the client's cognitive-developmental capacity.

In traditional psychotherapy, a considerable amount of attention has been given to the client's acquisition of insight and awareness. It is expected that the interpretation offered by the therapist to facilitate awareness will correspond to the truth as defined by the therapist's orientation. Yet this leads to a situation in which we must acknowledge many "truths," if we take into account the full spectrum of psychotherapies. An alternative point of view is that the efficacy of an interpretation does not reside in its truth value, but in its potential to dislodge the client's centered belief. Even "incorrect" interpretations may stimulate a decentering and accommodation process, resulting in structural modification. By "incorrect," in this context we simply mean *different* ways of conceiving self, world, or others than are customary for the client, regardless of whether these alternate viewpoints correspond to objective reality. There are several reasons for placing credence in this speculation, but in particular, support is derived from a constructivist orientation as observed in the work of Doise and his colleagues (Doise & Mugny, 1979; Doise, Mugny, & Perret-Clermont, 1975). Working with young children at a transitional stage of development, Doise was successful in accelerating stage advance by promoting conflict through social interaction among peers, as well as between subject and experimenter, in which the participants confronted each other with incorrect interpretations to Piagetian tasks. In this social matrix, the individual centrations of subjects are in conflict with one another. Yet, while none of the centrations is correct, the ensuing disequilibrium sets into motion a process of cognitive restructuring that culminates in a correct understanding with accurate explanations for the tasks at hand. This work is well worth contemplating in relation to clinical interpretation.

The foregoing comments by no means exhaust the potential application of the constructivist–developmental paradigm to traditional psychotherapy. For example, Piaget's assimilation-accommodation model has many fertile implications for exploring personality change and conducting therapy (Block, 1982; Rosen, 1985; Wachtel, 1981). However, I hope that they are sufficiently reflective of the paradigm's versatility to arouse the reader's interest.

## Implications for Selecting Clinical Interventions

We have seen how therapists' direct verbal communications should take into account the client's cognitive–structural developmental stages. The same concept should be kept in mind in the selection and design of treatment strategies. Kegan (1982) has carefully explicated this in relation to his constructivist version of the evolving self. Let us speculatively adapt Kegan's comments to Mr. Shore. Imagine that during his psychiatric hospitalization, Mr. Shore is required to participate as a community member on a ward that has been organized to provide milieu therapy. Such a therapy concept requires at least a Stage 3 interpersonal orientation for optimum success. Mr. Shore is somewhere between the Stage 1 embeddedness in his own impulses and the Stage 2 embeddedness in his own needs. He will be unable to meet the demands placed on him. His capacity for reciprocal exchange is limited at most to a rule of "I will do for you only so that you will in turn give me what I need." He is likely to be experienced by other people as manipulative, which is not surprising, since for him they are merely objects existing to meet his needs. Staff members will find him resistant and uncooperative. They will become frustrated and resort to pejorative labels, concluding that he is acting out and unsuited for therapy.

Perhaps this strikes a familiar chord; recall that Michael was not permitted to return to camp, his unacceptable behavior having been interpreted as willful misbehavior. Whether considering our speculative example about Mr. Shore, or the actual experience of Michael, I am suggesting that in neither case is the approach helpful to the individual involved. From a constructivist standpoint, the expectations being placed upon Mr. Shore and Michael are unrealistic. Neither one is currently capable of understanding what is being expected of him from the perspective of the authorities who are "calling the shots." Neither one is "bad," but merely acting in a way that is meaningful to himself, given his cognitive–structural limitations. The treatment solution for both Michael and his father lies in adopting a respectful attitude towards their present developmental status and implementing methods that will help them to evolve to higher stages, so that the environmental demands of milieu therapy, in the case of Mr. Shore, or of the camp setting, in Michael's case, can be constructively met.

Assertiveness training is a very popular approach in some therapeutic quarters. In some sense, it is a client at Stage 3, embedded in his or her interpersonal relationships, who will be seen as most in need of such training. Such a client conceives of the disruption or loss of significant relationship as a threat to the existence of his or her own self structure, an idea that is hardly conducive to appropriate assertiveness. For the same reason, however, it is this same client who will be the most vulnerable to and threatened by the prospect of assertiveness training. In this case, it may be that the most effective approach is an indirect one. If the therapist focuses on helping the client emerge from interpersonal embeddedness, the client will evolve beyond Stage 3 and hence become freer to risk assertiveness in relationships. Therapists who decide to offer assertiveness training to clients whose meaning-making activity is at Stage 3 should remain exquisitely sensitive to what they are asking of the clients, and should be prepared to provide maximum interpersonal support.

Another approach to selecting interventions from a constructivist perspective has been formulated by Abroms (1978), who has correlated discrete treatment goals with Kohlberg's six stages of moral reasoning. For example, at Stage 1 the emphasis is on assuring physical and material well-being; at Stage 3 there is an emphasis on the socialization process; and at Stage 6 the goal is "the synthesis of a cohesive self with an idealized super-ego, devoted to the realization of social justice . . ." (Abroms, 1978, p. 12). Actually, therapists must anticipate what it is that clients need in order to help them overcome the limitations of their present stage and benefit from the advantages inherent in the next stage. Thus, pleasure-driven individuals at Kohlberg's Stage 2 need the appropriate experiences to help them become socialized at Stage 3, where they are less likely to get into trouble and encounter rejection for offending the boundaries of other people (Abroms, 1978). Observe the following comment by a client who has made precisely this kind of transition: "It used to be, when I screwed up I worried that I was gonna get it; now when I screw up I worry that other people are going to worry" (Kegan, 1980, p. 375). Note that the focus of Mr. Shore's concerns, each time he approaches the front door of his home, is upon others' expectations of him to provide what he feels he cannot, rather than upon the meaning of the problematic events to those others. In treatment, at the same time that clients are being supplied with what is most necessary at their present level, they are being prepared for passage to the next one. As therapists dialogue with their clients, they afford them glimpses into the meanings of the next stage, which beckons them forward.

## Implications of Generating Techniques

The constructivist–developmental paradigm has been identified primarily as a conception of human development and not as a system of psychotherapy. Although this model does have significant implications for therapeutic practice, as I have tried to demonstrate in the preceding sections, it does not come readymade with a packaged set of techniques. Yet implicit in it are some suggestive strategies and tactics that have been explored recently (Edelson, 1978; Rosen, 1980, 1985; Selman, 1976a, 1980; Weiner, 1985).

A major approach that has been derived from a constructivist paradigm in order to help people with interpersonal dysfunction is *perspective-taking training* (see Urbain & Kendall, 1980, for a review of the literature). Any activity that fosters decentration from an individual's egocentric embeddedness and that promotes role-taking opportunities can be integrated into a perspective-taking treatment program. One approach is to have a group of people write a skit and then rotate playing each character. This activity is followed by a discussion about what the experience was like from each perspective. Probing questions can be asked to engage the participants in a process whereby they examine their inner thoughts and feelings from the perspective of each role as they played it. In addition, they look at how their thoughts and feelings about the other characters were modified by the assumption of diverse roles (Chandler, Greenspan, & Barenboim, 1974). This activity will not only foster decentration, but will go beyond that to assist individuals in moving towards the developmental capacity of coordinating multiple perspectives simultaneously.

Many creative variations of perspective-taking training are possible, limited only by the therapist's flexibility. In the case of the Shore family, it may be therapeutically effective to have them reenact various conflict situations that arise, with each member rotating through each other's role, and then follow up with the therapist leading the discussion. Michael's unhappiness and loneliness outside the family matrix, which are due largely to his unsuccessful attempts to make friends, may derive from his low level of perspective-taking and accompanying ontogenetic limitations in such social-reasoning domains as friendship and conflict-resolution. Participation in a perspective-taking training program could resolve much of his loneliness by improving his interpersonal reasoning and skills. Similarly, Mr. Shore is having employment difficulties and is presently undergoing some kind of vocational rehabilitation. We do not know the nature of the interpersonal skills training he is receiving, but I would venture to say that it would be much more effective if it is taking into account his developmental level and limited perspective-taking capabilities.

Role-taking abilities can also be advanced by training in referential communication (Chandler et al., 1974; Dickson, 1981), which utilizes the cognitive model by providing feedback when subjects transmit incorrect messages. Referential communication entails taking into account, when speaking, what the listener's precise informational needs are. Egocentrism is an impediment to doing this, since the speaker must be able to place himself or herself at the listener's perspective to identify what is needed. Training in referential communication increases both sociocentric speech and role-taking abilities. However, training in role-taking, while valuable in its own right, does not automatically increase referential communication, which seems to require skills that are specific to it. Hence, role-taking is a necessary, but not sufficient, component of referential communication.

There have been many successful attempts to advance the moral-stage reasoning of individuals. A pioneer in the field has been Turiel (1966), who succeeded by exposing subjects to two opposing solutions of an ethical dilemma; the solutions were at the same stage, which was also one stage above that of the subjects. For example, subjects at Stage 2 were given two contradictory resolutions, both of which were characterized by Level 3 cognitive–structural reasoning. The subjects were not given any correct answers. The disequilibrium induced by this cognitive conflict situation frequently resulted in a structural reorganization at a higher level.

The issue of developmental moral reasoning has special relevance to juvenile delinquency (Jurkovic, 1980) and adult offenders (Hickey & Scharf, 1980). Recent work in the field has concentrated upon organizing opportunities for inmates of correctional institutions to participate in democratic processes in what has become known as "justice-as-treatment" programs (Hickey & Scharf, 1980). In a comprehensive program, the total moral atmosphere of the correctional institution is changed. Prior to the change, the institution is likely to be operated on an autocratic basis by officials and guards. Most inmates see such institutions as governed by the rules embedded in Stages 1 and 2 of Kohlberg's developmental scheme. The majority of adolescent offenders are themselves at Stage 1 or 2, whereas the majority (75%) of adolescents and young adults who are crime-free are at Stage 3 or 4 (Kohlberg, Kauffman, Scharf, & Hickey, 1975). In a "just community," the inmates design a constitution of their own that will govern rights, privileges, rewards, and punishments within the institution. Guards are trained in advance to understand Kohlberg's stages and to lead discussion groups that will facilitate stage advance. When infractions of the new rules occur, inmates are assembled to discuss the incident and recommend a disciplinary course of action. They now constitute a cohesive self-government, in which each inmate has an individual vote and decision-making power. Such a transformed moral atmosphere does not occur overnight, and the role of the "therapeutic team" (a group of professionals trained in this approach) is multifaceted. The objective is to help the inmates progress to Stage 3, where they will have a sense of caring for other members and loyalty to the group. Progression to Stage 4, which sometimes occurs, introduces an even greater probability of behavioral stability in accord with the laws of society.

For many inmates, this experience affords them the first opportunity of their lives to enjoy a social context of mutual concern and fair exchange in relationships. The just community may be characterized as a democratic process in which rules are generated and conflict is resolved by individual participation. Ideally, community members conduct their discussions and make their decisions in an objective and impartial manner, tempered by a growing concern for each other's welfare. This is not the way it starts out, but is the goal toward which it progresses. The rate of recidivism is low in this approach (Kohlberg et al., 1975). This can be explained by the structural transformation that occurs in moral-stage progression, which facilitates the maintenance and generalization of gains.

So far, this discussion about moral atmosphere and a just community has been focused upon correctional institutions. However, I believe that the same sorts of considerations of fair and just exchanges, as illuminated by the Piaget-Kohlberg model, can be valuable in couples and family therapy. Indeed, the moral atmosphere of the family, the first institution to which most of us are exposed, will lay the groundwork for the moral sense we bring to the world. Applying these ideas to the Shore family would offer an exciting therapeutic challenge.

## Therapist-Client Relationship

A constructivist–developmental therapist maintains a stance of unconditional respect for the intrinsic worth of the client and the evolutionary meaning-making activities he or she is engaged in. The therapist is not value-free, however, for each advancing stage is recognized as being both psychologically and philosophically more adequate. As a result, there is a preconceived framework within which therapy proceeds and a goal towards which it is guided (Kegan, 1982). The relationship between therapist and client is not a uniformly stable one, but is subject to disequilibrating events and autoregulative activities in much the same way that individual development is (Voyat, 1983). The role of the therapist in relation to the client along an active-passive continuum will be highly variable. At times, the therapist will be very active, as when structuring and directing a training program. On other occasions, the therapist may be only relatively active—for example, when engaging in a Socratic dialogue with the intention of fostering glimpses into higher stage reasoning and when inducing cognitive conflict to promote structural reorganization. Finally, there will be times when the therapist will appear comparatively passive as he or she conveys an understanding of the client's personal paradigm for interpreting the world and demonstrates support as the client navigates the transition through uncharted waters to a newly constructed paradigm or self structure.

## LIMITATIONS OF THE MODEL

Currently it is a matter of some debate whether stages have quite the quality of structured wholeness that Piaget had maintained. There is certainly a reality of stage-mixture, particularly through transitional phases. Also, while an individual may exhibit a predominant stage, specific variables may activate the use of lower stages. It is generally agreed upon, however, that qualitatively different strategies of reasoning in physical, social, and moral domains *do* emerge in an invariant sequence with age progression.

A limitation to the constructivist–developmental paradigm is that it does not offer a single coherent practice model. It is conceivable that one might appear in the future. There is a strength in this limitation, however, since it implies a certain versatility that allows us to look at old practice from new perspectives and to creatively generate a diversity of novel procedures. Both of these implications have very practical consequences for clinical intervention strategies and tactics. With a few exceptions, however, the honing of new techniques has not yet reached a technically refined or sophisticated level.

## RESEARCH

The constructivist–developmental paradigm is the most extensively researched theory of human development. The research tapestry is made of cross-sectional, cross-cultural, and longitudinal strands. Although the field continues to evolve and its researchers often engage in robust debate, research findings are essentially supportive and promising. The vast spectrum of literature reporting the research is too great to identify here, but the reader wishing to keep abreast of the trends should consult the journals *Child Development* and *Human Development,* as well as the publications of major figures we have discussed: Piaget, Selman, Kohlberg, and Kegan. Most of the research has been with children and adolescents. There is a growing interest, however, in life-span development. Subjects from Kohlberg's longitudinal research on moral development are now in their late thirties and forties. Kegan has researched his model of an evolving self with adult psychiatric patients.

Perspective-taking training (Urbain & Kendall, 1980) and the "justice-as-treatment" model (Hickey & Scharf, 1980) have demonstrated their effectiveness in research endeavors. The general theory for developmental change based on a conflict strategy has been validated in many research projects, most notably those of Inhelder, Sinclair, and Bovet (1974) and Piaget (1974/1980). However, research on cognitive conflict has not yet been conducted in a therapeutic context.

Implications of the paradigm for traditional psychotherapy and for selecting conventional clinical interventions have not been researched thus far, but rather have received their support from theoretical analyses and clinical experience. There is certainly something logically compelling, for example, about saying that a therapist should take into account the client's developmental stage when formulating a communication or interpretation. Nevertheless, the absence of research in these areas is a challenging invitation to those who would wish to further strengthen the credibility of the paradigm's promise of usefulness for the therapeutic arena.

## SUMMARY

In this exposition of the constructivist–developmental paradigm, individuals have been presented as active agents who create meaning as they progress in their understanding of the physical, social, and moral aspects of the world. The process is one in which they are recurrently liberated from embeddedness in the constraints of earlier stages. Each advance offers them greater flexibility and autonomy through an evolving self, within the framework of wider and deeper social and psychological perspectives. Ultimately, development leads to a multisystems perspective—a recognition of the interdependence between systems and individuals. Cognitive conflict, the impetus towards the construction of greater structural adequacy, is seen as a positive force. Development moves through a hierarchical series of invariant stages. Each stage constitutes a higher-order reorganization and integration of sociocognitive structures, and results in a more adaptive way of knowing-and-being-in-the-world.

The conceptualization of human development from a constructivist viewpoint offers guidelines for traditional psychotherapy, for differentially selecting treatment strategies, and for generating novel clinical approaches. The full yield of the paradigm's therapeutic potential has yet to be realized.

I hope that this explanation of the developmental journey will give therapists the option to integrate the constructivist–developmental paradigm with their current orientation, in order to achieve a higher-order structural synthesis of greater clinical understanding, utility, and adaptability.

## REFERENCES

Abroms, G. (1978). The place of values in psychotherapy. *Journal of Marriage and Family Counseling, 4*, 3–17.

Anthony, E. J. (1956). The significance of Jean Piaget for child psychiatry. *British Journal of Medical Psychology, 29*, 20–34.

Anthony, E. J. (1957). The system makers: Piaget and Freud. *British Journal of Medical Psychology, 30*, 255–269.

Anthony, E. J. (1976). Freud, Piaget, and human knowledge: Some comparisons and contrasts. In Chicago Institute for Psychoanalysis (Ed.), *The annual of psychoanalysis* (Vol. 4, pp. 253–277). New York: International Universities Press.

Baldwin, J. M. (1906). *Social and ethical interpretations in mental development.* New York: Macmillan.

Barker, P. (1985). *Using metaphors in psychotherapy.* New York: Brunner/Mazel.

Basch, M. F. (1977). Development of psychology and explanatory theory in psychoanalysis. In Chicago Institute for Psychoanalysis (Ed.), *The annual of psychoanalysis* (Vol. 5, pp. 229–263). New York: International Universities Press.

Beck, A. T., Rush, A. J., Shaw, B. F., & Emery, G. (1979). *Cognitive therapy of depression.* New York: Guilford.

Blasi, A. (1980). Bridging moral cognition and moral action: A critical review of the literature. *Psychological Bulletin, 88*, 1–45.

Block, J. (1982). Assimilation, accommodation, and the dynamics of personality. *Child Development, 53*, 281–295.

Case, R. (1978). Intellectual development from birth to adulthood: A neo-Piagetian interpretation. In R. Siegler (Ed.), *Children's thinking: What develops?* (pp. 37–72). Hillsdale, NJ: Lawrence Erlbaum.

Chandler, M. J., Greenspan, S., & Barenboim, C. (1974). Assessment and training of role-taking and referential communication skills in institutionalized emotionally disturbed children. *Developmental Psychology, 10*, 456–553.

Cicchetti, D. (1984). The emergence of developmental psychopathology. *Child Development, 55*, 1–7.

Cohen, R., & Schleser, R. (1984). Cognitive development and clinical interventions. In A. W. Meyers & W. E. Craighead (Eds.), *Cognitive behavior therapy with children* (pp. 45–68). New York: Plenum.

Cowan, P. A. (1978). *Piaget with feeling.* New York: Holt, Rinehart & Winston.

Davis, L. V. (1985). Female and male voices in social work. *Social Work*, March-April, 106–113.

Dewey, J. (1930). *The quest for certainty.* New York: Minton, Balch.

Dickson, W. P. (Ed.). (1981). *Children's oral communication skills.* New York: Academic Press.

Doise, W., & Mugny, G. (1979). Individual and collective conflicts of centrations in cognitive development. *European Journal of Social Psychology, 9*, 105–108.

Doise, W., Mugny, G., & Perret-Clermont, A. (1975). Social interaction and the development of cognitive operations. *European Journal of Social Psychology, 5,* 367–383.

Edelson, J. L. (1978). A Piagetian approach to social work practice with children and adolescents. *Clinical Social Work, 6,* 3–12.

Elkind, D. (1974). *Children and adolescents: Interpretive essays on Jean Piaget.* New York: Oxford University Press.

Fast, I. (1985). *Event theory: A Piaget-Freud integration.* Hillsdale, NJ: Erlbaum.

Feffer, M. H. (1959). The cognitive implications of role-taking behavior. *Journal of Personality, 27,* 152–168.

Fischer, K. W. (1980). A theory of cognitive development: The control of hierarchies of skill. *Psychological Review, 87,* 477–531.

Flavell, J. H. (1963). *The developmental psychology of Jean Piaget.* Princeton: D. Van Nostrand.

Flavell, J. H. (1977). *Cognitive development.* Englewood Cliffs, NJ: Prentice-Hall.

Flavell, J. H. (1985). *Cognitive development* (2nd ed.). Englewood Cliffs, NJ: Prentice-Hall.

Flavell, J. H., Botkin, P. T., Fry, C. L., Wright, W., & Jarvis, P. E. (1968). *The development of role-taking and communication skills in children.* New York: Wiley.

Furth, H. G. (1980). *The world of grown-ups: Children's conceptions of society.* New York: Elsevier.

Gholson, B., & Rosenthal, T. L. (Eds.). (1984). *Applications of cognitive-developmental theory.* New York: Academic Press.

Gilligan, C. (1982). *In a different voice: Psychological theory and women's development.* Cambridge, MA: Harvard University Press.

Goldstein, A. P., Lopez, M., & Greenleaf, D. O. (1979). Introduction. In A. P. Goldstein & F. H. Kanfer (Eds.), *Maximizing treatment gains: Transfer enhancement in psychotherapy* (pp. 1–22). New York: Academic Press.

Gordon, D. (1978). *Therapeutic metaphors.* Cupertino, CA: META Publications.

Greenspan, S. I. (1979). *Intelligence and adaptation.* New York: International University Press.

Hickey, J. E., & Scharf, P. L. (1980). *Toward a just correctional system.* San Francisco: Jossey-Bass.

Inhelder, B., & Piaget, J. (1958). *The growth of logical thinking from childhood to adolescence* (A. Parsons & S. Milgram, Trans.). New York: Basic Books. (Original work published 1955)

Inhelder, B., & Piaget, J. (1969). *The early growth of logic in the child* (E. A. Lunzer & D. Papert, Trans.). New York: Norton. (Original work published 1959)

Inhelder, B., Sinclair, H., & Bovet, M. (1974). *Learning and the development of cognition* (S. Wedgwood, Trans.). Cambridge, MA: Harvard University Press.

Jurkovic, G. J. (1980). The juvenile delinquent as a moral philosopher: A structural-developmental perspective. *Psychological Bulletin, 88,* 709–727.

Kegan, R. (1977). Ego and truth: Personality and the Piaget paradigm. (Doctoral dissertation, Harvard University, 1977.) *American Doctoral Dissertations, 1976–1977,* 163.

Kegan, R. (1980). Making meaning: The constructive-developmental approach to persons and practice. *The Personnel and Guidance Journal, 58,* 373–380.

Kegan, R. (1982). *The evolving self.* Cambridge, MA: Harvard University Press.

Kegan, R., Noam, G. G., & Rogers, L. (1982). The psychologic of emotion: A neo-Piagetian view. In D. Cicchetti & P. Hesse (Eds.), *New directions for child development: Emotional development* (No. 2, pp. 105–128). San Francisco: Jossey-Bass.

Kohlberg, L. (1981). *Essays on moral development: Vol. 1. The philosophy of moral development.* New York: Harper & Row.

Kohlberg, L. (1984). *Essays on moral development: Vol. 2. The psychology of moral development.* New York: Harper & Row.

Kohlberg, L., Kauffman, K., Scharf, P., & Hickey, J. (1975). The just community approach to corrections: A theory. *Journal of Moral Education, 4,* 243–260.

Kuhn, D. (1972). Mechanisms of change in the development of cognitive structures. *Child Development, 43,* 833–844.

Mead, G. H. (1934). *Mind, self and society.* Chicago: University of Chicago Press.

Piaget, J. (1955). *The language and thought of the child* (M. Gabain, Trans.). Cleveland: Meridian. (Original work published 1923)

Piaget, J. (1960). *The child's conception of the world* (J. & A. Tomlinson, Trans.). Totowa, NJ: Littlefield, Adams. (Original work published 1926)

Piaget, J. (1962). Three lectures: The stages of the intellectual development in the child; The relation of affectivity to intelligence in the mental development; Will and action. *Bulletin of the Menninger Clinic, 26,* 120–145.

Piaget, J. (1963). *The origins of intelligence in the child* (M. Cook, Trans.). New York: Norton. (Original work published 1936)

Piaget, J. (1965). *The moral judgment of the child* (M. Gabain, Trans.). New York: Free Press. (Original work published 1932)

Piaget, J. (1969a). *Judgment and reasoning in the child* (M. Warden, Trans.). Totowa, NJ: Littlefield, Adams. (Original work published 1924)

Piaget, J. (1969b). *The child's conception of physical causality* (M. Gabain, Trans.). Totowa, NJ: Littlefield, Adams. (Original work published 1927)

Piaget, J. (1970). *Structuralism* (C. Maschler, Trans.). New York: Basic Books. (Original work published 1968)

Piaget, J. (1971). *The construction of reality in the child* (M. Cook, Trans.). New York: Ballantine. (Original work published 1936)

Piaget, J. (1972). *Psychology and epistemology* (A. Rosin, Trans.). New York: Viking. (Original work published 1970)

Piaget, J. (1973). *The child and reality* (A. Rosin, Trans.). New York: Grossman. (Original work published 1972)

Piaget, J. (1976). *The grasp of consciousness* (S. W. Wedgwood, Trans.). Cambridge, MA: Harvard University Press. (Original work published 1974)

Piaget, J. (1977). *The development of thought* (A. Rosin, Trans.). New York: Viking. (Original work published 1975)

Piaget, J. (1978). *Success and understanding* (A. J. Pomerans, Trans.). Cambridge, MA: Harvard University Press. (Original work published 1974)

Piaget, J. (1980). *Experiments in contradiction* (D. Coltman, Trans.). Chicago: University of Chicago Press. (Original work published 1974)

Piaget, J. (1981). *Intelligence and affectivity: Their relationship during child development* (T. A. Brown & C. E. Kaegi, Trans. and Eds.). Palo Alto: Annual Reviews Monograph. (Original work published 1954, in outline form)

Rhodes, M. L. (1985). Gilligan's theory of moral development as applied to social work. *Social Work,* March–April, 101–105.

Rosen, H. (1979). The development of sociomoral knowledge: A cognitive-structural approach. (Doctoral dissertation, Columbia University, 1979.) *Dissertation Abstracts International, 40,* 2397B.

Rosen, H. (1980). *The development of sociomoral knowledge.* New York: Columbia University Press.

Rosen, H. (1985). *Piagetian dimensions of clinical relevance.* New York: Columbia University Press.

Selman, R. L. (1971). Taking another's perspective: Role-taking development in early childhood. *Child Development, 42,* 1721–1734.

Selman, R. L. (1976a). Social-cognitive understanding: A guide to educational and clinical practice. In T. Lickona (Ed.), *Moral development and behavior* (pp. 299–316). New York: Holt, Rinehart & Winston.

Selman, R. L. (1976b). A developmental approach to interpersonal and moral awareness in young children: Some educational implications of levels of social perspective-taking. In T. C. Hennessy (Ed.), *Value and moral development* (pp. 142–167). New York: Paulist Press.

Selman, R. L. (1980). *The growth of interpersonal understanding.* New York: Academic Press.

Selman, R. L., & Byrne, D. F. (1974). A structural-developmental analysis of levels of role-taking in middle childhood. *Child Development, 45,* 803–806.

Serban, G. (1982). *The tyranny of magical thinking.* New York: Dutton.

Shantz, C. U. (1975). The development of social cognition. In E. M. Hetherington (Ed.), *Review of child development research* (Vol. 5, pp. 257–323). Chicago: University of Chicago Press.

Shantz, C. U. (1983). Social cognition. In J. H. Flavell & E. M. Markman (Eds.), *Handbook of child psychology: Cognitive development* (Vol. 3, pp. 495–555). New York: Wiley.

Siegler, R. (1986). *Children's thinking.* Englewood Cliffs, NJ: Prentice-Hall.

Smedslund, J. (1961). The acquisition of conservation of substance and weight in children. I. Introduction. *Scandinavian Journal of Psychology, 2,* 11–20.

Turiel, E. (1966). An experimental test of the sequentiality of developmental stages in the child's moral judgments. *Journal of Personality and Social Psychology, 3,* 611–618.

Turiel, E. (1974). Conflict and transition in adolescent moral development. *Child Development, 45,* 14–29.

Turiel, E. (1977). Conflict and transition in adolescent moral development. II. The resolution of disequilibrium through structural reorganization. *Child Development, 48,* 634–637.

Urbain, E. S., & Kendall, P. C. (1980). Review of social-cognitive problem-solving interventions with children. *Psychological Bulletin, 88,* 109–143.

Voyat, G. E. (1982). *Piaget systematized.* Hillsdale, NJ: Erlbaum.

Voyat, G. E. (1983). Conscious and unconscious. *Contemporary Psychoanalysis, 19,* 348–358.

Wachtel, P. L. (1981). Transference, schema, and assimilation. The relevance of Piaget to the psychoanalytic theory of transference. *The Annual of Psychoanalysis* (Vol. 8, pp. 59–76). New York: International Universities Press.

Walker, L. J. (1980). Cognitive and perspective-taking prerequisites for moral development. *Child Development, 51,* 131–140.

Weiner, M. L. (1985). *Cognitive experiential therapy: An integrative ego psychotherapy.* New York: Brunner/Mazel.

Wellman, H. M. (1985). The origins of metacognition. In D. L. Forrest-Pressley, G. E. MacKinnon, & T. G. Waller (Eds.), *Metacognition, cognition, and human performance* (pp. 1–30). New York: Academic Press.

Wolff, P. H. (1960). The developmental psychologies of Jean Piaget and psychoanalysis. *Psychological Issues, 2* (monograph 5). New York: International Universities Press.

# 15

# Cybernetic Epistemology

*Sophie Freud, Ph.D.*

The elegant name of my paradigm is adopted from Keeney (1983, p. 16), who proposed it in honor of Bateson, who thought that "cybernetics is the biggest bite out of the fruit of the Tree of Knowledge that mankind has taken in the last 2000 years" (1972, p. 476). I have chosen this paradigm because, at my late midlife stage of life, I am continuously and compellingly faced with the roundness of life, which is the central, deepest idea of cybernetics.

Epistemology refers to the premises that underlie our actions and thoughts. It is "a study of how people or systems of people know things and how they think they know things" (Keeney, 1983, p. 13). What we know and believe—our epistemology—leads us to construct the world in certain ways, and the way we construct the world leads us to know certain things in certain ways. Many of the premises and central philosophical principles that I will describe are taken from Bateson's ideas, as they appear in the essays collected in *Steps to an Ecology of Mind* (1972), and Hoffman's (1981) clarifying comments, as well as Keeney's (1983; Keeney & Ross, 1985) elaborations of "cybernetics of cybernetics." I also hope to integrate the overlapping and now confluent but somewhat independently developed stream of General Systems Theory as applied to autonomous living structures. For this latter exposition, I will draw upon the ideas developed by the General Systems Theory Committee of the American Group Psychotherapy Association, especially Durkin's (1981) and Brown's (1981) expositions of those ideas.

Modern cybernetics and General System Theory are particularly attractive to social workers because they represent deeply humanistic values. I agree with Bateson, who became quite desperate in his old age, in feeling that only a systemic ecological perspective would give us a possibility of survival in this age of nuclear weapons, pollution, and depletion of this planet's natural resources.

## THE CONCEPT OF THE PERSON AND THE HUMAN EXPERIENCE

Cybernetics is the study of the patterns and organizations that manifest themselves when human beings in a consensual social process draw distinctions upon an infinitely varied and indistinct world. We all participate in this social construction of reality. This does not mean that there is no reality; it simply means that our minds are structured to process the world in terms of space and time. Therefore, it is the structure of our minds that determines what reality is for us. Reality is also unknowable because it cannot be objectively observed; moreover, it changes in the process of being observed.

The world that is created and maintained through this process of drawing distinctions is ordered by an infinite number of interacting and hierarchically connected *feedback loops.* For Bateson, *mind* stood for the concept of a cybernetic system. Every system of interconnected parts with a self-corrective feedback structure is said to have mental characteristics. Mind is located in all of nature, both within systems and between systems, and thus serves as the interconnection between all living structures. The *interdependence and interconnectedness* of all life, phenomena, organizations, and behavior patterns is a central principle of cybernetics. There is both an ecological interconnectedness, which we can visualize as a net, and a circular interconnectedness that occurs through feedback between different levels of systems, which we may visualize as loops.

*Wisdom* consists of perceiving the whole circuitry of a transaction that is interconnected with other circuitries and that ultimately affects the whole ecology. The cause-and-effect concept of linear "punctuation" is rejected in favor of *circular causality.* (It is recognized that the decision on where a particular interaction started, referred to as punctuation, is arbitrary. Such a decision is determined by particular private or public, or perhaps political, purposes, rather than by absolute reality, which always remains uncertain.) The process of drawing distinctions and then creating our own punctuations on the stream of circular interactions gives us the freedom to create our own meaning. By drawing new distinctions, we can create new realities. We can also interrupt destructive interactions at any point in time, without having to seek causes in the past.

*Lack of wisdom* is defined as compulsive purposeful action that is guided by narrow common sense, by the view of partial arcs (i.e., sectors of the whole), and by blindness to the larger picture. Wars and pollution and exploitation are caused by our blindness to the fact that cruelty and injustice will inevitably reverberate through a circular system that is continually recycling itself. Victims and oppressors are recursively connected through feedback cycles. Masters rely on their slaves, and through that process they become incompetent and dependent upon their slaves (who thus in effect become their masters).

From the cybernetic viewpoint, our interest is no longer in common characteristics, and diagnostic categories are viewed as self-fulfilling prophecies and as "dormitive principles." (This phrase, which Bateson applied to situations in which a description, in the form of a label, erroneously stands for an explanation, comes from the dubious reasoning that opium puts people to sleep because it contains a dormitive [i.e., sleep-inducing] principle.) Our goal is the understanding of pattern and organization. *Behavior* is defined as communication (Watzlawick, Beavin, & Jackson, 1967), which emphasizes the interpersonal message value of all of our behavior. Others react to our communications, and we in turn react to their responses, in endless feedback cycles. When we define behavior as communication, we can understand that it happens *between* people, rather than inside them, and derives meaning from its being part of an ongoing flow of events in a particular *context*. It is context that gives meaning to communication. Even psychological attributes acquire their meaning only when they are considered as part of the stream of unfolding circular transactions.

According to this perspective, we are not studying events or objects but rather the *information* that is carried by them. Information is a central concept that replaces the concept of force and energy. In fact, there is no place in systems thinking for these concepts. In a world of patterns, events are triggered or released by differences rather than by force or energy. "Unilateral power," which is seen as a concept that is based on energy, is an epistemological error that nevertheless can become self-validating and destructive to the system, like any other such error. (That is, if people are convinced that unilateral power exists, they will act so as to bring it about.) Power cannot be located in one particular part of the system; it can only be located in the rules of interactions. Such rules cannot be changed by conscious purpose, because force cannot be applied to patterns. The attempt to have such unilateral control, like man's attempt at technological control of the ecosystem, creates catastrophe.

Because we create the world by drawing distinctions, *we are always a part of everything we observe.* Our reality is thus inevitably self-referential and nonobjective. Each perspective may be one particular truth and a partial arc of the whole. Different truths lead to different epistemologies—with different social, ecological, and political consequences. Ways of punctuating reality that ignore the cybernetic laws of recursive feedback and complementarity may lead to disaster.

Most destructive to our ecology is the false distinction that our Western culture draws between self and nonself, which blinds us to the recognition of our interdependence. The "self" is not an independent unit; it is the false reification of an improperly delimited part of a much larger field of interlocking processes. The unit of survival is not an isolated self, but an ecosystem. The "fittest" is the member that most contributes to the health of the ecosystem by adding diversity.

Apart from drawing the dangerous duality of self and nonself, we create many other dualities that lead to destructive consequences. Such Cartesian dualisms as means and end, mind and body, health and sickness, love and hate, and description and prescription are in reality two sides of a whole. They are *complementary* cybernetic polarities; that is, one side of the polarity loses meaning without the other side. There is, after all, no happiness unless we have experienced unhappiness, and vice versa. Cybernetic polarities are recursive, in that together they create circular processes that fold inward upon themselves. Therefore, if one side is maximized at the expense of the other, it becomes the opposite— and creates pathology. Even virtues carried to their extreme turn upon themselves. For example, too much love becomes possessiveness and overcontrol, and ultimately becomes as destructive as hate. Life without sickness and death would lead to overpopulation and ecological disaster. Life and death are thus not dualisms; they do not belong to an either–or system, but they belong together. There are also occasions when opposites may be one side of a larger cycle on a different level. For example, happiness versus sadness may be viewed as one side of the polarity of being in touch with one's feelings, as opposed to not being in touch with one's feelings. It is important to recreate awareness of both sides of the distinction, at whatever level may be chosen.

Of special interest, for the post-Freudian world, is the cybernetic concept of the polarity between *conscious* and *unconscious* processes. Freud saw the unconscious as a dangerous, potentially disruptive, sub-terranean force of unbridled emotions, whereas Bateson thought that unconscious processes may protect us against the sterility and destruc-tiveness of excessively purposeful and deliberate acts. He saw unconscious processes as sources of intuition, creativity, fantasy, art, and playfulness, and therefore a vital counterpart to conscious processes. He did agree with Freud that love is an intuitive feeling that cannot be purposeful and that comes from the unconscious. According to Bateson, love—as a corrective for conscious purpose and as manifest in the I-Thou relationship between human beings and their ecosystem—is a hoped-for solution to our present ecological threats.

Using a somewhat different meaning of the unconscious, Bateson also agreed with Freud that increased awareness may widen our perception of choices. He anchored the unconscious in cognitive (rather than emo-tional) processes and suggested that our belief systems and taken-for-granted premises, our maps of the world that direct our perceptions of differences that we perceive or unconsciously choose not to perceive, are outside of our awareness and thus, by definition, unconscious.

Individuation and relatedness can similarly be seen as cybernetic complementarities. It is only through secure attachment that we learn to individuate; therefore, we can say that individuation grows out of attachment. However, attachment also grows out of individuation: We know that true relatedness is only possible if we are individuated enough to recognize the otherness of our partner.

In the same spirit, we can see that interconnectedness is only one half of a cybernetic whole. The process of drawing distinctions presupposes an I or a YOU that draws such distinctions. We cannot postulate interconnectedness of living systems without also contemplating their *autonomy*. We can only speak of a system, its continuity over time, and its characteristics, if the system has the autonomous ability to regulate its interactions and preserve its organization in the face of an everchanging and disturbing environment.

Before we continue to examine additional concepts derived from cybernetics and systems thinking, we may find it helpful to create a larger context of meaning by turning to a historical perspective.

## HISTORICAL PERSPECTIVE

### General System Theory and Cybernetics

Although Bateson seemed to subsume ecology, communication theory, information theory, and systems theory under the roof of cybernetics, historically it appears that systems theory had priority and that cybernetic theory developed as a branch of systems theory. In any case, each of these ideas played a part in the development of the new paradigm that has revolutionized 20th-century thinking.

Remembering the cybernetic principle of interconnectedness, we can look for the way systems thinking and cybernetic ideas have grown out of the *Zeitgeist* of the 20th century. On the other hand, if we want to avoid premature punctuation, we can simply ask how these ideas *represent* our century. Just as Freud's metapsychology mirrored the laws of energy mechanics and conservation of energy of the 19th century, this new epistemology mirrors new ideas in the natural sciences, such as new views about *what* was to be investigated and *how* it was to be done. (See Durkin, 1981, and Auerswald, 1985, for background on the following ideas.)

Cybernetics is the study of patterns, organizations, and the interconnectedness of systems; its development paralleled physicists' attempts to understand patterns of interrelationships that integrate the parts into a whole. The rule of nonsummativity of the parts that make up a system (i.e., the whole is different from the sum of its parts) paralleled a similar discovery in quantum mechanics. The realization of uncertainty in the physical world replaced a deterministic mechanical perspective and made room for new speculations about the human creation of a shifting reality.

Most important was the idea that the investigator is not an objective external observer but is part of the phenomenon that is being investigated. In a similar vein, it was found that any phenomenon that is being studied changes through that act. The "objectivity" of science started to make room, at least in some circles, for the idea that scientists' findings are influenced by their values, making them responsible for the questions to be asked, the interpretations of the data, and the political implications of those interpretations.

In the 1920s, in this new climate, Ludwig von Bertalanffy tried to create mathematical models that would highlight the similar (isomorphic) global properties of all systems and that would lead to the creation of a General System Theory (GST). These beginning efforts then sprouted in many directions, including not only technical applications but also ecological applications and new ideas about the nature of equilibrium and stability (homeostasis) and change. In the 1940s, Norbert Wiener founded and worked on the science of cybernetics, which was based on the functioning of self-controlling networks. Initially, cybernetics was simply a description of self-governing circular feedback loops in mechanical systems. Later, technical applications of GST and cybernetics contributed to the development of computer sciences.

By the 1960s, the field of systems thinking and cybernetics had changed and expanded, as attempts were being made to apply similar principles to living organisms such as people, families, and other human groups. Many investigators, such as von Foerster, von Neumann, Ashby, Prigogine, Varela, and Maturana, added radically new ideas to both Wiener's original closed-system concepts and to von Bertalanffy's early formulations. Some of these thinkers were especially interested in the concepts of autonomy, autopoiesis, and self-reference of living structures, creating second-order cybernetics (the cybernetics of cybernetics).

Gregory Bateson, an anthropologist and philosopher, was perhaps the most important successor to von Bertalanffy. Bateson applied cybernetic and GST ideas to an ecological rather than a mechanical model of the world. A group of gifted researchers, including Don Jackson, Virginia Satir, Jay Haley, and John Weakland, assembled around Bateson at Stanford University during the 1950s (Broderick & Schrader, 1981) to study such topics as levels of learning, levels of meaning in face-to-face communication, the nature of fantasy, play, and paradox. This was a continuation of the work on the hierarchy of logical types that had been begun by Whitehead and Russell 40 years earlier.

Eventually, the group became interested in applying their ideas to the study of families that had schizophrenic members, which led to the publication of the seminal paper on the pathological nature of "double bind" communication (Bateson, Jackson, Haley, & Weakland, 1956). ("Double bind" refers to the idea that parents disqualify and mystify their children [in effect, drive them crazy] by giving them messages that are contradictory at different levels of communication, called metalevels.) Although this idea was highly innovative, it was still limited by the use of linear causality, and it focused on dyadic rather than truly systemic interactions.

The Palo Alto group also initiated the idea of applying cybernetic principles to families. However, they used a model of closed mechanical systems and were therefore led to emphasize the tendency of families towards self-corrective homeostasis. It was thought that families needed their symptomatic member—the somewhat arbitrarily identified patient—to maintain adaptation and homeostasis. No doubt, the rigidity they observed in the families with a schizophrenic member led them to this early formulation, which was later modified because of findings from research on living structures.

## Family Therapy

John Bell is often given credit for his pioneering work with families, which began in 1951, although Carl Whitaker had already experimented with seeing families in the early 1940s. Other important figures and centers* in the development of family therapy include:

1. The Family Mental Health Clinic at Jewish Family Service in New York City, founded by Nathan Ackerman in 1960 (and renamed the Ackerman Institute for Family Therapy after his death);
2. Theodore Lidz and his work group at Yale in the 1950s;
3. Lyman Wynne at The National Institute of Mental Health, joined by Murray Bowen in 1954;
4. The Philadelphia group that formed around Boszormenyi-Nagy beginning in 1957;
5. Don Jackson's founding of the Mental Research Institute in Palo Alto in 1959. (This institute became a center of communication studies, which led to the publication of *The Pragmatics of Human Communication*, Watzlawick et al., 1967, a seminal work on communication theory.)

---

*Many of these early family-centered efforts were directed at families with schizophrenic members, a situation for which outcome measures are still uncertain.

The founding of the journal *Family Process,* with the participation of many of these pioneers, is usually considered the point at which family therapy began to be thought of as a major therapeutic movement. Eventually, out of these beginning efforts, a number of individual schools of family therapy developed. Each had its own unique theoretical base and interventions that were founded on it, yet the great majority of them united under the umbrella of systemic thinking.

## The Founding of the Milan School

The method of intervention that I will focus on later in this chapter is the approach originated by the so-called Milan School. The Institute for Family Study in Milan, Italy, organized by Mara Selvini Palazzoli, began to conduct family therapy in 1967. From the beginning, research was an integral part of the Institute and was intimately connected with providing better service to its families (Selvini Palazzoli, Boscolo, Cecchin, & Prata, 1978).

Selvini Palazzoli's first book dealt with her experiences in treating anorexic girls. Results were disappointing until she started to see the girls with their families. After that, she experienced sudden, dramatic therapeutic successes. In 1972, the team initiated a new research program that, once again, directed efforts to families with schizophrenic children.

Eventually, the main staff consisted of four psychoanalytically trained family therapists who worked as a group: two as therapists and two (behind a one-way mirror) as supervisors. Above all, the Milan workers tried to fit their interventions to the new cybernetics of living systems, paying respect to the autonomy of living systems and the possibility of sudden transformations of those systems. They published their dramatic results in the late-1970s in *Paradox and Counterparadox* (1978), which had an immediate and ever-expanding impact on family therapy theory and practice around the world.

## KEY THEORETICAL CONSTRUCTS

After these theoretical expositions, we—I, the writer, and you, the reader—are ready, in our interconnectedness, for a more concrete approach to our paradigm. Since we are in the fortunate position of having the Shore family included in our common context, we can use that family to illustrate the theory.

## System Concepts

Cybernetic and systemic thinkers divide the world into systems (biological, social, psychological, geographical, etc.) with boundaries that can be drawn in various ways, for various purposes. For example, we can define the Shore family as a living system. Like any other system, it is composed of parts that are *interrelated in dynamic interaction.* The functioning of this family cannot be understood simply from the functioning of its members. (This is a system property called nonsummativity.)

Once a system has been created, it can be imagined as hierarchically nested in larger (supra) systems or smaller (sub) system configurations. Subsystems usually have fewer elements and a less complex organization than their suprasystems have. The Shore family can be viewed as a subsystem of its neighborhood, city, and society, and each member of the family is a subsystem of the family unit. All of these systems have certain isomorphic properties regarding boundaries, feedback, processes of stability and change, and autonomy and interdependence.

The very act of distinguishing a system creates *boundaries.* All living systems have boundaries that are more or less permeable and that define possible transactions. The Shore family has quite well-defined boundaries, and it is clear who does or does not belong to the family. However, although she is a family member, Rena is an adopted child, and her fantasies about her birth mother introduce some boundary problems.

There are also internal subsystem boundary problems. Charley acts like a little boy and Nancy treats him accordingly—or perhaps Nancy treats Charley like a little boy and Charley therefore acts accordingly. In any case, subsystem boundaries between generations are blurred, with mother all alone and overburdened in the executive system and with father's authority undermined. Rena's role is unclear: She is a child (Nancy's, Gram's, and even her birth mother's), but she also has occupied the role of grandmother since Gram's death. Families that have such blurred subsystem boundaries are called *enmeshed.* The Shore family is an excellent example of an enmeshed system.

One has the impression that the Shores' family boundaries have also become more rigid over the years, which has led to the family's increased isolation. Moreover, the system has shrunk as it has lost important extended family members. Because all parts of a system are interconnected, the system changes when some parts are removed. There is indication that the death of Charley's mother—and especially the deaths of the two powerful matriarchal women in this family, Gram and Aunt Flo—affected the functioning of the Shore family.*

---

* *Editor's note:* Actually, Aunt Flo is still alive; this was evidently not clear in the case material.

## Theories of Change

### *The autopoiesis\* of living systems*

Both the theories of living structure and the cybernetics of cybernetics have emphasized processes of autonomy in living systems. The responses of an autonomous system are determined by its own structure, rather than by external impacts; this concept is referred to as *structure determinism.*\*\* If we punctuate a system as autonomous, our interactions with it can only affect the system as a whole through *perturbations.* Squeezing a balloon, for example, can be viewed as a perturbation, because the process changes its shape (i.e., structure) without breaking its boundaries or fundamental organization. In response to perturbations, a system may change its structure to maintain its organization (which is its identity). Therefore, even though there may be ongoing structural change with every perturbation, there is a maintenance of organization. Organization pertains to the continuity of the system and is referred to by such words as "person," "identity," or "family." Loss of organization would mean the end of that system.

It is a fundamental requirement of any organism that it be coupled to its environment (the principle of *structural coupling*) and that people who live together organize themselves into particular patterns (the process of *co-evolution*). Any organism that has survived can be seen as adapted to its environment in the best way this organism has found, given its particular structure. Therefore, existing behavior is necessarily compatible with the environment; otherwise, it would be extinguished.

Such concepts imply that we cannot change another system in a unilateral direction, but that the system will determine how it shapes its response to us. This is reminiscent of Bateson's rejection of "force" as a correct cybernetic concept, as well as his insistence that it is impossible for one part of the system (for example, the therapist) to change the rest of the system (such as a family) in unilateral ways. If there were no structure determinism, similar actions would have similar effects on all systems *(instructive interaction)*, which is blatantly not the case. Rules about linear causality are based on instructive interaction.

These are powerful ideas that change the nature of therapy. They lead us to reject the metaphor of "healing" or impacting and substitute an image of disrupting ongoing interaction loops. According to this perspective, a therapist does not act on the family; instead, we observe the mutual perturbations of two co-evolving systems. This reminds us

---

\* *Autopoiesis* is a term used by Maturana and Varela to refer to "the order of process that generates and maintains the wholeness of autonomy of biological cells" (Keeney, 1983, p. 84).

\*\* See Dell (1985) for a more detailed exposition of many of these ideas.

of Harry Stack Sullivan's ideas of therapy as "participant observation." Indeed, Sullivan had intuitively arrived at many of these ideas and had incorporated them into his thinking.

Bateson emphasized the *external* interconnectedness of all living systems, whereas other scholars, such as Varela or Maturana, emphasized the *internal* interconnectedness, with organization as the focus of study. In second-order cybernetics, we do not speak of observing other systems, since objective observations are meaningless. We can only speak of *observing our observing* of other systems, such as a family. As we apply our ideas to individuals and families, we need to be aware of both the autonomy and the interconnectedness of systems.

### Constraints versus autonomy

Simple cybernetics uses a theory of *restraints* as an explanation for the outcome of development and events. It is thought that phenomena develop in particular directions because they had, or have, no alternative pathways. The cause of restraints can be the lack of alternative solutions, a particular feedback cycle, rigid unconscious belief systems, and lack of information. An important restraint is the redundancy that arises out of patterns, which means that we can guess about a total configuration from knowing parts of it. For example, from knowing the Shore children, we could guess that they are part of a problematic family system.

It seems as if restraints have a deterministic, freedom-restricting influence. If restraints are in a feedback cycle within systems, they can be of a higher order. On the other hand, if they are located in the system's structure, such as in a particular belief system, they can be within the autonomous system. Perhaps the most important restraint that makes change difficult is that each system is only part of a larger system, and "the part can never control the whole" (Bateson, 1972, p. 437).

In the Shore family, there are many areas of restraint from all the sources that have been mentioned. Both Nancy and Charley were raised under circumstances that helped them create certain assumptions about the world. They both learned to expect that fathers are either unreliable, or absent, or incompetent. They learned to long for and admire the glamour of the acting world. Together they have learned to anticipate disasters, to the point of creating them to ease the tension of anticipation. Nancy and Charley have both lived in a working-class or lower-middle-class socioeconomic environment, which has constrained many real opportunities for later achievements. Charley had limited formal education and therefore is limited to menial employment opportunities. Michael has lived under the restraints of illness all his life.

In addition to these restraints, there are powerful feedback processes within the family that limit the possibilities for each member. For example,

Charley's hopes to amount to something are constrained by his wife's utter contempt for his capacities. (This, of course, is only one arc that has been arbitrarily lifted out of a whole feedback cycle.) Many of the family's constraints also arise from higher level feedback processes, such as the school system, the summer camp, and the medical system. All the members of the Shore family have a limited perspective on alternative possibilities for their lives.

However, the theory of living structures also suggests that certain areas of freedom are possible for all living structures. Because these structures are autonomous systems with some capacity for self-regulation, they reach wholeness through such processes as development, maintenance, adaptation, differentiation, and self-maintaining boundary-strengthening activities. The Shore family does not succeed very well in some of these activities, yet there is a great deal of interdependence, and even positive mutual caretaking. For instance, both Nancy and Charley are conscientious parents, within their capacities. There is also some striving towards differentiation by the family's subsystems, such as Rena's efforts at growing up and separating from the family and Michael's persistence in wanting to act like a normal boy, in the face of contrary messages. Charley's efforts at wholeness consist of his not giving up and going on disability maintenance.

Living structures also have some capacity for self-transformation and some freedom for self-organization. Therapeutic efforts are based on these characteristics.

Although we are initially tempted to view restraints and autonomy as irreconcilable opposites, we are quickly led to recognize them as cybernetic complementarities. Restraints offer guidance and direction; without restraints, choices would be infinite—a situation that could not lead to development and to autonomous structure. Without autonomy, there would be no structure at all, and restraint would become meaningless. However, as individuals, we can lean towards one or the other polarity. For example, Bateson did not believe that we are "the captains of our soul" (1972, p. 438), yet he tried throughout his life to create differences that would make a difference to the world.

### Stability and change

We find the same kind of polarity between stability and change. Living systems have inherent capacities to maintain stability, order, regularity, and predictability in the face of disturbing environments (morphostasis), as well as differentiation, transformation, growth, and change (morphogenesis). These processes occur simultaneously and continuously in all living systems at all times. Systems change in order to maintain stability, and there must be some order so that change is possible.

A structure can only survive and become stable if it changes its structure to adapt to changing conditions that are both internal and external to the system. Stability and change are a cybernetic complementarity; neither is possible without the other. The interaction of these two processes is a flowing equilibrium that appears to be a steady state.

There have been a great many changes in the Shore family. Members have died, the children have grown up, there have been many illnesses and many misfortunes. The family has had difficulty dealing with all these changes; strong homeostatic forces keep the basic interaction patterns quite similar. There is a cycle of escalating misfortunes, accompanied by the mother's intense worrying, a final explosion of the issue at hand, and a temporary relaxation until the next crisis occurs. One might hope to introduce new ways for this family to change, creating cybernetic *change of change.*

### The feedback system

Cybernetic theory distinguishes three feedback processes: positive, negative, and evolutionary feedback. Morphostasis and morphogenesis are structural names for these feedback processes.

The concept of *negative feedback* comes from simple cybernetics and describes the process of maintaining homeostasis in self-corrective systems, such as steam engines or thermostats. Feedback processes also operate in all living systems, such as the body, which, for example, maintains its temperature at an even level in many different kinds of climates. The "calibration" or "set-point" (a metaphor taken from the thermostat) of a mechanical system is always set outside the system, primarily by human beings. In living systems we find different types of calibrations, usually several of them acting together. Some calibrations may be located in each of the subsystems, or in a higher level system. For example, the behavior of a child can be the calibration for a family, or the legal system (in the form of child-protective laws) can be a calibration at a higher level.

Just as we imagine systems to be nested in a hierarchical order, we can picture feedback loops in similar ways, with simple feedback processes at one level being modified at another higher level in a recursive hierarchical fashion. It is important to appreciate how lower level processes can impinge upon higher systemic levels, in a form of *entrapment* (such as bodily illness or addictions that invade the whole person). In a well-functioning system, feedback, in the form of new information, leads to new learning and self-corrective processes.

There are also several ways in which feedback processes can be damaged. For instance, feedback can become repetitive and equilibrium-maintaining without introducing new information. We then talk about a family's being "stuck." In addition, corrective behavior can "overshoot,"so that the system seems to be oscillating and is apparently out of control. However, such wild oscillations, which appear chaotic, may actually be part of a fairly rigid feedback system.

We find examples of both kinds of defective negative feedback processes in the Shore family. A simple negative feedback cycle, in which the calibration is within the family, is Nancy's being upset with Charley for lying to her, while he continues lying to her in order to protect her and to not upset her with bad news. This loop seems to be fairly repetitive and has not changed much over time.

A feedback cycle that involves a set-point outside the system might be Nancy's working in a nursing home to earn extra money to supplement her disability payments. Because society does not allow such activities, a higher order feedback (in the form of the legal system) keeps Nancy at home. In this case, the disability payments function to assure the family some stability in terms of basic economic maintenance, yet it is a stability that perpetuates chronic disability in both parents. The regulation of the social security system might be influenced by a particular administration, which in turn is connected in a feedback loop with individual voters who elect the administration, creating recursive feedback loops that cut across various levels of systems in both directions.

Another example of higher order feedback processes' maintaining lower order feedback processes in the family is the medical system. In this case, the medical system tends to act on partial arcs, without a view to long-range feedback processes and the whole circuitry. This demonstrates what Bateson called "lack of wisdom." Through their processes of diagnosing and medicating, members of the medical system have reinforced the family's own homeostatic tendencies. Moreover, the medical system creates and maintains problems by treating an *instance* of action (such as a manic-depressive episode or a convulsion) as a *category* of actions, a "condition." This is something that Bateson has warned us against. (Explaining Charley's difficulty by diagnosing it as "Bipolar depression" is a perfect example of Bateson's "dormitive principle," in which a label stands for an explanation.) Any intervention would have to take into account not only the family's own feedback cycles but also higher order feedback cycles with which the family's cycles are recursively connected.

The wisdom of knowing that short-range solutions may have unexpected long-range consequences when the whole circuitry is considered has important therapeutic implications. For example, it leads us to reflect upon the stigmatizing and identity-changing consequences of hospitalization for mental disturbances, or on the addictive consequences of prolonged therapy.

A vivid example of "overshooting" feedback in order to maintain family stability is Charley's effort to protect Nancy from Rena, which injures his daughter in the process. One could imagine that such an overshooting effort at maintaining equilibrium, which has already resulted in violence, could become habitual in this family, or even lead to a *runaway* of violence (in which violence begets more violence).

There is some controversy about the usefulness of the concept of *positive feedback,* which refers either to a set-point that amplifies rather than minimizes deviations, or to a condition in which a runaway in the form of an *escalating sameness* is created. We could imagine, for example, how Nancy's shame about her obesity leads her to stay home and hide and eat more to cover her loneliness and shame, which makes her even more obese—in a cycle of escalating sameness. Calibration here might come from an obesity-related illness, which would be a lower order feedback (her own body) involving higher order feedback processes (such as the medical system). Similarly, we could imagine how Nancy's contempt for Charley led him to become more incompetent, which increased her contempt for him (an escalating sameness), until Charley came down with a manic-depressive "condition" that served to regulate the interaction at a new, low level (with calibration being in both Charley and the medical system). In both of these instances, we can see how positive feedback really becomes negative feedback at a different level and eventually stops the runaway with a new kind of equilibrium. Positive and negative feedback are thus not intrinsically different, but are merely perspectives from different levels of systems.

Another solution to a runaway is the destruction of the system. (To take an extreme example, the arms race, which is seen as the epitome of a positive feedback runaway, might eventually get stopped by the destruction of the planet.) Although positive feedback may lead to change through a runaway, it is usually thought of more as an escalating sameness that aborts efforts at change, rather than as a true change.

Change that comes about through negative feedback processes has been called *first-order change* (Watzlawick, Weakland, & Fisch, 1974), regardless of whether it results from a simple internal family feedback or from the feedback of systems outside the family. We could punctuate the therapist's suggestion that Charley teach Michael to fish and to play miniature golf as a first-order intervention—or recognize that at least this was how the Shores utilized the idea, given their remarkable skill at merging external feedback into the family's habitual operations.

I suspect that not only the medical system but also a whole array of social workers has become a homeostatic part of this family. This situation illustrates Bateson's observation that, over time, systems become habituated to the continuing presence of people (the welfare system, the family service system) who wanted to help the system but who were neutralized by first-order homeostatic processes.

To be effective, interventions need to introduce *second-order change,* in which the rules that govern the usual feedback systems get changed. For example, within the Shore family, we could view the attempt to rent the downstairs apartment as a move that might introduce new differences, and perhaps second-order change. Here again, however, Nancy is prepared to transform this opportunity into a first-order change by adding the renting of the apartment to the large list of other happenings that make her anxious and that need to be worried about.

Because living systems can only maintain stability through ongoing fluctuations, there is an ever-present possibility that one such fluctuation (or oscillation) may suddenly lead the system into new directions. It could happen, for example, that the new family renting the downstairs apartment will bring in resources and information that will *not* get swallowed up by the family's homeostatic tendency but that will get utilized in new and unforeseen ways. Unexpected events may always occur and move the system from repetition to evolution. The term *evolutionary feedback* (Hoffman, 1981, p. 157) has been adopted from its use by the physicist Prigogine to characterize discontinuous change as a leap into the unknown.

In General System Theory, such evolutionary leaps are said to occur through the system's own decision to open its boundaries and make room for entropic processes (disorder, chaos)—what Bateson has called "random" elements—in a system that might have been overly regulated by negentropy (order, pattern, structure, regularity, specialization). Although such opening of boundaries is said to be an autonomous act, there is no fixed set-point, either inside or outside the system; and the final outcome remains unpredictable. Sometimes two systems, even those from different hierarchies, open their boundaries to each other; this may lead to the mutual drawing of new distinctions and to transformations. At its best, the therapeutic encounter can be such a transforming encounter. After such an episode of boundary opening, boundaries must then be closed to consolidate the change and restore order.

It is hoped that therapeutic interventions can facilitate the move from chronic recursive spirals to evolutionary leaps and second-order change. Therefore, a therapist would be wise to use a minimum of interventions to allow the system's self-healing processes to take over. As soon as a family has become "unstuck," they can be relied on to find, independently, a new structure that might serve them better.

Symptoms are often embedded in positive feedback processes. Although those processes rarely lead to a more favorable equilibrium, they can still be recognized as one way in which the system reaches for change.

## The Meaning of Symptoms

The reframing of the meaning of symptoms, from the expression of intrapsychic conflict to a particular interpersonal message, was an immediate implication of communication theory. From the cybernetic standpoint, there is a further transformation of the meaning: Symptoms can be viewed as an expression of a whole disturbed ecological network. Nevertheless, Freud's original hypothesis that a symptom was a compromise formation (between an instinctual wish and inhibiting forces) has remained intact in these two new meanings. For communication theorists, the symptom is a compromise between communicating and not communicating, or a possibility of communicating without having to take responsibility for the message. Similarly, in our current new (cybernetic) formulation, a symptom may be viewed as "a compromise between pressure for and against change" (Hoffman, 1981, p. 166). Although the symptom is often an abortive and maladaptive attempt to introduce change into a system, it may create enough disequilibrium to upset a family's usual self-corrective processes.

Nancy's back problem, for example, could be viewed as her self-sacrificing attempt to get Charley to take more responsibility in his role of father of the family, rather than an attempt to put him down through her superior competence. Actually, all the members of the Shore family show this exceptional readiness for personal self-sacrifice. At the same time, all those symptoms—such as Rena's messing up, or Michael's constant asthma attacks, or Charley's "condition"—reinforce the family's stuckness.

Symptoms may be viewed as indications about where the family therapist might begin to assist the family's own change efforts. There are schools of individual and family therapy in which the removal of the symptom is the goal, with the expectation that a system without a symptom will reorganize itself in a more functional manner. However, proponents of the Milan School direct their efforts at the relationship context for which the symptom is an expression. More specifically, their aim is to change the rules that maintain the family's transactional game (Selvini Palazzoli et al., 1978, p. 4).

In many situations, the symptom is actually a solution that has become the problem (Watzlawick et al., 1974), or at least the attempted solution to the symptom has become more problematic than the symptom itself. Here again, systemic theory joins hands with psychodynamic theory, in which some behaviors (e.g., alcoholism) may be viewed as an initial attempt at treating mental pain, but an attempt that has become more problematic than the pain it was meant to anesthetize.

Solutions to problems are created over time through trial and error. Once such solutions have been created and have proven themselves over time, some rigid families (and individuals) become extremely reluctant to give them up, lest they face worse alternatives. This pattern is strikingly demonstrated in the Shore family, in which Nancy's worrying and Charley's lying are obviously solutions that work in some measure but which also perpetuate the family problems.

## Personality Theory

Personality theory is inherent in all of the above ideas. A person is viewed as a system (divided into subsystems) and as a part of larger systems with feedback loops in both directions. If we take the perspective of the person as the focus of observation, we can punctuate him or her as an autonomous structure in which the set-point for behavior (the ideal state) is contained within the system. We can then study the organization, feedback cycles, and set-point of that particular system, without reference to other systems.

Such concepts as purpose, characteristics, resistance, pathology, and homeostasis are called *symbolic explanations* (Keeney, 1983, p. 106) and are meaningless when applied to an autonomous system. However, they become meaningful when the system is studied in relation to other systems. For example, we can call someone "passive-aggressive" or "masochistic" in relation to other human beings, although these attributes would be meaningless outside of an interpersonal context.

*Operational* explanations are those that refer to the autonomous system, such as to its organization of parts. Personal change might involve the disruption of people's own homeostatic devices, one of which could be their habitual ways of drawing distinctions and selecting the reality that is to be either attended to or ignored. In psychodynamic theory, these processes are called defenses, and operational (inner space) explanations are often preferred. Systemic therapists have found it more useful to use symbolic explanations, which focus on the many social systems with which people are involved through ongoing feedback loops.

A person, like any other system, is the product of a history of learning that affects its present state. People's history, in therapy, may become the source of the "random" in which new elements may be found to construct a new story for the family.

The power of family delegations, parental missions, and intergenerational loyalty has been emphasized by Stierlin and colleagues (Stierlin, Ruecker-Embden, Wetzel, & Wirsching, 1980). It might be useful to think of intergenerational legacies as feedback loops through the generations (even though it is a somewhat linear idea). One could hypothesize that even dead people can give imaginary feedback that would direct a course of action.

According to systemic thinking, dyadic relationships can be viewed as either *symmetrical,* in which the two partners define each other as equals, or *complementary,* in which the two partners have unequal social positions but interlocking matching needs (Watzlawick et al., 1967). Symmetrical partners can exchange advice, praise, or criticism, and conflicts tend to escalate into mutual violence. Complementary relationships are viewed as a dominant-submissive pattern, and conflict can lead to the disconfirmation of the "one-down" partner. Healthy relationships are apt to be a mixture of both patterns.

One could frame the Shore marriage either as a symmetrical escalation of incompetence or as a domination of Charley by Nancy (in a mother-son relationship). In treatment, it would be useful to introduce the possibility of some symmetry around competence, as well as an occasional reversal of complementarity, in which Charley could become the father and Nancy the little daughter.

## ASSESSMENT

An important principle of assessment is that the system's behavior is meaningful, purposeful, and the best adaptation for a particular system (given the history and current restraints and the distinctions that operate within the system). To understand the functioning of the system, we need to look at the *effects* of behavior, rather than attempt to find causes, which are, in any case, apt to be circular and therefore elusive.

Understanding a client's punctuations and distinctions is an important aspect of assessment. An examination of attempted solutions, which may be in the form of symptoms, may lead to hypotheses about the nature of perceived restraints.

In the Milan system, assessment starts with the formulation of hypotheses as soon as any information (no matter how preliminary) is gathered about the family. These hypotheses are then introduced into the system in the form of circular questions. They become modified or reinforced, depending on the family's reactions. For instance, denial and protest would lead to modifications; thoughtfulness and surprise would indicate reinforcement. The assessment is thus a dynamic process of feedback loops. Hypotheses need to be plausible and yet different enough from the causal belief system of the family to make a difference (Ugazio, 1985). Many of the hypotheses about the Shore family have been mentioned in the course of this exposition. During the assessment process, we can add a few more hypotheses to the picture.

Overall, the Shore family appears to be in perpetual chaos. However, this apparent chaos seems regulated by quite rigid homeostatic patterns. Those patterns can be illustrated by the following examples, which arbitrarily focus primarily on Nancy.

Nancy can be viewed as an extremely overburdened family caretaker. By her constant worrying about each family member, she makes everyone feel very valued. She offers Charley a mother, giving him the opportunity to not let go of his own mother, whom he lost prematurely. She sacrifices her competence as a nurse so that Charley will not feel too inferior to her. Her back disability also gives her more time to take care of the constant family emergencies; in addition, it reassures the rest of the family that she will not leave them and will always be around. It is also possible that her back disability and obesity protect Charley against having to demonstrate his manhood in sexual relations.

Charley, in turn, serves Nancy by reinforcing and appreciating her mother role, which is currently her major role. His determined incompetence lets her be the sole family caretaker, giving her life much value and importance. Besides, it is the traditional role of women in that family, and a disruption in that pattern might be an act of intergenerational disloyalty. Both Charley and the children contribute to Nancy's life by giving her much to worry about. Indeed, worrying seems to be the central meaning of her life. The repeated family catastrophes also allow Nancy to relax her vigilance for a short time and to demonstrate her competence in the face of disasters. Michael's illness, for example, allows Nancy to use her nursing skills and to continue to stay in touch with doctors. Rena's persistent "messing up" seems to have a similar purpose. Both children provide enough trouble so that Nancy cannot concentrate all her irritation and worrying on Charley. (If she were able to concentrate entirely on Charley, the situation might become a runaway.)

Rena has also spent her life serving the family, just as Nancy did before her. She took her turn trying to make Gram happy by providing her with a "movie star," after Nancy's mother and Nancy's husband failed in that role. Gram's death threatened to upset the family's equilibrium, and Rena stepped into Gram's role so she would not be missed too much. By not succeeding in college and getting on with her life, which might eventually separate her from her family, Rena demonstrates her family loyalty through repeated failures. However, she does have some yearning to leave the family and find an alternate one, which is expressed by her search for her birth mother.

This family shows strong homeostatic patterns across generations. On both sides, there is a family history of incompetent, invisible, or abandoning men. There is an intergenerational feedback system of mothers and daughters sacrificing their competence for each other. As a child, Nancy met her mother's needs by becoming Gram's angel and perhaps a future movie star. In adolescence, Nancy became fat in order not to threaten her aging mother's sexual attractiveness. Later, she would marry a "movie star" to make up for her mother's failure in that role; when that project failed, she offered her daughter as another candidate. Nancy even made sure that Gram's dire predictions about her marriage to Charley would become true.

We can thus see that there is an enormous amount of mutual caretaking in this family. Any solution to the family's problems will have to include other ways in which members might be able to take care of each other.

## TREATMENT OF CHOICE

I have chosen the Milan School to illustrate the cybernetic epistemology paradigm because I believe that its interventions, especially as they have been developed in centers throughout Europe (Campbell & Draper, 1985), Canada (Tomm, 1984a, 1984b), and Australia (White, 1986), are more closely matched to modern cybernetic and systemic thinking than are the interventions of most other schools. It also seemed that this particular approach was almost made-to-order for this rigid family, which appears deeply entrenched in its dysfunctional system. I believe that the Shores are the kind of family that could easily defeat most of the more traditionally oriented therapeutic approaches.

Although I will take the family as my unit of treatment, I would need to include some larger systems at some point in the course of therapy. I would then draw a boundary around the family and the representatives of the medical system and school system, and treat the whole unit with similar principles, as outlined below (Christofas, Goldsmith, Marx, Mason, & Peatfield, 1985). It might also be useful to do individual therapy, especially with the children; here again, I would use systemic principles.

## THE THERAPEUTIC PROCESS

### Techniques and Methods

I shall recapitulate the major therapeutic principles arising out of cybernetic epistemology and connect them with particular techniques as practiced by the Milan School and other related therapeutic approaches. Essentially, our goal is to change the nature of existing restraints, including the existing feedback cycles, people's cognitive maps, and the whole pattern that the system has formed.

One major principle is that we need to *disrupt* the whole ecology that is reflected by symptomatic behavior and *interrupt* the feedback cycles that maintain it. Such feedback cycles may be homeostatic or runaways. A great deal of creativity has gone into the invention of disruptive techniques. Most of them are quite similar and are often paradoxical, in that they seemingly aim at stability rather than at disruption. For example, it has been found useful to co-opt a family's tendency towards homeostasis by prescribing it. I will discuss a few of these techniques below.

*1. The family's way of seeing the world is accepted, but doubts are introduced by escalating it into the absurd*

We might accept Nancy's worry about the future, for example, but escalate it into all life spheres. We might talk of the danger of letting

Michael go to school, lest he have an unexpected asthma attack. We could recommend that the family go on tip-toe from now on, in order to not disturb the tenants downstairs. We could forbid Nancy to ever go out at all and perhaps recommend total bed rest for a month as a preventive measure. In short, we could view these escalations as methods of amplifying positive feedback and encouraging problem behavior.

*2. We could try to keep one part of the system still, in order to prevent the usual fluctuations that allow just enough change so that the system stays the same*

For example, we could talk about the danger of Rena's living on her own and could insist that she move back home, since her moving out was a homeostatic move that eased tension just enough so that the family could stay the same.

*3. We could "prescribe" the symptoms. This is yet another way of unsettling the equilibrium by pushing down too hard on one side*

In this instance, we could insist that Charley lie to Nancy at least once a day, or we could tell Nancy that she has to make one bad prophecy every week for each family member. The rationale for this approach is that it will help them view their lives and future dangers with more clarity. Such a procedure could even be constructed into a once-a-week ritual. These techniques address themselves to the ways in which the family habitually attempts to solve problems.

A second major principle is that we want to help the family members *draw new distinctions* and, through this process, change some of their belief systems. In the Milan method, which is based on circular questioning and therapeutic neutrality (Tomm, 1984b), circular interviewing has become the major way of introducing new ideas into the family. Much of the session is thus spent on what appears to be "mere questioning." However, this is the major way of conveying information.

The questions are phrased to embed prescriptions to the family. Questions explore the initial hypotheses, and verbal and nonverbal responses serve to confirm, broaden, or disprove a particular hypothesis. Because questions are meant to introduce new differences into the family, they are therefore *about* differences. They are asked in a circular fashion. Sometimes one family member is asked his or her opinion about one or more other family members or is asked to order a series of differences. The same question may be asked of several family members (to show differences in thinking within the family and to offer a *double description*), or different family members may be asked different questions.

*1. Inquiries may be made about differences between persons or relationships*

"Michael, who do you think would be more pleased if Rena returned to college, your father or your mother?"

"Rena, do you agree with Michael's view?"

"Nancy (Charley, Rena, Michael), do you think Charley gets more upset when Rena messes up or when Michael messes up?"

"Nancy, do you think the family would be better or worse off if Michael started not to tell you truthfully all the bad things that always happen at school and if Charley started to tell you the whole truth about upsetting matters?"

"Rena, when your father and Michael quarrel, does your mother tend to side with Michael or with your father?"

"Michael, do you agree with Rena on that?" "Nancy, do you see it the same way?" A question about family sequences can follow the answer: "What does your father do if your mother sides with Michael?"

"Charley, do you think Nancy is more angry with you, or less angry with you, when Michael gets sick?"

"Rena, is Nancy easier to live with, or harder to live with, right after Michael has an asthma attack?"

*2. Inquiries may be about a series of differences*

"Rena, who in the family, including yourself, do you think would be most pleased if your mother got over her backache and returned to nursing? And second pleased? And least pleased?"

"Michael, who forgets the most things when they are sent on an errand? And second most? And the least?"

"Michael, who do you think is the most pessimistic about your father's getting a steady job? And next? And who is the most optimistic?"

"Rena, who is most convinced that Michael needs medication for epilepsy? And next? And least? Who is most convinced that Michael misbehaved at camp because he wanted to be sent home rather than because he could not manage to behave better? And second? And least?"

*3. Inquiry could also involve triads*

"Rena, what do you think your mother would say if we asked her who would miss her worrying the most?"

"Charley, what do you think Nancy would worry about most, if Rena finds her birth mother?"

*4. It is very important that questions introduce a measure of confusion and chaos, in order to unsettle the system*

"Rena, if your father and mother got divorced, who do you think would get remarried first?" "Michael, do you agree with Rena? What sort of a person would your mother hope to marry next?" "Nancy, do you agree with Michael?" "Charley, what could Nancy do that would make you ask her for a divorce? And under what circumstances do you think she would ask you for a divorce?"

"Nancy, if Charley and Rena both decided to go to college, who do you think would mess up first? How do you think they would mess up?"

*5. It is considered very important to put the most feared events "on the table"*

"Nancy, if Charley commits suicide, who in the family would be most sad? And next sad? And least sad?" "Rena, do you think your mother would gain more weight or lose some weight if your father committed suicide?"

*6. Inquiries may be about the meaning that people attribute to each other's behavior*

"Nancy, do you think Rena's messing up is meant to defy you, or make you worry about her?" "Michael, do you think your parents think that Rena's looking for her birth mother means that she is disappointed with them?"

*7. Questions may concern relationship differences in the past*

"Michael, do you think Rena was closer to Mother or to Gram?"

"Nancy, who do you think loved her daughter the most—Gram, or your mother, or yourself? And the least?"

"Charley, who do you think made you feel more like a little boy, your mother or your wife? To whom are you more grateful for being such a good mother?"

"Charley, if Gram were still alive, and Rena became a famous actress, who would be happier—Gram or Nancy?"

*8. Questions about temporal differences may be important, to show the family that things have been different or, in the case of hypothetical questions about the future, to show how things could be different*

"Nancy, when you first got married, who loved the other more—you or Charley?" "Charley, do you agree with her? And who loves the other more now?"

"Michael, do you think Rena messed up more before Gram died or after Gram died?"

"Nancy, do you think Charley was more optimistic about his life before his mother died, or less optimistic? Did Gram have a better opinion of Charley before you were married or after you were married?"

"Charley, do you think Nancy was more impatient with you before you had your condition, or after you had your condition?" "Michael, do you agree with your father's view?"

"Rena, do you think there would be more fighting in the family if your father goes on disability, or less fighting? What if your father started to work in a steady job, would that make for more or less fighting?"

"Michael, if your father's tests show that he is not very smart, do you expect that there would be more or less fighting in the family? And if the tests show that he is actually very smart, would that make for more or less fighting?"

"Charley, if you were still not working and if Nancy's health improved and she went back to nursing, would she expect you to help with the cooking and housecleaning?"

"Michael, if your mother's weight problem led to a health crisis and she had to be hospitalized, do you think Rena would move back home and take care of the family? If your mother were to die and Rena were to move back home and take care of the family, would she also gain weight like your mother?"

"Charley, if Nancy had a health crisis, would it just discourage her further or might it motivate her to join Weight Watchers?"

Therapists do not ask only circular questions. They also ask linear questions about sequences, and they ask family members directly about their own perceptions, plans, hopes, and the like. White (1986), for example, has elaborated a series of very ingenious questions, in which he first asks each family member how he or she can participate in continuing the present state of the family—a "conservative option" (p. 174). He then asks each family member what he or she might do to improve the family situation—a "radical option" (p. 174)—and what difficulties might need to be anticipated. This strategy might work well with the Shore family.

A third major proposition of this approach is that we need to introduce alternate maps of reality that the family can use in its problem-solving attempts. Here again, we find new, ingenious techniques that largely overlap with the initial paradoxical strategies.

Alternating a particular reality is best done through repunctuation of particular sequences; this is referred to as *reframing*. In our earlier assessment section, we repunctuated many family interactions that might sometimes be seen as destructive under the framework of mutual caretaking. In the Milan School, such radical reframing, which has been called *positive connotation,* was usually introduced at the end of the session as an introduction either to some prescription, such as a family ritual, or to some family task. Initially, such positive connotation was merely a rationale for a paradoxical prescription, although it turned out to be a powerful intervention in its own right. It is easy to see how positive connotation could introduce confusion, surprise, and even absurdity into the system.

However, it is important to appreciate that reframing is not merely "trickery" but also reconnects the dismembered side of the polarity. We can bring competence into a picture in which only incompetence is visible, or altruism into a picture that appears only to be exploitation, because we know that the opposite must also be true on some level. Positive connotations can thus be presented with seriousness and respect.

Another reframing technique consists of exploring the *family history,* in the hope that it might provide meaning-making frameworks. With the Shore family, for example, one has the impression that Gram was a powerful figure whose various legacies may have contributed to the family's stuckness. Talking about each family member's relationship to Gram—perhaps through the perspective of another family member—might be very useful.

The prescribing of *family rituals* is yet another way in which the Milan School tries to introduce new differences into the family system. Rituals can have many functions for different families (Imber-Black, 1986): They celebrate and affirm change (divorce, remarriage, reconciliation); they provide a context for the expression of strong emotions; they promote transformations while maintaining sameness; they punctuate comings and goings in the family; they resolve contradictions by incorporating contradictory elements; they bury the past; and so on.

Rituals are meant to disconnect families from their usual roles and positions. Rituals may also be used as a wedge to be inserted in order to highlight an idea at the center of a family's belief system that may be expressed in a dysfunctional family rule. In addition, the therapist may seek out one rigid sequence and ask that it be acted out on purpose, or opposite rituals may be prescribed on alternating days to highlight contradictions in the family. Rituals may also introduce novelty and provide the random elements around which a family can reorganize itself. The prescribed ritual is thus as much a *message* to the family as it is a *task* that should be performed. The family's nonperformance of a ritual is simply treated as information about the family.

## Therapist-Client Relationship

After hypothesizing and circular questioning, *therapeutic neutrality* is the next most important principle of the Milan approach. The Milan therapist has great respect for the system's ability for self-transformation and considers his or her interventions to be only a trigger that might release the family's own self-corrective solutions. There is thus an emphasis on minimal interference, and no guidance is given about the direction in which the family should change. However, even though tenacity of purpose is contrary to cybernetic thinking, such neutrality about the nature of change may often be more of a pretense than a reality (White, 1986).

In the Milan approach, it is thought to be very important that the therapist not become more invested in change than the family is, thus carefully avoiding a symmetrical struggle about change. Earlier, I noted some ways in which rigid families may manage to obstruct any change efforts. In the Milan model, therapists are extremely careful not to take sides in such maneuvers. They appreciate the need for the system to be as it is, and do not blame, praise, or pass any moral judgments. They take a nonreactive stance and resist linear traps, alliances, and entanglements. Families are usually seen once every three weeks or once a month, and such long intervals have proved to be further blocks to the family's instant reactivity and their ability to defeat the therapists. In some ways, therefore, the Milan School joins those other schools of family therapy that view a contest between family system and therapy system as a prerequisite for change.

## Course of Treatment

A family such as the Shores is generally seen every three weeks by a team of two therapists. Arrangements could be made so that their current social worker, who has presumably referred the family, could become the family's co-therapist, under supervision, _if_ he or she is not too enmeshed with the family. The family therapy system, as "meta" to the current social work system, would have to judge the extent to which the family's social worker has become part of the dysfunctional system that is the target of change and has helped to maintain it, or the extent to which he or she has been able to maintain his or her separate boundaries (Selvini Palazzoli, Boscolo, Cecchin, & Prata, 1980). As I suggested before, at some point representatives of other systems, such as the medical system, will be included. They will be seen as "included" in the client group as contributors to the problem, and their efforts—however much lacking in "wisdom"—will then be positively connoted. The usual methods would apply to this larger unit as well.

A combination of all of the above-mentioned methods would be used to introduce new differences into the family. It is customary to have a break towards the end of the session in order to construct a useful final intervention. These final interventions were initially considered the most important aspect of the Milan method, although those who use the method now think that it is the circular questioning with its embedded subtle messages, rather than the final pronouncement, that triggers change in families.

Nevertheless, for the sake of our illustration, we shall present our assessment to the Shore family at the end of the first session, with the assumption that the questions around these initial hypotheses have yielded productive answers. It is important that any final session-prescription contains both suggestions for sameness and suggestions for change. We shall thus emphasize the mutual caretaking and sacrifice of competence for the sake of family loyalty. Everyone's behavior is thus important to the family; but, with time, family members could think of one or two new ways with which they could show their family loyalty. We shall then prescribe the following family ritual:

> Everyone in the family has lost people who were very important to them, and this family has been so busy that nobody has had time to mourn. We believe that many of the family problems are related to these unmourned losses. Your family will have to meet four times between the first and second session, on Sunday afternoons for one hour. Each week belongs to one family member, starting with the oldest member and ending with the youngest. The person whose week it is will decide what family members are to participate, and for whom he or she wants to mourn. Each person can use this mourning time in any way they want to, and direct other family members to participate in the ways that will be most helpful to the mourner.

If the family members carried out the task, they would have found that each member had quite different plans. They would have been required to attend to each other in a way that is probably unusual in this family and would have gotten new information about what each member cares about, thus effecting small differentiating steps. Even though the exercise would introduce highly novel elements into this family, the family will still operate in the spirit of enmeshment.

In the second session, the therapists will demand feedback about the ritual. Questions might then revolve around past family figures and the loyalty needs that are connected with them. At the end of the second session, a second family ritual will be prescribed:

> This family has had many worries in the past and it is important that these worries not be swept under the table. There are also many talents and strengths in this family that deserve to be noticed.
> You will have three weeks before the next meeting. You are to meet twice a week, on Tuesday and Friday evenings. On Tuesdays,

each family member will predict some unfortunate outcome for every other family member. On Fridays, each family member will predict a fortunate outcome for each family member. The same good and bad outcomes may be predicted every week, or people may invent new outcomes. Since it is important that the therapist learn about these predictions, we shall ask Nancy to keep track, in writing, of all the good predictions, and Charley to make a list of all the bad predictions.

The reader will recognize how we have prescribed an insidious and central family process—worrying and negative self-fulfilling prophecy—but have asked that it be done more deliberately and in a slightly different way. I will now leave the rest of the family sessions and interventions to the fertile imagination of the reader.

## LIMITATIONS OF THE MODEL

Although the implications of systemic and cybernetic thinking are extremely humanistic and could be seen as a last attempt to rescue the eco-system in which we have to survive, they also contain some possibilities for political distortions. Some people might emphasize the *autonomy* of living systems (with its theory of structure determinism) and neglect the cybernetic polarity of *connectedness,* as well as the whole area of restraints that limit autonomy. It is indeed difficult to keep both polarities in mind, and yet it is essential that we do so.

In a similar vein, it is politically unnerving to eliminate the concept of unilateral power. Unless we punctuate a cycle of oppression, the negation of unilateral power can implicate the victim, as well as the victimizer. Indeed, this has led to a clash between feminists and systemic thinkers. We will need to find some way out of this dilemma. It is also true, however, that the balance of power may shift as oppressed people become aware of their own strengths.

When the emphasis is on the present, insufficient respect might be paid to a system's development over time. It is possible that the systemic model does not pay enough respect to the history of systems. Further integration between systems theory and the latest theories about the development of the self will be a challenging area of research and theory-building.

## RESEARCH

Research on systems theory and cybernetic theory goes on throughout the world, at the frontier of many sciences,* and even a cursory review

---

* For example, it has been said that Bateson, an anthropologist, pointed to Humberto Maturana, a biologist, as his spiritual successor.

would be a daunting task. The new *Journal of Strategic and Systemic Therapy* would probably be the best way to keep up with the latest clinically oriented systemic research. In addition, the established journal, *Family Process,* seems to be the source of many seminal articles. *The Journal of Marital and Family Therapy* also carries reports on the forefront of work in systemic thinking. *Order Out of Chaos* (Prigogine & Stenger, 1984) might be of interest to many readers. Maturana and Varela's *The Tree of Knowledge* (1987) has recently been translated into English and should prove to be a groundbreaking book.

## SUMMARY

The reader must appreciate that the above thoughts, grouped around cybernetics but comprising General Systems Theory, ecology, and communication theory, are a profoundly and radically new world view that stands for progress and hope at the end of the 20th century. Unlike psychoanalytic theory, it is not a view that grew out of clinical practice. Instead, this new understanding of the world was developed by philosophers, scientists, and biologists. With time, these thoughts reached out into clinical practice and changed our approach to human beings in psychic pain.

This approach draws our attention to the fateful *interconnectedness* and *interdependence* of all living matter on earth. We are focused towards the *context* in which events occur and are given meaning. Our views have shifted from linear explanations to *circular repetitive feedback cycles,* in which people in families and social groups and nations become trapped. Disputes arise over correct *punctuations* of these recursive interactions, but we, as cyberneticists, believe that causes are illusive and shifting. Our former world of facts and certainty has become a world created by human beings drawing certain distinctions upon chaos, with language being our most important tool for doing this. There are no observations in which we are not part of the observed, and "objectivity" and "subjectivity" become meaningless concepts. The old polarities of "I" and "Thou," sane and insane, happy and unhappy, conscious and unconscious, have become wholes that belong together—and whenever we find an isolated pole, we start to look for its complementarity.

With this new belief system, we have given up archeological digs into people's pasts, because problems and conflicts are no longer viewed as arising from the inner space of human beings. Instead, they are seen as part of the intricate patterns that connect human beings in small and ever-larger interlocking circles of groups. Instead of attempting to locate blame, we seek to understand these repetitive feedback cycles, knowing that they must be disrupted before change can occur. With a new respect for the limits of our power to change others, we merely attempt to introduce new distinctions and to unsettle an equilibrium that has outlived its usefulness.

I started writing this chapter as a detached observer, interested in presenting a new way of thinking about life. My reasons for writing it were ambition, duty, a wish for academic visibility—all of them *symbolic explanations*, relying on you as an audience. As I absorbed myself for many weeks in these ideas, in a different way than I had done before, my world view changed forever. Cybernetic ideas captured my imagination and transformed my view of the universe. The project became an autonomous enterprise and the meaning of writing it shifted to the project itself, in that I worked on it for its own sake, for *operational* reasons. The writing of this chapter was thus both an autonomous act and an interrelated act, depending on our punctuation.

As I end this chapter, I return to you, dear reader, without whom this chapter would have no further existence. Without you this chapter would not have been written, and my spiritual transformation could not have happened. Therefore, you have changed my thinking, as I hope I may have changed yours. We are recursively interconnected.

## REFERENCES

Auerswald, E. H. (1985). Thinking about thinking in family therapy. *Family Process, 24,* 1–12.

Bateson, G. (1972). *Steps to an ecology of mind.* New York: Ballantine Books.

Bateson, G., Jackson, D. D., Haley, J., & Weakland, J. (1956). Toward a theory of schizophrenia. *Behavioral Sciences, 1,* 251–264.

Broderick, C. B., & Schrader, S. S. (1981). The history of professional and family therapy. In A. S. Gurman & D. P. Kniskern (Eds.), *Handbook of family therapy* (pp. 17–25). New York: Brunner/Mazel.

Brown, D. T. (1981). Learning general system theory through an experiential workshop. In J. E. Durkin (Ed.), *Living groups* (pp. 284–293). New York: Brunner/Mazel.

Campbell, D., & Draper, R. (Eds.). (1985). *Applications of systemic family therapy: The Milan approach.* London: Grune & Stratton.

Christofas, S., Goldsmith, A., Marx, P., Mason, B., & Peatfield, P. (1985). Working systematically with disadvantaged families and the professional network: Sharing is caring but meta is better. In D. Campbell & R. Draper (Eds.), *Applications of systemic family therapy: The Milan approach* (pp. 163–171). London: Grune & Stratton.

Dell, P. F. (1985). Understanding Bateson and Maturana: Toward a biological foundation for the social sciences. *Family Process, 11,* 1–20.

Durkin, J. E. (1981). Foundations of autonomous living structure. In J. E. Durkin (Ed.), *Living groups* (pp. 24–59). New York: Brunner/Mazel.

Hoffman, L. (1981). *Foundations of family therapy.* New York: Basic Books.

Imber-Black, E. (1986). *Recent innovations in family therapy.* Presented at The Family Institute of Cambridge (MA), March 15.

Keeney, B. P. (1983). *Aesthetics of change.* New York: The Guilford Press.

Keeney, B. P., & Ross, J. M. (1985). *Mind in therapy. Constructing systemic family therapies.* New York: Basic Books.

Maturana, H. R., & Varela, F. J. (1987). *The tree of knowledge: The biological roots of human understanding.* Boston, MA: New Science Library.

Prigogine, I., & Stenger, I. (1984). *Order out of chaos.* New York: Bantam.

Selvini Palazzoli, M., Boscolo, L., Cecchin, G., & Prata, G. (1978). *Paradox and counterparadox: A new model in the therapy of the family in schizophrenic transaction*. New York: Jason Aronson.

Selvini Palazzoli, M., Boscolo, L., Cecchin, G., & Prata, G. (1980). The problem of the referring person. *Journal of Marital and Family Therapy, 6,* 3-7.

Stierlin, H., Ruecker-Embden, I., Wetzel, N., & Wirsching, M. (1980). *The first interview with the family*. New York: Brunner/Mazel.

Tomm, K. (1984a). One perspective on the Milan systemic approach: Part I. Overview of development, theory, and practice. *Journal of Marital and Family Therapy, 10,* 113–125.

Tomm, K. (1984b). One perspective on the Milan systemic approach: Part II. Description of session format, interviewing style and interventions. *Journal of Marital and Family Therapy, 10,* 253–271.

Ugazio, V. (1985). Hypothesis making: The Milan approach revisited. In D. Campbell & R. Draper (Eds.), *Applications of systemic family therapy: The Milan approach* (pp. 23–32). London: Grune & Stratton.

Watzlawick, P., Beavin, J. H., & Jackson, D. D. (1967). *The pragmatics of human communication*. New York: Norton.

Watzlawick, P., Weakland, J., & Fisch, R. (1974). *Change: Principles of problem formation and problem resolution*. New York: Norton.

White, M. (1986). Negative explanation, restraint, and double description: A template for family therapy. *Family Process, 25,* 169–184.

# 16

# Evolving a Personal Philosophy of Practice: Towards Eclecticism

## *Hugh Rosen, D.S.W.*

*I suppose it is tempting, if the only tool you have is a hammer, to treat everything as if it were a nail.*—Abraham Maslow, 1966

Social work practice is enormous in its breadth. It may engage individuals, couples, groups, families, or communities as the client unit. It takes place in such diverse settings as schools, clinics, hospitals, prisons, adoption and family agencies, industry, and private practice. The practitioner participates in a wide range of functions encompassing treatment, advocacy, brokerage, prevention, community organization, service coordination, and crisis intervention. Many fields of knowledge contribute to social work practice, including ego psychology, psychoanalysis, communication theory, behavioral theory, systems theory, ecology, role theory, crisis theory, and group dynamics. It is not unlikely that new trends in cognitive science and information-processing theories will eventually be drawn upon.

There are several generic texts on social work practice, including Goldstein (1973), Pincus and Minahan (1973), Siporin (1975), and Lowenberg (1977). Other volumes specifically address clinical social work: for example, Strean (1978), Rosenblatt and Waldfogel (1983), Saari (1986), and Turner (1986). Some works on clinical practice are at a metatheoretical level and serve as an orienting framework for the practice of *all* clinical models (e.g., Saari, 1986), while others provide a *particular* practice model (Fischer & Gochros, 1975; Hollis, 1972; Reid, 1978; Reid & Epstein, 1977;

Turner, 1978). Meyer (1983) has advanced an eco-systems perspective, which does not constitute a practice model but instead is an overarching conceptual framework for guiding assessment and the selection of intervention models (see Chapter 12 of this book). It facilitates taking into account the complex variables of any given case and avoids the premature delimiting in assessment that would occur by initially viewing the case through the lens of a single model. Germain and Gitterman (1980) have developed a practice model that adopts an ecological orientation, emphasizing the adaptive match between the individual and his or her environment.

Distinctively clinical social work focuses upon the person-in-situation gestalt. There is a recognition of the continuing reciprocal process in which the individual who is interacting with the environment both shapes it and is shaped by it. Interventions are designed not only to influence the client's psychological and internal forces, but also his or her social and physical environment. Effective clinical social work enhances the client's social functioning and overall competence in living. In my opinion, all good psychotherapy is ultimately psychosocial in character. Psychotherapists who ignore the person-in-situation gestalt do so at their own risk, and at the risk of the client as well.

In this chapter, I propose to address some central issues and questions that I think are of special interest and relevance to all helping professionals who engage clients in a therapeutic relationship. I will not attempt to provide a brave new model for practicing clinical social work—do we really need another one? Nor is it my intention to be exhaustive, definitive, or dogmatic. I *will* offer some speculation, interweaving some personal impressions with observations from the literature. The tone I hope to convey is invitational: an invitation to you to grapple with this commentary and to forge from it personal perspectives that will guide you in the development of your own clinical practice philosophy.

## THEORETICAL MONISM AND METHODOLOGICAL PLURALISM

At this point, I would like to stake out the parameters of my own preferences regarding clinical theory and practice. It is not possible to embark upon a discussion or study in a completely neutral manner, inductively collecting and assembling raw data in a way that is totally value-free. When people approach new experiences, they bring with them personal theories, explicit or implicit, that influence what data they will seek, see, and select. Further, since raw data can be interpreted in more than one way, people's own prior theories will influence how they will *interpret* new facts and events (Kuhn, 1972).

I find that when I talk about what has caused a relatively stable therapeutic change in an individual, I am a theoretical monist, but in relation to practice models and techniques, I am a methodological pluralist. Looking across the range of therapeutic models, one sees too much of value among them to justify adopting a single model to the exclusion of all others (for a similar view, see Fischer, 1978; Lazarus, 1981; and Siporin, 1979). Clinical interventions may be designed to alter affective, behavioral, cognitive, or environmental systems. A linear, causal view is not adequate to describe what takes place as these systems interact reciprocally with one another. For example, the therapist may wish to have the client institute a behavioral change, but this will not occur without some level of motivation. However, once the client has begun to carry out the new behavior, he or she may very well feel differently about himself or herself. Hence, affect and behavior reciprocally interact with one another.

Yet affect and behavior that do not have an undergirding cognitive structure are likely to prove to be ephemeral. A cathartic experience may indeed leave the client feeling good temporarily, but if it does not lead to a cognitive modification, it is not likely to produce any enduring or stabilized change. A structure, by definition, is relatively permanent and stable, although it is subject to modification. Karasu (1986) suggests, "Although heightened arousal under conditions of cognitive organization helps to unfreeze an attitude, it does not necessarily lead to a new solution unless it is followed by cognitive learning" (p. 691). He proposes that the primary role of affective arousal in therapy is to render the client more receptive to cognitive intervention and change.

Engaging in new behaviors may also have a significant impact upon cognitive organization. The behaviors engaged in during a college experience, military training, or a love affair have been known to induce a profound change in one's assumptive world. It is this change, and not the behaviors themselves, that will stabilize and govern the individual's future behaviors. I want to stress that although the multiple systems we have been discussing are reciprocally interactive (hence the influence between any two of them is bidirectional), it is necessary to produce a cognitive-structural change in order to achieve relative *permanence* of therapeutic gain. This conceptualization allows for a plurality of techniques and models, yet it acknowledges the necessity of cognitive change to derive enduring therapeutic benefit. Raimy (1975, 1976) has documented at length that a wide range of apparently diverse therapeutic models employ different cognitive review techniques aimed at correcting clients' misconceptions. As he states, "Unfortunately for those who hope that they have found the one and only true path to success in psychological treatment, there seem to be innumerable pathways to achieving change in misconceptions and in their associated maladjusted behaviors" (Raimy, 1976, p. 212).

## INFLUENCES ON CHOOSING A THERAPEUTIC MODEL

The quest for a "one and only true path" seems never-ending. Some therapists are simply bewildered by the almost limitless array of approaches they find themselves confronted with. Corsini (1981) has listed 250, and he has probably overlooked a few.

What are the influences that lead a therapist to adopt one approach over another? Without embarking on a journey of psychodynamic speculation, I would simply like to articulate several significant variables. To begin, there is the fortuitous factor: A student may simply happen to enroll in a school that promotes one approach over all others. From that time forward it is in the student's best interest to master the proffered model. (Whether it is in the client's best interest is a separate question.) Similarly, in a field placement, the student may be assigned a supervisor who advocates a single model over all others. As the student achieves an increasing degree of competence in practicing that one model, he or she is reinforced intrinsically by a sense of accomplishment and by social reward from the school and the supervisor. Furthermore, if students are in a position to observe a significant charismatic figure practicing the approach they are being asked to learn, then they will further internalize that approach in conformity with the principles of modeling (Bandura, 1977). Sometimes the practice approach pursued by an individual may be based upon his or her personal therapy experience. Throughout the learning process, a differentiation and integration of cognitive structures occurs, which produces a personal knowledge paradigm that embraces the theoretical model being practiced.

In other instances, one may deliberately seek to master a particular model because of the intrinsic appeal it seems to hold. In such cases, the model may readily be assimilated into the individual's personal paradigm. There occurs a kind of "click," based upon an ideological fit. Alternatively, a similar clicking into place may occur when there is a fit between model and personality; the theoretical nature and practice demands of the model may be congenial to the personality strengths and limitations of the therapist. For example, a somewhat distant individual or someone who is uncomfortable with spontaneous exchanges might find it most comfortable to practice classical psychoanalysis, with its advocacy of a neutral stance on the part of the therapist, who interacts minimally with the client. (This is not to deny that the analytic endeavor calls upon the analyst to resonate empathetically and discerningly to the client's material in order to construct meaning from the experience of free association.) On the other hand, an individual with an expressive and extroverted personality may favor one of the experiential therapies: for example, the gestalt approach. Along the same lines, a "cerebrally oriented" therapist who seeks intellectual activity may lean towards the cognitive psychotherapies. This is an oversimplification, of course, for certainly psychoanalysis is also an intellectual endeavor from the analyst's perspective. Therefore, it might be more accurate to suggest that a cerebrally oriented individual with a propensity towards maintaining distance would be inclined towards practicing classical analysis, whereas one who favors collaborative interaction would lean towards a model such as Beck's cognitive therapy.

Messer (1986) has articulated a scheme that differentiates several major therapeutic approaches in terms of the vision of reality that each reflects. A therapist would be expected to embrace that model which is perceived to be most akin to his or her own version of reality: comic, romantic, ironic, or tragic. The therapist's ideology, personality, and world view may incline him or her towards one particular practice model. However, it is likely that each therapeutic approach can claim adherents who represent a variety of personality and cognitive styles.

Finally, once an individual has invested a considerable amount of time and money to master a model, he or she has an economic motive to continue practicing it and to resist investing heavily in learning new or alternative approaches. There is also a diminished status involved in becoming a student or trainee once again.

Observe that I have had nothing to say here about the needs of the client. Ultimately, those must be paramount. Here, however, I have attempted to simply describe several variables that influence what leads a therapist to adopt and continue practicing a particular therapeutic model.

## CHANGING PARADIGMS

The work of Kuhn (1972), a philosopher of science, may illuminate our understanding of how it is that we tend to cling to a single model, even when it may not prove to be adequate in all cases, and in the face of mounting evidence that alternative approaches have therapeutic merit as well. In science, the core assumptions of a paradigm are unquestioned by those scientists who embrace the paradigm. A paradigm is a conceptual–interpretive *framework*—an interlocking network of presuppositions, assumptions, attitudes, beliefs, premises, expectations, and values. It is a construal of reality that orients a person to the world and that guides him or her in the selection of problems and methodology for conducting research programs. The paradigm directs scientific inquiry within a particular field; it focuses observations and data collection upon a certain range. Questions and data outside of that range or field of inquiry are excluded. According to Kuhn, the theories of two opposing paradigms are held to be incommensurate; that is, they cannot be compared, because the concepts of one are untranslatable into the concepts of the other (Newton-Smith, 1981).

There are several strategies that serve to preserve the structure of a paradigm when it is confronted with contrary evidence. The evidence may simply be ignored, denied, or disqualified. It may be regarded as trivial and therefore not worthy of attention. It could be assimilated into the paradigm and in the process become so distorted that it no longer poses a threat. Still another response could be to change peripheral aspects of the paradigm, while leaving the core assumptions intact. However, as the paradigm proves to be less and less adaptive, and as contrary evidence that poses a threat to the core assumptions persists, a crisis is induced. As Mahoney (1980) has commented about this process, "The cogency of its theoretical foundations are then placed in doubt and the period of crisis is marked by extensive emotionality, desperate attempts to salvage the system, and sometimes a retreat to blind faith in earlier assumptions" (p. 175). Eventually, the old paradigm is abandoned and a new one is adopted. In fact, before the old one is likely to be given up, a competing paradigm must be available. When this does occur, there is receptivity to new data, and the old data are now reinterpreted from a different perspective. Prior to this, the "true believers" of paradigm *A* would only examine paradigm *B* from their own perspective, failing or refusing to understand paradigm *B* on its own terms.

There is much in the literature on psychotherapy—with its denunciations and polemical battles—that would tend to support this interpretation. The proponents of one model rarely modify its underlying theories to accommodate new perspectives or new findings that come from outside its fold; when they *do* pay attention to alternative approaches, it is usually to denounce them. Yet this scenario does not completely capture the contemporary scene. In fact, one might argue that the extent to which a group or individual is locked into and isolated within a paradigm serves as a measure of pathology. (See Mahoney, 1980, for an interesting discussion about the analogy he draws between Kuhn's remarks on scientific paradigms and the personal paradigms of clients in psychotherapy.)

Popper (1982) rejects Kuhn's thesis on the incommensurability of competing paradigms and refers to it as "The Myth of the Framework." His comments on this are worth citing:

The Myth of the Framework is, in our time, the central bulwark of irrationalism. My counter-thesis is that it simply exaggerates a difficulty into an impossibility. The difficulty of discussion between people brought up in different frameworks is to be admitted. But nothing is more fruitful than such a discussion; than the culture clash which has stimulated some of the greatest intellectual revolutions. (pp. 56–57)

Thus in science, as distinct from theology, a critical comparison of the competing theories . . . is always possible. . . . In science (and only science) can we say that we have made genuine progress: that we know more than we did before. (p. 57)

Fortunately, we are witnessing vigorous attempts to communicate in an empathic and understanding way across frameworks. Converging trends in psychotherapy have been highlighted by Goldfried (1982) and Patterson (1986). Turner (1986) has conducted a comparative assessment of practice models generated both from within and from outside of the social work profession. The result is an illumination of the interconnectedness among theoretical practice models. Norcross (1986a) tackles the growing trend towards eclectic practice by assembling many voices on the subject in one volume.

## THE NATURE OF ECLECTICISM

The eclectic movement raises the issue of the "truth" of a theory. To the extent that a person adopts a theoretical model as the embodiment of the absolute truth, to that *same* extent will he or she resist giving serious consideration to adopting an eclectic stance. From a practitioner's viewpoint, it may be more adaptive to think of theories in terms of their utility in bringing about the desired effects, rather than to consider their actual truth value. Theories are like maps. They either possess the necessary information to help you get to where you want to go, or they do not. A map may even accurately reflect what the mapmaker intended, yet not serve someone else's particular purpose well. For example, a map of a particular terrain could either include or omit buried treasure, military installations, caches of food, and roads designed for walking, horseback-riding, or driving. If you are traveling through a desert, you would surely want your map to inform you about where food and water can be found. A map that does not will be of limited value, even though what it depicts may be accurate. Similarly, if you are setting out to help someone overcome a simple phobia, you may want a map that identifies the contours of systematic desensitization (Wolpe, 1982), whereas if your goal is to assist someone who is depressed, you may find that a cognitive therapy map proves to be of optimum benefit (Beck, Rush, Shaw, & Emery, 1979). In any event, as general semanticists are fond of saying, "The map is not the territory." Stated more directly by Goldfried and Padawer (1982), "Our theoretical notions and research findings do not encompass all of clinical reality" (p. 33).

The successful outcome of a particular intervention and a given theoretical explanation for its efficacy may not necessarily be linked as cause and effect. Several alternative explanations may be equally plausible. The essential question is: Which of them is the greatest help to the therapist when he or she is designing effective future clinical interventions? A particular explanation may be useful within a certain range of operation, but any attempt to use it outside that range will come to an impasse. That is a signal that an alternative theory and intervention design are called for. At a metatheoretical level, what should perhaps be paramount is the development of our map-making skills, rather than our quest for the one true map or set of maps.

I believe that our training programs rely too heavily on indoctrinating students into practicing the methods preferred by their professors, rather than on promoting creativity and innovation. Practitioners who have been encouraged to develop in the latter mode may be less likely to feel frustration or despair when lost in the therapeutic maze; they will be more likely to respond by drawing their own therapeutic maps to find their way. I do not mean to say, however, that students' training should not be grounded in conventional wisdom and contemporary research. After mastering such fundamentals, students have the sanction to be inventive. Hariman (1986) states, "The successful practice of psychotherapy depends on the *disciplined creativeness of a fertile, trained imagination,* not on routine manipulation of strategies or psychotherapy, no matter how well tested they are" (pp. 12–13). Occasionally, we should pause to ponder the question of who gave Freud the "right" to encourage free association, Perls the right to set up the "two chair dialogue," Ellis the right to engage in disputational encounters, or Frankl the right to use paradoxical intention.

According to Norcross (1986b), anywhere from one third to one half of clinicians who are active today refer to themselves as "eclectic" and disavow exclusive allegiance to a single school of therapy. (Jayaratne, 1982, found that a plurality—47%—of eclectic social work clinicians use a psychoanalytic approach more than any other. Given the profession's traditional reliance upon that orientation, it would appear that even among eclectics there is a strong conservative tendency.)

What exactly *is* eclecticism? It means merely that the clinician does not conduct his or her practice from the limited view of a single therapeutic model. However, at this stage in the movement's development we cannot know from the label "eclectic" just what it is that the practitioner *does* do. The term "eclecticism" has had a pejorative connotation for some time, because of the general impression that its adherents practice a haphazard type of therapy, unsystematically trying first one technique and then another until, in shotgun fashion, they hit the target. Yet this represents the antithesis of a contemporary conceptualization of eclecticism. Eclectic practice models are moving in the direction of systematization, comprehensiveness, and, in most cases, integration. What is most promising about the goal of eclecticism is articulately captured by Norcross (1986a):

> Eclecticism strives to tailor the method to the patient's personality, problem, motivation, and so on in order to maximize treatment success. To the degree that therapists are able to modify and broaden their practices to fit the patient's needs and characteristics, the benefits are potentiated. This is truly the promise of eclecticism: integrated, prescriptive, psychosocial treatment based on patients' needs rather than therapists' preferences. (p. 15)

In its purest and simplest form, eclecticism means selecting *from a variety of clinical models* those techniques that seem to work best in a given situation, and applying those skills and methods to promoting the client's psychosocial welfare. Implied in this open-minded approach to clinical utility is an empirical foundation. The key question for the eclectically oriented clinician is: "What specific therapeutic intervention produces specific changes in specific patients under specific conditions?" (Strupp, 1978). The therapist in search of answers to this question must turn to the practice and research literature.

An excellent example of modern-day research with a particular therapeutic model is that which is being conducted by Beck and his colleagues (Kovacs, 1980; Kovacs, Rush, Beck, & Hollon, 1981; Rush, Beck, Kovacs, & Hollon, 1977; Wright & Beck, 1983). Beck has developed a generic model of cognitive therapy that can be applied across a wide range of psychosocial and sexual disorders. However, it has been tested (and has received substantial research validation) primarily in the treatment of depression. Beck and Emery (1985) have recently published a volume on the application of cognitive therapy to the treatment of anxiety; one can reasonably anticipate that the same careful research afforded to the treatment of depression will be extended to this field of inquiry.

It is such an approach to research that nurtures the eclectic endeavor. The more widely this type of research occurs, the greater will be the empirical resource pool which the eclectic therapist can draw upon. Of course, if a single model were to march across the research terrain, consistently demonstrating its superiority as it steps from one problem area to the next, we would then have grounds for adopting it to the exclusion of all other approaches, including eclecticism. Thus far, however, no such model has appeared. For example, even Freud, whom many might think of as a single-model loyalist, pointed out the limitations of psychoanalysis and circumscribed the population with whom it should be practiced.

## CRITERIA FOR CHOOSING MODELS AND TECHNIQUES

At this juncture, I would like to introduce some criteria that may prove useful to the eclectic therapist for evaluating any particular model or technique. We have already identified the central pragmatic question: *Does the model or technique work,* given the particular needs of the client and the context?

Despite the centrality of that criterion, there is a superordinate concern that will always take precedence: *Is it ethical?* Any approach to helping that violates fundamental ethical principles should automatically be ruled out; there must be no compromise in this area. (A presupposition here is that the therapist will have a clear set of ethical principles guiding his or her practice and will have a capacity for high-level moral reasoning to resolve complex dilemmas when they arise.)

There are several additional points to consider. *Does the method work quickly*—or at least more quickly than other available models, all other things being equal? I have never understood the complacency of those whose practice in a given case will admittedly often take many years, sometimes even 10 or more. Such therapists sometimes not only do not seem to have the impetus to discover briefer methods, but they also are often cynically critical of those who do. They label as "superficial" those therapists who utilize methods that have been pruned of excess theoretical baggage. Yet these same critics seem unconcerned with examining the therapeutic efficacy of the briefer methods; they assume that, because those methods are not based upon the critics' own belief system, a priori they cannot work. As for theory, the presupposition seems to be that the more complex it is, the better it must be. However, this is neither self-evident nor empirically substantiated.

Still another question is whether the assumed efficacy of the model is due to features that it has in common with all other approaches or to specific features that clearly distinguish it from alternative schools. This issue is of considerable importance and will be returned to shortly.

Another consideration is a fiscal one, which is related to the time span required to implement the method. *How does the method compare in cost-efficiency with other methods?* Therapists are often uncomfortable with— and sometimes even disdainful of—monetary considerations. This is a limitation that should be overcome as part of the therapist's personal and professional development. Taking the cost-effectiveness of a method into account amounts to fiscal responsibility.

*Do the results of the method under examination generalize beyond the clinical office and spread through other areas of the client's life?* If they do not, the method may only be of limited value. A therapeutic procedure that takes longer to implement but has a greater potential for generalization may be preferable to one that produces swifter results but does not generalize. Hence, the selection process sometimes requires a balancing of one advantage over another.

Related to generalization is the issue of maintenance. *Is the model or method one that leads to the sustainment of gains beyond the termination of treatment?* This is a question that can be answered only by follow-up contacts. In some instances, clients have been known to make their greatest progress in the months immediately subsequent to treatment. It is as if, during the course of therapy, seeds were planted that only later began to sprout.

A major consideration in choosing a paradigm for clinical practice has to do with testing of the model: *How well does it hold up under investigation?* If there is to be a science of psychotherapy and particularly of eclectic psychotherapy, then the theories and techniques involved must be testable. They must be potentially falsifiable; if a proposition is not falsifiable, it cannot enter the domain of science and is not distinguishable from religious propositions. For example, if a religious person prays and the prayer is answered, he or she may say that God has heard the prayer and has responded. If the outcome of the prayer is not as wished for, the person may say that God has heard the prayer and answered with a greater wisdom than he or she, being only human, possesses. Hence, the proposition that God answers all prayers is not falsifiable. It is not necessarily incorrect, but we will never know for certain; whether or not the proposition is accepted depends on faith. However, faith is within the realm of religion, whereas demonstration is within the realm of science. The question of whether the same experimental paradigm used in the natural sciences is appropriate for all research in psychotherapy is a separate issue that deserves extensive consideration in its own right.

Finally, *can people be trained to practice the method or model?* If not, then its value is severely curtailed. If a method *can* be taught, but has a training process as lengthy and restricted as that of orthodox psychoanalysis, for example, then its social utility is limited, regardless of any inherent value it may possess.


## THREE ECLECTIC MODELS

At present, eclectic psychotherapy is not represented by a single unified and comprehensive paradigm that would serve as an adequate guide to all practitioners and researchers. What eclectics have in common is simply their disavowal of allegiance to only one approach and their advocacy of an empirical orientation to practice. Major position statements can be found in the work of Fischer (1978), Garfield (1980), Lazarus (1981), Beutler (1983), Hart (1983), and Prochaska and DiClemente (1984). The

*Handbook of Eclectic Psychotherapy*, edited by Norcross (1986a), is an excellent compendium on the subject.

For our purposes, I would like to introduce three leading models of eclecticism. The first is embodied in the work of Lazarus (1981), who has advanced the practice of *technical eclecticism*. Lazarus has abandoned the idea of attempting to organize a theoretical integration across schools, because of what he sees as the logical incompatibility between systems. Observe his comments on the subject:

> If we look closely at the theories, metatheories, and assumptions that underlie the different psychotherapeutic systems, contradictory notions and divergent points of reference are readily discerned. These differences are not merely terminological or semantic—they often go to the core of fundamental differences in ideology and rest on entirely different epistemological foundations. (Lazarus, 1986, p. 67)

Without necessarily embracing any of the underlying theories, Lazarus freely borrows techniques from the various approaches, seeks empirical validation for his choices, and is willing to exercise some flexibility in trying out techniques on an exploratory basis. While it eschews theoretical integration across schools, Lazarus's approach is systematic in offering a conceptual framework for the assessment and tracking of the multimodal variables that he has distinctly organized (i.e., behavior, affect, sensation, imagery, cognition, interpersonal, and biology). Furthermore, his orientation is not atheoretical, for he professes that it is founded upon Bandura's social learning theory. Lazarus also draws upon general system theory, and on group and communication theory as well. In his writings, however, Lazarus gives less attention to his use of these theories than he does to his multimodal framework.

Prochaska and DiClemente (1986) represent a second type of eclecticism. They have developed a complexly integrated system of psychotherapy in which they emphasize a spirit of *collaboration and rapprochement* among the many diverse schools. Their model has three major dimensions: change processes, levels of change, and stages of change. These three dimensions are based upon a comparative analysis of 24 major systems of psychotherapy (Prochaska, 1984) and are receiving increasing research attention. This orientation is especially useful in helping to identify what types of interventions might be useful at particular stages. For example, there are four basic stages: precontemplation, contemplation, action, and maintenance. Ten change processes are drawn eclectically from the various schools, encompassing such variables as insight, catharsis, and reinforcement. Not all change processes are equally appropriate for each stage, as Prochaska and DiClemente point out:

Once it is clear what stage of change a client is in, the therapist would know what processes to apply in order to help the client progress to the next stage of change. Rather than apply change processes in a haphazard or trial-and-error approach, eclectic therapists can begin to use change processes in a much more systematic style. (1986, p. 166)

Each of five levels of change is arranged hierarchically in order of severity, ranging from "symptom/situational" (least severe) to "intrapersonal conflicts" (most severe). Theoretically, the client who is being treated for any one of these levels of disorder will traverse the stages of precontemplation, contemplation, action, and maintenance.

The third type of eclecticism I want to discuss is one proposed by Beutler (1986). A pivotal point in his *systematic* eclectic model is the adaptation of techniques and methods to clients' characteristics. Beutler proposes that researchers look at such questions as the optimum match between therapist and clients on various dimensions, the most appropriate procedure for a particular client, and considerations that should come into play with respect to altering methods as time progresses during a course of therapy. While he advocates the appropriate selection of a wide range of techniques drawn from the many available therapeutic models, Beutler has adopted "interpersonal influence models of social persuasion" as a superordinate conceptual framework for systematically understanding and organizing the therapeutic enterprise. He believes that this framework offers many advantages, not the least of which is the provision of a common language and viewpoint that transcend all schools and has the potential to unify therapists from diverse orientations. He further emphasizes the centrality in all psychotherapies of the clinician's role as a persuasive agent who must convince the client that the therapist is "credible, trustworthy, supportive, and knowledgeable" (Beutler, 1986, p. 99). This succinct formulation offers only a glimpse into the incisive and synthesizing effort reflected in Beutler's work; I hope that he will continue building upon it.

## THE COMMONALITIES VERSUS SPECIFIC TECHNIQUES CONTROVERSY

It would seem that the general question of whether psychotherapy works has been answered—and the answer is affirmative (Luborsky, Singer, & Luborsky, 1975; Meltzoff & Kornreich, 1970; Smith & Glass, 1977). What has not been established is the clear and consistent superiority of any one therapeutic model over another (Lambert, 1986; Luborsky et al., 1975; Strupp, 1978). In a careful examination of the evidence, Stiles, Shapiro, and Elliot (1986) state, "A substantial body of evidence and

opinion points to the conclusion that the outcomes of different psychotherapies with clinical populations are equivalent" (p. 166). They
stress that this conclusion about similar outcomes is in sharp contrast to
the apparent differences among the techniques of various schools; these
techniques flow from a school's underlying theories, which often contradict theories from competing schools.

Some writers, on the other hand, are opposed to the theory of equivalence of all psychotherapies. Kazdin and Wilson (1978) and Frances,
Sweeney, and Clarkin (1985) have argued persuasively that *specific* techniques, when properly matched to client and problem, *do* prove highly
effective. These findings seem to be moving us in two opposing directions,
each of which has the potential for enriching our understanding of both
the therapeutic process and its change mechanisms. One direction is
towards an increasingly more fine-grained research analysis of specific
techniques that interact with a diversity of client characteristics and
problem areas. The emphasis here is upon *micro* analysis in process and
outcome research, rather than the more global and undifferentiated type
of analysis. The other direction is towards a keener appreciation of the
therapeutically efficacious common elements that are present in the
conduct of therapy, regardless of one's orientation. Anyone struggling
to develop a personal philosophy of practice would want to be aware
of the ramifications of both of these directions.

Frank (1974, 1976) has been in the forefront of those who subscribe
to the premise that it is the common elements present in all schools of
psychotherapy that account for the benefit derived by the client. His
thesis is that the essential ingredient in psychotherapy is the restoration
of the client's morale, and that this component of the therapeutic process
is shared with religious healers in cultures throughout the world. His
position is succinctly formulated in this passage:

> Features common to all types of psychotherapy combat a major
> source of distress and disability of persons who seek psychothera-
> peutic help. The source of this distress may be termed demorali-
> zation—a sense of failure or of powerlessness to affect oneself and
> one's environment. Psychotherapies may combat the patient's de-
> moralization not only by alleviating his specific symptoms of sub-
> jective distress and disordered behavior but also . . . by employing
> measures to restore his self-confidence and to help him find more
> effective ways of mastering his problems. (Frank, 1974, p. xvi)

The spectrum of technical diversity across schools is thus seen to be
united by the common achievement of restoring the client's morale,
instilling self-confidence, and promoting coping skills. A related unifying
concept that may well be the result of all psychotherapeutic efforts is a
sense of *self-efficacy*. Bandura (1984) defines self-efficacy as a person's

subjective judgment that he or she possesses, and can successfully implement, the behavioral skills necessary to attain a desired objective. If the wide variety of techniques throughout the therapies all succeed, at a higher level of abstraction, in restoring morale and promoting self-efficacy, then one can readily understand how at least *macro* level research finds an equivalence of outcomes.

Change in therapy requires a modification of the client's assumptive world. No matter how diverse their techniques may be, all orientations work towards this end (Frank, 1974). The assumptive world comprises a network of attitudes, beliefs, and expectations. This is a position clearly congenial to that of Raimy (1975), who maintains that all therapies correct misconceptions of the client's self through techniques that amount to a cognitive review (see also Beck, 1976).

The strongest argument in the commonality camp has been made by Patterson (1985), who has cogently marshaled evidence for his position that the most important conditions for therapeutic change inhere in the therapeutic relationship itself. Patterson is openly anti-technique. He feels that the *necessary* and *sufficient* ingredients for the achievement of maximum therapeutic benefits are empathic understanding, genuineness or congruence, and respect or unconditional positive regard—of which nonpossessive warmth is considered an aspect (see also Rogers, 1957). There are no substitutes, and if these ingredients are present in the therapist, then no special techniques are necessary. Whenever a course of psychotherapy has been successful, we can reasonably infer that empathy, genuineness, and respect were operative regardless of which therapeutic orientation and techniques were adhered to. Of course, for these therapist attributes to be effective, it is essential that the client perceive or experience them on some level. Patterson urges a strongly philosophical orientation that views all people as inherently good. The *goal* of psychotherapy is to facilitate the process that leads to the client's self-actualization. It is the *function* of psychotherapy to deal with the client's emotional and social deprivation, which are the impediments to self-actualization.

There are still more common elements that range across the therapies (Frank, 1974; Garfield, 1980). In all therapy cases, disturbed individuals are seeking help from socially sanctioned healers who have a belief in the efficacy of the actions that both they and the clients will carry out during the course of treatment. Clients generally have an expectancy for improvement, are engaged in self-observation, and are provided with coherent rationales for understanding themselves and their problems. They find themselves in the presence of someone who listens sympathetically and respectfully as they share their feelings, thoughts, and secrets. They gain insight and emotional release through participation in a set of healing rituals that are initiated by the therapist and which are based upon the rationale of the model being practiced.

Thus far we have been examining the viewpoints of therapists. What do clients have to say for themselves about their experience in therapy? When *clients* reveal their *own* perceptions about what it has been like for them to be in psychotherapy, they emphasize the relationship and the therapist's personality, rather than the techniques or differentiating characteristics of the model practiced by the therapist. Strupp, Fox, and Lessler (1969) conducted an extensive study with outpatients (many of whom had been previously hospitalized) who were receiving private treatment from psychoanalytically oriented psychiatrists. The researchers found that a positive attitude towards the therapist was significantly related to a successful therapy outcome. Whether in brief-oriented or long-term intensive therapy, those patients who judged their therapy to be successful found their therapists to be "warm, attentive, interested, understanding, and respectful" (Strupp, Fox, & Lessler, 1969, p. 116). In addition, Strupp (1976) believes that the therapist's leverage for helping the patient to learn and the patient's receptivity to change are greatest when their interpersonal relationship *re-creates* a parent–child connection between them. In this relationship, the therapist's attitudes are those of "respect, interest, understanding, tact, maturity, and a firm belief in his or her ability to help" (p. 97). For Strupp, the establishment of such a relationship provides a power base for the therapist to operate from; hence, its importance should not be minimized.

A study by Sloane, Staples, Cristol, Yorkston, and Whipple (1975) has considerable relevance to our interest in clients' views of what is meaningful to them in psychotherapy. Three prominent behavior therapists and a comparable group of psychoanalytically oriented therapists each provided individual treatment to 10 different patients over a four-month period. Treatment was conducted in accordance with each therapist's orientation. This study was well designed and is often cited as an exemplar of psychotherapy research. Its results proved surprising, even unsettling, to many. Both therapy groups made gains significantly greater than those of a control group that received no treatment. However, there were no significant differences in outcome between the two therapy groups, even though the clinicians were clearly employing techniques and procedures that were specific to their respective orientations.

An analysis of one of the sessions revealed that there were no differences between the two sets of therapists on variables of interpersonal exploration and unconditional positive regard. However, the researchers rated the behavior therapists as significantly higher on such variables as accurate empathy, interpersonal contact, and genuineness. This finding should go a long way towards destroying the myth that behavior therapy is necessarily impersonal and mechanical. It also raises some questions about the roles of empathy and genuineness. Since the behavior therapists scored significantly higher with respect to these dimensions, why didn't their patients rate significantly higher in outcome? Possibly there is a ceiling on the gain that can be attributed to these factors; the amount necessary to reach that ceiling may have been reached by the psychoanalytically oriented therapists as well.

This study highlights another vital issue: How much of the gains reported in the behavior therapy literature can be credited to such therapist attributes, rather than to individual technologies? This is especially relevant because behavior therapists seem to have as many of these attributes as the psychodynamically oriented clinicians do. (In fact, behavior therapists sometimes have them in greater abundance.)

How did the patients in the study by Sloane and his colleagues perceive their therapy? The majority of patients from both groups who were rated with a successful outcome emphasized the importance of dimensions that were present in common between the two orientations. None of the patients emphasized technical aspects that would have differentiated one therapy from the other. What they found *most* helpful were the therapist's personality and the fact that he helped them to understand themselves and their problems, as well as the encouragement he gave them to face and participate in activities that they had had difficulties with. In general, they cited the meaningfulness of having an understanding person to talk over their problems with. Other important factors were the therapists' perceived capabilities and the confidence they demonstrated in the patients' potential for change. From this description, it would be impossible to infer the orientation of the therapists. Yet from the perspective of the observers, the therapists were clearly conducting traditional psychoanalytically oriented therapy or behavioral therapy.*

What is one to make of this dichotomy between the common ingredients of a good relationship and the specific techniques that differentiate each school of therapy? No doubt the dispute will go on for some time to come. I, for one, see no reason to choose between the two. Commonalities most assuredly *do* exist—and cannot be dismissed cavalierly. Smith, Glass, and Miller (1980) go so far as to state, "The weight of the evidence that now rests in the balance so greatly favors the general factors interpretation of therapeutic efficacy that it can no longer be ignored by researchers and theoreticians" (p. 186). Yet there is something distinctly counterintuitive about accepting the conclusion that no technical intervention whatever can have any precise effect. Moreover, there is a plethora of behavior therapy research that strongly argues the case for differential effects of specific techniques (Kazdin & Wilson, 1978; Rachman & Wilson, 1980).

---

* For more information on this topic, see also Cooley and Lajoy, 1980; Lazarus, 1971; and Lorr, 1965.

It is important to keep in mind that even though a given ingredient of the therapeutic process may cut across all models, it may still constitute a technical intervention. I would not characterize warmth, empathy, and genuineness as technical interventions. They are attributes of the therapist that produce conditions for client growth. However, recall Raimy's thesis that all major models of psychotherapy engage clients in a cognitive review that produces a correction in misconceptions of self. The form that the review takes may vary greatly among the diverse models, but the effect of certain procedures operationalized by each model is the same. Hence, what appears to be superficially diverse at a perceptual and behavioral level is actually identical at a higher order conceptual level. This interpretation is consistent with a structuralist position, since it emphasizes both surface and deep structures (Gardner, 1972).

We can shine some light on the controversy of commonalities versus specific techniques by comparing it to a father's playing a constructive parental role as he teaches his son various skills over the years. Let us say that the boy has learned from the father how to swim, drive, and hunt. The father relates to the child in a warm and empathic manner, confident that the child will grow and acquire the necessary skills in the process. The father's attitude and mode of relating create a climate for receptive learning in the child. Much more than that, they lead to construction of a self that is confident in its ability to perform and to be loved. This is an abstract achievement that generalizes across situations and is maintained through time. However, it does not in itself generate new skills. In order to teach the child how to swim, hunt, and drive, the father had to employ specific techniques beyond merely exhibiting warmth and empathy. In fact, differential techniques were necessary in going from one activity to another.

Let us carry this analogy over into the therapeutic context. It may be very beneficial for clients to experience the therapist's warmth, empathy, and genuineness. However, this will not necessarily lead to their becoming appropriately assertive with exploitive employers or to their crossing over a bridge about which they have a phobia. A subjective sense of self-worth and an objective attainment of competence go hand in hand along the therapeutic journey. Experiencing the therapist as a genuine, warm, open, and caring human being may very possibly be a new experience for the clients, one that will make them more willing to risk being assertive or more willing to cross the bridge. However, there are specific procedures and tactics that have been differentially designed to promote such behaviors. One does not learn to drive a car by mastering the breast stroke or, for that matter, by merely being praised.

I have had the good fortune to observe Erving and Miriam Polster conduct several demonstrations at a gestalt therapy workshop. These two masterly practitioners have co-authored the premiere gestalt therapy text

(Polster & Polster, 1974). Gestalt therapy is a highly experiential form of therapy with an existential orientation and is generally associated with affectively based techniques. I was quite pleasantly surprised to witness the wide-ranging skill and versatility of both therapists. I could clearly identify their skillful deployment of assertiveness training, modified systematic desensitization, cognitive restructuring, behavioral rehearsal, coaching, and the identification and challenging of underlying assumptions. Presumably the Polsters generated and processed all these from the perspective of the gestalt therapy model. A remark that Erving Polster made towards the end of the workshop was particularly interesting to me. He commented, "In doing gestalt therapy, there may be only one moment identifiable as gestalt therapy, but that moment may be crucial." It seems to me that in practice the Polsters are unquestionably eclectic, despite the fact that they are so inextricably linked to the gestalt model. Virtuosos at drawing upon a variety of techniques from multiple sources, they are anchored in a unified theory and philosophy (in their case, that of gestalt therapy). And *that* makes a critical difference.

In connection with some of the above observations, it is worthwhile to inquire into the recommendations arrived at by Smith et al. (1980) upon the completion of their extensive meta-analytic study on the benefits of psychotherapy. They suggest:

> Our findings warn against an eclecticism in practice that fails to differentiate into one type or the other of psychotherapy. One of the paradoxes of psychotherapy . . . may be that although all therapies are equally effective, one must choose only one to learn and practice. (p. 185)

Ultimately, however, Smith and his colleagues make a plea for pluralism. They advocate a therapeutic world in which each therapist learns and practices one model well, while at the same time recognizing that that model does not represent exclusive, absolute truth. Further, pluralism entails a respect for other models and the fostering of a climate in which they will flourish alongside of one's own. In the absence of evidence testifying to the clear superiority of one clinical practice model over another, this would seem to be a reasonable position to adopt (Prochaska, 1984). It brings to mind a metaphor used by Miriam Polster at the previously mentioned workshop. She suggested that we imagine a room containing several original paintings by great artists such as Rembrandt, Picasso, and Renoir. "Which one has the truth?" she asked. "Well," she added, "the same may be said for theories and models of therapy. Each has grasped and contains elements of the truth." Of course, one could use that perspective to justify adopting an eclectic orientation.

## A GENERIC CORE STRATEGY FOR ECLECTIC PRACTICE

I recommend that someone who is considering taking the eclectic approach go about it in one of two ways: either by first mastering a single model from which he or she can then venture into other, less-known areas, or by developing a coherent and generic core out of which he or she can radiate towards different techniques and models. A generic core would not be embedded in any one approach; it would comprise a general set of conditions, skills, and values that would serve as an orienting framework out of which the practitioner would operate regardless of how wide-ranging the selection and use of specific techniques would be.

I would like to propose a model for this approach, but I should caution the reader that there are alternative configurations that he or she may put together out of his or her own judgment and experience. At the heart of this conceptualization is the "I-Thou" relationship that was described by Buber (1958). In such a relationship there is an emphasis upon what takes place *between* two people. Each relates to the other in a way that acknowledges the other person's internal life; there is no possibility of one's being exploited by the other. Interaction between the two people creates a "dialogical" (rather than a purely psychological) experience. The focus or emphasis is upon the interchange between the two and the experience of mutual confirmation that can occur (Friedman, 1985).

The germ of Buber's philosophy is contained in a story he tells about himself at a time in his life when he was preoccupied with religious mysticism (Buber, 1947). One afternoon, following a morning of absorption in "religious enthusiasm," Buber received a visit from a young man. Although his spirit was not in the meeting, Buber nevertheless was friendly and polite. He failed, however, to discern the true purpose of his guest's visit. Later he discovered that the young man was "no longer alive" and that he had come to Buber for help in making an important decision. Buber writes poignantly:

> He had come to me, he had come in this hour. What do we expect when we are in despair and yet go to a man? Surely a presence by means of which we are told that nevertheless there is a meaning. (1947, p. 14)

Building upon Buber's philosophy and widening the context to include the therapeutic situation, I advocate that therapists adopt an existential *attitude*, a stance that involves no particular technique and that can be inclusive of many approaches (Bergantino, 1981; Bugental, 1981; Krill, 1986). Important concepts that need to be considered in developing this existential attitude are authenticity, commitment, encounter, immediacy, responsibility, dialogue, and choice. These concepts involve deeply felt values and beliefs that one must authentically choose to commit oneself to, for without commitment, one is merely espousing these in bad faith.

The therapeutic model developed by Carl Rogers is an example of an existentially oriented approach. The conditions for growth that Rogers has singled out as being sufficient and necessary serve as excellent factors to integrate into the committed eclectic's operational core. Empathic understanding, nonpossessive warmth, and genuineness may seem like elusive abstractions. However, there *are* training methods that have successfully helped students and practitioners develop in these and related areas (Carkhuff, 1969a, 1969b; Fischer, 1978; Ivey, 1980, 1983; Ivey & Authier, 1978). Such training increases therapists' communication skills, which contribute towards making them more effective helpers. Because the skills involved are central to optimizing effective communication and interpersonal functioning, it follows that clients' psychosocial functioning will also be greatly improved with their increasing acquisition of them.

A developmental framework is important to a core configuration, in order to view the client within a longitudinal framework covering past, present, and potential future. In my own work, I have adopted the constructivist paradigm (presented in Chapter 14 of this book), which offers a dialectical progression of subject-object relations through various stages of development, as well as an explanatory concept to account for transformational changes.

A person who is forging a core configuration should always have some ultimate goal in mind. My choice for a transcendent goal is borrowed from Ivey (1980), who recommends "intentionality." He puts it this way:

> The person who acts with intentionality has a sense of capability. He or she can generate alternative behaviors in a given situation and "approach" a problem from different vantage points. The intentional, fully functioning individual is not bound to one course of action but can respond in the moment to changing life situations and look forward to longer term goals. (p. 8)

One can readily appreciate that this is an appropriate goal for any creative therapist to adopt, whether he or she chooses to practice clinically from a single model of therapy or from an eclectic framework. In fact, intentionality is a desirable superordinate goal for both therapist *and* client.

Another building block in the construction of the core is a conceptual system for conducting case assessments. At the *macro* level, one may usefully adopt the eco-systems approach because of its comprehensiveness (Meyer, 1983; see also Chapter 12 in this book). The eco-systems model encompasses the multivariable matrix of any case unit; hence, its careful application will assure that the appropriate subsystems that are in need of intervention will be identified. At the *micro* level, Lazarus' multimodal assessment framework will serve to clarify those aspects of the total person that the therapist should be designing and selecting interventions for (Lazarus, 1981). It will also illuminate the sequential order in which these aspects (such as affect, cognition, behavior, and sensation) are interacting with one another. Recognition of this tracking sequence will serve as a further guide to well-targeted interventions. Although it is rather comprehensive, the multimodal approach *does* leave out the client's spirituality, which the therapist will not want to overlook.

Almost all of the pieces of the core configuration are now in place: the I-Thou relationship, an existential stance, conditions of growth, communication skills, a developmental paradigm, a superordinate goal, and assessment tools. These afford the therapist a philosophical and skill-based grounding from which to responsibly practice eclectic psychotherapy.

There is one final and essential requirement, however, and that is the criterion for selecting specific strategies and techniques of clinical intervention. Empirical validation is the standard that one will want to embrace. Assuming that it is ethical, a method that is reported in the literature as one that has produced the most effective results when applied to the treatment of particular problems with specified populations under certain circumstances, and that has been adequately replicated, is one that can be responsibly practiced. Emotional allegiance to the theoretical source of the method, or to its charismatic founder, should not enter into the decision-making process. The extent to which we may responsibly deviate from this empirical criterion for the selection of explicit methods is a matter of personal judgment (each of us must decide for himself or herself in the existential moment with the client), but depart from it we must, if we wish to be creative, intentional clinicians.

I am reminded of something that Carl Rogers said at the 1985 conference on the evolution of psychotherapy. He said that he regards himself as both a scientist and an artist, but that it is not the scientist who enters the clinical office. We must all decide for ourselves who it is that enters that office. Perhaps our quest for a personal philosophy of practice will move towards an integration of these two polarities, so that they may engage in a mutually enhancing dialogue that can only benefit our clients.

## REFERENCES

Bandura, A. (1977). *Social learning theory.* Englewood Cliffs, NJ: Prentice-Hall.
Bandura, A. (1984). Recycling misconceptions of perceived self-efficacy. *Cognitive Therapy and Research, 8,* 231–255.

Beck, A. T. (1976). *Cognitive therapy and the emotional disorders.* New York: International Universities Press.

Beck, A. T., & Emery, G. (1985). *Anxiety disorders and phobias: A cognitive perspective.* New York: Basic Books.

Beck, A. T., Rush, A. J., Shaw, B. F., & Emery, G. (1979). *Cognitive therapy of depression.* New York: Guilford.

Bergantino, L. (1981). *Psychotherapy: Insight and style.* Boston: Allyn & Bacon.

Beutler, L. E. (1983). *Eclectic psychotherapy: A systematic approach.* New York: Pergamon.

Beutler, L. E. (1986). Systematic eclectic psychotherapy. In J. C. Norcross (Ed.), *Handbook of eclectic psychotherapy* (pp. 94–131). New York: Brunner/Mazel.

Buber, M. (1947). *Between man and man* (G. R. Smith, Trans.). London: Kegan, Paul, Trench, Trubner & Co.

Buber, M. (1958). *I and thou* (2nd rev. ed.). New York: Charles Scribner's Sons.

Bugental, J. F. T. (1981). *The search for authenticity: An existential-analytic approach to psychotherapy.* New York: Irvington Publishers.

Carkhuff, R. R. (1969a). *Helping and human relationships: Vol. I. Selection and training.* New York: Holt, Rinehart & Winston.

Carkhuff, R. R. (1969b). *Helping and human relationships: Vol. II. Practice and research.* New York: Holt, Rinehart & Winston.

Cooley, E. J., & Lajoy, R. (1980). Therapeutic relationship and improvement as perceived by clients and therapists. *Journal of Clinical Psychology, 36,* 562–570.

Corsini, R. J. (1981). *Handbook of innovative therapies.* New York: Wiley.

Corsini, R. J. (1984). *Current psychotherapies* (3rd ed.). Itasca, IL: F. E. Peacock.

Fischer, J. (1978). *Effective caseworker practice: An eclectic approach.* New York: McGraw-Hill.

Fischer, J., & Gochros, H. L. (1975). *Planned behavior change: Behavior modification in social work.* New York: Free Press.

Frances, A., Sweeney, J., & Clarkin, J. (1985). Do psychotherapies have specific effects? *American Journal of Psychotherapy, 39,* 159–174.

Frank, J. D. (1974). *Persuasion and healing* (rev. ed.). Baltimore: Johns Hopkins University Press.

Frank, J. D. (1976). Restoration of morale and behavior change. In A. Burton (Ed.), *What makes behavior change possible?* (pp. 73–95). New York: Brunner/Mazel.

Friedman, M. (1985). *The healing dialogue in psychotherapy.* New York: Jason Aronson.

Gardner, H. (1972). *The quest for mind.* New York: Knopf.

Garfield, S. L. (1980). *Psychotherapy: An eclectic approach.* New York: Wiley.

Germain, C. B., & Gitterman, A. (1980). *The life model of social work practice.* New York: Columbia University Press.

Goldfried, M. R. (Ed.). (1982). *Converging themes in psychotherapy.* New York: Springer.

Goldfried, M. R., & Padawer, W. (1982). Current status and future directions in psychotherapy. In M. R. Goldfried (Ed.), *Converging themes in psychotherapy* (pp. 3–49). New York: Springer.

Goldstein, H. (1973). *Social work practice.* Columbia: University of South Carolina Press.

Hariman, J. (1986). Coupures epistemologiques. *International Journal of Eclectic Psychotherapy, 5,* 5–15.

Hart, J. (1983). *Modern eclectic therapy: A functional orientation to counseling and psychotherapy.* New York: Plenum.

Hollis, F. (1972). *Casework: A psychosocial therapy* (2nd ed.). New York: Random House.

Ivey, A. E. (1980). *Counseling and psychotherapy: Skills, theories, and practice.* Englewood Cliffs, NJ: Prentice-Hall.

Ivey, A. E. (1983). *Intentional interviewing and counseling.* Monterey, CA: Brooks/Cole.

Ivey, A. E., & Authier, J. (1978). *Microcounseling* (2nd ed.). Springfield, IL: Charles C Thomas.

Jayaratne, S. (1982). Characteristics and theoretical orientations of clinical social workers: A national survey. *Journal of Social Service Research, 4,* 17–30.

Karasu, T. B. (1986). The specificity versus nonspecificity dilemma: Toward identifying therapeutic change agents. *American Journal of Psychiatry, 143,* 687–695.

Kazdin, A. E., & Wilson, G. T. (1978). *Evaluation of behavior therapy: Issues, evidence, and research strategies.* Lincoln, NE: University of Nebraska Press.

Kovacs, M. (1980). The efficacy of cognitive and behavior therapies for depression. *American Journal of Psychiatry, 137,* 1495–1501.

Kovacs, M., Rush, J., Beck, A. T., & Hollon, S. D. (1981). Depressed outpatients treated with cognitive therapy or pharmacotherapy. *Archives of General Psychiatry, 38,* 33–39.

Krill, D. F. (1986). Existential social work. In F. J. Turner (Ed.), *Social work treatment* (3rd ed., pp. 181–217). New York: The Free Press.

Kuhn, T. S. (1972). *The structure of scientific revolutions* (2nd ed.). Chicago: University of Chicago Press.

Lambert, M. J. (1986). Implications of psychotherapy outcome for eclectic psychotherapy. In J. C. Norcross (Ed.), *Handbook of eclectic psychotherapy* (pp. 436–462). New York: Brunner/Mazel.

Lazarus, A. A. (1971). *Behavior therapy and beyond.* New York: McGraw-Hill.

Lazarus, A. A. (1981). *The practice of multimodal therapy.* New York: McGraw-Hill.

Lazarus, A. A. (1986). Multimodal therapy. In J. C. Norcross (Ed.), *Handbook of eclectic psychotherapy* (pp. 65–93). New York: Brunner/Mazel.

Lorr, M. (1965). Client perception of therapists. *Journal of Consulting Psychology, 29,* 146–149.

Lowenberg, F. (1977). *Fundamentals of social intervention.* New York: Columbia University Press.

Luborsky, L., Singer, B., & Luborsky, L. (1975). Comparative studies of psychotherapies: Is it true that "Everybody has won and all must have prizes"? *Archives of General Psychiatry, 32,* 995–1008.

Mahoney, M. J. (1980). Psychotherapy and the structure of personal revolutions. In M. J. Mahoney (Ed.), *Psychotherapy process* (pp. 157–179). New York: Plenum.

Maslow, A. H. (1966). *The psychology of science: A reconnaissance* (pp. 15–16). New York: Harper & Row.

Meltzoff, J., & Kornreich, M. (1970). *Research in psychotherapy.* New York: Atherton.

Messer, S. B. (1986). Eclecticism in psychotherapy: Underlying assumptions, problems, and trade-offs. In J. C. Norcross (Ed.), *Handbook of eclectic psychotherapy* (pp. 379–397). New York: Brunner/Mazel.

Meyer, C. H. (Ed.). (1983). *Clinical social work in the eco-systems perspective.* New York: Columbia University Press.

Newton-Smith, W. H. (1981). *The rationality of science.* Boston: Routledge & Kegan Paul.

Norcross, J. C. (Ed.). (1986a). *Handbook of eclectic psychotherapy.* New York: Brunner/Mazel.

Norcross, J. C. (1986b). Eclectic psychotherapy: An introduction and overview. In J. C. Norcross (Ed.), *Handbook of eclectic psychotherapy* (pp. 3–24). New York: Brunner/Mazel.

Patterson, C. H. (1985). *The therapeutic relationship: Foundations for an eclectic psychotherapy.* Monterey, CA: Brooks/Cole.

Patterson, C. H. (1986). *Theories of counseling and psychotherapy.* New York: Harper & Row.

Pincus, A., & Minahan, A. (1973). *Social work practice.* Itasca, IL: F. E. Peacock.

Polster, I., & Polster, M. (1974). *Gestalt therapy integrated.* New York: Vintage.

Popper, K. (1982). Normal science and its dangers. In I. Lakatos & A. Musgrave (Eds.), *Criticism and the growth of knowledge* (pp. 51–58). Cambridge, England: Cambridge University Press.

Prochaska, J. O. (1984). *Systems of psychotherapy: A transtheoretical analysis* (2nd ed.). Homewood, IL: Dorsey Press.

Prochaska, J. O., & DiClemente, C. C. (1984). *The transtheoretical approach: Crossing traditional boundaries of therapy.* Homewood, IL: Dow Jones-Irwin.

Prochaska, J. O., & DiClemente, C. C. (1986). The transtheoretical approach. In J. C. Norcross (Ed.), *Handbook of eclectic psychotherapy* (pp. 163–200). New York: Brunner/Mazel.

Rachman, S., & Wilson, G. T. (1980). *The effects of psychological therapy.* Oxford: Pergamon.

Raimy, V. (1975). *Misunderstandings of the self.* San Francisco: Jossey-Bass.

Raimy, V. (1976). Changing misconceptions as the therapeutic task. In A. Burton (Ed.), *What makes behavior change possible?* (pp. 197–226). New York: Brunner/Mazel.

Reid, W. J. (1978). *The task-centered system.* New York: Columbia University Press.

Reid, W. J., & Epstein, L. (Eds.). (1977). *Task-centered practice.* New York: Columbia University Press.

Rogers, C. R. (1957). The necessary and sufficient conditions for therapeutic personality change. *Journal of Consulting Psychology, 21,* 95–103.

Rosenblatt, A., & Waldfogel, D. (Eds.). (1983). *The handbook of clinical social work.* San Francisco: Jossey-Bass.

Rush, A. J., Beck, A. T., Kovacs, M., & Hollon, S. (1977). Comparative efficacy of cognitive therapy and pharmacotherapy in the treatment of depressed outpatients. *Cognitive Therapy and Research, 1,* 17–37.

Saari, C. (1986). *Clinical social work treatment: How does it work?* New York: Gardner Press.

Siporin, M. (1975). *Introduction to social work practice.* New York: Macmillan.

Siporin, M. (1979). Practice theory for clinical social work. *Clinical Social Work Journal, 7,* 75–89.

Sloane, R. B., Staples, F. R., Cristol, A. H., Yorkston, N. J., & Whipple, K. (1975). *Psychotherapy versus behavior therapy.* Cambridge, MA: Harvard University Press.

Smith, M. L., & Glass, G. V. (1977). Meta-analysis of psychotherapy outcome studies. *American Psychologist, 132,* 752–760.

Smith, M. L., Glass, G. V., & Miller, T. I. (1980). *The benefits of psychotherapy.* Baltimore: The Johns Hopkins University Press.

Stiles, W. B., Shapiro, D. A., & Elliot, R. (1986). Are all psychotherapies equivalent? *American Psychologist, 41,* 165–180.

Strean, H. S. (1978). *Clinical social work: Theory and practice.* New York: The Free Press.

Strupp, H. H. (1976). The nature of the therapeutic influence and its basic ingredients. In A. Burton (Ed.), *What makes behavior change possible?* (pp. 96–112). New York: Brunner/Mazel.

Strupp, H. H. (1978). Psychotherapy research and practice: An overview. In S. L. Garfield & E. Bergin (Eds.), *Handbook of psychotherapy and behavior change* (2nd ed., pp. 3–22). New York: John Wiley & Sons.

Strupp, H. H., Fox, R. E., & Lessler, K. (1969). *Patients view their psychotherapy.* Baltimore: The Johns Hopkins University Press.

Turner, F. J. (1978). *Psychosocial therapy: A social work perspective.* New York: The Free Press.

Turner, F. J. (Ed.). (1986). *Social work treatment: Interlocking theoretical approaches* (3rd ed.). New York: The Free Press.

Wolpe, J. (1982). *The practice of behavior therapy* (3rd ed.). New York: Pergamon.

Wright, J. H., & Beck, A. T. (1983). Cognitive therapy of depression. *Hospital and Community Psychiatry, 34,* 1119–1127.

# EPILOGUE

## THE SHORES—ONE YEAR FOLLOW-UP

*Editor's note:* When I met with the Shores exactly one year after I interviewed them for "The Case," I was struck by the difference in their attitudes. Although family members still had problems and were still involved with social services, they demonstrated a sense of optimism that had not been present earlier. Nancy no longer expressed the concern that after the book was published she would run from social worker to social worker, trying to do everything suggested. All the family members expressed anticipation about soon being able to see the finished book. They were humble about their contribution ("It wasn't anything"), but at the same time they were proud of their participation.

Because the Shores were not my clients, I do not know what kinds of therapeutic paradigms they were exposed to during the year. I only know for certain that there was some treatment. The experience of telling their story in depth, uncluttered by clinical intervention, and "going public" has also surely had some impact on family members and on the family as a whole. It remains to be seen how they will make use of what we have written.

### Nancy

During the past year, both of Nancy's parents developed cancer. Her mother's was a relatively minor skin cancer, but her father's was terminal. Shortly before he lapsed into a coma, Nancy and her father talked about her childhood. Her father was genuinely surprised about her feelings of

413

abandonment and he reassured her of his love. Nancy also talked with her mother, who reassured her that her preoccupations with friends and career during Nancy's childhood were caused by her own unhappiness, not by a lack of love for or a lack of interest in Nancy.

Nancy worries about Michael more than ever, but her panic attacks occur less frequently and with less impact. She has spent a year in individual therapy and feels that the treatment has given her permission "to stop feeling guilty for everything, to stop trying to control everyone, and to stop worrying about what people think." She no longer feels compelled to return to work or school.

### Charley

One year later, Charley has still not read the case study. He no longer attends the vocational rehabilitation program, but otherwise his life is much the same as it was last year. His relationship with Michael is still poor, perhaps worse. Weekly performances at the comedy club are still fun. The best news is that the family is hopeful because Charley has kept a job as a trash collector for five months. If he is retained beyond the six-month probationary period, he will be virtually guaranteed the municipal union job.

### Rena

Six months ago, Rena found her birth mother. Aunt Flo's employer, an attorney, was able to give Rena the name of her birth mother and the name of the state in which she lived. Rena called every woman in the state with that name—a common one at that—until she found her. After an initial "infatuation" with her birth mother, the discovery of a half-sister close to her age, and the uncovering of the facts about her birth, Rena settled down to a job in a medical office (which she has held for seven months). She is talking about applying to nursing school and is in an "on again, off again" relationship with a young man. Rena eventually got off the waiting list and entered therapy. She dropped out after nine months because she did not like her therapist.

### Michael

The past year has been a mixed one for Michael. He has not had any asthma attacks. The summer brought a successful camp experience at a new camp, and he was invited to return as a counselor-in-training.

Although he has retained a few friends from camp, they are all much younger. He speaks less of his sadness, his differentness, and his loneliness, but he clearly remains an outcast among his peers. Michael is still a loyal Boy Scout and has been appointed the troop scribe by his scout leaders. He also attends a religious educational program and frequently coaxes the rest of the family into participating in religious rituals at home. An adolescent therapy group he entered early in the year has recently been disbanded because of a drop in membership.

# AUTHOR INDEX

# SUBJECT INDEX